Advanced Business Finance
FI 414

Charles Hadlock
Assem Safieddine

Selected Materials from Corporate Finance, Fourth Edition, by

Stephen A. Ross
Yale University

Randolph W. Westerfield
University of Southern California

Jeffrey Jaffe
Wharton School of Business
University of Pennsylvania

The ***McGraw-Hill*** *Companies*
Primis Custom Publishing

New York St. Louis San Francisco Auckland Bogota
Caracas Lisbon London Madrid Mexico Milan Montreal
New Delhi Paris San Juan Singapore Sydney Tokyo Toronto

The **McGraw·Hill** *Companies*

Materials were selected from:

Corporate Finance, Fourth Edition, by Stephen A. Ross, Randolph W. Westerfield and Jeffrey Jaffe.

Within this custom text pp. 1-257.

ADVANCED BUSINESS FINANCE

ISBN 0-07-229769-7

Printed in the United States of America.

1 2 3 4 5 6 7 8 9 0 QD 9 0 9 8

Editor: Karen Perry
Printer/Binder: Quebecor

Table of Contents

CHAPTER

12 Risk, Return, and Capital Budgeting

Our text has devoted a number of chapters to net-present-value (NPV) analysis. We pointed out that a dollar to be received in the future was worth less than a dollar received today for two reasons. First, there is the simple time-value-of-money argument in a riskless world. If you have a dollar today, you can invest it in the bank and receive more than a dollar by some future date. Second, a risky dollar is worth less than a riskless dollar. Consider a firm expecting a \$1 cash flow. If actuality exceeds expectations (revenues are especially high or expenses are especially low), perhaps \$1.10 or \$1.20 will be received. If actuality falls short of expectations, perhaps only \$0.80 or \$0.90 will be received. This risk is unattractive to the typical firm.

Our work on NPV allowed us to precisely value riskless cash flows. That is, we discounted by the riskless interest rate. However, because most real-world cash flows in the future are risky, business demands a procedure for discounting risky cash flows. This chapter applies the concept of net present value to risky cash flows.

Let us review what previous work in the text has to say about NPV. In earlier chapters we learned that the basic NPV formula for an investment that generates cash flows (C_t) in future periods is

$$\text{NPV} = C_0 + \sum_{t=1}^{T} \frac{C_t}{(1+r)^t}$$

For risky projects, expected incremental cash flows $\overline{C}_t$ are placed in the numerator, and the NPV formula becomes

$$\text{NPV} = C_0 + \sum_{t=1}^{T} \frac{\overline{C}_t}{(1+r)^t}$$

In this chapter, we will learn that the discount rate used to determine the NPV of a risky project can be computed from the CAPM (or APT). For example, if an all-equity firm is seeking to value a risky project, such as renovating a warehouse, the firm will determine the required return, r_S, on the project by using the SML. We call r_S the firm's **cost of equity** capital.

When firms finance with both debt and equity, the discount rate to use is the project's overall cost of capital. The overall cost of capital is a weighted average of the cost of debt and the cost of equity.

12.1 The Cost of Equity Capital

Whenever a firm has extra cash, it can take one of two actions. On the one hand, it can pay out the cash immediately as a dividend. On the other hand, the firm can invest

FIGURE 12.1 Choices of a Firm with Extra Cash

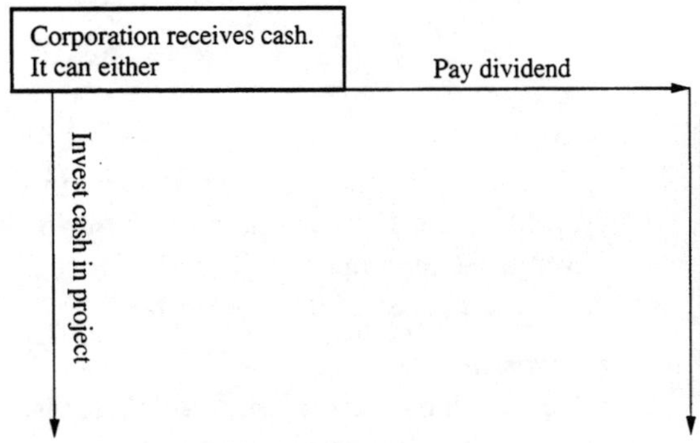

Stockholders want the firm to invest in a project only if the expected return on the project is at least as great as that of a financial asset of comparable risk.

extra cash in a project, paying out the future cash flows of the project as dividends. Which procedure would the stockholders prefer? If a stockholder can reinvest the dividend in a financial asset (a stock or bond) with the same risk as that of the project, the stockholders would desire the alternative with the highest expected return. In other words, the project should be undertaken only if its expected return is greater than that of a financial asset of comparable risk. This is illustrated in Figure 12.1. This discussion implies a very simple capital-budgeting rule: The discount rate of a project should be the expected return on a financial asset of comparable risk.

From the firm's perspective, the expected return is the cost of equity capital. If we use the CAPM model for returns, the expected return on the stock will be

$$\overline{R} = R_F + \beta \times (\overline{R}_M - R_F) \tag{12.1}$$

where R_F is the risk-free rate and $\overline{R}_M - R_F$ is the difference between the expected return on the market portfolio and the riskless rate. This difference is often called the expected *excess* market return.[1]

We now have the tools to estimate a firm's cost of equity capital. To do this, we need to know three things:

- The risk-free rate, R_F
- The market-risk premium, $\overline{R}_M - R_F$
- The company beta, β_i

• ***Example***

Suppose the stock of the Quatram Company, a publisher of college textbooks, has a beta (β) of 1.3. The firm is 100-percent equity financed, that is, it has no debt. Quatram is considering a number of capital-budgeting projects that will double its size. Because these new projects are similar to the firm's existing ones, the average beta on the new projects is assumed to be equal to Quatram's existing beta. The risk-free rate is 7 percent. What is the appropriate discount rate for these new projects, assuming a market-risk premium of 8.5 percent?

[1] Of course, we can use the *k*-factor APT model (Chapter 11) and estimate several beta coefficients. However, for our purposes it is sufficient to estimate a single beta.

Now we can estimate the cost of equity r_S for Quatram as

$$\begin{aligned} r_S &= 7\% + (8.5\% \times 1.3) \\ &= 7\% + 11.05\% \\ &= 18.05\% \end{aligned}$$

Two key assumptions were made in this example: (1) The beta risk of the new projects is the same as the risk of the firm, and (2) the firm is all-equity financed. Given these assumptions, it follows that the cash flows of the new projects should be discounted at the 18.05-percent rate. •

• ***Example***

Suppose Alpha Air Freight is an all-equity firm with a beta of 1.21. Further suppose the market-risk premium is 8.5 percent, and the risk-free rate is 6 percent. We can determine the expected return on the common stock of Alpha Air Freight by using the SML of equation (12.1). We find that the expected return is

$$6\% + (1.21 \times 8.5\%) = 16.3\%$$

Because this is the return that shareholders can expect in the financial markets on a stock with a β of 1.21, it is the return they expect on Alpha Air Freight's stock.

Further suppose Alpha is evaluating the following non–mutually exclusive projects:

Project	*Project's Beta (β)*	*Project's Expected Cash Flows Next Year*	*Project's Internal Rate of Return*	*Project's NPV When Cash Flows Are Discounted at 16.3%*	*Accept or Reject*
A	1.21	$140	40%	$20.4	Accept
B	1.21	$120	20%	$ 3.2	Accept
C	1.21	$110	10%	−$ 5.4	Reject

Each project initially costs $100. All projects are assumed to have the same risk as the firm as a whole. Because the cost of equity capital is 16.3 percent, projects in an all-equity firm are discounted at this rate. Projects *A* and *B* have positive NPVs, and *C* will have a negative NPV. Thus, only *A* and *B* will be accepted.[2] This is illustrated in Figure 12.2. •

[2] In addition to the SML, the dividend-valuation model presented earlier in the text can be used to represent the firm's cost of equity capital. Using this model, the present value (P) of the firm's expected dividend payments can be expressed as

$$P = \frac{\text{Div}_1}{(1 + r_S)} + \frac{\text{Div}_2}{(1 + r_S)^2} + \cdots + \frac{\text{Div}_N}{(1 + r_S)^N} + \cdots \qquad \text{(a)}$$

where r_S is the required return of shareholders and the firm's cost of equity capital. If the dividends are expected to grow at a constant rate, g, equation (a) reduces to

$$P = \frac{\text{Div}_1}{r_S - g} \qquad \text{(b)}$$

Equation (b) can be reformulated as

$$r_S = \frac{\text{Div}_1}{P} + g \qquad \text{(c)}$$

We can use equation (c) to estimate r_S. Div_1/P is the dividend yield expected over the next year. An estimate of the cost of equity capital is determined from an estimate of Div_1/P and g.

The dividend-valuation model is generally considered both less theoretically sound and more difficult to practically apply than the SML. Hence, examples in this chapter calculate cost of equity capital using the SML approach.

FIGURE 12.2 Using the Security-Market Line to Estimate the Risk-Adjusted Discount Rate for Risky Projects

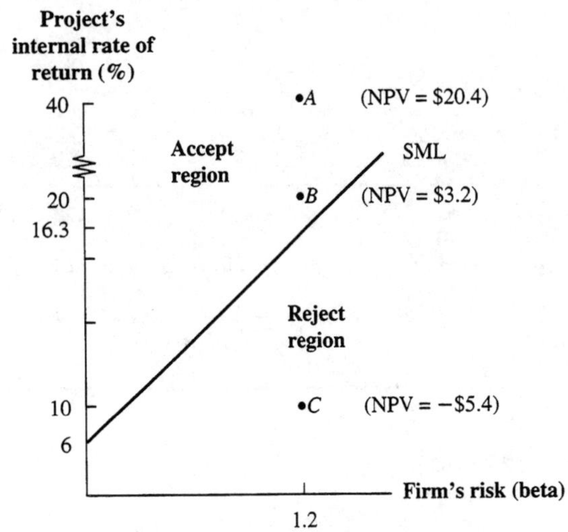

The diagonal line represents the relationship between the cost of equity capital and the firm's beta. An all-equity firm should accept a project whose internal rate of return is greater than the cost of equity capital, and should reject a project whose internal rate of return is less than the cost of equity capital. (The above graph assumes that all projects are as risky as the firm.)

In the previous example we assumed that the company beta was known. Of course, beta must be estimated in the real world. We pointed out earlier that the beta of a security is the standardized covariance of a security's return with the return on the market portfolio. The formula for security *i*, first given in Chapter 10, is

$$\text{Beta of security } i = \frac{\text{Cov}(R_i, R_M)}{\text{Var}(R_M)} = \frac{\sigma_{i,M}}{\sigma_M^2}$$

In words, the beta is the covariance of a security with the market, divided by the variance of the market. Because we calculated both covariance and variance in earlier chapters, calculating beta involves no new material.

• ***Example (Advanced)***
Suppose we sample the returns on the stock of the General Tool Company and the returns on the S&P 500 Index for four years. They are tabulated as follows:

Year	*General Tool Company* R_G	*S&P 500 Index* R_M
1	−10%	−40%
2	3	−30
3	20	10
4	15	20

We can calculate beta in six steps.

TABLE 12.1 Calculating Beta

(1) Year	(2) Rate of Return on General Tool (R_G)	(3) General Tool's Deviation from Average Return* ($R_G - \bar{R}_G$)	(4) Rate of Return on Market Portfolio	(5) Market Portfolio's Deviation from Average Return† ($R_M - \bar{R}_M$)	(6) Deviation of General Tool Multiplied by Deviation of Market Portfolio	(7) Squared Deviation of Market Portfolio
1	−0.10	−0.17 (−0.10 − 0.07)	−0.40	−0.30	0.051 [(−0.17) × (−0.30)]	0.090 [(−0.30) × (−0.30)]
2	0.03	−0.04	−0.30	−0.20	0.008	0.040
3	0.20	0.13	0.10	0.20	0.026	0.040
4	0.15	0.08	0.20	0.30	0.024	0.090
	Avg = 0.07		Avg = −0.10		Sum: 0.109	Sum: 0.260

Beta of General Tool: $0.419 = \frac{0.109}{0.260}$.

* Average return for General Tool is 0.07.

† Average return for market is −0.10.

1. Calculate average return on each asset:

Average Return on General Tool:

$$\frac{-0.10 + 0.03 + 0.20 + 0.15}{4} = 0.07\ (7\%)$$

Average Return on Market Portfolio:

$$\frac{-0.40 - 0.30 + 0.10 + 0.20}{4} = -0.10\ (-10\%)$$

2. For each asset, calculate the deviation of each return from the asset's average return determined above. This is presented in columns 3 and 5 of Table 12.1.
3. Multiply the deviation of General Tool's return by the deviation of the market's return. This is presented in column 6. This procedure is analogous to our calculation of covariance in an earlier chapter. The procedure will be used in the numerator of the beta calculation.
4. Calculate the squared deviation of the market's return. This is presented in column 7. This procedure is analogous to our calculation of variance in Chapter 9. The procedure will be used in the denominator of the beta calculation.
5. Take the sum of column 6 and the sum of column 7. They are

Sum of Deviation of General Tool Multiplied by Deviation of Market Portfolio:

$$0.051 + 0.008 + 0.026 + 0.024 = 0.109$$

Sum of Squared Deviation of Market Portfolio:

$$0.090 + 0.040 + 0.040 + 0.090 = 0.260$$

Measuring Company Betas

The basic method of measuring company betas is to estimate:

$$\frac{\text{Cov}(R_{it}, R_{Mt})}{\text{Var}(R_{Mt})}$$

Using $t = 1, 2, \ldots, T$ observations

Problems

1. Betas may vary over time.
2. The sample size may be inadequate.
3. Betas are influenced by changing financial leverage and business risk.

Solutions

1. Problems 1 and 2 (above) can be moderated by more sophisticated statistical techniques.
2. Problem 3 can be lessened by adjusting for changes in business and financial risk.
3. Look at average beta estimates of several comparable firms in the industry.

6. The beta is the sum of column 6 divided by the sum of column 7. This is

Beta of General Tool:

$$0.419 = \frac{0.109}{0.260} \quad \bullet$$

Concept Questions

- How does one calculate the discount rate from the beta?
- What are the two key assumptions we used when calculating the discount rate?
- What are the six steps needed to calculate beta?

12.2 Determinants of Beta

The regression analysis approach in the previous section doesn't tell us where beta comes from. The beta of a stock does not come out of thin air. Rather, it is determined by the characteristics of the firm. We consider three factors: the cyclical nature of revenues, operating leverage, and financial leverage.

Cyclicality of Revenues

The revenues of some firms are quite cyclical. That is, these firms do well in the expansion phase of the business cycle and do poorly in the contraction phase. Empirical evidence suggests high-tech firms, retailers, and automotive firms fluctuate with the business cycle. Firms in industries such as utilities, railroads, food, and airlines are less dependent upon the cycle. Because beta is the standardized covariability of a stock's return with the market's return, it is not surprising that highly cyclical stocks have high betas.

It is worthwhile to point out that cyclicality is not the same as variability. For example, a movie-making firm has highly variable revenues because hits and flops are not easily predictable. However, because the revenues of a studio are more dependent on the quality of its releases than upon the phase of the business cycle, motion-picture companies are not particularly cyclical. In other words, stocks with high standard deviations need not have high betas, a point we have stressed before.

Operating Leverage

We distinguished fixed costs from variable costs earlier in the text. At that time, we mentioned that fixed costs do not change as quantity changes. Conversely, variable costs increase as the quantity of output rises. This difference between variable and fixed costs allows us to define operating leverage.

• ***Example***

Consider a firm that can choose either technology *A* or technology *B* when making a particular product. The relevant differences between the two technologies are displayed below:

Technology A	Technology *B*
Fixed cost: \$1,000/year Variable cost: \$8/unit Price: \$10/unit Contribution margin: \$2 (\$10 − \$8)	Fixed cost: \$2,000/year Variable cost: \$6/unit Price: \$10/unit Contribution margin: \$4 (\$10 − \$6)

Technology *A* has lower fixed costs and higher variable costs than does technology *B*. Perhaps technology *A* involves less mechanization than does *B*. Or, the equipment in *A* may be leased whereas the equipment in *B* must be purchased. Alternatively, perhaps technology *A* involves few employees but many subcontractors, whereas *B* involves only highly skilled employees who must be retained in bad times. Because technology *B* has both lower variable costs and higher fixed costs, we say that it has higher **operating leverage.**[3]

Figure 12.3 graphs costs under both technologies. The slope of each total-cost line represents variable costs under a single technology. The slope of *A*'s line is steeper, indicating greater variable costs.

Because the two technologies are used to produce the same products, a unit price of \$10 applies for both cases. We mentioned in an earlier chapter that contribution margin is the difference between price and variable cost. It measures the incremental profit from one additional unit. Because the contribution margin in *B* is greater, its technology is riskier. An unexpected sale increases profit by \$2 under *A* but increases profit by \$4 under *B*. Similarly, an unexpected sale cancellation reduces profit by \$2

[3] The actual definition of operating leverage is

$$\frac{\text{Change in EBIT}}{\text{EBIT}} \times \frac{\text{Sales}}{\text{Change in sales}}$$

where EBIT is the earnings before interest and taxes. That is, operating leverage measures the percentage change in EBIT for a given percentage change in sales or revenues. It can be shown that operating leverage increases as fixed costs rise and as variable costs fall.

FIGURE 12.3 Illustration of Two Different Technologies

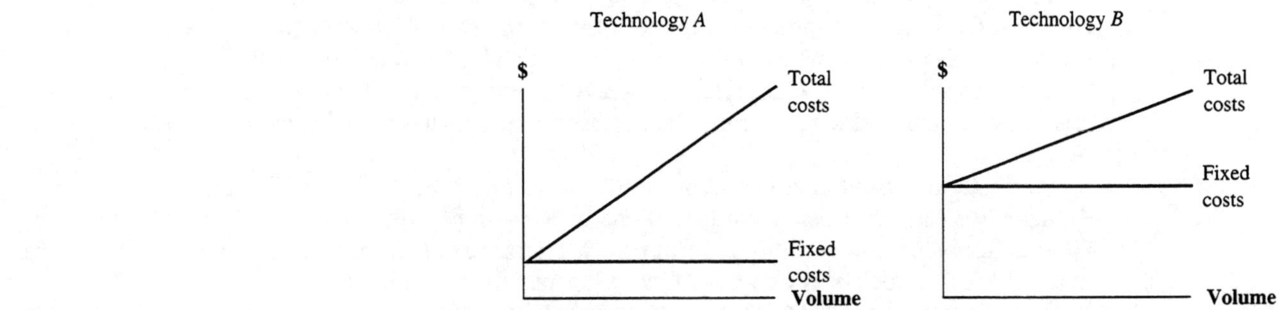

Technology *A* has higher variable costs and lower fixed costs than does technology *B*. Technology *B* has higher operating leverage.

FIGURE 12.4 Illustration of the Effect of a Change in Volume on the Change in Earnings before Interest and Taxes (EBIT)

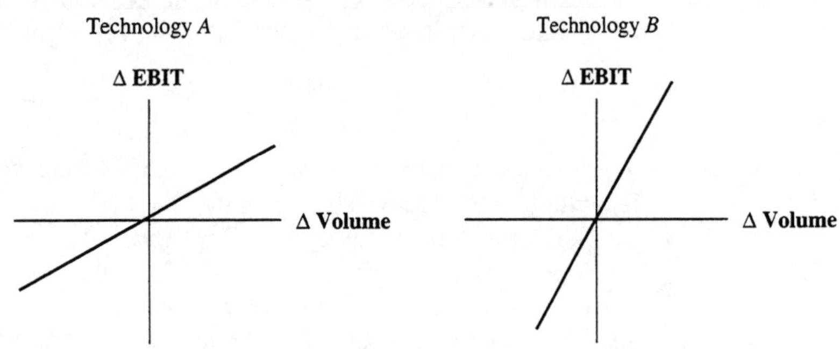

Technology *B* has lower variable costs than *A*, implying a higher contribution margin. The profits of the firm are more responsive to changes in volume under technology *B* than under *A*.

under *A* but reduces profit by $4 under *B*. This is illustrated in Figure 12.4. This figure shows the change in earnings before interest and taxes for a given change in volume. The slope of the right-hand graph is greater, indicating that technology *B* is riskier. •

The cyclicality of a firm's revenues is a determinant of the firm's beta. Operating leverage magnifies the effect of cyclicity on beta. As mentioned earlier, business risk is generally defined as the risk of the firm without financial leverage. Business risk depends both on the responsiveness of the firm's revenues to the business cycle and on the firm's operating leverage.

While the above discussion concerns firms, it applies to projects as well. If one cannot estimate a project's beta in another way, one can examine the project's revenues and operating leverage. Those projects whose revenues appear strongly cyclical and whose operating leverage appears high are likely to have high betas. Conversely, weak cyclicality and low operating leverage implies low betas. As mentioned earlier, this approach is unfortunately qualitative in nature. Because start-up projects have little data, quantitative estimates of beta generally are not feasible.

Financial Leverage and Beta

As suggested by their names, operating leverage and financial leverage are analogous concepts. Operating leverage refers to the firm's fixed costs of *production*. Financial leverage is the extent to which a firm relies on debt and a levered firm is a firm with some debt in its capital structure. Because a *levered* firm must make interest payments regardless of the firm's sales, financial leverage refers to the firm's fixed costs of *finance*.

Consider our discussion in section 10.8 concerning the beta of Jelco, Inc. In that example, we estimated beta from the returns of Jelco *stock*. Similarly, we estimated General Tool's beta in section 12.1 from stock returns. Thus, in each case, we estimated the firm's stock or **equity beta.** One will generally be estimating the equity beta in the real world, since beta is typically estimated from returns on stock. Actually, a firm has an asset beta as well as an equity beta. As the name suggests, the **asset beta** is the beta of the assets of the firm. The asset beta may also be thought of as the beta of the common stock had the firm been financed with only equity.

Imagine an individual who owns all of the firm's debt and all of its equity. In other words, this individual owns the entire firm. What is the beta of her portfolio of the firm's debt and equity?

As with any portfolio, the beta of this portfolio is a weighted average of the betas of the individual items in the portfolio. Hence, we have

$$\beta_{\text{Asset}} = \frac{\text{Debt}}{\text{Debt} + \text{Equity}} \times \beta_{\text{Debt}} + \frac{\text{Equity}}{\text{Debt} + \text{Equity}} \times \beta_{\text{Equity}} \tag{12.2}$$

where β_{Equity} is the beta of the equity of the *levered* firm. Notice that the beta of debt is multiplied by Debt/(Debt + Equity), the percentage of debt in the capital structure. Similarly, the beta of equity is multiplied by the percentage of equity in the capital structure. Because the portfolio contains both the debt of the firm and the equity of the firm, the beta of the portfolio is the *asset beta.* As we said above, the asset beta can also be viewed as the beta of the common stock had the firm been all-equity.

The beta of debt is very low in practice. If we make the commonplace assumption that the beta of debt is zero, we have

$$\beta_{\text{Asset}} = \frac{\text{Equity}}{\text{Debt} + \text{Equity}} \times \beta_{\text{Equity}} \tag{12.3}$$

Because Equity/(Debt + Equity) must be below 1 for a levered firm, it follows that $\beta_{\text{Asset}} < \beta_{\text{Equity}}$. Rearranging the above equation, we have

$$\beta_{\text{Equity}} = \beta_{\text{Asset}}\left(1 + \frac{\text{Debt}}{\text{Equity}}\right)$$

The equity beta will always be greater than the asset beta with financial leverage.[4]

Concept Questions

- What are determinants of equity betas?
- What is the difference between an asset beta and an equity beta?

[4] It can be shown that the relationship between a firm's asset beta and its equity beta with corporate taxes is

$$\beta_{\text{Equity}} = \beta_{\text{Asset}}\left[1 + (1 - T_C)\frac{\text{Debt}}{\text{Equity}}\right]$$

See Chapter 17 for more details.

12.3 Extensions of the Basic Model

The Firm versus the Project: Vive la Difference

We now assume that the risk of a project differs from that of the firm, while going back to the all-equity assumption. We began the chapter by pointing out that each project should be paired with a financial asset of comparable risk. If a project's beta differs from that of the firm, the project should be discounted at the rate commensurate with its own beta. This is a very important point because firms frequently speak of a *corporate discount rate.* (*Hurdle rate, cutoff rate, benchmark,* and *cost of capital* are frequently used synonymously.) Unless all projects in the corporation are of the same risk, choosing the same discount rate for all projects is incorrect.

• ***Example***
D. D. Ronnelley Co., a publishing firm, may accept a project in computer software. Noting that computer software companies have high betas, the publishing firm views the software venture as more risky than the rest of its business. It should discount the project at a rate commensurate with the risk of software companies. For example, it might use the average beta of a portfolio of publicly traded software firms. Instead, if all projects in D. D. Ronnelley Co. were discounted at the same rate, a bias would result. The firm would accept too many high-risk projects (software ventures) and reject too many low-risk projects (books and magazines). This point is illustrated in Figure 12.5. •

The D. D. Ronnelley example assumes that the proposed project has identical risk to that of the software industry, allowing the industry beta to be used. However, the beta of a new project may be greater than the beta of existing firms in the same

FIGURE 12.5 Relationship between the Firm's Cost of Capital and the Security Market Line

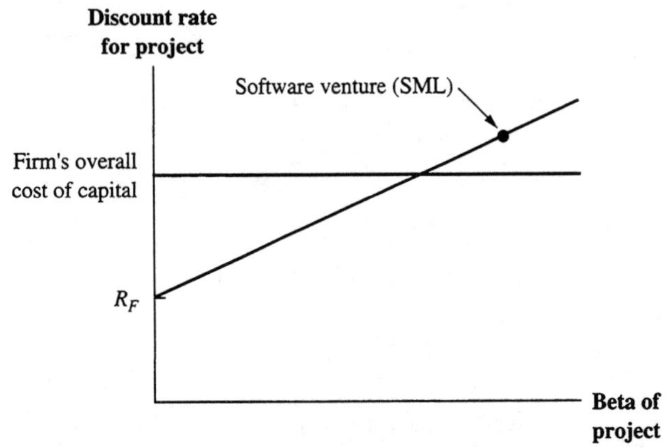

Use of a firm's cost of capital may lead to incorrect capital-budgeting decisions. Projects with high risk, such as the software venture for D. D. Ronnelley Co., should be discounted at a high rate. By using the firm's cost of equity, the firm is likely to accept too many high-risk projects.

Projects with low risk should be discounted at a low rate. By using the firm's cost of capital, the firm is likely to reject too many low-risk projects.

industry because the very newness of the project likely increases its responsiveness to economywide movements. For example, a start-up computer venture may fail in a recession while IBM, DEC, or Control Data will still be around. Conversely, in an economywide expansion, the venture may grow much faster than the old-line computer firms.

Fortunately, a slight adjustment is all that is needed here. The new venture should be assigned a somewhat higher beta than that of the industry to reflect added risk. The adjustment is necessarily ad hoc, so no formula can be given. Our experience indicates that this approach is widespread in practice today.

However, a problem does arise for the rare project constituting its own industry. For example, consider the firms providing consumer shopping by television. Today, one can obtain a reasonable estimate for the beta of this industry, since a few of the firms have publicly traded stock. However, when the ventures began in the 1980s, any beta estimate was suspect. At that time, no one knew whether shopping by TV belonged in the television industry, the retail industry, or in an entirely new industry.

What beta should be used in the rare case when an industrywide beta is not appropriate? One approach, which considers the determinants of the project's beta, was treated earlier in this chapter. Unfortunately, that approach is only qualitative in nature.

The Cost of Capital with Debt

Section 12.1 showed how to choose the discount rate when a project is all-equity financed. In this section, we discuss an adjustment when the project is financed with both debt and equity.

Suppose a firm uses both debt and equity to finance its investments. If the firm pays r_B for its debt financing and r_S for its equity, what is the overall or average cost of its capital? The cost of equity is r_S, as discussed in earlier sections. The cost of debt is the firm's borrowing rate, r_B. If a firm uses both debt and equity, the cost of capital is a weighted average of each. This works out to be

$$\frac{S}{S+B}r_S + \frac{B}{S+B}r_B$$

The weights in the formula are, respectively, the proportion of total value represented by the equity

$$\left(\frac{S}{S+B}\right)$$

and the proportion of total value represented by debt

$$\left(\frac{B}{S+B}\right)$$

This is only natural. If the firm had issued no debt and was therefore an all-equity firm, its average cost of capital would equal its cost of equity, r_S. At the other extreme, if the firm had issued so much debt that its equity was valueless, it would be an all-debt firm, and its average cost of capital would be its cost of debt, r_B.

Of course, interest is tax deductible at the corporate level (to be treated in more detail in Chapter 15). The after-tax cost of debt is

$$\begin{array}{c}\text{Cost of debt}\\ \text{(after corporate tax)}\end{array} = r_B \times (1 - T_C)$$

Assembling these results, we get the average cost of capital (after tax) for the firm:

$$\text{Average cost of capital} = \left(\frac{S}{S+B}\right) \times r_S + \left(\frac{B}{S+B}\right) \times r_B \times (1 - T_C) \qquad (12.4)$$

Because the average cost of capital is a weighting of its cost of equity and its cost of debt, it is usually referred to as the **weighted average cost of capital r_{WACC}**, and from now on we will use this term.

• ***Example***

We can compute the r_{WACC} for a firm whose debt has a market value of $40 million and whose stock has a market value of $60 million (3 million outstanding shares of stock, each selling for $20 per share). The firm pays a 15-percent rate of interest on its new debt and has a beta of 1.41. The corporate tax rate is 34 percent. (Assume that the SML holds, that the risk premium on the market is 8.5 percent, and that the current Treasury bill rate is 11 percent.)

To compute the r_{WACC} using equation (12.4), we must know (1) the after-tax cost of debt, $r_B \times (1 - T_C)$, (2) the cost of equity, r_S, and (3) the proportions of debt and equity used by the firm. These three values are computed below.

1. The pretax cost of debt is 15 percent, implying an after-tax cost of 9.9 percent [15% × (1 − 0.34)].
2. The cost of equity capital is computed by using the SML:

$$\begin{aligned} r_S &= R_F + \beta \times [\bar{R}_M - R_F] \\ &= 11\% + 1.41 \times 8.5\% \\ &= 23.0\% \end{aligned}$$

3. The proportions of debt and equity are computed from the market values of debt and equity. Because the market value of the firm is $100 million ($40 million + $60 million), the proportions of debt and equity are 40 and 60 percent, respectively.

The cost of equity, r_S, is 23.0 percent, and the after-tax cost of debt, $r_B \times (1 - T_C)$, is 9.9 percent. B is $40 million and S is $60 million. Therefore,

$$\begin{aligned} r_{WACC} &= \frac{B}{B+S} \times r_B \times (1 - T_C) + \frac{S}{B+S} \times r_S \\ &= \left(\frac{40}{100} \times 9.9\%\right) + \left(\frac{60}{100} \times 23.0\%\right) = 17.8\% \end{aligned}$$

This procedure is presented in chart form below:

(1) *Financing Components*	(2) *Market Values*	(3) *Weight*	(4) *Cost of Capital (after corporate tax)*	(5) *Weighted cost of Capital*
Debt	$ 40,000,000	0.40	15% × (1 − 0.34) = 9.9%	4.0%
Equity	$ 60,000,000	0.60	11% + 1.41 × 8.5% = 23.0%	13.8%
	$100,000,000	1.00		17.8%

The weights we used in the previous example were market-value weights. Market-value weights are more appropriate than book-value weights because the market values of the securities are closer to the actual dollars that would be received from their sale. •

• ***Example***

Suppose that a firm has a current debt-equity ratio of 0.6, a cost of debt of 15.15 percent, and a cost of equity of 20 percent. The corporate tax rate is 34 percent.

Our first step calls for transforming the debt-to-equity (B/S) ratio to a debt-to-value ratio. A B/S ratio of 0.6 implies 6 parts debt for 10 parts equity. Since value is equal to the sum of the debt plus the equity, the debt-to-value ratio is $\frac{6}{6+10} = 0.375$. Similarly, the equity-to-value ratio is $\frac{10}{6+10} = 0.625$. The r_{WACC} will then be

$$r_{\text{WACC}} = \left(\frac{S}{S+B}\right) \times r_S + \left(\frac{B}{S+B}\right) \times r_B \times (1 - T_C)$$

$$= .625 \times 20\% + .375 \times 15.15\% \times (.66) = 16.25\%$$

Suppose the firm is considering taking on a warehouse renovation that is expected to yield cost savings of $12 million a year for six years. Using the NPV equation and discounting the six years of expected cash flows from the renovation at the r_{WACC}, we have[5]

$$\begin{aligned} \text{NPV} &= -\$50 + \frac{\$12}{(1 + r_{\text{WACC}})} + \cdots + \frac{\$12}{(1 + r_{\text{WACC}})^6} \\ &= -\$50 + \$12 \times A^6_{.1625} \\ &= -\$50 + (12 \times 3.66) \\ &= -\$6.07 \end{aligned}$$

Should the firm take on the warehouse renovation? The project has a negative NPV using the firm's r_{WACC}. This means that the financial markets offer superior projects in the same risk class (namely, the firm's risk class). The answer is clear: The firm should reject the project. •

12.4 Summary and Conclusions

Earlier chapters on capital budgeting assumed that projects generate riskless cash flows. The appropriate discount rate in that case is the riskless interest rate. Of course, most cash flows from real-world capital-budgeting projects are risky. This chapter discusses the discount rate when cash flows are risky.

1. A firm with excess cash can either pay a dividend or make a capital expenditure. Because stockholders can reinvest the dividend in risky financial assets, the expected return on a capital-budgeting project should be at least as great as the expected return on a financial asset of comparable risk.
2. The expected return on any asset is dependent upon its beta. Thus, we showed how to estimate the beta of a stock. The appropriate procedure employs regression analysis on historical returns.

[5] This discussion of WACC has been implicitly based on perpetual cash flows. However, an important paper by J. Miles and R. Ezzel, "The Weighted Average Cost of Capital, Perfect Capital Markets and Project Life: A Clarification," *Journal of Financial and Quantitative Analysis* (September 1980), shows that the WACC is appropriate even when cash flows are not perpetual.

3. We considered the case of a project whose beta risk was equal to that of the firm. If the firm is unlevered, the discount rate on the project is equal to

$$R_F + \beta \times (\overline{R}_M - R_F)$$

where $\overline{R}_M$ is the expected return on the market portfolio and R_F is the risk-free rate. In words, the discount rate on the project is equal to the CAPM's estimate of the expected return on the security.
4. If the project's beta differs from that of the firm, the discount rate should be based on the project's beta. The project's beta can generally be estimated by determining the average beta of the project's industry.
5. The beta of a company is a function of a number of factors. Perhaps the three most important are

    - Cyclicality of revenues
    - Operating leverage
    - Financial leverage

6. Sometimes one should not use the average beta of the project's industry as an estimate of the beta of the project. In this case, one can estimate the project's beta by considering the project's cyclicality of revenues and its operating leverage. This approach is qualitative in nature.
7. If a firm uses debt, the discount rate to use is the r_{WACC}. In order to calculate r_{WACC}, the cost of equity and the cost of debt applicable to a project must be estimated. If the project is similar to the firm, the cost of equity can be estimated using the SML for the firm's equity. Conceptually, a dividend-growth model could be used as well, though it is likely to be far less accurate in practice.

Key Terms

Suggested Readings

The following article contains a superb discussion of some of the subtleties of using WACC for project evaluation:

Miles, J., and R. Ezzel. "The Weighted Average Cost of Capital, Perfect Capital Markets and Project Life: A Clarification." *Journal of Financial and Quantitative Analysis* 15 (September 1980).

This is an excellent article on how to use the SML in project evaluation:

Weston, J. F. "Investment Decisions Using the Capital Asset Pricing Model." *Financial Management* (Spring 1973).

The classical papers on the stability of risk measures are

Blume, M. "On the Assessment of Risk." *Journal of Finance* (March 1971).

Sharpe, W., and G. Cooper. "Risk-Return Classes of New York Stock Exchange Common Stocks 1931–1967." *Financial Analysts Journal* (March/April 1972).

An excellent treatment of practical issues is contained in

Rosenberg, B., and A. Rudd. "The Corporate Uses of Beta." In *Issues in Corporate Finance.* New York: Stern Stewart Putnam and Macklis, 1983.

Questions and Problems

Beta and the Cost of Equity

12.1 Furniture Depot, Inc., is an all-equity firm with a beta of 0.95. The market-risk premium is 9 percent and the risk-free rate is 5 percent. The company must decide whether or not to undertake the project that requires an immediate investment of $1.2 million and will generate annual after-tax cash flows of $340,000 at year-end for 5 years. If the project has the same risk as the firm as a whole, should Furniture Depot undertake the project?

12.2 The returns for the past five years on Douglas stock and the New York Stock Exchange Composite Index (NYSE) are listed below.

Douglas	*NYSE*
−0.05	−0.12
0.05	0.01
0.08	0.06
0.15	0.10
0.10	0.05

a. What is the average returns on Douglas stock and on the market?
b. Compute the beta of Douglas stock.

12.3 Mitsubishi Inc., is a levered firm with a debt-to-equity ratio of 0.25. The beta of common stock is 1.15, while the beta of debt is 0.3. The market-risk premium is 10 percent and the risk-free rate is 6 percent. The corporate tax rate is 35 percent. The SML holds for the company.
a. If a new project of the company has the same risk as the common stock of the firm, what is the cost of equity on the project?
b. If a new project of the company has the same risk as the overall firm, what is the weighted average cost of capital on the project?

12.4 The correlation between the returns on Ceramics Craftsman, Inc., and the returns on the S&P 500 is 0.675. The variance of the returns on Ceramics Craftsman, Inc., is 0.004225, and the variance of the returns on the S&P 500 is 0.001467. What is the beta of Ceramics Craftsman stock?

12.5 The returns from the past 12 quarters on Travis Manufacturing and the market are listed below.

Travis	*Market*
−0.009	0.023
0.051	0.058
−0.001	−0.020
−0.045	−0.050
0.085	0.071
0.000	0.012
−0.080	−0.075
0.020	0.050
0.125	0.120
0.110	0.049
−0.100	−0.030
0.040	0.028

a. What is the beta of Travis Manufacturing stock?
b. Is Travis's beta higher or lower than the beta of the average stock?

12.6 The following table lists possible rates of return on two risky assets, *M* and *J*. The table also lists their joint probabilities, that is, the probability that they will occur simultaneously.

R_M	R_J	Prob(R_M, R_J)
0.16	0.16	0.10
0.16	0.18	0.06
0.16	0.22	0.04
0.18	0.18	0.12
0.18	0.20	0.36
0.18	0.22	0.12
0.20	0.18	0.02
0.20	0.20	0.04
0.20	0.22	0.04
0.20	0.24	0.10

a. List the possible values for R_M and the probabilities that correspond to those values.
b. Compute the following items for R_M.
   i. expected value
   ii. variance
   iii. standard deviation
c. List the possible values for R_J and the probabilities that correspond to those values.
d. Compute the following items for R_J.
   i. expected value
   ii. variance
   iii. standard deviation
e. Calculate the covariance and correlation coefficient of R_M and R_J.
f. Assume *M* is the market portfolio. Calculate the beta coefficient for security *J*.

12.7 If you use the stock beta and the security market line to compute the discount rate for a project, what assumptions are you implicitly making?

12.8 Pacific Cosmetics is evaluating a project to produce a perfume line. Pacific currently produces no-body scent products. Pacific Cosmetics is an all-equity firm.
a. Should Pacific Cosmetics use its stock beta to evaluate the project?
b. How should Pacific Cosmetics compute the beta to evaluate the project?

12.9 The following table lists possible rates of return on Blue Jay, Inc.'s stock and debt, and on the market portfolio. The corporate tax rate is 35 percent. The corresponding probabilities are also listed.

State	*Probability*	*Return on Equity (%)*	*Return on Debt (%)*	*Return on the Market (%)*
1	0.1	3%	8%	5%
2	0.3	8	8	10
3	0.4	20	10	15
4	0.2	15	10	20

a. What is the beta of Blue Jay debt?
b. What is the beta of Blue Jay stock?
c. If the debt-to-equity ratio of Blue Jay is 0.5, what is the asset beta of Blue Jay, Inc.?

12.10 Is the discount rate for the projects of a levered firm higher or lower than the cost of equity computed using the security market line? Why? (Consider only projects that have similar risk to that of the firm.)

12.11 What factors determine the beta of a stock? Define and describe each.

Weighted Average Cost of Capital

12.12 The equity beta for National Napkin Company is 1.29. National Napkin has a debt-to-equity ratio of 1.0. The expected return on the market is 13 percent. The risk-free rate is 7 percent. The cost of debt capital is 7 percent. The corporate tax rate is 35 percent.
a. What is National Napkin's cost of equity?
b. What is National Napkin's weighted average cost of capital?

12.13 Calculate the weighted average cost of capital for the Luxury Porcelain Company. The book value of Luxury's outstanding debt is $60 million. Currently, the debt is trading at 120 percent of book value and is priced to yield 12 percent. The 5 million outstanding shares of Luxury stock are selling for $20 per share. The required return on Luxury stock is 18 percent. The tax rate is 25 percent.

12.14 M. Silberman Co. has 20 million shares of common stock outstanding that is currently being sold for $25 per share. The firm's debt is publicly traded at 95 percent of its face value of $180 million. The cost of debt is 10 percent and the cost of equity is 20 percent. What is the weighted average cost of capital for the firm? Assume the corporate tax rate is 40 percent.

12.15 Calgary Industries, Inc., is considering a new project that costs $25 million. The project will generate aftertax (year-end) cash flows of $7 million for five years. The firm has a debt-to-equity ratio of 0.75. The cost of equity is 15 percent and the cost of debt is 9 percent. The corporate tax rate is 35 percent. It appears that the project has the same risk of the overall firm. Should Calgary take on the project?

CHAPTER 15 Capital Structure: Basic Concepts

Previous chapters of this book examined the capital-budgeting decision. We pointed out that this decision concerns the left-hand side of the balance sheet. The last two chapters began our discussion of the capital-structure decision,[1] which deals with the right-hand side of the balance sheet.

In general, a firm can choose any capital structure that it wants. It can issue floating-rate preferred stock, warrants, convertible bonds, caps, and callers. It can arrange lease financing, bond swaps, and forward contracts. Because the number of instruments is so large, the variations in capital structures are endless. We simplify the analysis by considering only common stock and straight debt in this chapter. The "bells and whistles," as they are called on Wall Street, must await later chapters of the text.

Our results in this chapter are basic. First we discuss the capital-structure decision in a world with neither taxes nor other capital-market imperfections. Surprisingly, we find that the capital-structure decision is a matter of indifference in this world. We next argue that there is a quirk in the U.S. tax code that subsidizes debt financing. Finally, we show that an increase in the firm's value from debt financing leads to an increase in the value of the equity.

15.1 The Capital-Structure Question and the Pie Theory

How should a firm choose its debt-equity ratio? More generally, what is the best capital structure for the firm? We call our approach to the capital-structure question the **pie model.** If you are wondering why we chose this name, just take a look at Figure 15.1. The pie in question is the sum of the financial claims of the firm, debt and equity in this case. We *define* the value of the firm to be this sum. Hence, the value of the firm, V, is

$$V \equiv B + S \tag{15.1}$$

where B is the market value of the debt and S is the market value of the equity. Figure 15.1 presents two possible ways of slicing this pie between stock and debt: 40 percent–60 percent and 60 percent–40 percent. If the goal of the management of the firm

[1] It is conventional to refer to choices regarding debt and equity as *capital-structure decisions.* However, the term *financial-structure decisions* would be more accurate, and we use the terms interchangeably.

FIGURE 15.1 Two Pie Models of Capital Structure

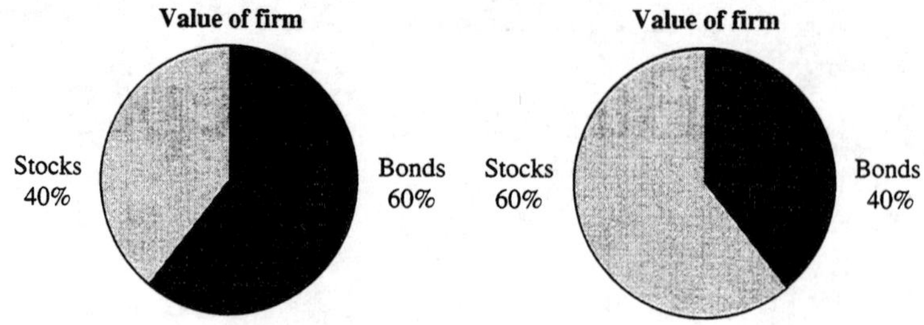

is to make the firm as valuable as possible, then the firm should pick the debt-equity ratio that makes the pie—the total value, *V*—as big as possible.

This discussion begs two important questions:

1. Why should the stockholders in the firm care about maximizing the value of the entire firm? After all, the value of the firm is, by definition, the sum of both the debt and the equity. Instead, why should the stockholders not prefer the strategy that maximizes their interests only?
2. What is the ratio of debt to equity that maximizes the shareholders' interests?

Let us examine each of the two questions in turn.

Concept Question

- What is the pie model of capital structure?

15.2 Maximizing Firm Value versus Maximizing Stockholder Interests

The following example illustrates that the capital structure that maximizes the value of the firm is the one that financial managers should choose for the shareholders.

• ***Example***

Suppose the market value of the J. J. Sprint Company is $1,000. The company currently has no debt, and each of J. J. Sprint's 100 shares of stock sells for $10. A company such as J. J. Sprint with no debt is called an *unlevered* company. Further suppose that J. J. Sprint plans to borrow $500 and pay the $500 proceeds to shareholders as an extra cash dividend of $5 per share. After the issuance of debt, the firm becomes *levered.* The investments of the firm will not change as a result of this transaction. What will the value of the firm be after the proposed restructuring?

Management recognizes that, by definition, only one of three outcomes can occur from restructuring. Firm value after restructuring can be either (1) greater than the original firm value of $1,000, (2) equal to $1,000, or (3) less than $1,000. After consulting with investment bankers, management believes that restructuring will not change firm value more than $250 in either direction. Thus, they view firm values of $1,250, $1,000, and $750 as the relevant range. The original capital structure and these three possibilities under the new capital structure are presented below.

	No debt (original capital structure)	Value of debt plus Equity after Payment of Dividend (three possibilities)		
		I	*II*	*III*
Debt	0	\$500	\$500	\$500
Equity	\$1,000	750	500	250
Firm value	\$1,000	\$1,250	\$1,000	\$750

Note that the value of equity is below \$1,000 under any of the three possibilities. This can be explained in one of two ways. First, the chart shows the value of the equity *after* the extra cash dividend is paid. Since cash is paid out, a dividend represents a partial liquidation of the firm. Consequently, there is less value in the firm for the equityholders after the dividend payment. Second, in the event of a future liquidation, stockholders will be paid only after bondholders have been paid in full. Thus, the debt is an encumbrance of the firm, reducing the value of the equity.

Of course, management recognizes that there are infinite possible outcomes. The above three are to be viewed as *representative* outcomes only. We can now determine the payoff to stockholders under the three possibilities:

	Payoff to Shareholders after Restructuring		
	I	*II*	*III*
Capital gains	−\$250	−\$500	−\$750
Dividends	500	500	500
Net gain or loss to stockholders	\$250	0	−\$250

No one can be sure ahead of time which of the three outcomes will occur. However, imagine that managers believe that outcome *I* is most likely. They should definitely restructure the firm because the stockholders would gain \$250. That is, although the price of the stock declines by \$250 to \$750, they receive \$500 in dividends. Their net gain is \$250 = −\$250 + \$500. Also, notice that the value of the firm would rise by \$250.

Alternatively, imagine that managers believe that outcome *III* is most likely. In this case they should not restructure the firm because the stockholders would expect a \$250 loss. That is, the stock falls by \$750 to \$250 and they receive \$500 in dividends. Their net loss is −\$250 = −\$750 + \$500. Also, notice that the value of the firm would fall by \$250.

Finally, imagine that the managers believe that outcome *II* is most likely. Restructuring would not affect the stockholders' interest because the net gain to stockholders in this case is zero. Also, notice that the value of the firm is unchanged if outcome *II* occurs. •

This example explains why managers should attempt to maximize the value of the firm. In other words, it answers question (1) in section 15.1. In this example, changes in capital structure benefit the stockholders *if and only if* the value of the firm increases. Conversely, these changes hurt the stockholders if and only if the value of the firm decreases. This result holds generally for capital-structure changes of many different types.[2] Thus, managers should choose the capital structure that they believe will have the highest firm value because this capital structure is most beneficial to the firm's stockholders.

Note however that the example does not tell us which of the three outcomes is most likely to occur. Thus, it does not tell us whether debt should be added to J. J. Sprint's capital structure. In other words, it does not answer question (2) in section 15.1. This second question is treated in the next section.

Concept Question

- Why should financial managers choose the capital structure that maximizes the value of the firm?

15.3 Can an Optimal Capital Structure Be Determined?

Modigliani and Miller: Proposition I (No Taxes)

The previous section shows that the capital structure producing the highest firm value is the one most beneficial to the shareholders. In the present section, we would have liked to determine the particular capital structure that produces the highest firm value. Unfortunately, as you will see, we are unable to do this. Modigliani and Miller (MM) have a convincing argument that a firm cannot change the total value of its outstanding securities by changing the proportions of its capital structure. In other words, the value of the firm is always the same under different capital structures. In *still* other words, no capital structure is any better or worse than any other capital structure for the firm's stockholders. This rather pessimistic result is the famous **MM Proposition I.**[3]

To see how MM Proposition I works, consider an unlevered firm that generates expected earnings of *Earn* per year. The firm does not retain any earnings, so its earnings are all paid out as dividends. The value of this unlevered firm is denoted as V_U. Further consider an individual buying 15 percent of the company. He pays $.15V_U$ initially and expects to receive $.15Earn$ as dividends each year. This transaction can be illustrated as follows:

Strategy I (buying 15% of unlevered firm)

Initial Investment	*Expected Dividend per Year*
$.15V_U$	$.15Earn$

Now consider a levered firm, i.e., a firm with both stock and debt in its capital structure. The value of the stock is denoted by S_L, and the value of the bonds is denoted B. As mentioned earlier, the value of the firm is, by definition, the sum of its stock plus its bonds. Thus, the value of the levered firm, V_L, is equal to $S_L + B$. Except for the difference in capital structure, we assume that this firm is identical to the unlev-

[2] This result may not hold exactly in the more complex case where debt has a significant possibility of default. Issues of default are treated in the next chapter.

[3] The original paper appeared in 1958: F. Modigliani and M. Miller, "The Cost of Capital, Corporation Finance and the Theory of Investment," *American Economic Review* (June 1958).

ered firm above. This means that the levered firm is expected to generate yearly earnings before interest payments of *Earn.* Now assume that the bondholders receive interest payments of *Int,* implying that the stockholders expect to receive annual dividends of (*Earn* − *Int*). A person buying 15 percent of the stock of this levered firm pays $.15S_L$ initially and expects to receive .15(*Earn* − *Int*) each year. This transaction can be illustrated as:

Strategy II (buying 15% of the stock of the levered firm)

Initial Investment	*Expected Dividend per Year*
$.15S_L$	.15(*Earn* − *Int*)

Strategy II is more risky than strategy I because strategy II involves corporate leverage. This difference in risk occurs because bondholders receive their interest in full before the stockholders receive anything. (Much more will be said on the effect of leverage on risk later in this chapter.)

Now consider Robert Heiler, an arbitrageur, who is contemplating a third, and more complex, strategy. He plans to:

1. Borrow $.15B_L$ from either a bank or, more likely, a brokerage house. (If the brokerage house is the lender, we say that Mr. Heiler is *going on margin.*)
2. Use the borrowed proceeds plus his own funds to buy 15 percent of the stock of the unlevered firm.

This strategy is illustrated as follows:

Strategy III (buying 15% of the stock of the unlevered firm by a combination of one's own funds plus personal borrowing)

Initial Investment	*Expected Net Dividend per Year after Payment of Interest*
$.15V_U - .15B_L$	.15*Earn* − .15*Int*

Note that it costs $.15V_U$ to buy 15 percent of the unlevered firm. However, since our arbitrageur borrows $.15B_L$, he only pays the difference, $.15V_U - .15B_L$, out of his own pocket. Also, his expected net dividends per year is .15*Earn* − .15*Int* because he must pay interest on the money he borrowed.[4]

Now let us compare strategy III with strategy II, the comparison that Modigliani and Miller use to establish their important capital proposition I. We compare both the expected net dividends per year and the initial investments of the two strategies. Notice that the expected net dividends each period are equal for the two strategies.

The initial investments of the two strategies are:

Initial investment of Strategy II	*Initial investment of strategy III*
$.15\ S_L$	$.15V_U - .15B_L$

Because the net dividends on the two strategies are identical, the initial investments *must* be identical as well. Otherwise, one investment would be cheaper than the other, and no rational person would buy the expensive asset. Consequently, its price would then fall until the two initial investments became equal.

[4] We are assuming that an individual can borrow at the same interest rate as the firm. Though many students believe that this assumption is unrealistic, we show later that it is quite plausible in the real world.

Inspection of the two initial investments above indicates that equality of initial investment occurs when $V_U = S_L + B_L$. Since $S_L + B_L$ is equal to V_L by definition, equality of initial investment occurs when $V_U = V_L$. This proves that

> **MM Proposition I (no taxes): The value of the unlevered firm is the same as the value of the levered firm, that is, $V_L = V_U$.**

Though this discussion may strike you as mathematical, the intuition can be explained as follows. Suppose that our result did not hold. For example, suppose that the value of the levered firm were actually greater than the value of the unlevered firm, that is, $V_L > V_U$. Our arbitrageur, Mr. Heiler, could borrow on his own account and invest in the stock of the unlevered company. He would get the same net dividend each year as if he had invested in the levered firm. However, his cost would be less because $V_L > V_U$. The strategy would not be unique to Mr. Heiler. Given $V_L > V_U$, no rational individual would ever invest in the levered firm. Anyone desiring shares in the levered firm would get the same dollar return more cheaply by borrowing to finance a purchase of the unlevered firm's shares. The equilibrium result would be, of course, that the value of the levered firm would fall and the value of the unlevered firm would rise until $V_L = V_U$. At this point, individuals would be indifferent between strategy II and strategy III.

This is perhaps the most important example in all of corporate finance. In fact, it is considered the beginning point of modern managerial finance. Before MM, the effect of leverage on the value of the firm was considered complex and convoluted. Modigliani and Miller show a blindingly simple result: If levered firms are priced too high, rational investors will simply borrow on personal account to buy shares in unlevered firms. This substitution is oftentimes called *homemade leverage.* As long as individuals borrow (and lend) on the same terms as the firm, they can duplicate the effects of corporate leverage on their own.

The above example shows that leverage does not affect the value of the firm. Since we showed earlier that stockholders' welfare is directly related to the firm's value, the example indicates that changes in capital structure cannot affect the stockholders' welfare.

Concept Questions

- State MM Proposition I. What are its assumptions?
- How can a shareholder undo a firm's financial leverage?

15.4 Financial Leverage and Firm Value: An Example

Trans Am Corporation currently has no debt in its capital structure. The chief financial officer, Ms. Morris, is considering issuing debt to buy back some of its equity. Both its current and proposed capital structures are presented in Table 15.1. The firm's assets are $8,000,000. There are 400,000 shares of the all-equity firm, implying a market value per share of $20. The proposed debt issue is for $4,000,000, leaving $4,000,000 in equity. The interest rate is 10 percent.

TABLE 15.1 Financial Structure of Trans Am Corporation

	Current	*Proposed*
Assets	$8,000,000	$8,000,000
Debt	0	$4,000,000
Equity (market and book)	$8,000,000	$4,000,000
Interest rate	10%	10%
Market value/share	$20	$20
Shares outstanding	400,000	200,000

The proposed capital structure has leverage, whereas the current structure is all equity.

TABLE 15.2 Alternative Capital Structures for Trans Am Corporation

	Current Structure: No Debt			Proposed Structure: Debt = $4,000,000		
	Recession	*Expected*	*Expansion*	*Recession*	*Expected*	*Expansion*
Return on assets (ROA)	5%	15%	25%	5%	15%	25%
Earnings before interest (EBI)	$400,000	$1,200,000	$2,000,000	$400,000	$1,200,000	$2,000,000
Interest	0	0	0	$400,000	$400,000	$400,000
Earnings after interest	$400,000	$1,200,000	$2,000,000	0	$800,000	$1,600,000
Return on equity (ROE) = Earnings after interest/Equity	5%	15%	25%	0	20%	40%
Earnings per share (EPS)	$1.00	$3.00	$5.00	0	$4.00	$8.00

When EBI is high, Trans Am has higher EPS and ROE with the proposed structure than with the current structure. When EBI is low, Trans Am has lower EPS and ROE with the proposed structure. Thus, the equityholders bear more risk with the proposed structure.

Ms. Morris believes the firm's stockholders will be better off with a debt issue. To justify her conclusion, she has prepared Table 15.2, which shows both the company's current structure and its proposed structure under three different, *equally probable* economic scenarios. Ms. Morris is ultimately interested in comparing both return on equity (ROE) and earnings per share (EPS) under the two capital structures. ROE is the ratio of earnings after interest to equity. Under the current capital structure, ROE is expected to be 15 percent (= $1,200,000/$8,000,000). Under the current capital structure, EPS is expected to be $3 (= $1,200,000/400,000), where 400,000 is the number of shares outstanding.

She concludes from her analysis that

1. The effect of financial leverage depends on the company's earnings before interest. If earnings before interest is equal to $1,200,000, the return on equity (ROE) is higher under the proposed structure. If earnings before interest is equal to $400,000, the ROE is higher under the current structure.

FIGURE 15.2 Financial Leverage: EPS and EBI for the Trans Am Corporation

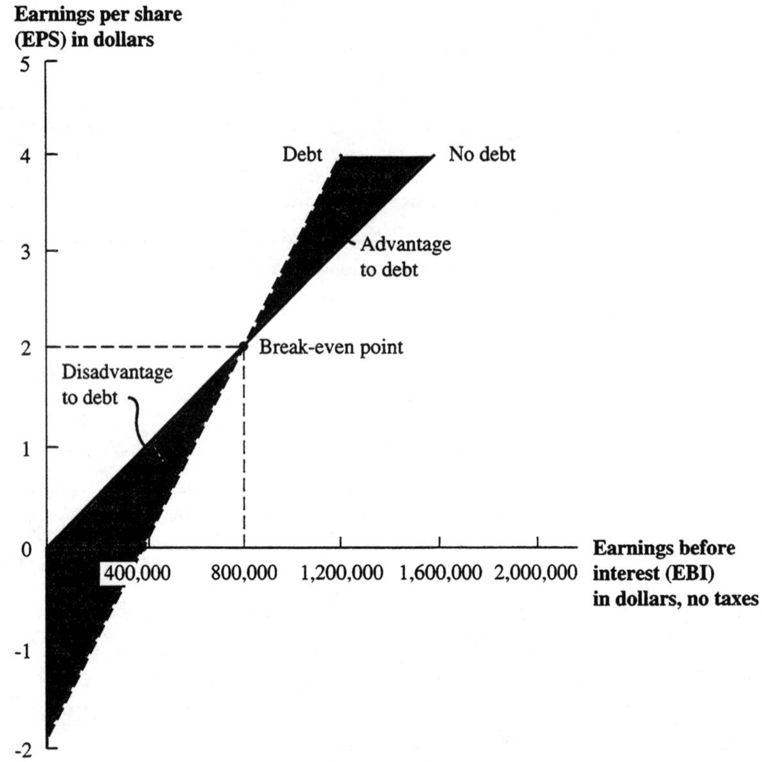

This is represented in a graph of hers, which we have reproduced as Figure 15.2. The solid line represents the case of no leverage. The line begins at the origin, indicating that earnings per share (EPS) would be zero if earnings before interest (EBI) were zero. The EPS rises in tandem with a rise in EBI.

The dotted line represents the case of $4,000,000 of debt. Here, EPS is negative if EBI is zero. This follows because $400,000 of interest must be paid regardless of the firm's profits.

Now consider the slopes of the two lines. The slope of the dotted line (the line with debt) is higher than the slope of the solid line. This occurs because the levered firm has *fewer* shares of stock outstanding than does the unlevered firm. Therefore, any increase in EBI leads to a greater rise in EPS for the levered firm because the earnings increase is distributed over fewer shares of stock.

Because the dotted line has a lower intercept but a higher slope, the two lines must intersect. The *break-even* point occurs at $800,000 of EBI. Were earnings before interest to be $800,000, both firms would produce $2 of earnings per share (EPS). Because $800,000 is break-even, earnings above $800,000 lead to greater EPS for the levered firm. Earnings below $800,000 lead to greater EPS for the unlevered firm.

2. Because expected earnings before interest is $1,200,000, she reasons that the stockholders are better off under the proposed capital structure.

Mr. Siegel, a financial consultant hired by the Trans Am Corporation, argues that the analysis in point (1) is correct, but the conclusion in point (2) is incorrect. He states that the shareholders of Trans Am can borrow on personal account if they want to

TABLE 15.3 Payoff and Cost to Shareholders of Trans Am Corporation under the Proposed Structure and under the Current Structure with Homemade Leverage

Trans Am: Proposed Capital Structure	*Recession*	*Expected*	*Expansion*
EPS (taken from last line of Table 15.2)	$0	$4	$8
Earnings per 100 shares	$0	$400	$800
Initial cost = 100 shares @ $20/share = $2,000			

Homemade Leverage by Shareholders of Trans Am	*Recession*	*Expected*	*Expansion*
Earnings per 200 shares in current Trans Am	$1 × 200 = $200	$3 × 200 = $600	$5 × 200 = $1,000
Interest at 10% on $2,000	−$200	−$200	−$200
Net	$0	$400	$800
Initial cost = 200 shares @ $20/share − $2,000 = $2,000 (Cost of stock, Cost of debt)			

Investor receives the same payoff whether she (1) buys shares in a levered corporation or (2) buys shares in an unlevered firm and borrows on personal account. Her initial investment is the same in either case. Thus, the firm neither helps nor hurts her by adding debt to capital structure.

duplicate the company's proposed financial leverage. The consultant considers an investor who would buy 100 shares of the proposed levered equity. Alternatively, the investor could buy 200 shares of the unlevered firm, partially financing his purchase by borrowing $2,000. Both the cost and the payoff from the two strategies will be the same. Thus, Mr. Siegel concludes that Trans Am is neither helping nor hurting its stockholders by restructuring. In other words, the investor is not receiving anything from corporate leverage that he or she could not achieve on his or her own. His calculations are presented in Table 15.3.

His sidekick, Stuart Weiss, then stated, "This is nothing more than a discussion of the Modigliani-Miller relationship. Because individuals can create homemade leverage, there is no need for corporate leverage." He then related the story of the world's stupidest criminal. It seems someone hijacked a commercial airplane, commanding it to go to Washington, D.C. However, Washington, D.C. was the scheduled destination anyway. Mr. Weiss concluded, "The hijacker's action neither helped nor hurt the passengers. Similarly, a change in corporate leverage can neither help nor hurt the stockholders."

A Key Assumption

The MM result hinges on the assumption that individuals can borrow as cheaply as corporations. If, alternatively, individuals can only borrow at a higher rate, one can easily show that corporations can increase firm value by borrowing.

Is this assumption of equal borrowing costs a good one? Individuals who want to buy stock and borrow can do so by establishing a margin account with the broker. Under this arrangement, the broker loans the individual a portion of the purchase price. For example, the individual might buy $10,000 of stock by investing $6,000 of her own funds and borrowing $4,000 from the broker. Should the stock be worth

$9,000 on the next day, the individual's net worth or equity in the account would be $5,000 = $9,000 − $4,000.[5]

The broker fears that a sudden price drop will cause the equity in the individual's account to be negative, implying that the broker may not get her loan repaid in full. To guard against this possibility, stock exchange rules require that the individual make additional cash contributions (replenish her margin account) as the stock price falls. Because (1) the procedures for replenishing the account have developed over many years, and (2) the broker holds the stock as collateral, there is little default risk to the broker.[6] In particular, if margin contributions are not made on time, the broker can sell the stock in order to satisfy her loan. Therefore, brokers generally charge low interest, with many rates being only slightly above the risk-free rate.

By contrast, corporations frequently borrow using illiquid assets (e.g., plant and equipment) as collateral. The costs to the lender of initial negotiation and ongoing supervision, as well as of working out arrangements in the event of financial distress, can be quite substantial. Thus, it is difficult to argue that individuals must borrow at higher rates than can corporations.[7]

This is, of course, the argument of MM Proposition I.

Concept Questions

- Describe financial leverage.
- What is levered equity?
- How can a shareholder of Trans Am undo the company's financial leverage?

15.5 Modigliani and Miller: Proposition II (No Taxes)

At a corporate meeting where both Ms. Morris and Mr. Siegel presented their viewpoints, a corporate officer said, "Well, maybe it does not matter whether the corporation or the individual levers—as long as some leverage takes place. Leverage benefits investors. After all, the investor's expected return rises with the amount of leverage present." He then pointed out that, from Table 15.2, the expected return on unlevered equity is 15 percent while the expected return on levered equity is 20 percent.

Mr. Siegel replied, "Not necessarily. Though the expected return rises with leverage, the *risk* rises as well." Mr. Siegel's point can be seen from an examination of Table 15.2. With earnings before interest (EBI) varying between $400,000 and $2,000,000, earnings per share (EPS) for the stockholders of the unlevered firm vary between $1.00 and $5.00. EPS for the stockholders of the levered firm vary between $0 and $8.00. This greater range for the EPS of the levered firm implies greater risk for the levered firm's stockholders. In other words, levered stockholders have better

[5] We are ignoring the one-day interest charge on the loan.

[6] Had this text been published before October 19, 1987, when stock prices declined by more than 20 percent, we might have used the phrase "virtually no" risk instead of "little."

[7] One caveat is in order. Initial margin or borrowing is currently limited by law to 50 percent of value. Certain companies, like financial institutions, borrow over 90 percent of their firm's market value. Individuals borrowing against the stock of all-equity corporations cannot duplicate the debt of these highly levered corporations.

returns in good times than do unlevered stockholders but have worse returns in bad times. Table 15.2 also shows greater range for the ROE of the levered firm's stockholders. The above interpretation concerning risk applies here as well.

The same insight can be taken from Figure 15.2. The slope of the line for the levered firm is greater than the slope of the line for the unlevered firm. This also means that the levered stockholders have better returns in good times than do unlevered stockholders but have worse returns in bad times, implying greater risk with leverage. In other words, the slope of the line measures the risk to stockholders, since the slope indicates the responsiveness of ROE to changes in firm performance (earnings before interest).

Since levered equity has greater risk, it should have greater expected returns as compensation. The market only *requires* a 15 percent expected return for the unlevered equity, but it requires a 20 percent expected return for the levered equity.

This type of reasoning allows us to develop **MM Proposition II.** Here, MM argue that the expected return on equity is positively related to leverage, because the risk of equity increases with leverage.

To develop this position recall from Chapter 12 that the firm's weighted average cost of capital, r_{WACC}, can be written as[8]:

$$\frac{B}{B+S} \times r_B + \frac{S}{B+S} \times r_S \qquad (15.2)$$

where

r_B is the interest rate, also called the cost of debt
r_S is the expected return on equity, also called the *cost of equity* or the *required return on equity*
r_{WACC} is the firm's weighted average cost of capital
B is the value of debt
S is the value of stock or equity

Formula (15.2) is quite intuitive. It simply says that a firm's weighted average cost of capital is a weighted average of its cost of debt and its cost of equity. The weight applied to debt is the proportion of debt in the capital structure, and the weight applied to equity is the proportion of equity in the capital structure. Calculations of r_{WACC} from (15.2) for both the unlevered and the levered firm are presented in Table 15.4.

An implication of MM Proposition I is that r_{WACC} is a constant for a given firm, regardless of the capital structure.[9] For example, Table 15.4 shows that r_{WACC} for TransAm is 15%, with or without leverage.

Let us now define r_0 to be the *cost of capital for an all-equity firm.* For the Trans Am Corp., r_0 is calculated as:

$$r_0 = \frac{\text{Expected earnings to unlevered firm}}{\text{Unlevered equity}} = \frac{\$1{,}200{,}000}{\$8{,}000{,}000} = 15\%$$

As can be seen from Table 15.4, r_{WACC} is equal to r_0 for Trans Am. In fact, r_{WACC} must always equal r_0 in a world without corporate taxes.

[8] Since we do not have taxes here, the cost of debt is r_B, not $r_B(1 - T_C)$ as it was in Chapter 12.

[9] This statement holds in a world of no-taxes. It does not hold in a world with taxes, a point to be brought out later in this chapter (see Figure 15.6).

TABLE 15.4 Cost of Capital Calculations for Trans Am

$$r_{WACC} = \frac{B}{B+S} \times r_B + \frac{S}{B+S} \times r_S$$

Unlevered firm: $$15\% = \frac{0}{\$8{,}000{,}000} \times 10\%^* + \frac{\$8{,}000{,}000}{\$8{,}000{,}000} \times 15\%^\dagger$$

Levered firm: $$15\% = \frac{\$4{,}000{,}000}{\$8{,}000{,}000} \times 10\%^* + \frac{\$4{,}000{,}000}{\$8{,}000{,}000} \times 20\%^\ddagger$$

*10% is the interest rate.

†From the "expected" column in Table 15.2, we learn that expected earnings after interest for the unlevered firm are $1,200,000. From Table 15.1, we learn that equity for the unlevered firm is $8,000,000. Thus, r_S for the unlevered firm is:

$$\frac{\text{Expected earnings after interest}}{\text{Equity}} = \frac{\$1{,}200{,}000}{\$8{,}000{,}000} = 15\%$$

‡From the "expected" column in Table 15.2, we learn that expected earnings after interest for the levered firm are $800,000. From Table 15.1, we learn that equity for the levered firm is $4,000,000. Thus, r_S for the levered firm is

$$\frac{\text{Expected earnings after interest}}{\text{Equity}} = \frac{\$800{,}000}{\$4{,}000{,}000} = 20\%.$$

Proposition II states the expected return on equity, r_S, in terms of leverage. The exact relationship, derived by setting $r_{WACC} = r_0$ and then rearranging (15.2), is[10]

MM Proposition II (no taxes):

$$r_S = r_0 + \frac{B}{S}(r_0 - r_B) \tag{15.3}$$

Equation (15.3) states that the required return on equity is a linear function of the firm's debt-to-equity ratio. Examining equation (15.3), we see that if r_0 exceeds the debt rate, r_B, then the cost of equity increases with increases in the debt-equity ratio, B/S.[11] Note that equation (15.3) holds for Trans Am in its levered state:

$$.20 = .15 + \frac{\$4{,}000{,}000}{\$4{,}000{,}000}(.15 - .10)$$

Figure 15.3 graphs equation (15.3). As you can see, we have plotted the relation between the cost of equity, r_S, and the debt-equity ratio, B/S, as a straight line. What

[10] This can be derived from (15.2) by setting $r_{WACC} = r_0$

$$\frac{B}{B+S} r_B + \frac{S}{B+S} r_S = r_0 \tag{15.2}$$

Multiplying both sides by $(B + S)/S$ yields:

$$\frac{B}{S} r_B + r_S = \frac{B+S}{S} r_0$$

We can rewrite the right-hand side as

$$\frac{B}{S} r_B + r_S = \frac{B}{S} r_0 + r_0$$

Moving $(B/S)\, r_B$ to the right-hand side and rearranging yields:

$$r_S = r_0 + \frac{B}{S}(r_0 - r_B) \tag{15.3}$$

[11] Normally, r_0 should exceed r_B. That is, because even unlevered equity is risky, it should have an expected return greater than that on riskless debt.

FIGURE 15.3 The Cost of Equity, the Cost of Debt, and the Weighted Average Cost of Capital: MM Proposition II with No Corporate Taxes

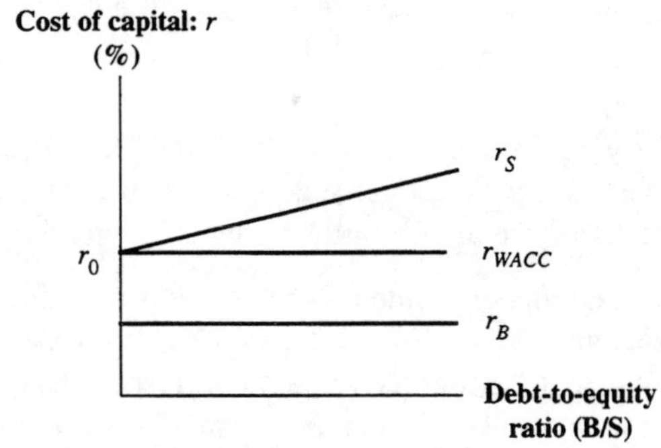

$r_S = r_0 + (r_0 - r_B)B/S$
r_S is the cost of equity
r_B is the cost of debt
r_0 is the cost of capital for an all-equity firm
r_{WACC} is a firm's weighted average cost of capital. In a world with no taxes, r_{WACC} for a levered firm is equal to r_0.

The cost of equity capital, r_S is positively related to the firm's debt-equity ratio. The firm's weighted average cost of capital, r_{WACC}, is invariant to the firm's debt-equity ratio.

we witness in equation (15.3) and illustrate in Figure 15.3 is the effect of leverage on the cost of equity. As the firm raises the debt-equity ratio, each dollar of equity is levered with additional debt. This raises the risk of equity and therefore the required return, r_S, on the equity.

Figure 15.3 also shows that r_{WACC} is unaffected by leverage, a point we made above.

Example Illustrating Proposition I and Proposition II

• ***Example***

Luteran Motors, an all-equity firm has expected earnings of $10 million per year in perpetuity. The firm pays all of its earnings out as dividends, so that the $10 million may also be viewed as the stockholders' expected cash flow. There are 10 million shares outstanding, implying expected annual cash flow of $1 per share. The cost of capital for this unlevered firm is 10 percent. In addition, the firm will soon build a new plant for $4 million. The plant is expected to generate additional cash flow of $1 million per year. These figures can be described as

Current Company	*New Plant*
Cash flow: $10 million	Initial outlay: $4 million
Number of outstanding shares: 10 million	Additional annual cash flow: $1 million

The project's net present value is

$$-\$4 \text{ million} + \frac{\$1 \text{ million}}{0.1} = \$6 \text{ million}$$

assuming that the project is discounted at the same rate as the firm as a whole. Before the market knows of the project, the *market-value* balance sheet of the firm is

LUTERAN MOTORS
Balance sheet (all equity)

Old assets: $\frac{\$10 \text{ million}}{0.1} = \$100 \text{ million}$	Equity: $100 million (10 million shares of stock)

The value of the firm is $100 million, because the cash flow of $10 million per year is capitalized at 10 percent. A share of stock sells for $10 ($100 million/10 million) because there are 10 million shares outstanding. •

The market-value balance sheet is a useful tool of financial analysis. Because students are often thrown off guard by it initially, we recommend extra study here. The key is that the market-value balance sheet has the same form as the balance sheet that accountants use. That is, assets are placed on the left-hand side whereas liabilities and owners' equity are placed on the right-hand side. In addition, the left-hand side and the right-hand side must be equal. The difference between a market value balance sheet and the accountant's balance sheet is in the numbers. Accountants value items in terms of historical cost (original purchase price less depreciation), whereas financial people value items in terms of market value.

The firm will either issue $4 million of equity or debt. Let us consider the effect of equity and debt financing in turn.

Stock Financing

Imagine that the firm announces that, in the near future, it will raise $4 million in equity in order to build a new plant. The stock price, and therefore the value of the firm, will rise to reflect the positive net present value of the plant. According to efficient markets, the increase occurs immediately. That is, the rise occurs on the day of the announcement, not on the date of either the onset of construction of the power plant or the forthcoming stock offering. The market-value balance sheet becomes

LUTERAN MOTORS
Balance sheet
(upon announcement of equity issue to construct plant)

Old assets	$100 million	Equity	$106 million (10 million shares of stock)
NPV of plant:			
$-\$4 \text{ million} + \frac{\$1 \text{ million}}{0.1} =$	6 million		
Total assets	$106 million		

Note that the NPV of the plant is included in the market-value balance sheet. Because the new shares have not yet been issued, the number of outstanding shares remains 10 million. The price per share has now risen to $10.60 ($106 million/10 million) to reflect news concerning the plant.

Shortly thereafter, $4 million of stock is issued or *floated.* Because the stock is selling at $10.60 per share, 377,358 ($4 million/$10.60) shares of stock are issued. Imagine that funds are put in the bank *temporarily* before being used to build the plant. The market-value balance sheet becomes

LUTERAN MOTORS
Balance sheet
(upon issuance of stock but before construction begins on plant)

Old assets	$100 million	Equity	$110 million (10,377,358 shares of stock)
NPV of plant:	6 million		
Proceeds from new issue of stock (currently invested in bank)	4 million		
Total assets	$110 million		

The number of shares outstanding is now 10,377,358 because 377,358 new shares were issued. The price per share is $10.60 ($110,000,000/10,377,358). Note that the price has not changed. This is consistent with efficient capital markets, because stock price should only move due to new information.

Of course, the funds are placed in the bank only temporarily. Shortly after the new issue, the $4 million is given to a contractor who builds the plant. To avoid problems in discounting, we assume that the plant is built immediately. The balance sheet then becomes

LUTERAN MOTORS
Balance sheet
(upon completion of the plant)

Old assets	$100 million	Equity	$110 million (10,377,358 shares of stock)
PV of plant: $\frac{\$1 \text{ million}}{0.1}$ =	10 million		
Total assets	$110 million		

Though total assets do not change, the composition of the assets does change. The bank account has been emptied to pay the contractor. The present value of cash flows of $1 million a year from the plant are reflected as an asset worth $10 million. Because the building expenditures of $4 million have already been paid, they no longer represent a future cost. Hence, they no longer reduce the value of the plant. According to efficient capital markets, the price per share of stock remains $10.60.

Expected yearly cash flow from the firm are $11 million, $10 million of which comes from the old assets and $1 million from the new. The expected return to equityholders is

$$r_S = \frac{\$11 \text{ million}}{\$110 \text{ million}} = 0.10$$

Because the firm is all equity, $r_S = r_0 = 0.10$.

Debt Financing

Alternatively, imagine that the firm announces that, in the near future, it will borrow $4 million at 6 percent to build a new plant. This implies yearly interest payments of $240,000 ($4,000,000 × 6%). Again the stock price rises immediately to reflect the positive net present value of the plant. Thus, we have

LUTERAN MOTORS
Balance sheet
(upon announcement of debt issue to construct plant)

Old assets	\$100 million	Equity	\$106 million (10 million shares of stock)
NPV of plant: $-\$4\text{ million} + \dfrac{\$1\text{ million}}{0.1}$ =	6 million		
Total assets	\$106 million		

The value of the firm is the same as in the equity financing case because (1) the same plant is to be built and (2) MM prove that debt financing is neither better nor worse than equity financing.

At some point, \$4 million of debt is issued. As before, the funds are placed in the bank temporarily. The market-value balance sheet becomes

LUTERAN MOTORS
Balance sheet
(upon debt issuance but before construction begins on plant)

Old assets	\$100 million	Debt	\$4 million
NPV of plant	6 million	Equity	106 million (10 million shares of stock)
Proceeds from debt issue (currently invested in bank)	4 million		
Total assets	\$110 million	Debt plus equity	\$110 million

Note that debt appears on the right-hand side of the balance sheet. The stock price is still \$10.60, in accordance with our discussion of efficient capital markets.

Finally, the contractor receives \$4 million and builds the plant. The market value balance sheet becomes

LUTERAN MOTORS
Balance sheet
(upon completion of the plant)

Old assets	\$100 million	Debt	\$ 4 million
PV of plant	10 million	Equity	106 million (10 million shares of stock)
Total assets	\$110 million	Debt plus equity	\$110 million

The only change here is that the bank account has been depleted to pay the contractor. The equityholders expect yearly cash flow after interest of

$$\underset{\text{Cash flow on old assets}}{\$10{,}000{,}000} + \underset{\text{Cash flow on new assets}}{\$1{,}000{,}000} - \underset{\text{Interest: } \$4\text{ million} \times 6\%}{\$240{,}000} = \$10{,}760{,}000$$

The equityholders expect to earn a return of

$$\frac{\$10{,}760{,}000}{\$106{,}000{,}000} = 10.15\%$$

This return of 10.15 percent for levered equityholders is higher than the 10 percent return for the unlevered equityholders. This result is sensible because, as we argued earlier, levered equity is riskier. In fact, the return of 10.15 percent should be exactly what MM Proposition II predicts. This prediction can be verified by plugging values into

$$r_S = r_0 + \frac{B}{S} \times (r_0 - r_B) \tag{15.3}$$

We obtain

$$10.15\% = 10\% + \frac{\$4{,}000{,}000}{\$106{,}000{,}000} \times (10\% - 6\%)$$

This example was useful for two reasons. First, we wanted to introduce the concept of market-value balance sheets, a tool that will prove useful elsewhere in the text. Among other things, this technique allows one to calculate the price per share of a new issue of stock. Second, the example illustrates three aspects of Modigliani and Miller:

1. The example is consistent with MM Proposition I because the value of the firm is $110 million after either equity or debt financing.
2. Students are often more interested in stock price than in firm value. We show that the stock price is always $10.60, regardless of whether debt or equity financing is used.
3. The example is consistent with MM Proposition II. The expected return to equityholders rises from 10 to 10.15 percent, just as formula (15.3) states. This rise occurs because the equityholders of a levered firm face more risk than do the equityholders of an unlevered firm.

MM: An Interpretation

The Modigliani-Miller results indicate that managers of a firm cannot change its value by repackaging the firm's securities. Though this idea was considered revolutionary when it was originally proposed in the late 1950s, the MM model and arbitrage proof have since met with wide acclaim.[12]

MM argue that the firm's overall cost of capital cannot be reduced as debt is substituted for equity, even though debt appears to be cheaper than equity. The reason for this is that, as the firm adds debt, the remaining equity becomes more risky. As this risk rises, the cost of equity capital rises as a result. The increase in the cost of the remaining equity capital offsets the higher proportion of the firm financed by low-cost debt. In fact, MM prove that the two effects exactly offset each other, so that both the value of the firm and the firm's overall cost of capital are invariant to leverage.

MM use an interesting analogy to food. They consider a dairy farmer with two choices. On the one hand, he can sell whole milk. On the other hand, by skimming he can sell a combination of cream and low-fat milk. Though the farmer can get a high price for the cream, he gets a low price for the low-fat milk, implying no net gain. In fact, imagine that the proceeds from the whole-milk strategy were less than those from the cream–low-fat-milk strategy. Arbitrageurs would buy the whole milk, perform the skimming operation themselves, and resell the cream and low-fat milk separately. Competition between arbitrageurs would tend to boost the price of whole milk until proceeds from the two strategies became equal. Thus, the value of the farmer's milk is invariant to the way in which the milk is packaged.

[12] Both Merton Miller and Franco Modigliani were awarded separate Nobel Prizes, in part for their work on capital structure.

Food found its way into this chapter earlier, when we viewed the firm as a pie.[13] MM argue that the size of the pie does not change, no matter how stockholders and bondholders divide it. MM say that a firm's capital structure is irrelevant; it is what it is by some historical accident. The theory implies that firms' debt-equity ratios could be anything. They are what they are because of whimsical and random managerial decisions about how much to borrow and how much stock to issue.

Although scholars are always fascinated with far-reaching theories, students are perhaps more concerned with real-world applications. Do real-world managers follow MM by treating capital-structure decisions with indifference? Unfortunately for the theory, virtually all companies in certain industries, such as banking, choose high debt-to-equity ratios. Conversely, companies in other industries, such as pharmaceuticals, choose low debt-to-equity ratios. In fact, almost any industry has a debt-to-equity ratio to which companies in that industry adhere. Thus, companies do not appear to be selecting their degree of leverage in a frivolous or random manner. Because of this, financial economists (including MM themselves) have argued that real-world factors may have been left out of the theory.

Though many of our students have argued that individuals can only borrow at rates above the corporate borrowing rate, we disagreed with this argument earlier in the chapter. But when we look elsewhere for unrealistic assumptions in the theory, we find two.[14]

1. Taxes were ignored.
2. Bankruptcy costs and other agency costs were not considered.

We will turn to taxes shortly. Bankruptcy costs and other agency costs will be treated in the next chapter.

Concept Questions

- Why does the expected return on equity rise with firm leverage?
- What is the exact relationship between the expected return on equity and firm leverage?
- How are market-value balance sheets set up?

15.6 Taxes

The Basic Insight

The previous part of this chapter showed that firm value is unrelated to debt in a world without taxes. We now show that, in the presence of corporate taxes, the firm's value is positively related to its debt. The basic intuition can be seen from a pie chart, such as the one in Figure 15.4. Consider the all-equity firm on the left. Here, both equityholders and the IRS have claims on the value of the firm. The value of the all-equity firm is, of course, that part of the pie owned by the equityholders. The proportion going to taxes is simply a cost.

[13] Other authors have also brought food into discussions on capital structure. For example, Stewart Myers in "The Search for Optimal Capital Structure," *Midland Corporate Finance Journal* (Spring 1983), used chicken. Abstracting from the extra costs in cutting up poultry, he argues that all of the chicken parts should, in sum, sell for no more than a whole chicken.

[14] MM were aware of both of these issues, as can be seen in their original paper.

In Professor Miller's Words . . .

The Modigliani-Miller results are not easy to understand fully. This point is related in a story told by Merton Miller.[15]

"How difficult to summarize briefly the contribution of the [Modigliani-Miller] papers was brought home to me very clearly last October after Franco Modigliani was awarded the Nobel Prize in Economics in part—but, of course, only in part—for the work in finance. The television camera crews from our local stations in Chicago immediately descended upon me. 'We understand,' they said, 'that you worked with Modigliani some years back in developing these M and M theorems and we wonder if you could explain them briefly to our television viewers.'

" 'How briefly?' I asked.

" 'Oh, take ten seconds,' was the reply.

"Ten seconds to explain the work of a lifetime! Ten seconds to describe two carefully reasoned articles, each running to more than thirty printed pages and each with sixty or so long footnotes! When they saw the look of dismay on my face, they said, 'You don't have to go into details. Just give us the main points in simple, common-sense terms.'

"The main point of the first or cost-of-capital article was, in principle at least, simple enough to make. It said that in an economist's ideal world of complete and perfect capital markets and with full and symmetric information among all market participants, the total market value of all the securities issued by a firm was governed by the earning power and risk of its underlying real assets and was independent of how the mix of securities issued to finance it was divided between debt instruments and equity capital. . . .

"Such a summary, however, uses too many short-handed terms and concepts, like perfect capital markets, that are rich in connotations to economists but hardly so to the general public. So I thought, instead, of an analogy that we ourselves had invoked in the original paper. . . .

" 'Think of the firm,' I said, 'as a gigantic tub of whole milk. The farmer can sell the whole milk as is. Or he can separate out the cream and sell it at a considerably higher price than the whole milk would bring. (That's the analog of a firm selling low-yield and hence high-priced debt securities.) But, of course, what the farmer would have left would be skim milk with low butterfat content and that would sell for much less than whole milk. That corresponds to the levered equity. The M and M proposition says that if there were no costs of separation (and, of course, no government dairy support programs), the cream plus the skim milk would bring the same price as the whole milk.'

"The television people conferred among themselves and came back to inform me that it was too long, too complicated, and too academic.

" 'Don't you have anything simpler?' they asked. I thought of another way that the M and M proposition is presented these days, which emphasizes the notion of market completeness and stresses the role of securities as devices for 'partitioning' a firm's payoffs in each possible state of the world among the group of its capital suppliers.

" 'Think of the firm,' I said, 'as a gigantic pizza, divided into quarters. If now you cut each quarter in half in eighths, the M and M proposition says that you will have more pieces but not more pizza.'

"Again there was a whispered conference among the camera crew, and the director came back and said:

" 'Professor, we understand from the press release that there were two M and M propositions. Can we try the other one?' "

[Professor Miller tried valiantly to explain the second proposition, though this was apparently even more difficult to get across. After his attempt:]

"Once again there was a whispered conversation. They shut the lights off. They folded up their equipment. They thanked me for giving them the time. They said that they'd get back to me. But I knew that I had somehow lost my chance to start a new career as a packager of economic wisdom for TV viewers in convenient ten-second bites. Some have the talent for it . . . and some just don't."

---

[15] Taken from *GSB Chicago*, University of Chicago (Autumn 1986).

FIGURE 15.4 Two Pie Models of Capital Structure under Corporate Taxes

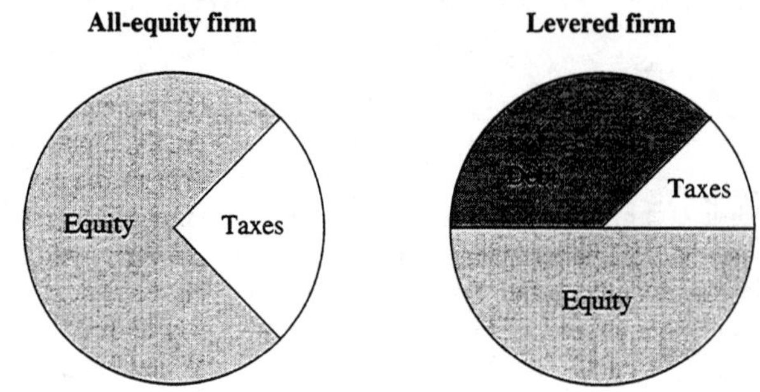

The levered firm pays less than does the all-equity firm. Thus, the sum of the debt plus the equity of the levered firm is greater than the equity of the unlevered firm.

The pie on the right for the levered firm shows three claims: equityholders, debtholders, and taxes. The value of the levered firm is the sum of the value of the debt and the value of the equity. In selecting between the two capital structures in the picture, a financial manager should select the one with the highest value. Assuming that the total area is the same for both pies,[16] value is maximized for that capital structure paying the least in taxes. In other words, the manager should choose the capital structure that the IRS hates the most.

We will show that, due to a quirk in U.S. tax law, the proportion of the pie allocated to taxes is less for the levered firm than it is for the unlevered firm. Thus, managers should select high leverage.

The Quirk in the Tax Code

• ***Example***

The Water Products Company is evaluating two financing plans. The Water Products Company has a corporate tax rate, T_C, of 35 percent and expected earnings before interest and taxes (EBIT) of $1 million. Under plan *I*, Water Products has no debt in its capital structure. Under plan *II*, the company would have $4,000,000 of debt, B. The cost of debt, r_B, is 10 percent.

The chief financial officer for Water Products makes the following calculations:

	Plan I	*Plan II*
Earnings before interest and corporate taxes (EBIT)	$1,000,000	$1,000,000
Interest ($r_B B$)	0	(400,000)
Earnings before taxes (EBT) = (EBIT − $r_B B$)	1,000,000	600,000
Taxes ($T_C = 0.35$)	(350,000)	(210,000)
Earnings after corporate taxes (EAT) = [(EBIT − $r_B B$) × (1 − T_C)]	650,000	390,000
Total cash flow to both stockholders and bondholders [EBIT × (1 − T_C) + $T_C r_B B$]	$650,000	$790,000

The most relevant numbers for our purposes are the two on the bottom line. Here, we see that more cash flow reaches the owners of the firm (both stockholders and bondholders) under plan *II*. The difference is $140,000 = $790,000 − $650,000. It

[16] Under the MM propositions developed earlier, the two pies should be of the same size.

does not take one long to realize the source of this difference. The IRS receives less taxes under plan *II* (\$210,000) than it does under plan *I* (\$350,000). The difference here is \$140,000 = \$350,000 − \$210,000.

This difference[17] occurs because the IRS treats interest differently than it does earnings going to stockholders. Interest totally escapes corporate taxation, whereas earnings after interest but before corporate taxes (EBT) are taxed at the 35-percent rate. We can express this relationship algebraically below.

We will assume in this discussion that all cash flows are constant (that is, perpetual without growth). If EBIT is the total cash flow of the firm before interest and taxes, and if we ignore the effect of depreciation and other items such as taxes, then the taxable income of an all-equity firm is simply

$$\text{EBIT}$$

For an all-equity firm, total taxes are

$$\text{EBIT} \times T_C$$

where T_C is the corporate tax rate. Earnings after corporate taxes are

$$\text{EBIT} \times (1 - T_C) \tag{15.4}$$

For a levered firm, taxable income is

$$\text{EBIT} - r_B B$$

Total taxes in a levered firm are

$$T_C \times (\text{EBIT} - r_B B)$$

Cash flow going to the stockholders in a levered firm is

$$\text{EBIT} - r_B B - T_C \times (\text{EBIT} - r_B B) = (\text{EBIT} - r_B B) \times (1 - T_C)$$

Cash flow going to both the stockholders and the bondholders in a levered firm is

$$\text{EBIT} \times (1 - T_C) + T_C r_B B \tag{15.5}$$

which quite explicitly depends on the amount of debt financing.

The key can be seen by comparing the difference between expressions (15.4) and (15.5). The difference, $T_C r_B B$, is the extra cash flow going to **investors** in the levered firm. We use the term *investors* to mean both stockholders and bondholders. It is also the extra funds not going to the IRS.

Let us calculate this difference for Water Products:

$$T_C r_B B = 35\% \times 10\% \times \$4{,}000{,}000 = \$140{,}000$$

This is the same number that we calculated above. •

Value of the Tax Shield

The discussion above shows a tax advantage to debt or, equivalently, a tax disadvantage to equity. We now want to value this advantage. We previously said that the cash

[17] Note that stockholders actually receive more under Plan I (\$650,000) than under Plan II (\$390,000). Students are often bothered by this since it seems to imply that stockholders are better off without leverage. However, remember that there are more shares outstanding in Plan I than in Plan II. A full-blown model would show that earnings *per share* are higher with leverage.

flow of the levered firm each period is greater than the cash flow of the unlevered firm by

$$T_C r_B B \tag{15.6}$$

Expression (15.6) is often called the *tax shield from debt.*

As long as the firm expects to be in a positive tax bracket, we can assume that the cash flow in expression (15.6) has the same risk as the interest on the debt. Thus, its value can be determined by discounting at the interest rate, r_B. Assuming that the cash flows are perpetual, the value of the tax shield is

$$\frac{T_C r_B B}{r_B} = T_C B$$

Value of the Levered Firm

We have just calculated the present value of the tax shield from debt. Our next step is to calculate the value of the levered firm. We showed above that the after-tax cash flow to the stockholders in the levered firm is

$$\text{EBIT} \times (1 - T_C) + T_C r_B B \tag{15.5}$$

The first term in expression (15.5) is the after-tax cash flow in the unlevered firm. The value of an unlevered firm (that is, a firm with no debt) is the present value of $\text{EBIT} \times (1 - T_C)$,

$$V_U = \frac{\text{EBIT} \times (1 - T_C)}{r_0}$$

where

V_U = Present value of an unlevered firm
$\text{EBIT} \times (1 - T_C)$ = Firm cash flows after corporate taxes
T_C = Corporate tax rate
r_0 = The cost of capital to an all-equity firm. As can be seen from the formula, r_0 now discounts *after-tax* cash flows.

The second part of the cash flows, $T_C r_B B$, is the tax shield. To determine its value, the tax shield should be discounted at r_B.

As a consequence, we have[18]

MM Proposition I (corporate taxes):

$$V_L = \frac{\text{EBIT} \times (1 - T_C)}{r_0} + \frac{T_C r_B B}{r_B} \tag{15.7}$$
$$= V_U + T_C B$$

Equation (15.7) is MM Proposition I under corporate taxes. The first term in equation (15.7) is the value of the cash flows of the firm with no debt tax shield. In other words,

[18] This relationship holds when the debt level is assumed to be constant through time. A different formula would apply if the debt-equity ratio was assumed to be a constant over time. For a deeper treatment of this point, see J. A. Miles and J. R. Ezzel, "The Weighted Average Cost of Capital, Perfect Capital Markets and Project Life," *Journal of Financial and Quantitative Analysis* (September 1980).

this term is equal to V_U, the value of the all-equity firm. The value of the firm is the value of an all-equity firm plus $T_C B$, the tax rate times the value of the debt. $T_C B$ is the present value of the tax shield in the case of perpetual cash flows.[19]

The Water Products example reveals that, because the tax shield increases with the amount of debt, the firm can raise its total cash flow and its value by substituting debt for equity. We now have a clear example of why the capital structure does matter: By raising the debt-equity ratio, the firm can lower its taxes and thereby increase its total value. The strong forces that operate to maximize the value of the firm would seem to push it toward an all-debt capital structure.

• ***Example***

Divided Airlines is currently an unlevered firm. It is considering a capital restructuring to allow \$200 of debt. The company expects to generate \$153.85 in cash flows before interest and taxes, in perpetuity. The corporate tax rate is 35 percent, implying after-tax cash flows of \$100. Its cost of debt capital is 10 percent. Unlevered firms in the same industry have a cost of equity capital of 20 percent. What will the new value of Divided Airlines be?

The value of Divided Airlines will be equal to[20]

$$\begin{aligned} V_L &= \frac{\text{EBIT} \times (1 - T_C)}{r_0} + T_C B \\ &= \frac{\$100}{0.20} + (0.35 \times \$200) \\ &= \$500 + \$70 \\ &= \$570 \end{aligned}$$

Because $V_L = B + S$, the value of levered equity, S, is equal to \$570 − \$200 = \$370. The value of Divided Airlines as a function of leverage is illustrated in Figure 15.5. •

Expected Return and Leverage under Corporate Taxes

MM Proposition II under no taxes posits a positive relationship between the expected return on equity and leverage. This result occurs because the risk of equity increases

---

[19] The following example calculates the present value if we assume the debt has a finite life. Suppose the Maxwell Company has \$1 million in debt with an 8-percent coupon rate. If the debt matures in two years and the cost of debt capital, r_B, is 10 percent, what is the present value of the tax shields if the corporate tax rate is 35 percent? The debt is amortized in equal installments over two years.

Year	*Loan balance*	*Interest*	*Tax shield*	*Present value of Tax shield*
0	\$1,000,000			
1	\$500,000	\$80,000	0.35 × \$80,000	\$25,454.54
2	0	\$40,000	0.35 × \$40,000	11,570.25
				\$37,024.79

The present value of the tax savings is

$$\text{PV} = \frac{0.35 \times \$80{,}000}{1.10} + \frac{0.35 \times \$40{,}000}{(1.10)^2} = \$37{,}024.79$$

The Maxwell Company's value is higher than that of a comparable unlevered firm by \$37,024.79

[20] Note that, in a world with taxes, r_0 is used to discount *after-tax* cash flows.

with leverage. The same intuition also holds in a world of corporate taxes. The exact formula is[21]

MM Proposition II (corporate taxes):

$$r_s = r_0 + \frac{B}{S} \times (1 - T_C) \times (r_0 - r_B) \tag{15.8}$$

Applying the formula to Divided Airlines, we get

$$r_S = 0.2351 = 0.20 + \frac{200}{370} \times (1 - 0.35) \times (0.20 - 0.10)$$

This calculation is illustrated in Figure 15.6.

We can check this calculation by discounting at r_S to determine the value of the levered equity. The algebraic formula for levered equity is

$$S = \frac{(\text{EBIT} - r_B B) \times (1 - T_C)}{r_S} \tag{15.9}$$

The numerator is the expected cash flow to levered equity after interest and taxes. The denominator is the rate at which the cash flow to equity is discounted.

For Divided Airlines we get[22]

$$\frac{(\$153.85 - 0.10 \times \$200)(1 - 0.35)}{0.2351} = \$370 \tag{15.9$'$}$$

the same result we obtained earlier.

---

[21] This relationship can be shown as follows: Given MM Proposition I under taxes, a levered firm's market-value balance sheet can be written as

V_U = Value of unlevered firm	B = Debt
$T_C B$ = tax shield	S = Equity

The value of the unlevered firm is simply the value of the assets without benefit of leverage. The balance sheet indicates that the firm's value increases by $T_C B$ when debt of B is added. The expected cash flow *from* the left-hand side of the balance sheet can be written as

$$V_U r_0 + T_C B r_B \tag{a}$$

Because assets are risky, their expected rate of return is r_0. The tax shield has the same risk as the debt, so its expected rate of return is r_B.

The expected cash *to* bondholders and stockholders together is

$$S r_S + B r_B \tag{b}$$

Expression (*b*) reflects the fact that stock earns an expected return of r_S and debt earns the interest rate r_B.

Because all cash flows are paid out as dividends in our no-growth perpetuity model, the cash flows going into the firm equal those going to stakeholders. Hence (a) and (b) are equal:

$$S r_S + B r_B = V_U r_0 + T_C B r_B \tag{c}$$

Dividing both sides of (c) by S, subtracting $B r_B$ from both sides, and rearranging yields

$$r_S = \frac{V_U}{S} \times r_0 - (1 - T_C) \times \frac{B}{S} r_B \tag{d}$$

Because the value of the levered firm, V_L, equals $V_U + T_C B = B + S$, it follows that $V_U = S + (1 - T_C) \times B$. Thus, (d) can be rewritten as

$$r_S = \frac{S + (1 - T_C) \times B}{S} \times r_0 - (1 - T_C) \times \frac{B}{S} r_B \tag{e}$$

Bringing the terms involving $(1 - T_C) \times \frac{B}{S}$ together produces (15.8).

[22] The calculation suffers slightly from rounding error because we only carried the discount rate, 0.2351, out to four decimal places.

FIGURE 15.5 The Effect of Financial Leverage on Firm Value: MM with Corporate Taxes in the Case of Divided Airlines

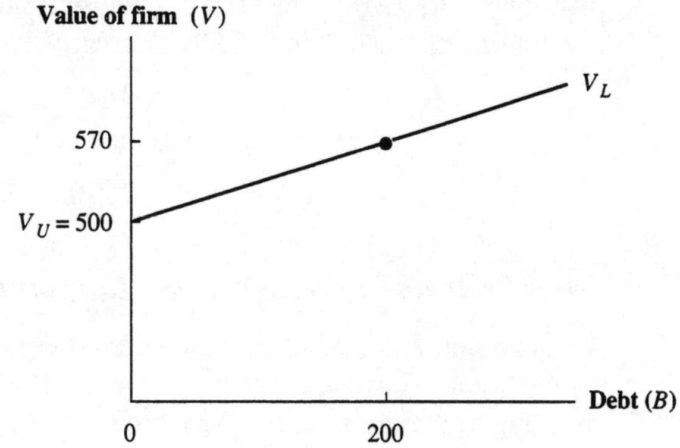

$$V_L = V_U + T_C B$$
$$= \$500 + (0.35 \times \$200)$$
$$= \$570$$

Debt reduces Divided's tax burden. As a result, the value of the firm is positively related to debt.

FIGURE 15.6 The Effect of Financial Leverage on the Cost of Debt and Equity Capital

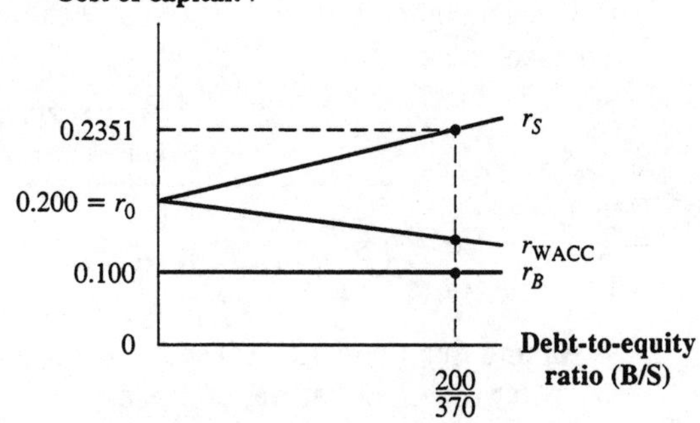

$$r_s = r_0 + (1 - T_C)(r_0 - r_B)B/S$$
$$= 0.20 + \left(0.65 \times 0.10 \times \frac{200}{370}\right)$$
$$= 0.2351$$

Financial leverage adds risk to the firm's equity. As compensation, the cost of equity rises with the firm's risk.

The Weighted Average Cost of Capital r_{WACC} *and Corporate Taxes*

In Chapter 12, we defined the weighted average cost of capital (with corporate taxes) as

$$r_{WACC} = \frac{B}{V_L} r_B (1 - T_C) + \frac{S}{V_L} r_S$$

For Divided Airlines, r_{WACC} is equal to

$$r_{WACC} = \left(\frac{200}{570} \times .10 \times .65\right) + \left(\frac{370}{570} \times .2351\right)$$
$$= .1754$$

Divided Airlines has reduced its r_{WACC} from .20 (with no debt) to .1754 with reliance on debt. This result is intuitively pleasing because it suggests that, when a firm lowers its r_{WACC}, the firm's value will increase. Using the r_{WACC} approach, we can confirm that the value of Divided Airlines is $570.

$$V_L = \frac{\text{EBIT} \times (1 - T_C)}{r_{WACC}}$$
$$= \$570$$

Stock Price and Leverage under Corporate Taxes

At this point, students often believe the numbers—or at least are too intimidated to dispute them. However, they think we have asked the wrong question. "Why are we choosing to maximize the value of the firm?" they will say. "If managers are looking out for the stockholder's interest, why aren't they trying to maximize stock price?" If this question occurred to you, you have come to the right section.

Our response is twofold: First, we showed in the first section of this chapter that the capital structure that maximizes firm value is also the one that most benefits the interests of the stockholders.[23]

However, that general explanation is not always convincing to students. As a second procedure, we calculate the stock price of Divided Airlines both before and after the exchange of debt for stock. We do this by presenting a set of market-value balance sheets. The market-value balance sheet for the company in its all-equity form can be represented as

DIVIDED AIRLINES
Balance sheet (all-equity firm)

Physical assets: $\frac{\$153.85}{0.20} \times (1 - 0.35) = \$500$		Equity	$500 (100 shares)

Assuming that there are 100 shares outstanding, each share is worth $5 = $500/100.

Next imagine that the company announces that, in the near future, it will issue $200 of debt to buy back $200 of stock. We know from our previous discussion that the value of the firm will rise to reflect the tax shield of debt. According to efficient capital markets, the increase occurs immediately. That is, the rise occurs on the day of the announcement, not on the date of the debt-for-equity exchange. The market-value balance sheet now becomes

DIVIDED AIRLINES
Balance sheet
(upon announcement of debt issue)

Physical assets	$500	Equity	$570 (100 shares)
Present value of tax shield: $T_C B = 35\% \times \$200 =$	70		
Total Assets	$570		

Note that the debt has not yet been issued. Therefore, only equity appears on the right-hand side of the balance sheet. Each share is now worth $570/100 = $5.70, implying

[23] At that time, we pointed out that this result may not exactly hold in the more complex case where debt has a significant possibility of default. Issues of default are treated in the next chapter.

that the stockholders have benefited by $70. The equityholders gain because they are the owners of a firm that has improved its financial policy.

The introduction of the tax shield to the balance sheet is frequently perplexing to students. Although physical assets are tangible, the ethereal nature of the tax shield bothers many students. However, remember that an asset is any item with value. The tax shield has value because it reduces the stream of future taxes. The fact that one cannot touch the shield in the way that one can touch a physical asset is a philosophical, not a financial, consideration.

At some point, the exchange of debt for equity occurs. Debt of $200 is issued, and the proceeds are used to buy back shares. How many shares of stock are repurchased? Because shares are now selling at $5.70 each, the number of shares that the firm acquires is $200/$5.70 = 35.09. This leaves 64.91 (100 − 35.09) shares of stock outstanding. The market-value balance sheet is now

DIVIDED AIRLINES
Balance sheet
(after exchange has taken place)

Physical assets	$500	Equity (100 − 35.09 = 64.91 shares)	$370
Present value of tax shield	70	Debt	200
Total assets	$570	Debt plus equity	$570

Each share of stock is worth $370/64.91 = $5.70 after the exchange. Notice that the stock price does not change on the exchange date. As we mentioned above, the stock price moves on the date of the announcement only. Because the shareholders participating in the exchange receive a price equal to the market price per share after the exchange, they do not care whether they exchange their stock or not.

This example was provided for two reasons. First, it shows that an increase in the value of the firm from debt financing leads to an increase in the price of the stock. In fact, the stockholders capture the entire $70 tax shield. Second, we wanted to provide more work with market-value balance sheets.

Concept Questions

- What is the quirk in the tax code making a levered firm more valuable than an otherwise-identical unlevered firm?
- What is MM Proposition I under corporate taxes?
- What is MM Proposition II under corporate taxes?

15.7 Summary and Conclusions

1. We began our discussion of capital-structure policy by arguing that the particular capital structure that maximizes the value of the firm is also the one that provides the most benefit to the stockholders.
2. In a world of no taxes, the famous Proposition I of Modigliani and Miller proves that the value of the firm is unaffected by the debt-to-equity ratio. In other words, financial policy is a matter of indifference in that world. The authors obtain their results by showing that either a high or a low corporate ratio of debt to equity can be offset by homemade leverage. The result hinges on the assumption that individuals can borrow at the same rate as corporations, an assumption we believe to be quite plausible.

3. MM's Proposition II in a world without taxes states

$$r_S = r_0 + \frac{B}{S}(r_0 - r_B)$$

This implies that the expected rate of return on equity (also called the *cost of equity* or the *required return on equity*) is positively related to the firm's leverage. This makes intuitive sense, because the risk of equity rises with leverage, a point illustrated by the different sloped lines of Figure 15.2.

4. While the above work of MM is quite elegant, it does not explain the empirical findings on capital structure very well. MM imply that the capital-structure decision is a matter of indifference, while the decision appears to be a weighty one in the real world. To achieve real-world applicability, we next considered corporate taxes.

5. In a world with corporate taxes but no bankruptcy costs, firm value is an increasing function of leverage. The formula for the value of the firm is

$$V_L = V_U + T_C B$$

Expected return on levered equity can be expressed as

$$r_S = r_0 + (1 - T_C) \times (r_0 - r_B) \times \frac{B}{S}$$

Here, value is positively related to leverage. This result implies that firms should have a capital structure almost entirely composed of debt. Because real-world firms select more moderate levels of debt, the next chapter considers modifications to the results of this chapter.

Key Terms

Suggested Readings

The classic papers by Modigliani and Miller are

Modigliani, F., and M. H. Miller. "The Cost of Capital, Corporation Finance, and the Theory of Investment." *American Economic Review* (June 1958).

Modigliani, F., and M. H. Miller. "Corporate Income Taxes and the Cost of Capital: A Correction." *American Economic Review* (June 1963).

A more recent perspective on the above papers is provided by

Miller, M. "The Modigliani-Miller Propositions after 30 Years" in D. Chew, ed., *The New Corporate Finance: Where Theory Meets Practice* (New York: McGraw-Hill, 1993).

Questions and Problems

Capital Structure without Taxes

15.1 Nadus Corporation and Logis Corporation are identical in every way except their capital structures. Nadus Corporation, an all-equity firm, has 5,000 shares of stock outstanding; each share sells for \$20. Logis Corporation uses leverage in its capital structure. The market value of Logis Corporation's debt is $25,000. Logis's cost of debt is 12 percent. Each firm is expected to have earnings before interest of $350,000. Neither firm pays taxes.

Suppose you want to purchase the same portion of the equity of each firm. Assume you can borrow money at 12 percent.

a. What is the value of Nadus's stock?
b. What is the value of Logis's stock?
c. What will your costs and returns be if you buy 20 percent of each firm's equity?
d. Which investment is riskier? Why?
e. Construct an investment strategy for Nadus stock that replicates the investment returns of Logis stock.
f. What is the value of Logis Corporation?
g. If the value of Logis's assets is $135,000 and you can invest up to 20 percent of the Logis stock, what should you do?

15.2 Acetate, Inc., has common stock with a market value of $20 million and debt with a market value of $10 million. The cost of the debt is 14 percent. The current Treasury-bill rate is 8 percent, and the expected market premium is 10 percent. The beta on Acetate's equity is 0.9.

a. What is Acetate's debt-equity ratio?
b. What is the firm's overall required return?

15.3 You invest $100,000 in the stock of the Liana Rope Company. To make the investment, you borrowed $75,000 from a friend at a cost of 10 percent. You expect your equity investment to return 20 percent. There are no taxes. What would your return be if you did not use leverage?

15.4 Levered, Inc., and Unlevered, Inc., are identical companies with identical business risk. Their earnings are perfectly correlated. Each company is expected to earn $96 million per year in perpetuity, and each company distributes all its earnings. Levered's debt has a market value of $275 million and provides a return of 8 percent. Levered's stock sells for $100 per share, and there are 4.5 million outstanding shares. Unlevered has only 10 million outstanding shares worth $80 each. Unlevered has no debt. There are no taxes. Which stock is a better investment?

15.5 The Veblen Company and the Knight Company are identical in every respect except that Veblen Company is not levered. The market value of Knight Company's 6-percent bonds is $1 million. The financial statistics for the two firms appear below. Neither firm pays taxes.

	Veblen	*Knight*
Net operating income	$ 300,000	$ 300,000
Interest on debt	0	60,000
Earnings available to common stock	$ 300,000	$ 240,000
Required return on equity	0.125	0.140
Market value of stock	$2,400,000	$1,714,000
Market value of debt	0	$1,000,000
Market value of the firm	$2,400,000	$2,714,000
Overall required return	0.125	0.110
Debt-equity ratio	0	0.584

a. An investor who is also able to borrow at 6 percent owns $10,000 worth of Knight stock. Can he increase his net return by borrowing money to buy Veblen stock? If so, show the strategy.
b. According to Modigliani and Miller, what kind of investors will attempt this strategy? When will the process cease?

15.6 No Lights At Wrigley, Inc. (NLAW), is a Hong Kong–based corporation that sells sunglasses. The firm pays no corporate taxes, and its shareholders pay no personal income taxes. NLAW currently has 100,000 shares outstanding worth $50 each; the firm has no debt.

Consider three stockholders of NLAW, Ms. *A*, Ms. *B*, and Ms. *C*. All three women have good access to capital markets, so they can lend and borrow at 20 percent, the same rate at which the firm lends and borrows. The value of their holdings and their overall borrowing and lending positions are listed below.

	Value of NLAW Shares	*Total Borrowing*	*Total Lending*
Ms. *A*	$10,000	$2,000	0
Ms. *B*	$50,000	0	$6,000
Ms. *C*	$20,000	0	0

NLAW desires a ratio of debt to total capital of 0.20. To meet that desire, suppose the firm issues $1 million in risk-free debt and uses the funds to repurchase 20,000 shares.

The three stockholders wish to keep the risk of their portfolios unchanged. Show the value of their holdings and their borrowing and lending positions after they have adjusted their portfolios.

15.7 Rayburn Manufacturing is currently an all-equity firm. The firm's equity is worth $2 million. The cost of that equity is 18 percent. Rayburn pays no taxes.

Rayburn plans to issue $400,000 in debt and to use the proceeds to repurchase stock. The cost of debt is 10 percent.

a. After Rayburn repurchases the stock, what will the firm's overall costs of capital be?
b. After the repurchase, what will the cost of equity be?
c. Explain your result in (*b*).

15.8 Strom, Inc., has 250,000 outstanding shares of stock that sell for $20 per share. Strom, Inc., currently has no debt. The appropriate discount rate for the firm is 15 percent. Strom's earnings last year were $750,000. The management expects that if no changes affect the assets of the firm, the earnings will remain $750,000 in perpetuity. Strom pays no taxes.

Strom plans to buy out a competitor's business at a cost of $300,000. Once added to Strom's current business, the competitor's facilities will generate earnings of $120,000 in perpetuity. The competitor has the same risk as Strom, Inc.

a. Construct the market-value balance sheet for Strom before the announcement of the buyout is made.
b. Suppose Strom uses equity to fund the buyout.
  i. According to the efficient-market hypothesis, what will happen to Strom's price?
  ii. Construct the market-value balance sheet as it will look after the announcement.
  iii. How many shares did Strom sell?
  iv. Once Strom sells the new shares of stock, how will its accounts look?
  v. After the purchase is finalized, how will the market-value balance sheet look?
  vi. What is the return to Strom's equityholders?
c. Suppose Strom uses 10-percent debt to fund the buyout.
  i. Construct the market-value balance sheet as it will look after the announcement.
  ii. Once Strom sells the bonds, how will its accounts look?
  iii. What is the cost of equity?
  iv. Explain any difference in the cost of equity between the two plans.
  v. Use MM Proposition II to verify the answer in (*iii*).
d. Under each financing plan, what is the price of Strom stock after the buyout?

15.9 The Gulf Power Company is an electric utility that is planning to build a new conventional power plant. The company has traditionally paid out all earnings to the stockholders as dividends, and financed capital expenditures with new issues of common stock. There is no debt or preferred stock presently outstanding. Data on the company and the new power plant follow. Assume all earnings streams are perpetuities.

Company Data
Current annual earnings: $27 million
Number of outstanding shares: 10 million

New Power Plant
Initial outlay: $20 million
Added annual earnings: $3 million

Management considers the power plant to have the same risk as existing assets. The current required rate of return on equity is 10 percent. Assume there are no taxes and no costs of bankruptcy.

a. What will the total market value of Gulf Power be if common stock is issued to finance the plant?

b. What will the total market value of the firm be if $20 million in bonds with an interest rate of 8 percent are issued to finance the plant? Assume the bonds are perpetuities.

c. Suppose Gulf Power issues the bonds. Calculate the rate of return required by stockholders after the financing has occurred and the plant has been built.

15.10 Suppose there are no taxes, no transaction costs, and no costs of financial distress. In such a world, are the following statements true, false, or uncertain? Explain your answers.

a. If a firm issues equity to repurchase some of its debt, the price of the remaining shares will rise because those shares are less risky.

b. Moderate borrowing does not significantly affect the probability of financial distress or bankruptcy. Hence, moderate borrowing will not increase the required return on equity.

15.11 *a.* List the three assumptions that lie behind the Modigliani-Miller theory.

b. *Briefly* explain the effect of each upon the conclusions of the theory for the real world.

15.12 The Digital Sound Corporation has 1 million shares of common stock outstanding at $10 per share. It is an all equity firm. Susan Wang is CEO at Wang Finance Ltd. She wants to acquire a stake of 1 percent of the firm but has not decided among the three possible financing choices. She can borrow 20 percent, 40 percent, or 60 percent of the money she needs at a constant interest rate of 10 percent a year. The return on equity of the Digital Sound Corporation is 15 percent. Assume that she is in a MM no-tax world.

a. How much dollar return can Susan expect to earn from her investment each year under each of the three financing alternatives respectively?

b. What are Susan's returns on equity on each financing choice respectively?

c. From parts *a* and *b,* what inference can she draw about the return on equity of a leveraged firm?

15.13 Old Fashion Corp. is an all-equity firm famous for its antique furniture business. If the firm uses 36 percent leverage through issuance of long-term debt, the CFO predicts that there is a 20 percent chance that the ROE will be 10 percent, 40 percent chance that the ROE will be 15 percent, and 40 percent chance that the ROE will be 20 percent. The firm is tax exempt. Explain whether the firm should change its capital structure if the forecast of the CFO changes to 30 percent, 50 percent, and 20 percent chances respective for the three ROE possibilities.

15.14 Sunrise Industries Corp. is planning to repurchase part of its common stock in the open market by issuing corporate debt. As a result, the debt to equity ratio is expected to rise from 40 percent to 50 percent. The annual interest payment on its outstanding debt amounts to $0.75 million with an interest rate at 10 percent. The expected earnings before interest is $3.75 million. There are no taxes in the country where Sunrise operates. (Treat the debt and earnings as perpetuities to simplify calculation).

a. What is the total value of Sunrise Industries Corp.?

b. What is the expected return on equity before and after the announcement of the stock repurchase plan?
c. How would the stock price change at the announcement of the repurchase?

Capital Structure with Corporate Taxes

15.15 The market value of a firm with $500,000 of debt is $1,700,000. EBIT are expected to be a perpetuity. The pretax interest rate on debt is 10 percent. The company is in the 34-percent tax bracket. If the company was 100-percent equity financed, the equityholders would require a 20-percent return.
a. What would the value of the firm be if it was financed entirely with equity?
b. What is the net income to the stockholders of this levered firm?

15.16 An all-equity firm is subject to a 30-percent corporate tax rate. Its equityholders require a 20-percent return. The firm's initial market value is $3,500,000, and there are 175,000 shares outstanding. The firm issues $1 million of bonds at 10 percent and uses the proceeds to repurchase common stock. Assume there is no change in the costs of financial distress for the firm. According to MM, what is the new market value of the equity of the firm?

15.17 Streiber Publishing Company, an all-equity firm, generates perpetual earnings before interest and taxes (EBIT) of $2.5 million per year. Streiber's after-tax, all-equity discount rate is 20 percent. The company's tax rate is 34 percent.
a. What is the value of Streiber Publishing?
b. If Streiber adjusts its capital structure to include $600,000 of debt, what is the value of the firm?
c. Explain any difference in your answers.
d. What assumptions are you making when you are valuing Streiber?

15.18 Olbet, Inc., is a nongrowth company in the 35-percent tax bracket. Olbet's perpetual EBIT is $1.2 million per annum. The firm's pretax cost of debt is 8 percent and its interest expense per year is $200,000. Company analysts estimate that the unlevered cost of Olbet's equity is 12 percent.
a. What is the value of this firm?
b. What does the calculation in (*a*) imply about the correct level of debt?
c. Is the conclusion correct? Why or why not?

15.19 Green Manufacturing, Inc., plans to announce that it will issue $2,000,000 of perpetual bonds. The bonds will have a 6-percent coupon rate. Green Manufacturing currently is an all-equity firm. The value of Green's equity is $10,000,000 and there are 500,000 shares outstanding. After the sale of the bonds, Green will maintain the new capital structure indefinitely. The expected annual pretax earnings of Green are $1,500,000. Those earnings are also expected to remain constant into the foreseeable future. Green is in the 40-percent tax bracket.
a. What is Green's current overall required return?
b. Construct Green Manufacturing's market-value balance sheet as it looks before the announcement of the debt issue.
c. What is the market-value balance sheet after the announcement?
d. How many shares of stock will Green retire?
e. What will the accounts show after the restructuring has taken place?
f. What is Green's cost of equity after the capital restructuring?

15.20 The Nikko Company has perpetual EBIT of $4 million per year. The after-tax, all-equity discount rate r_0 is 15 percent. The company's tax rate is 35 percent. The cost of debt capital is 10 percent, and Nikko has $10 million of debt in its capital structure.
a. What is Nikko's value?
b. What is Nikko's r_{WACC}?
c. What is Nikko's cost of equity?

15.21 Eureka Space Technology Group (an all-equity firm) is announcing a $100 million R&D project, which is expected to drastically improve its satellite launching technology by reducing its annual launching costs from $500 million to $475 million. The firm can either finance the project through retained earnings or a new bond issue. The firm's cost of equity capital is 12.5%. The prevailing market rate of interest for comparable corporate bonds is 8 percent. Currently, the firm has 15 million shares of stocks outstanding at $32.5 a share. The firm has sufficient earnings to fully utilize the corporate tax shield if the project is debt financed. Assume the relevant marginal corporate tax rate is 35 percent.

a. Which financing method, retained earnings or external debt financing, would you recommend to the management and why?

b. What is the resulting PV of the firm from each of these two financing methods?

c. What do you expect will be the stock market stock price response to the two different methods?

d. Explain the intuition behind the results in part *c.*

CHAPTER

16 Capital Structure: Limits to the Use of Debt

One question a student might ask is, "Does the MM theory with taxes predict the capital structure of typical firms?" The answer is, unfortunately, "no." The theory states that $V_L = V_U + T_C B$. According to this equation, one can always increase firm value by increasing leverage, implying that firms should issue maximum debt. This is inconsistent with the real world, where firms generally employ only moderate amounts of debt.

However, the MM theory tells us *where to look* when searching for the determinants of capital structure. For example, the theory ignores bankruptcy and its attendant costs. Because these costs are likely to get out of hand for a highly levered firm, the moderate leverage of most firms can now easily be explained.

In addition, the MM theory ignores personal taxes. In the real world, the *personal* tax rate on interest is higher than the *effective* personal tax rate on equity distributions. Thus, the personal tax penalties to bondholders tend to offset the tax benefits to debt at the corporate level. Even when bankruptcy costs are ignored, this idea can be shown to imply that there is an optimal amount of debt for the economy as a whole. The implications of bankruptcy costs and personal taxes are examined in this chapter.

16.1 Costs of Financial Distress

Bankruptcy Risk or Bankruptcy Cost?

As mentioned throughout the previous chapter, debt provides tax benefits to the firm. However, debt puts pressure on the firm, because interest and principal payments are obligations. If these obligations are not met, the firm may risk some sort of financial distress. The ultimate distress is *bankruptcy,* where ownership of the firm's assets is legally transferred from the stockholders to the bondholders. These debt obligations are fundamentally different from stock obligations. While stockholders like and expect dividends, they are not legally entitled to dividends in the way bondholders are legally entitled to interest and principal payments.

We show below that bankruptcy costs, or more generally financial distress costs, tend to offset the advantages to debt. We begin by positing a simple example of bankruptcy. All taxes are ignored to focus only on the costs of debt.

• ***Example***

The Knight Corporation plans to be in business for one more year. It forecasts a cash flow of either \$100 or \$50 in the coming year, each occurring with 50-percent probability. The firm has no other assets. Previously issued debt requires payments of $49 of interest and principal. The Day Corporation has identical cash flow prospects but has $60 of interest and principal obligations. The cash flows of these two firms can be represented as

	Knight Corp.		Day Corp.	
	Boom Times (prob. 50%)	*Recession (prob. 50%)*	*Boom Times (prob. 50%)*	*Recession (prob. 50%)*
Cash flow	$100	$50	$100	$50
Payment of interest and principal on debt	49	49	60	50
Distribution to stockholders	$51	$1	$40	0

For Knight Corporation in both boom times and recession and for Day Corporation in boom times, cash flow exceeds interest and principal payments. In these situations, the bondholders are paid in full and the stockholders receive any residual. However, the most interesting of the four columns involves Day Corporation in a recession. Here, the bondholders are owed $60, but the firm has only $50 in cash. Since we assumed that the firm has no other assets, the bondholders cannot be satisfied in full. If bankruptcy occurs, the bondholders will receive all of the firm's cash, and the stockholders will receive nothing. Importantly, the stockholders do not have to come up with the additional $10 (= $60 − $50). Corporations have limited liability in America and most other countries, implying that bondholders cannot sue the stockholders for the extra $10.[1]

We assume that (1) both bondholders and stockholders are risk-neutral and (2) the interest rate is 10 percent. Due to this risk neutrality, cash flows to both stockholders and bondholders are to be discounted at the 10-percent rate.[2] We can evaluate the debt, the equity, and the entire firm for both Knight and Day as follows;

$$S_{\text{KNIGHT}} = \$23.64 = \frac{\$51 \times \frac{1}{2} + \$1 \times \frac{1}{2}}{1.10} \qquad S_{\text{DAY}} = \$18.18 = \frac{\$40 \times \frac{1}{2} + 0 \times \frac{1}{2}}{1.10}$$

$$B_{\text{KNIGHT}} = \$44.54 = \frac{\$49 \times \frac{1}{2} + \$49 \times \frac{1}{2}}{1.10} \qquad B_{\text{DAY}} = \$50 = \frac{\$60 \times \frac{1}{2} + \$50 \times \frac{1}{2}}{1.10}$$

$$V_{\text{KNIGHT}} = \$68.18 \qquad V_{\text{DAY}} = \$68.18$$

Note that the two firms have the same value, even though Day runs the risk of bankruptcy. Furthermore, notice that Day's bondholders are valuing the bonds with their

[1] There are situations where the limited liability of corporation can be "pierced." Typically, fraud or misrepresentation must be present.

[2] Normally, one assumes that investors are *averse* to risk. In that case, the cost of debt capital, r_B, is less than the cost of equity capital, r_S, which rises with leverage as shown in the previous chapter. In addition, r_B may rise when the increase in leverage allows the possibility of default.

For simplicity, we assume *risk neutrality* in this example. This means that investors are indifferent to whether risk is high, low, or even absent. Here, $r_S = r_B$, because risk-neutral investors do not demand compensation for bearing risk. In addition, neither r_S nor r_B rises with leverage. Because the interest rate is 10 percent, our assumption of risk neutrality implies that $r_S = 10\%$ as well.

Though financial economists believe that investors are risk-averse, they frequently develop examples based on risk-neutrality to isolate a point unrelated to risk. This is our approach, because we want to focus on bankruptcy costs—not bankruptcy risk. The same qualitative conclusions from this example can be drawn in a world of risk aversion, albeit with *much* more difficulty for the reader.

eyes open. Though the promised payment of principal and interest is \$60, the bondholders are willing to pay only \$50. Hence, their *promised* return or yield is

$$\frac{\$60}{\$50} - 1 = 20\%$$

Day's debt can be viewed as a *junk bond,* because the probability of default is so high. As with all junk bonds, bondholders demand a high promised yield.

Day's example is not realistic because it ignores an important cash flow to be discussed below. A more realistic set of numbers might be

DAY CORP.

	Boom times (prob. 50%)	*Recession (prob. 50%)*	
Earnings	\$100	\$50	$S_{DAY} = \$18.18 = \dfrac{\$40 \times \frac{1}{2} + 0 \times \frac{1}{2}}{1.10}$
Debt repayment	60	35	$B_{DAY} = \$43.18 = \dfrac{\$60 \times \frac{1}{2} + \$35 \times \frac{1}{2}}{1.10}$
Distribution to stockholders	\$40	0	$V_{DAY} = \$61.36$

Why do the bondholders receive only \$35 in a recession? If cash flow is only \$50, bondholders will be informed that they are not paid in full. These bondholders are likely to hire lawyers to negotiate or even to sue the company. Similarly, the firm is likely to hire lawyers to defend itself. Further costs will be incurred if the case gets to a bankruptcy court. These fees are always paid before the bondholders get paid. Thus, we are assuming that bankruptcy costs total \$15 (\$50 − 35).

The value of the firm is now \$61.36, an amount below the \$68.18 figure calculated earlier. By comparing Day's value in a world with no bankruptcy costs to Day's value in a world with these costs, we conclude

> The possibility of bankruptcy has a negative effect on the value of the firm. However, it is not the *risk* of bankruptcy itself that lowers value. Rather it is the *costs* associated with bankruptcy that lower value.

The explanation follows from our pie example. In a world of no bankruptcy costs, the bondholders and the stockholders share the entire pie. However, bankruptcy costs eat up some of the pie in the real world, leaving less for the stockholders and bondholders.

Because the bondholders are aware that they receive little in a recession, they pay a low price. In this case, their promised return is

$$\frac{\$60}{\$43.18} - 1 = 39.0\%$$

The bondholders are paying a fair price if they are realistic about both the probability and the cost of bankruptcy. It is the *stockholders* who bear these future bankruptcy costs. To see this, imagine that Day Corporation was originally all equity. The stockholders want the firm to issue debt with a promised payment of \$60 and use the proceeds to pay a dividend. If there had been no bankruptcy costs, our results show that bondholders would pay \$50 to purchase debt with a promised payment of \$60. Hence, a dividend of $50 could be paid to the stockholders. However, if bankruptcy costs exist, bondholders would only pay $43.18 for the debt. In that case, only a dividend of $43.18 could be paid to the stockholders. Because the dividend is less when bankruptcy costs exist, the stockholders are hurt by bankruptcy costs. •

Concept Questions

- What does risk neutrality mean?
- Can one have bankruptcy risk without bankruptcy costs?
- Why do we say that stockholders bear bankruptcy costs?

16.2 Description of Costs

The above example showed that bankruptcy costs can lower the value of the firm. In fact, the same general result holds even if a legal bankruptcy is prevented. Thus, *financial distress costs* may be a better phrase than *bankruptcy costs.* It is worthwhile to describe these costs in more detail.

Direct Costs of Financial Distress: Legal and Administrative Costs of Liquidation or Reorganization

As mentioned earlier, lawyers are involved throughout all the stages before and during bankruptcy. With fees often in the hundreds of dollars an hour, these costs can add up quickly. A wag once remarked that bankruptcies are to lawyers what blood is to sharks. In addition, administrative and accounting fees can substantially add to the total bill. And if a trial takes place, we must not forget expert witnesses. Each side may hire a number of these witnesses to testify about the fairness of a prepared settlement. Their fees can easily rival those of lawyers or accountants. (However, we personally look upon these witnesses more kindly, because they are frequently drawn from the ranks of finance professors.)

These direct costs have recently been estimated. While large in absolute amount, they are actually small as a percentage of firm value. White, Altman, and Weiss estimated the direct costs of financial distress to be about 3 percent of the market value of the firm.[3] In a study of direct financial distress costs of 20 railroad bankruptcies, Warner found that net financial distress costs were, on average, 1 percent of the market value of the firm seven years before bankruptcy and were somewhat larger percentages as bankruptcy approached (for example, 2.5 percent of the market value of the firm three years before bankruptcy).[4]

[3] M. J. White, "Bankruptcy Costs and the New Bankruptcy Code," *Journal of Finance* (May 1983); and E. I. Altman, "A Further Empirical Investigation of the Bankruptcy Cost Question," *Journal of Finance* (September 1984). More recently, Lawrence A. Weiss, "Bankruptcy Resolution: Direct Costs and Violation of Priority of Claims," *Journal of Financial Economics* 27 (1990), estimates that direct costs of bankruptcy are 3.1 percent of the value of the firm. Ferris, Jayaraman, and Makhija, "Direct Costs of Bankruptcy: Evidence from Filings of Liquidations and Reorganizations by Small Firms, 1981–1991," unpublished manuscript, Georgia Institute of Technology, 1993, report very high direct cost in smaller firms. At initiation of bankruptcy, the direct costs are about 28 percent of assets.

[4] J. B. Warner, "Bankruptcy Costs: Some Evidence," *Journal of Finance* (May 1977).

Warner pointed out that

> It is the *expected* cost of bankruptcy that is the relevant measure of bankruptcy costs. . . . Suppose, for example, that a given railroad picks a level of debt such that bankruptcy would occur on average once every 20 years (i.e., the probability of going bankrupt is 5 percent in any given year). Assume that when bankruptcy occurs, the firm would pay a lump sum penalty equal to 3 percent of its now current market value. . . .
>
> [Then], the firm's expected cost of bankruptcy is equal to fifteen one-hundredths of one percent of its now current market value.

Indirect Costs of Financial Distress

Impaired Ability to Conduct Business

Bankruptcy hampers conduct with customers and suppliers. Sales are frequently lost because of both fear of impaired service and loss of trust. For example, many loyal Chrysler customers switched to other manufacturers when Chrysler skirted insolvency in the 1970s. These buyers questioned whether parts and servicing would be available were Chrysler to fail. Sometimes the taint of impending bankruptcy is enough to drive customers away. For example, gamblers avoided Atlantis casino in Atlantic City after it became technically insolvent. Gamblers are a superstitious bunch. Many reasoned, "If the casino itself cannot make money, how can I expect to make money there." A particularly outrageous story concerned two unrelated stores both named Mitchells in New York City. When one Mitchells declared bankruptcy, customers stayed away from both stores. In time, the second store was forced to declare bankruptcy as well.

Though these costs clearly exist, it is quite difficult to estimate them. Altman has estimated that both direct and indirect costs are frequently greater than 20 percent of firm value.[5]

Agency Costs

When a firm has debt, conflicts of interest arise between stockholders and bondholders. Because of this, stockholders are tempted to pursue selfish strategies. These conflicts of interest, which are magnified when financial distress is incurred, impose

---

[5] Altman, op. cit. "A Further Empirical Investigation."

David M. Cutler and Lawrence H. Summers, "The Costs of Conflict Resolution and Financial Distress: Evidence from the Texaco-Pennzoil Litigation," *Rand Journal of Economics* 19 (1988), estimate the indirect costs of Texaco's 1987 bankruptcy to be about 9 percent of the firm's value. Steven N. Kaplan, "Campeau's Acquisition of Federated: Value Added or Destroyed," *Journal of Financial Economics* 24 (1989), finds the indirect costs of financial distress for Campeau to be very small.

The work of L. Lang and R. Stulz, "Contagious and Competitive Intra-industry Effects of Bankruptcy Announcements: An Empirical Analysis," *Journal of Financial Economics* (August 1992), and I. Opler and S. Titman, "The Indirect Costs of Financial Distress," Working Paper, Southern Methodist University, 1993, suggest indirect financial distress costs are substantial. T. Opler, "Controlling Financial Distress Costs in LBO's," *Financial Management* (Autumn 1993) shows that LBO financing techniques can be expected to reduce the costs of financial distress.

A fascinating and provocative set of articles by Robert Haugen and Lemma Senbet ("The Insignificance of Bankruptcy Costs to the Theory of Optimal Capital Structure," *Journal of Finance* (May 1978); "New Perspectives on Information Asymmetry and Agency Relationships," *Journal of Financial and Quantitative Analysis* (November 1979); "Bankruptcy and Agency Costs: Their Significance to the Theory of Optimal Capital Structure," *Journal of Financial and Quantitative Analysis* (March 1988)) argue that financial distress should, at most, only slightly impair the firm's ability to conduct business. They say that customers, employees, and so on, are concerned with the tenure of the *firm,* which is fundamentally a function of its asset characteristics. This tenure should not be dependent on the way the assets are financed.

agency costs on the firm. We describe three kinds of selfish strategies that stockholders use to hurt the bondholders and help themselves. These strategies are costly because they will lower the market value of the whole firm.

Selfish Investment Strategy #1: Incentive to Take Large Risks Firms near bankruptcy oftentimes take great chances, because they feel that they are playing with someone else's money. To see this, imagine a levered firm considering two *mutually exclusive* projects, a low-risk one and a high-risk one. There are two equally likely outcomes, recession and boom. The firm is in such dire straits that should a recession hit, it will come near to bankruptcy with one project and actually fall into bankruptcy with the other. The cash flows for the firm if the low-risk project is taken can be described as

Low-Risk Project

	Probability	*Value of Firm*	=	*Stock*	+	*Bonds*
Recession	0.5	$100	=	0	+	$100
Boom	0.5	$200	=	$100	+	$100

If recession occurs, the value of the firm will be $100, and if boom obtains, the value of the firm will be $200. The expected value of the firm is $150 (0.5 ×$100 + 0.5 × $200).

The firm has promised to pay bondholders $100. Shareholders will obtain the difference between the total payoff and the amount paid to the bondholders. In other words, the bondholders have the prior claim on the payoffs, and the shareholders have the residual claim.

Now suppose that another, riskier project can be substituted for the low-risk project. The payoffs and probabilities are as follows:

High-Risk Project

	Probability	*Value of Firm*	=	*Stock*	+	*Bonds*
Recession	0.5	$50	=	0	+	$50
Boom	0.5	$240	=	$140	+	$100

The expected value of the *firm* is $145 (0.5 × $50 + 0.5 × $240), which is lower than the expected value of the firm with the low-risk project. Thus, the low-risk project would be accepted if the firm were all equity. However, note that the expected value of the *stock* is $70 (0.5 × 0 + 0.5 × $140) with the high-risk project, but only $50 (0.5 × 0 + 0.5 × $100) with the low-risk project. Given the firm's present levered state, stockholders will select the high-risk project.

The key is that, relative to the low-risk project, the high-risk project increases firm value in a boom and decreases firm value in a recession. The increase in value in a boom is captured by the stockholders, because the bondholders are paid in full (they receive $100) regardless of which project is accepted. Conversely, the drop in value in a recession is lost by the bondholders, because they are paid in full with the low-risk project but receive only $50 with the high-risk one. The stockholders will receive nothing in a recession anyway, whether the high-risk or low-risk project is selected. Thus, financial economists argue that stockholders expropriate value from the bondholders by selecting high-risk projects.

A story, perhaps apocryphal, illustrates this idea. It seems that Federal Express was near financial collapse within a few years of its inception. The founder, Frederick

TABLE 16.1 Example Illustrating Incentive to Underinvest

	Firm without Project		Firm with Project	
	Boom	Recession	Boom	Recession
Firm cash flows	$5,000	$2,400	$6,700	$4,100
Bondholders' claim	4,000	2,400	4,000	4,000
Stockholders' claim	$1,000	0	$2,700	$ 100

The project has positive NPV. However, much of its value is captured by bondholders. Rational managers, acting in the stockholdewrs' interest, will reject the project.

Smith, took $20,000 of corporate funds to Las Vegas in despair. He won at the gaming tables, providing enough capital to allow the firm to survive. Had he lost, the banks would simply have received $20,000 less when the firm reached bankruptcy.

Selfish Investment Strategy #2: Incentive toward Underinvestment Stockholders of a firm with a significant probability of bankruptcy often find that new investment helps the bondholders at the stockholders' expense. The simplest case might be a real estate owner facing imminent bankruptcy. If he took $100,000 out of his own pocket to refurbish the building, he could increase the building's value by, say, $150,000. Though this investment has a positive net present value, he will turn it down if the increase in value cannot prevent bankruptcy. "Why," he asks, "should I use my own funds to improve the value of a building that the bank will soon repossess?"

This idea is formalized by the following simple example. Consider a firm with $4,000 of principal and interest payments due at the end of the year. It will be pulled into bankruptcy by a recession because its cash flows will be only $2,400 in that state. The firm's cash flows are presented in the left-hand side of Table 16.1. The firm could avoid bankruptcy in a recession by raising new equity to invest in a new project. The project costs $1,000 and brings in $1,700 in either state, implying a positive net present value. Clearly it would be accepted in an all-equity firm.

However, the project hurts the stockholders of the levered firm. To see this, imagine the old stockholders contribute the $1,000 *themselves*.[6] The expected value of the stockholders' interest without the project is $500(0.5 × $1,000 + 0.5 × $0). The expected value with the project is $1,400(0.5 × $2,700 + 0.5 × $100). The stockholders' interest rises by only $900($1,400 − $500) while costing $1,000.

The key is that the stockholders contribute the full $1,000 investment, but the stockholders and bondholders *share* the benefits. The stockholders take the entire gain if boom times occur. Conversely, the bondholders reap most of the cash flow from the project in a recession.

The discussion of selfish strategy 1 is quite similar to the discussion of selfish strategy 2. In both cases, an investment strategy for the levered firm is different from the one for the unlevered firm. Thus, leverage results in distorted investment policy. Whereas the unlevered corporation always chooses projects with positive net present value, the levered firm may deviate from this policy.

[6] The same qualitative results will obtain if the $1,000 is raised from new stockholders. However, the arithmetic becomes much more difficult since we must determine how many new shares are issued.

Selfish Investment Strategy #3: Milking the Property Another strategy is to pay out extra dividends or other distributions in times of financial distress, leaving less in the firm for the bondholders. This is known as *milking the property,* a phrase taken from real estate. Strategies 2 and 3 are very similar. In strategy 2, the firm chooses not to raise new equity. Strategy 3 goes one step further, because equity is actually withdrawn through the dividend.

Summary of Selfish Strategies

The above distortions occur only when there is a probability of bankruptcy or financial distress. Thus, these distortions *should not* affect, say, IBM because bankruptcy is not a realistic possibility for a blue-chip firm such as this. In other words, IBM's debt will be virtually risk-free, regardless of the projects it accepts. Because the distortions are related to financial distress, we have included them in our discussion of the "Indirect Costs of Financial Distress."

Who pays for the cost of selfish investment strategies? We argue that it is ultimately the stockholders. Rational bondholders know that, when financial distress is imminent, they cannot expect help from stockholders. Rather, stockholders are likely to choose investment strategies that reduce the value of the bonds. Bondholders protect themselves accordingly by raising the interest rate that they require on the bonds. Because the stockholders must pay these high rates, they ultimately bear the costs of selfish strategies. The relationship between stockholders and bondholders is very similar to the relationship between Erroll Flynn and David Niven, good friends and movie stars in the 1930s. Niven reportedly said that the good thing about Flynn was that you knew exactly where you stood with him. When you needed his help, you could always count on him to let you down.

Concept Questions

- What is the main direct cost of financial distress?
- What are the indirect costs of financial distress?
- Who pays the costs of selfish strategies?

16.3 Can Costs of Debt Be Reduced?

As U.S. senators are prone to say, "A billion here, a billion there. Pretty soon it all adds up."[7] Each of the costs of financial distress we mentioned above is substantial in its own right. The sum of them may well affect debt financing severely. Thus, managers have an incentive to reduce these costs. We now turn to some of their methods. However, it should be mentioned at the outset that methods below can, at most, reduce the costs of debt. They cannot *eliminate* them entirely.

[7] The original quote is generally attributed to Senator Everett Dirksen. In the 1950s, he reportedly said, "A *million* here, a *million* there. Pretty soon it all adds up." Government spending has increased since that time.

Protective Covenants

Because the stockholders must pay higher interest rates as insurance against their own selfish strategies, they frequently make agreements with bondholders in hopes of lower rates. These agreements, called **protective covenants,** are incorporated as part of the loan document (or *indenture*) between stockholders and bondholders. The covenants must be taken seriously since a broken covenant can lead to default. Protective covenants can be classified into two types: negative covenants and positive covenants.

A **negative covenant** limits or prohibits actions that the company may take. Here are some typical negative covenants:

1. Limitations are placed on the amount of dividends a company may pay.
2. The firm may not pledge any of its assets to other lenders.
3. The firm may not merge with another firm.
4. The firm may not sell or lease its major assets without approval by the lender.
5. The firm may not issue additional long-term debt.

A **positive covenant** specifies an action that the company agrees to take or a condition the company must abide by. Here are some examples:

1. The company agrees to maintain its working capital at a minimum level.
2. The company must furnish periodic financial statements to the lender.

These lists of covenants are not exhaustive. We have seen loan agreements with more than 30 covenants.

Smith and Warner examined public issues of debt in 1975 and found that 91 percent of the bond indentures included covenants that restricted the issuance of additional debt, 23 percent restricted dividends, 39 percent restricted mergers, and 36 percent limited the sale of assets.[8]

Protective covenants should reduce the costs of bankruptcy, ultimately increasing the value of the firm. Thus, stockholders are likely to favor all reasonable covenants. To see this, consider three choices by stockholders to reduce bankruptcy costs.

1. *Issue No Debt.* Because of the tax advantages to debt, this is a very costly way of avoiding conflicts.
2. *Issue Debt with No Restrictive and Protective Covenants.* In this case, bondholders will demand high interest rates to compensate for the unprotected status of their debt.
3. *Write Protective and Restrictive Covenants into the Loan Contracts.* If the covenants are clearly written, the creditors may receive protection without large costs being imposed on the shareholders. They will happily accept a lower interest rate.

Thus, bond covenants, even if they reduce flexibility, can increase the value of the firm. They can be the lowest-cost solution to the stockholder-bondholder conflict. A list of typical bond covenants and their uses appears in Table 16.2.

---

[8] C. W. Smith and J. B. Warner, "On Financial Contracting: An Analysis of Bond Covenants," *Journal of Financial Economics* 7 (1979).

TABLE 16.2 Loan Covenants

Covenant type	*Shareholder Action or Firm Circumstances*	*Reason for Covenant*
Financial-statement signals 1. Working capital requirement 2. Interest coverage 3. Minimum net worth	As firm approaches financial distress, shareholders may want firm to make high-risk investments.	Shareholders lose value before bankruptcy; bondholders hurt much more in bankruptcy than shareholders (limited lability); bondholders hurt by *distortortion of investment that leads to increases in risk.*
Restrictions on asset disposition 1. Limit dividends 2. Limit sale of assets 3. Collateral and mortgages	Shareholders attempt to transfer corporate assets to themselves.	Limits the ability of shareholders to transfer assets to themselves and to *underinvest.*
Restrictions on switching assets	Shareholders attempt to increase risk of firm.	Increased firm risk helps shareholders; bondholders hurt by *distortion of investment that leads to increases in risk.*
Dilution 1. Limit on leasing 2. Limit on further borrowing	Shareholders may attempt to issue new debt of equal or greater priority.	Restricts *dilution of the claim of existing bondholders.*

Consolidation of Debt

One reason bankruptcy costs are so high is that different creditors (and their lawyers) fight with each other. This problem can be alleviated by proper arrangement of bondholders and stockholders. For example, perhaps one, or at most a few, lenders can shoulder the entire debt. Should financial distress occur, negotiating costs are minimized under this arrangement. In addition, bondholders can purchase stock as well. In this way, stockholders and debtholders are not pitted against each other, because they are not separate entities. This appears to be the approach in Japan where large banks generally take significant stock positions in the firms to which they lend money.[9] Debt-equity ratios in Japan are far higher than those in the United States.

16.4 Integration of Tax Effects and Financial Distress Costs

Modigliani and Miller argue that the firm's value rises with leverage in the presence of corporate taxes. Because this implies that all firms should choose maximum debt, the theory does not predict the behavior of firms in the real world. Other authors have suggested that bankruptcy and related costs reduce the value of the levered firm.

The integration of tax effects and distress costs appears in Figure 16.1. The diagonal straight line in the figure represents the value of the firm in a world without bankruptcy costs. The ∩-shaped curve represents the value of the firm with these costs.

[9] Legal limitations may prevent this practice in the United States.

FIGURE 16.1 The Optimal Amount of Debt and the Value of the Firm

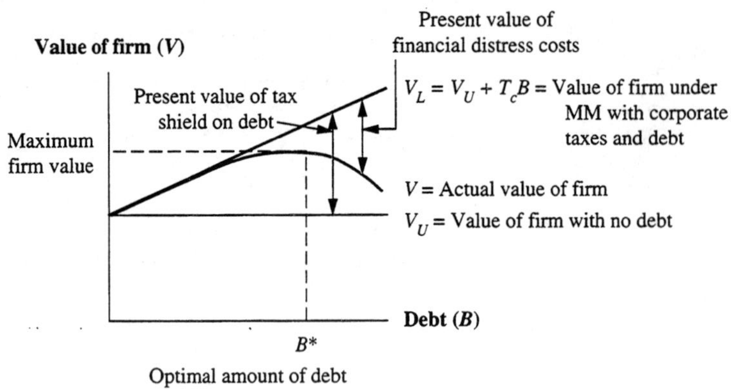

The tax shield increases the value of the levered firm. Financial distress costs lower the value of the levered firm. The two offsetting factors produce an optimal amount of debt at B^*.

The ∩-shaped curve rises as the firm moves from all equity to a small amount of debt. Here, the present value of the distress costs is minimal because the probability of distress is so small. However, as more and more debt is added, the present value of these costs rises at an *increasing* rate. At some point, the increase in the present value of these costs from an additional dollar of debt equals the increase in the present value of the tax shield. This is the debt level maximizing the value of the firm and is represented by B^* in Figure 16.1. In other words, B^* is the optimal amount of debt. Bankruptcy costs increase faster than the tax shield beyond this point, implying a reduction in firm value from further leverage.

The above discussion presents two factors that affect the degree of leverage. Unfortunately, no formula exists at this time to exactly determine the optimal debt level for a particular firm. This is because bankruptcy costs cannot be expressed in a precise way. The last section of this chapter offers some rules of thumb for selecting a debt-equity ratio in the real world.

Our situation reminds one of a quote of John Maynard Keynes. He reputedly said that, although most historians would agree that Queen Elizabeth I was both a better monarch and an unhappier woman than Queen Victoria, no one has yet been able to express the statement in a precise and rigorous formula.

Pie Again

Critics of the MM theory often say that MM fails when we add such real-world issues as taxes and bankruptcy costs. Taking that view, however, blinds critics to the real value of the MM theory. The pie approach offers a more constructive way of thinking about these matters and the role of capital structure.

Taxes are just another claim on the cash flows of the firm. Let G (for government and taxes) stand for the market value of the government's claim to the firm's taxes. Bankruptcy costs are also another claim on the cash flows. Let us label their value with an L (for lawyers?). The bankruptcy costs are cash flows paid from the firm's cash flows in a bankruptcy. The cash flows to the claim L rise with the debt-equity ratio.

The pie theory says that all of these claims are paid from only one source, the cash flows (CF) of the firm. Algebraically, we must have

FIGURE 16.2 The Pie Model with Real-World Factors

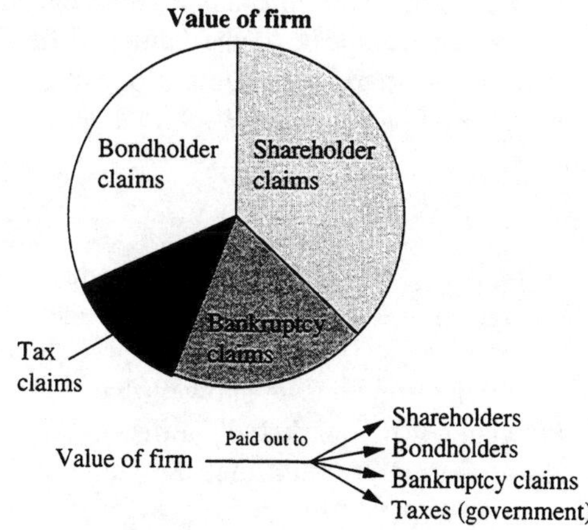

$$
\begin{gathered}
\text{CF} = \text{Payments to stockholders} \\
+ \\
\text{Payments to bondholders} \\
+ \\
\text{Payments to the government} \\
+ \\
\text{Payments to lawyers} \\
+ \\
\text{Payments to any and all other claimants} \\
\text{to the cash flows of the firm}
\end{gathered}
$$

Figure 16.2 shows the new pie. No matter how many slices we take and no matter who gets them, they must still add up to the total cash flow. The value of the firm, V_T, is unaltered by the capital structure. Now, however, we must be broader in our definition of the firm's value

$$V_T = S + B + G + L$$

We previously wrote the firm's value as

$$S + B$$

when we ignored taxes and bankruptcy costs.

Nor have we even begun to exhaust the list of financial claims to the firm's cash flows. To give an unusual example, everyone reading this book has an economic claim to the cash flows of General Motors. After all, if you are injured in an accident, you might sue GM. Win or lose, GM will expend resources dealing with the matter. If you think this is farfetched and unimportant, ask yourself what GM might be willing to pay every man, woman, and child in the country to have them promise that they would never sue GM, no matter what happened. The law does not permit such payments, but that does not mean that a value to all of those potential claims does not exist. We guess that it would run into the billions of dollars, and, for GM or any other company, there should be a slice of the pie labeled *LS* for "potential lawsuits."

This is the essence of the MM intuition and theory: V is V(CF) and depends on the total cash flow of the firm. The capital structure cuts it into slices.

There is, however, an important difference between claims such as those of stockholders and bondholders on the one hand and those of government and potential litigants in lawsuits on the other. The first set of claims are **marketed claims,** and the second set are **nonmarketed claims.** One difference is that the marketed claims can be bought and sold in financial markets, and the nonmarketed claims cannot.

When we speak of the value of the firm, generally we are referring just to the value of the marketed claims, V_M, and not the value of nonmarketed claims, V_N. What we have shown is that the total value,

$$\begin{aligned} V_T &= S + B + G + L \\ &= V_M + V_N \end{aligned}$$

is unaltered. But, as we saw, the value of the marketed claims, V_M, can change with changes in the capital structure in general and the debt-equity ratio in particular.

By the pie theory, any increase in V_M must imply an identical decrease in V_N. In an efficient market we showed that the capital structure will be chosen to maximize the value of the marketed claims, V_M. We can equivalently think of the efficient market as working to minimize the value of the nonmarketed claims, V_N. These are taxes and bankruptcy costs in the previous example, but they also include all the other nonmarketed claims such as the *LS* claim.

Concept Questions

- List all the claims to the firm's assets.
- Describe marketed claims and nonmarketed claims.
- How can a firm maximize the value of its marketed claims?

16.5 Shirking and Perquisites: A Note on Agency Cost of Equity

The chapter has focused on agency costs of debt so far. However, we would be remiss if we failed to mention an important agency cost of equity. A discussion of this cost of equity is contained in a well-known quote from Adam Smith:[10]

> The directors of such [joint-stock] companies, however, being the managers of other people's money than of their own, it cannot well be expected that they should watch over it with the same anxious vigilance with which the partners in a private copartnery frequently watch over their own. Like the stewards of a rich man, they are apt to consider attention to small matters as not for their master's honour, and very easily give themselves a dispensation from having it. Negligence and profusion, therefore, must always prevail, more or less, in the management of the affairs of such a company.

This elegant prose can be restated in modern-day vocabulary. An individual will work harder for a firm if she is one of its owners than if she is just an employee. In addition, the individual will work harder if she owns a large percentage of the company than if she owns a small percentage. This idea has an important implication for capital structure, which we illustrate with the following example.

• ***Example***
Ms. Pagell is an owner-entrepreneur running a computer-services firm worth \$1 million. She currently owns 100 percent of the firm. Because of the need to expand, she

[10] Adam Smith, *The Wealth of Nations* [1776], Cannon edition (New York: Modern Library 1937), p. 700, as quoted in M. C. Jensen and W. Meckling, "Theory of the Firm: Managerial Behavior, Agency Costs, and Ownership Structure," *Journal of Financial Economics* 3 (1978).

must raise another $2 million. She can either issue $2 million of debt at 12-percent interest or issue $2 million in stock. The cash flows under the two alternatives are presented below:

	Debt Issue				Stock Issue			
	Cash Flow	*Interest*	*Cash Flow to Equity*	*Cash Flow to Ms. Pagell (100% of equity)*	*Cash Flow*	*Interest*	*Cash Flow to Equity*	*Cash Flow to Ms. Pagell ($33\frac{1}{3}$ of equity)*
6-hour days	$300,000	$240,000	$ 60,000	$ 60,000	$300,000	0	$300,000	$100,000
10-hour days	400,000	240,000	160,000	160,000	400,000	0	400,000	133,333

Like any entrepreneur, Ms. Pagell can choose the degree of intensity with which she works. In our example, she can either work a 6- or a 10-hour day. With the debt issue, the extra work brings her $100,000 ($160,000 − $60,000) more income. However, with a stock issue she retains only a one-third interest in the equity. Thus, the extra work brings her only $33,333 ($133,333 − $100,000). Being only human, she is likely to work harder if she issues debt. In other words, she has more incentive to *shirk* if she issues equity.

In addition, she is likely to obtain more *perquisites* (a big office, a company car, more expense-account meals) if she issues stock. If she is a one-third stockholder, two thirds of these costs are paid for by the other stockholders. If she is the sole owner, any additional perquisites reduce her equity stake. Thus, as the firm issues more equity, she will increase both leisure time and work-related perquisites. The leisure time and work-related amenities are called agency costs, because managers of the firm are agents of the stockholders.[11] •

This example is quite applicable to a small company considering a large stock offering. Because a manager-owner will greatly dilute his or her share in the total equity in this case, a significant drop in work intensity or a significant increase in fringe benefits is possible. However, the example may be less applicable for a large corporation with many stockholders. For example, consider a large company like General Motors going public for the umpteenth time. The typical manager there already has such a small percentage stake in the firm that any temptation for negligence has probably been experienced before. An additional offering cannot be expected to increase this temptation.

Who bears the burden of these agency costs? If the new stockholders invest with their eyes open, they do not. Knowing that Ms. Pagell may work short hours, they will pay only a low price for the stock. Thus, it is the owner who is hurt by agency costs. However, Ms. Pagell can protect herself to some extent. Just as stockholders reduce bankruptcy costs through protective covenants, an owner may allow monitoring by new stockholders. However, though proper reporting and surveillance may reduce the agency costs of equity, these techniques are unlikely to eliminate them.

It is commonly suggested that leveraged buyouts (LBOs) significantly reduce the above cost of equity. In an LBO, a purchaser (usually a team of existing management)

[11] As previously discussed, agency costs are generally defined as the costs from the conflicts of interest among stockholders, bondholders, and managers.

buys out the stockholders at a price above the current market. In other words, the company goes private since the stock is placed in the hands of only a few people. Because the managers now own a substantial chunk of the business, they are likely to work harder than when they were simply hired hands.[12]

Going private is one way to reduce the agency costs of equity. Another way is to increase the firm's reliance on debt. Michael Jensen has observed that the interest payments on debt can absorb excess cash flow that firms may have been tempted to spend on wasteful perquisites.[13] He argues that debt forces the firm to pay the cash flow to bondholders instead of wasting the cash flow on perquisites.

Effect of Agency Costs of Equity on Debt-Equity Financing

Before our discussion of agency costs of equity in the current section, we stated that the change in the value of the firm when debt is substituted for equity is the difference between (1) the tax shield on debt minus (2) the increase in the costs of financial distress (including the agency costs of debt). Now, the change in the value of the firm is (1) the tax shield on debt plus (2) the reduction in the agency costs of equity minus (3) the increase in the costs of financial distress (including the agency costs of debt). The optimal debt-equity ratio would be higher in a world with agency costs of equity than in a world without these costs. However, because the agency costs of debt are so significant, the costs of equity do not imply 100-percent debt financing.

Concept Questions

- What are agency costs?
- Why are shirking and perquisites considered an agency cost of equity?
- How do agency costs of equity affect the firm's debt-equity ratio?

16.6 Growth and the Debt-Equity Ratio

While the trade-off between the tax shield and bankruptcy costs (as illustrated in Figure 16.1) is the "standard model" of capital structure, it has its critics. For example, some point out that bankruptcy costs in the real world appear to be much smaller than the tax subsidy. Thus, the model implies that the optimal debt/value ratio should still be near 100 percent, an implication at odds with reality.[14]

An important new idea is that growth implies significant equity financing, even in a world with low bankruptcy costs.[15] To explain the idea, we first consider an example of a no-growth firm. Next, we examine the effect of growth on firm leverage.

[12] One professor we know introduces his classes to LBOs by asking the students three questions:

1. How many of you have ever owned your own car?
2. How many of you have ever rented a car?
3. How many of you took better care of the car you owned than the car you rented?

Just as it is human nature to take better care of your own car, it is human nature to work harder when you own more of the company.

[13] Michael C. Jensen, "Agency Costs of Free Cash Flow, Corporate Finance Takeovers," *American Economic Review* 76 (1986), pp. 323–39.

[14] See Merton Miller's Presidential Address to the American Finance Association, reprinted as "Debt and Taxes," *Journal of Finance* (May 1977).

[15] This new idea is introduced and analyzed in J. L. Berens and C. L. Cuny, "Inflation, Growth and Capital Structure," unpublished paper, University of California at Irvine, June 1993.

No-Growth

Imagine a world of perfect certainty[16] where a firm has Earnings before Interest and Taxes (EBIT) of \$100. In addition, the firm has issued \$1000 of debt at an interest rate of 10 percent, implying interest payments of \$100 per year. The cash flows to the firm are:

Date	1	2	3	4 . . .
Earnings before interest and taxes (EBIT)	\$100	\$100	\$100	\$100 . . .
Interest	−100	−100	−100	−100 . . .
Taxable income	0	0	0	0

The firm has issued just enough debt so that all EBIT is paid out as interest. Since interest is tax-deductible, the firm pays no taxes. In this example, the equity is worthless because stockholders receive no cash flows. Since debt is worth \$1,000, the firm is also valued at \$1,000. Therefore, the debt-to-value ratio is 100 percent (= \$1,000/\$1,000).

Had the firm issued less than \$1,000 of debt, the corporation would have positive taxable income and, consequently, would have ended up paying some taxes. Had the firm issued more than \$1,000 of debt, interest would have exceeded EBIT, causing default. Consequently, the optimal debt-to-value ratio is 100 percent.

Growth

Now imagine another firm that also has EBIT of \$100 at date 1 but is growing at 5 percent per year.[17] To eliminate taxes, this firm also wants to issue enough debt so that interest equals EBIT. Since EBIT is growing at 5 percent per year, interest must also grow at this rate. This is achieved by increasing debt by 5 percent per year.[18] The debt and income levels are:

Date	0	1	2	3	4 . . .
Debt	\$1,000	\$1,050	\$1,102.50	\$1,157.63 . . .	
New debt issued		50	52.50	55.13 . . .	
EBIT		\$100	\$105	\$110.25	\$115.76 . . .
Interest		−100	−105	−110.25	−115.76 . . .
Taxable income		\$0	\$0	\$0	\$0

Note that interest on a particular date is always 10 percent of the debt on the previous date. Debt is set so that interest is exactly equal to EBIT. As in the no-growth case, the levered firm has the maximum amount of debt at each date. Default would occur if interest payments were increased.

Because growth is 5 percent per year, the value of the firm is:[19]

$$V_{Firm} = \frac{\$100}{.10 - .05} = \$2,000$$

[16] The same qualitative results occur under uncertainty, though the mathematics is more troublesome.

[17] For simplicity, assume that growth is achieved without earnings retention. The same conclusions would be reached with retained earnings, though the arithmetic would become more involved. Of course, growth without earnings retention is less realistic than growth with retention.

[18] Since the firm makes no real investment, the new debt is used to buy back shares of stock.

[19] The firm can also be valued by a variant of (15.7):

$$\begin{aligned} V_L &= \quad V_U \quad + \quad PVTS \\ &= \frac{\$100(1 - T_C)}{.10 - .05} + \frac{T_C \times \$100}{.10 - .05} = \$2,000 \end{aligned}$$

Because of firm growth, both V_U and $PVTS$ are growing perpetuities.

The equity at date 0 is the difference between the value of the firm at that time, \$2,000, and the debt of \$1,000. Hence, equity must be equal to \$1,000[20] implying a debt-to-value ratio of 50 percent (= \$1,000/\$2,000). Note the important difference between the no-growth and the growth example. The no-growth example has no equity; the value of the firm is simply the value of the debt. With growth, there is equity as well as debt.

As we mentioned earlier, any further increase in debt would lower the value of the firm in a world with bankruptcy costs. Thus, with growth, the optimal amount of debt is less than 100%. Note, however, that bankruptcy costs need not be as large as the tax subsidy. In fact, even with infinitesimally small bankruptcy costs, firm value would decline if promised interest rose above \$100 in the first year. The key to this example is that *today's* interest is set equal to *today's* income. While the introduction of future growth opportunities increases firm value, it does not increase the current level of debt needed to shield today's income from today's taxes. Since equity is the difference between firm value and debt, growth increases the value of equity.

The above example captures an essential feature of the real world: growth. The same conclusion is reached in a world of inflation but no growth opportunities.[21] The result of this section, that 100 percent debt financing is suboptimal, holds whether growth opportunities and/or inflation is present. Since most firms have growth opportunities and since inflation has been with us for most of this century, this section's example is based on realistic assumptions. The basic point is this: High-growth firms will have lower debt ratios than low-growth firms.

Concept Question

- How do growth opportunities decrease the advantage of debt financing?

16.7 Personal Taxes

So far in the chapter, we have considered corporate taxes only. Unfortunately, the IRS does not let us off that easily. Income to individuals is taxed at marginal rates up to 39.6 percent. To see the effect of personal taxes on capital structure, we have reproduced our Water Products example (from Section 15.6) below.

	Plan I	*Plan II*
EBIT	\$1,000,000	\$1,000,000
Interest ($r_B B$)	0	(400,000)
Earnings before taxes (EBT = EBIT − $r_B B$)	1,000,000	600,000
Taxes ($T_C = 0.35$)	(350,000)	(210,000)
Earnings after taxes [EAT = (EBIT − $r_B B$) × (1 − T_c)]	650,000	390,000
Add back interest ($r_B B$)	0	400,000
Total cash flow to all investors [EBIT × (1 − T_C) + $T_C r_B B$]	\$650,000	\$790,000

[20] Students are often surprised that equity has value when taxable income is zero. Actually, the equityholders are receiving cash flow each period, since new debt is used to buy back stock.

[21] Notice that we restricted the debt to bonds with level coupon payments. Suppose, instead, that the firm had begun at date 0 by issuing debt-carrying coupons of \$105 in year one, \$110.25 in year 2, \$115.76 in year 3, and so on. Since there is no uncertainty in our example, these coupons are just the annual EBIT of the firm. At an interest rate of 10% such a bond would carry a price of \$2,000, which is the entire value of the firm. Thus, the proceeds from the bond issue would equal the value of the firm and the firm would be capitalized as an all-debt firm.

Keep in mind that the important feature of debt is that it is a contractual commitment by the firm to make scheduled payments to the holder. While these payments are usually in the form of level coupons, they also may vary over time. (continued on next page)

As presented above, this example considers corporate but not personal taxes. To treat these personal taxes, we first assume that all earnings after taxes are paid out as dividends. Because dividends and interest are both taxed at the same personal rate (we assume 28 percent), we have

	Plan I		*Plan II*	
Dividends	$650,000		$390,000	
Personal taxes on dividends (Personal rate = 28%)	(182,000)		(109,200)	
Dividends after personal taxes		$468,000		$280,800
Interest	0		$400,000	
Taxes on interest	0		(112,000)	
Interest after personal taxes		0		288,000
Total cash flow to both bondholders and stockholders after personal taxes		$468,000		$568,800

Total taxes paid at both corporate and personal levels are

Plan *I*:	$350,000 Corporate taxes	+	$182,000 Personal taxes on dividends			=	$532,000
Plan *II*:	$210,000 Corporate taxes	+	$109,200 Personal taxes on dividends	+	$112,000 Personal taxes on interest	=	$431,200

Total cash flow to all investors after personal taxes is greater under plan *II*. This must be the case because (1) total cash flow was higher when personal taxes were ignored and (2) all cash flows (both interest and dividends) are taxed at the same personal tax rate. Thus, the conclusion that debt increases the value of the firm still holds. However, the above analysis assumed that all earnings are paid out in dividends. In reality, a firm may repurchase shares in lieu of dividends, a strategy resulting in lower personal taxes than would have occurred with dividends.[22] Alternatively, dividends may be deferred through retention of earnings. Thus, the effective personal tax rate on distributions to stockholders is likely to be below the personal tax rate on interest.

Technically, the same conclusion is reached under inflation in a world with financial institutions similar to those in the U. S. But the conclusion will not hold if indexed bonds are issued and/or only real payments are tax-deductible.

[22] Under the current U.S. tax code, dividends are taxed at an individual's marginal tax rate. Long-term capital gains are taxed at the lower of (*a*) the individual's marginal tax bracket or (*b*) 28 percent.

Interestingly, individuals face higher taxes on a dividend than on a long-term capital gain of equal size, even if tax rates on the two forms of income are the same. To see this, imagine a firm where all stockholders own 10 shares, each selling for $20. On the one hand, the firm can pay out a $2 dividend per share. Here, each stockholder would receive $20 of dividends and pay taxes of

$$T_S \times \$20$$

where T_S is the tax rate on both dividends and capital gains. On the other hand, the firm could repurchase one tenth of all the outstanding shares at the market price. Assuming that all shareholders participate in the repurchase, each shareholder would sell one share of stock. Because a share sells for $20, total payout from the firm is the same for the repurchase as it is for the dividend. Upon receiving $20, the shareholder's gain on the sale would be $\$20 - P_0$. Here, P_0 is the price at which the share was originally purchased. This implies a capital gains tax of

$$(\$20 - P_0) \times T_S$$

To illustrate this tax rate differential, let us assume that the effective personal tax rate on distributions to stockholders, T_S, is 10 percent and the personal tax rate on interest, T_B, is 50 percent.[23] The cash flows for the two plans are

	Plan I		*Plan II*	
Distributions to stockholders	$650,000		$390,000	
Personal taxes on stockholder distributions (at 10% tax rate)	(65,000)		(39,000)	
Distribution to stockholders after personal taxes		$585,000		$351,000
Interest	0		400,000	
Taxes on interest (at 50% tax rate)	0		(200,000)	
Interest after personal taxes		0		200,000
Total cash flow to both bondholders and stockholders after personal taxes		$585,000		$551,000

Total taxes paid at both personal and corporate levels are

Plan *I*:	$350,000 Corporate taxes	+	$65,000 Personal taxes on dividends			=	$415,000
Plan *II*:	$210,000 Corporate taxes	+	$39,000 Personal taxes on dividends	+	$200,000 Personal taxes on interest	=	$449,000

In this scenario, the total cash flows are higher under plan *I* than under plan *II*. Though the example is expressed in terms of cash flows, we would expect the value of the firm to be higher under plan *I* than under plan *II*. Which plan does the IRS dislike the most? Clearly, the IRS dislikes plan *I* more because lower total taxes are paid. The increase in corporate taxes under the all-equity plan is more than offset by the decrease in personal taxes.

Interest receives a tax deduction at the corporate level. Equity distributions may be taxed at a lower rate than interest at the personal level. The above examples illustrate that total tax at all levels may either increase or decrease with debt, depending on the tax rates in effect.

The Miller Model

Valuation under Personal and Corporate Taxes

The previous example calculated *cash flows* for the two plans under personal and corporate taxes. However, we have made no attempt to determine firm *value* so far. It can

[23] This 50-percent tax rate was possible under previous tax codes, where the highest marginal rate was 70 percent. However, it is not possible today.

be shown that the value of the levered firm can be expressed in terms of an unlevered firm as[24]

$$V_L = V_U + \left[1 - \frac{(1 - T_C) \times (1 - T_S)}{(1 - T_B)}\right] \times B \qquad (16.1)$$

T_B is the personal tax rate on ordinary income, such as interest, and T_S is the personal tax rate on equity distributions.

If we set $T_B = T_S$, (16.1) reduces to

$$V_L = V_U + T_C B \qquad (16.2)$$

which is the result we calculated for a world of no personal taxes. Hence, the introduction of personal taxes does not affect our valuation formula as long as equity distributions are taxed identically to interest at the personal level.

However, the gain from leverage is reduced when $T_S < T_B$. Here, more taxes are paid at the personal level for a levered firm than for an unlevered firm. In fact, imagine that $(1 - T_C) \times (1 - T_S) = 1 - T_B$. Formula (16.1) tells us there is no gain from leverage at all! In other words, the value of the levered firm is equal to the value of the unlevered firm. This lack of gain occurs because the lower corporate taxes for a levered firm are *exactly* offset by higher personal taxes. The above results are presented in Figure 16.3.

- ***Example***

Acme Industries anticipates a perpetual pretax earnings stream of $100,000 and faces a 35-percent corporate tax rate. Investors discount the earnings stream after corporate taxes at 15 percent. The personal tax rate on equity distributions is 12 percent, and the personal tax rate on interest is 28 percent. Acme currently has an all-equity capital structure but is considering borrowing $120,000 at 10 percent.

---

[24] Stockholders receive

$$(\text{EBIT} - r_B B) \times (1 - T_C) \times (1 - T_S)$$

Bondholders receive

$$r_B B \times (1 - T_B)$$

Thus, the total cash flow to all stakeholders is

$$(\text{EBIT} - r_B B) \times (1 - T_C) \times (1 - T_S) + r_B B \times (1 - T_B)$$

which can be rewritten as

$$\text{EBIT} \times (1 - T_C) \times (1 - T_S) + r_B B \times (1 - T_B) \times \left[1 - \frac{(1 - T_C) \times (1 - T_S)}{1 - T_B}\right] \qquad \text{(a)}$$

The first term in (a) is the cash flow from an unlevered firm after all taxes. The value of this stream must be V_U, the value of an unlevered firm. An individual buying a bond for B receives $r_B B \times (1 - T_B)$ after all taxes. Thus, the value of the second term in (a) must be

$$B \times \left[1 - \frac{(1 - T_C) \times (1 - T_S)}{1 - T_B}\right]$$

Therefore, the value of the stream in (a), which is the value of the levered firm, must be

$$V_U + \left[1 - \frac{(1 - T_C) \times (1 - T_S)}{1 - T_B}\right] \times B$$

FIGURE 16.3 Effect of Financial Leverage on Firm Value with Both Corporate and Personal Taxes

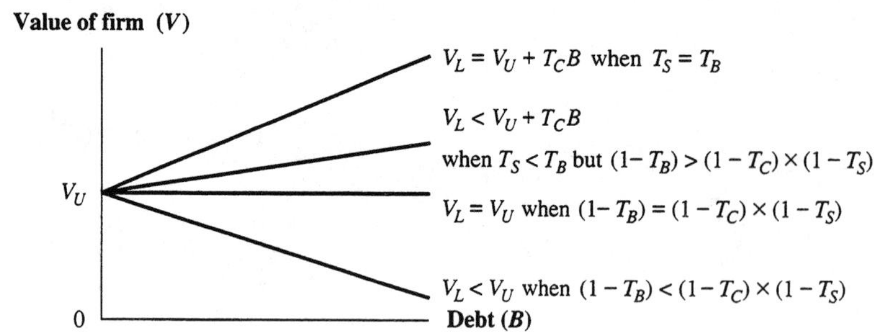

T_C is the corporate tax rate.
T_B is the personal tax rate on interest.
T_S is the personal tax rate on dividends and other equity distributions.
Both personal taxes and corporate taxes are included. Bankruptcy costs and agency costs are ignored.
The effect of debt on firm value depends on T_S, T_C, and T_B.

The value of the all-equity firm is[25]

$$V_U = \frac{\$100{,}000 \times (1 - 0.35)}{0.15} = \$433{,}333$$

The value of the levered firm is

$$V_L = \$433{,}333 + \left[1 - \frac{(1 - 0.35) \times (1 - 0.12)}{(1 - 0.28)}\right] \times \$120{,}000 = \$458{,}000$$

The advantage to leverage here is \$458,000 − \$433,333 = \$24,667. This is much smaller than \$42,000 = 0.35 × \$120,000 = $T_C B$, which would have been the gain in a world with no personal taxes.

Acme had previously considered the choice years earlier when T_B = 50% and T_S = 18%. Here,

$$V_L = \$433{,}333 + \left[1 - \frac{(1 - 0.35) \times (1 - 0.18)}{(1 - 0.50)}\right] \times \$120{,}000 = \$425{,}413$$

In this case, $V_L < V_U$. Hence, Acme was wise not to increase leverage years ago. The inequality occurs because the personal tax rate on interest is much higher than the personal tax rate on equity distributions. In other words, the reduction in corporate taxes from leverage is more than offset by the increase in taxes from leverage at the personal level. •

The Miller model provides an elegant description of the capital-structure decision. However, critics of the model commonly focus on two related areas:

[25] Alternatively, we could have said that investors discount the earnings stream after *both* corporate and personal taxes at 13.20 percent [15% × (1 − 0.12)]:

$$V_U = \frac{\$100{,}000 \times (1 - 0.35) \times (1 - 0.12)}{0.1320} = \$433{,}333$$

Thus, the same value for the unlevered firm would apply.

FIGURE 16.4 Value of the Firm under the Miller Model when Interest Deductibility is Limited to Earnings

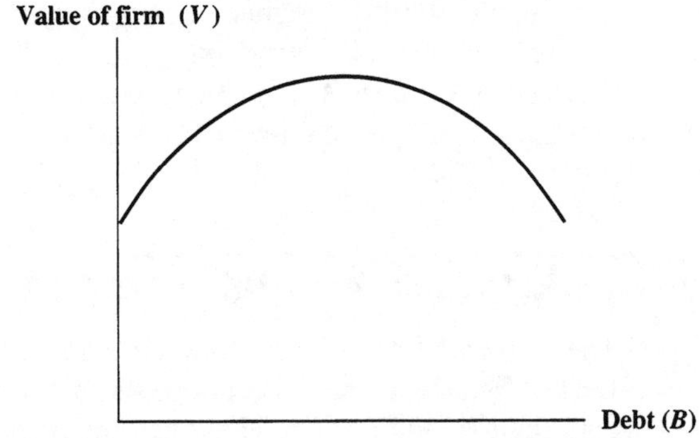

The Miller model with limited deductibility of interest leads to a U-shaped graph similar to the one presented in Figure 16.1. The U shape in Figure 16.1 arose from the trade-off between corporate taxes and bankruptcy costs.

1. *Tax Rates in the Real World.* Both Figure 16.3 and the previous example show that the relationship between firm value and leverage depends on personal and corporate tax rates. Consider the period from 1987 to 1992, when the corporate tax rate in the United States was 34 percent and the highest personal tax rate was 31 percent. Under the assumption that $T_S = 0$, equation (15.7) becomes

$$V_L = V_U + \left[1 - \frac{(1 - 0.34) \times (1 - 0)}{1 - 0.31}\right] \times B = V_U + 0.043B$$

Since $0.043 > 0$, there is a gain from leverage. Under the more plausible assumption that T_S is positive, the gain to leverage is even greater. And, while the corporate tax rate of 34 percent applied to essentially all corporations, most individuals were in tax brackets well below 31 percent, so the gain from leverage was likely even greater still. Thus, the Miller model predicted *all*-debt financing from 1987 to 1992, clearly a result at odds with reality.

More recently, the highest possible corporate tax rate in the United States has been less than the highest personal tax rate. Depending on the distribution of both T_B and T_S across individuals, leverage today may increase, decrease, or have no effect on firm value.

2. *Unlimited Tax Deductibility.* The above discussion shows that an empirical prediction of Miller's work was false from 1987 to 1992. Perhaps the problem lies in a missing assumption in the model. For example, critics point out that corporations have unlimited interest deductibility in the model. In reality, firms can deduct interest only to the extent of profits. Thus, the expected tax benefits of debt financing under this real-world assumption are clearly less than under the assumption of unlimited deductibility. Two effects are likely to result. First, corporations are likely to supply less debt, reducing the interest rate. Second, the first unit of debt is more likely to increase firm value than the last unit, because the interest on later units may not be deductible.

The results of limited deductibility are provided in Figure 16.4. Because the interest rate is now lower than that in the strict Miller model, firm value should rise when debt is first added to the capital structure. However, as more and more debt is issued, the full deductibility of the interest becomes less likely. Firm value still increases, but at a lower and lower rate. At some point, the probability of tax deductibility is low enough that an incremental dollar of debt is as costly to the firm as an incremental dollar of equity. Firm value then decreases with further leverage.[26]

This graph looks surprisingly like the curve in Figure 16.1 where the trade-off between the tax shield and bankruptcy costs is illustrated. Thus, a key change in assumptions may explain why firms are never all-debt financed, even when T_C is high relative to T_B.

16.8 How Firms Establish Capital Structure

The theories of capital structure are among the most elegant and sophisticated in the field of finance. Financial economists should (and do!) pat themselves on the back for contributions in this area. However, the practical applications of the theories are less than fully satisfying. Consider that our work on net present value produced an *exact* formula for evaluating projects. Conversely, the most we can say on capital structure is provided in either Figure 16.1 or Figure 16.4; the optimal capital structure involves a trade-off between taxes and costs of debt. No exact formula is available for evaluating the optimal debt-equity ratio. Because of this, we turn to evidence from the real world.

The following empirical regularities are worthwhile to consider when formulating capital-structure policy.

1. *Most Corporations Have Low Debt-Asset Ratios.* In fact, historically most U.S. corporations use less debt than equity financing. Many of these corporations pay substantial amounts in taxes, and the corporate tax has been an important source of government revenue. Figure 14.4 in Chapter 14 shows the debt-to-asset value for U.S. industrial firms. The measures are in accounting (that is, book) values for the years 1977 to 1992. It shows that debt ratios rose in the 1980s. Notice that the debt ratios are low; they are usually less than 50 percent. In 1992, the U.S. corporate debt-to-asset ratio was 50 percent. Although most corporations have low debt-asset ratios, they nevertheless pay substantial taxes. In 1995 corporate taxes were several hundred billion dollars. It is clear that corporations do not issue debt up to the point that tax shelters are used up. Figure 16.5 shows the debt-to-total value ratios of firms in several countries. Differences in accounting procedures make this figure difficult to interpret. However, the debt ratio of U.S. and Canadian firms is the lowest. There must be limits to the amount of debt corporations can issue.
2. *Changes in Financial Leverage Affect Firm Value.* In an important study, Masulis examined the effect of announcements of change in capital structure on stock prices.[27] Table 16.3 is an example of the type of results that Masulis

[26] H. DeAngelo and R. Masulis, "Optimal Capital Structure under Corporate and Personal Taxation," *Journal of Financial Economics* (March 1980), posit a model where interest on debt is not the firm's only tax shield. Investment tax credits, depreciation, and depletion are examples of other tax shields. The authors show results similar to those in this section.

[27] R. Masulis, "The Effects of Capital Structure Change on Security Prices: A Study of Exchange Offers," *Journal of Financial Economics* 8 (1980). More recently, M. Cornett and N. Travlos, "Information Effects Associated with Debt-in-Equity and Equity-in-Debt Exchange Offers," *Journal of Finance* 44 (1989); T. Copeland and Won Heum Lee, "Exchange Offers and Swaps: New Evidence," *Financial Management* 20 (1991); and K. Shah, "The Nature of Information Conveyed by Pure Capital Structure Changes," *Journal of Financial Economics* 36 (1994) have examined exchange offers.

FIGURE 16.5 Estimated Ratios of Debt to Total Value (accounting value) of Nonfinancial Firms, Various Countries (1992)

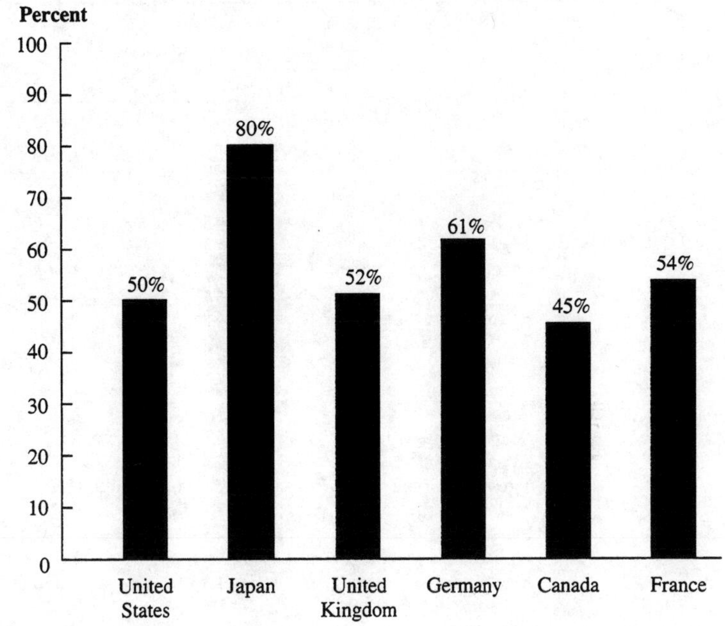

Source: OECD financial statistics.

TABLE 16.3 Rates of Return on Common Stock from Initial Announcement of Offers Increasing and Decreasing Leverage

Increasing Leverage			*Decreasing Leverage*		
Event Day	*Portfolio Daily Returns (%)*	*Percentage of Stock Returns > 0*	*Event Day*	*Portfolio Daily Returns (%)*	*Percentage of Stock Returns > 0*
−10	0.38	42.0	−10	−0.54	28.0
−9	0.34	31.0	−9	1.02	44.0
−8	0.03	43.0	−8	0.17	39.0
−7	0.53	41.0	−7	0.13	33.0
−6	0.40	36.0	−6	1.43	33.0
−5	0.29	42.0	−5	−0.43	30.0
−4	0.16	31.0	−4	−0.09	30.0
−3	0.62	43.0	−3	0.60	46.0
−2	0.15	40.0	−2	1.20	36.0
−1	0.50	38.0	−1	0.74	49.0
0	4.51	69.0	0	−2.98	11.0
1	3.12	58.0	1	−2.39	25.0
2	0.00	37.0	2	0.06	30.0
3	0.71	27.0	3	−0.60	33.0
4	0.21	40.0	4	0.26	28.0
5	0.09	34.0	5	0.46	32.0
6	0.54	26.0	6	0.30	21.0
7	0.15	30.0	7	0.31	35.0
8	0.26	27.0	8	0.39	39.0
9	0.06	39.0	9	−0.14	37.0
10	0.19	37.0	10	−0.47	29.0

From R. Masulis, "The Effects of Capital Structure Policy Change on Security Prices: A Study of Exchange Offers," *Journal of Financial Economics* 8 (1980), pp. 158–59.

TABLE 16.4 Debt-equity Ratios for Different Industries in the United States and Japan in 1983

	Net debt to:		Number of companies in the sample		
Industry	*Book-value equity*	*Market-value equity*	*Japan*	*United States*	*Total*
Nonferrous metals	3.791	1.106	11	13	24
General chemicals	2.945	1.256	21	16	37
Steel	1.973	1.665	35	35	70
Paper	1.732	1.364	16	25	41
Paint	1.548	0.614	7	5	12
Petroleum refining	1.548	1.117	6	33	39
Audio equipment	1.539	0.631	7	10	17
Textiles	1.405	1.296	29	23	52
Cement	1.298	1.366	6	10	16
Glass	1.213	1.087	5	8	13
Soaps and detergents	1.143	0.683	6	8	14
Apparel	1.021	0.951	14	41	55
Tires and rubber	1.021	0.835	8	14	22
Motor vehicles	0.922	0.594	9	6	15
Plastics	0.843	0.792	18	25	43
Agricultural machinery	0.836	1.082	5	5	10
Electrical machinery	0.813	0.376	14	12	26
Construction machinery	0.688	0.810	6	12	18
Electronic parts	0.614	0.358	19	34	53
Motor vehicle parts	0.488	0.500	20	16	36
Machine tools	0.472	0.425	10	15	25
Photo equipment	0.468	0.222	7	7	14
Alcoholic beverages	0.427	0.284	8	10	18
Communication equipment	0.356	0.186	15	24	39
Confectionery	0.326	0.286	6	5	11
Pharmaceuticals	0.194	0.079	25	23	48
Household appliances	0.102	0.244	13	13	26

From W. C. Kester, "Capital and Ownership Structure: A Comparison of United States and Japanese Manufacturing Corporations," *Financial Management* (Spring 1986).

obtained. The table shows the effect of announcing increases and decreases in financial leverage on abnormal returns on common stock. Notice that when firms announce an increase in leverage, there is a large increase in firm value (4.51 percent on day 0 and 3.12 percent on day 1). When they announce a decrease in leverage, there is a decrease in firm value (−2.98 percent on day 0 and −2.39 percent on day 1). These are percentages of total firm value. Several conclusions emerge from the Masulis study. First, stock price increases from increased leverage and stock price decreases from decreased leverage are consistent with a tax benefit from debt. Second, since a reduction in leverage lowers firm value, managers may not be acting in the best interests of the shareholders when leverage is lowered. Third, there is little evidence that bankruptcy costs have a significant effect.

3. *There Are Differences in the Capital Structures of Different Industries.* Table 16.4 is from a paper by Kester.[28] He looks at the debt-equity ratios in Japan and the United States, by industry. It can be deduced easily from looking at

[28] W. C. Kester, "Capital and Ownership Structure: A Comparison of United States and Japanese Manufacturing Corporations," *Financial Management* (Spring 1986).

the table that there is a wide variation in industrial debt-equity ratios. For example, using market values, Kester finds the debt-equity ratio for firms in the steel industry to be 1.665 and for firms in the pharmaceutical industry to be 0.079.

We do not have a unique formula that can establish a debt-equity ratio for all companies. However, there is evidence that firms behave as if they had target debt-equity ratios.[29] From a theoretical perspective and from empirical research, we present four important factors in the final determination of a target debt-equity ratio:

1. *Taxes.* If a company has (and will continue to have) taxable income, an increased reliance on debt will reduce taxes paid by the company and increase taxes paid by some bondholders. If corporate tax rates are higher than bondholder tax rates, there is value from using debt.
2. *Types of Assets.* Financial distress is costly, with or without formal bankruptcy proceedings. The costs of financial distress depend on the types of assets that the firm has. For example, if a firm has a large investment in land, buildings, and other tangible assets, it will have smaller costs of financial distress than a firm with a large investment in research and development. Research and development typically has less resale value than land; thus, most of its value disappears in financial distress.
3. *Uncertainty of Operating Income.* Firms with uncertain operating income have a high probability of experiencing financial distress, even without debt. Thus, these firms must finance mostly with equity. For example, pharmaceutical firms have uncertain operating income because no one can predict whether today's research will generate new drugs. Consequently, these firms issue little debt. By contrast, the operating income of utilities generally has little uncertainty. Relative to other industries, utilities use a great deal of debt.
4. *Pecking Order and Financial Slack.*[30] We first talked about the idea of a pecking order in our discussion of the financing patterns of U.S. and foreign firms in Chapter 14. The pecking-order theory states that firms prefer internal equity (i.e., retained earnings) to external financing. And, if funding requirements exceed retained earnings, debt issues are preferred to equity issues. This pecking order can be explained by two factors.

   - External financing is expensive because of the large fees paid to investment bankers.
   - It is hard for shareholders to accurately price external equity when managers know more about the firm than shareholders ("asymmetric information"). This fact can lead to a reluctance of shareholders to accept new equity issues.

   If firms prefer retained earnings over external financing, they may use less debt than is implied by taxes and financial distress costs. This is particularly true for highly profitable firms where retained earnings are likely to exceed

---

[29] The classic studies showing that firms may have target debt ratios are P. Marsh, "The Choice between Equity and Debt: An Empirical Study," *Journal of Finance* (March 1981); and R. A. Taggart, "A Model of Corporate Financing Decisions," *Journal of Finance* (December 1977).

[30] The pecking-order theory is generally attributed to S. C. Myers, "The Capital Structure Puzzle,"*Journal of Finance* 39 (July 1984).

funding requirements. The pharmaceutical industry is a good example since it has high profits and low leverage. (However, remember that the previous reason "uncertainty of operating income" can also explain low debt in the pharmaceutical industry.)

The pecking-order theory has at least two other implications. First, firms will hoard cash during good times to avoid the need to finance externally during bad times. Economists refer to the cash build-up as *financial slack.* Second, the pecking-order theory does not imply a well-defined target debt-to-equity ratio. Rather, the ratio varies as capital expenditures and retained earnings change.

One final note is in order. Because no formula supports them, the above four points may seem too nebulous to assist financial decision-making. Their industry's debt-equity ratio is an important factor for the capital-structure decisions of many real-world firms. While this may strike some as a cowardly approach, it at least keeps firms from deviating far from accepted practice. After all, the existing firms in any industry are the survivors. Therefore, one should pay at least some attention to their decisions.

Concept Questions

- List the empirical regularities we observe for corporate capital structure.
- What are the factors to consider in establishing a debt-equity ratio?

16.9 The Decision to Use More Debt: The Case of Goodyear Tire and Rubber[31]

What actually happens when a particular firm decides to use more debt? We look at the experiences of Goodyear Tire and Rubber to try to answer this question. Goodyear's increased reliance on debt illustrates many of the important points of this chapter.

Goodyear Tire and Rubber is a well-known manufacturer of rubber products. Automotive products account for about 60 percent of its sales. By 1986 Goodyear Tire and Rubber had become the world's largest manufacturer of tires. Goodyear had worked hard to obtain a reputation for outstanding quality in "high performance" tires. Although Goodyear was the world's leader in making tires, it had encountered difficulties when it tried to diversify into oil and gas and to build an oil pipeline from Texas to California.

In December 1986, Goodyear Tire and Rubber started a cash tender offer for 40 million of its shares at $50 per share. This represented a 50 percent premium over its share price two months earlier. The stock market's reaction was to substantially increase Goodyear's stock price. Why did Goodyear buy back almost one half of its outstanding stock? One reason was the threat of a takeover. Several weeks earlier, the company had reached an agreement with a group headed by feared raider Sir James Goldsmith to acquire his stake in Goodyear for $49.50 per share. The purpose of Goodyear's acquisition of its own stock was to buy out the Goldsmith group's posi-

[31] Alan Shapiro writes about the Goodyear Tire and Rubber Company in "Corporate Stakeholders and Corporate Responsibility," *USC Business* (Summer 1991). See also "Goodyear Tire and Rubber: 1988," Harvard Business School Case 284-177, for a description of Goodyear Tire and Rubber's restructuring and the aftermath. An upbeat article on Goodyear's current prospects appears in "Gault on Fixing Goodyear's Flat," *Fortune,* July 15, 1991.

tion and to make Goodyear more "shark repellent" for other raiders. The buyout was financed with new debt and with cash from sales of major assets. The result was to significantly increase Goodyear's reliance on debt.

Goodyear's type of financial restructuring is often called a *levered recapitalization. Recapitalization* is an imprecise term that refers to changes on the right-hand side of a firm's balance sheet. When the effect is to increase a firm's reliance on debt, it is called a *levered recapitalization,* and usually it involves repurchasing stock and new borrowing. The net effect of Goodyear's recapitalization on its balance sheet was to increase its long-term debt-to-equity ratio from 28.4 percent in 1985 to 150.2 percent in 1988 (see table below).

GOODYEAR TIRE AND RUBBER
(in millions)

	1985	*1986*	*1987*	*1988*	*1989*	*1990*
Long-term debt	$ 997.5	$2,487.5	$3,282.4	$3,044.8	$2,963.4	$3,286.4
Equity	$3,507.4	$3,002.6	$1,834.4	$2,027.1	$2,143.8	$2,097.9
Shares outstanding	216.2	194.2	114.0	114.9	115.6	117.0
Return on equity (ROE)	8.6%	9.2%	24.0%	17.7%	13.8%	negative

Was Goodyear's levered recapitalization a good decision? There are benefits and costs from any levered recapitalization. Clues can be gleaned from the stock market. The stock market's reaction to Goodyear's levered recapitalization was very positive. On the day Goodyear's levered recapitalization was announced, Goodyear's stock jumped by over 20 percent.

Benefits

1. *Tax Benefits.* It is well-known that new debt can increase a firm's value by reducing its taxes. There is no doubt that Goodyear's tax burden has been substantially reduced due to increased reliance on debt. Goodyear's interest expense increased from $101 million in 1985 to $282 million in 1987, and Goodyear's taxable income was reduced.
2. *Lower Agency Costs.* It is often argued that leverage reduces the agency costs arising between management and shareholders. Therefore, the new debt from the levered recapitalization can be thought of as a type of a control device for the shareholders of Goodyear. In 1982 Goodyear had embarked on a diversification program by acquiring Celeron, an oil and gas company. The acquisition of Celeron was followed by several other diversification attempts. Most importantly, Goodyear decided to construct a crude oil pipeline from Texas to California. Shareholders did not react favorably to Goodyear's diversification program, and its stock price fell 65 percent (relative to the S&P 500 Index) over the three and one-half years after 1982. It can be argued that this is a classic case of management pursuing selfish short-sighted goals at the expense of shareholders. Goodyear's diversification program imposed agency costs on its shareholders. Goodyear's levered recapitalization probably prevented it from further diversification because Goodyear was forced to sell most of its non-tire assets to service its new debt. It sold Celeron Oil in December 1987. By borrowing an amount equal to the present value of Goodyear's excess cash flow that could be used to acquire other firms, Goodyear's management has been effectively prevented from further diversification.

Costs

1. *Financial Distress.* When firms such as Goodyear increase their reliance on debt, they also increase the likelihood of financial distress. Financial distress can be formal bankruptcy. So far, Goodyear has not filed for bankruptcy. However, financial distress may occur without bankruptcy. After the levered recapitalization, Goodyear's debt was downgraded by Moody's and Standard & Poor's. This may be evidence of financial distress. Goodyear lost money in 1990 and its ROE was negative. More importantly, financial distress means doing particularly harmful things such as the selfish strategies that we talked about previously. Goodyear has said that it has been forced to cut down on planned research and development and capital spending because of its reliance on debt. Its level of capital spending decreased from about $1.5 billion in 1986 to $754 million in 1988. This may be evidence of financial distress. If so, this is one of the costs imposed upon Goodyear because of its levered recapitalization.
2. *Financial Slack.* The new debt has increased Goodyear's leverage well beyond traditional industry norms. Up to 1985 Goodyear had relied on little debt, leading some industry analysts in 1985 to contend that Goodyear had excess debt capacity (i.e., *financial slack*). However, the excess cash flows that supported Goodyear's borrowing in 1986 and 1987 disappeared in 1988. By the end of 1988 Goodyear had used up all of its financial slack. Loss of financial slack can preclude strategic options if competitors increase capital spending or lower prices. Many analysts believe this is what happened when in 1989 Bridgestone, Goodyear's main competitor, announced its intention to increase its capital spending in the North American tire market. Goodyear could not counter by increasing its own level of capital spending. The only way Goodyear could do so would have been by issuing new equity. But firms do not like to issue new equity because it is very expensive and it is the lowest financing option on the pecking order.

Part of Goodyear's decision to use more debt can be analyzed in terms of a trade-off between the tax benefits of debt and the costs of financial distress. However, the Goodyear experience shows that agency costs and financial slack are also factors in a firm's decision to use debt.

Postscript

Today Goodyear is still the world's largest rubber manufacturer. Its oil pipeline was profitable for the first time in 1994. (But Goodyear is trying to sell its pipeline.) Goodyear almost went broke in 1990–1991 and was forced to cut its dividend for the first time since the 1930s. In 1991 it hired a new CEO, Stanley Gault, who was hailed as CEO of the year in 1992 (by *Financial World*). In 1993 Goodyear's ROE was close to 18 percent and its long-term debt reduced to about $1 billion. Capital spending remained very low at about $450 million.

16.10 Summary and Conclusions

1. We mentioned in the last chapter that, according to theory, firms should create all-debt capital structures under corporate taxation. Because firms generally assume

moderate amounts of debt in the real world, the theory must be missing something at this point. We point out in this chapter that costs of financial distress cause firms to restrain their issuance of debt. These costs are of two types: direct and indirect. Lawyers' and accountants' fees during the bankruptcy process are examples of direct costs. We mentioned four examples of indirect costs:

Impaired ability to conduct business.
Incentive to take on risky projects.
Incentive toward underinvestment.
Distribution of funds to stockholders prior to bankruptcy.

2. Because the above costs are substantial and the stockholders ultimately bear them, firms have an incentive for cost reduction. We suggest three cost-reduction techniques:

   Protective covenants.
   Repurchase of debt prior to bankruptcy.
   Consolidation of debt.

3. Because costs of financial distress can be reduced but not eliminated, firms will not finance entirely with debt. Figure 16.1 illustrates the relationship between firm value and debt. In the figure, firms select the debt-to-equity ratio at which firm value is maximized.
4. While the trade-off between the tax shield and the cost of financial distress is the "standard model" of capital structure, it is not the only model. A recent paper by Berens and Cuny argues that significant equity financing can be explained by real growth and inflation, even in a world of low bankruptcy costs.
5. The results so far have ignored personal taxes. If distributions to equityholders are taxed at a lower effective personal tax rate than are interest payments, the tax advantage to debt at the corporate level is partially offset. In fact, the corporate tax advantage to debt is eliminated if

$$(1 - T_C) \times (1 - T_S) = (1 - T_B)$$

6. Debt-to-equity ratios vary across industries. From a theoretical perspective and from empirical research, we present four factors determining the target debt-to-equity ratio:
   a. *Taxes.* Firms with high taxable income should rely more on debt than firms with little taxable income.
   b. *Types of Assets.* Firms with a high percentage of intangible assets such as research and development should have low debt. Firms with primarily tangible assets should have higher debt.
   c. *Uncertainty of Operating Income.* Firms with high uncertainty of operating income should rely mostly on equity.
   d. *Pecking Order.* The most profitable firms will use less debt because they have sufficient internal equity for all positive NPV projects.
      Some firms will accumulate financial slack to avoid using external equity.

Key Terms

Agency costs 421
Protective covenants 424
Negative covenant 424
Positive covenant 424
Marketed claims 428
Nonmarketed claims 428

Suggested Readings

An excellent collection of recent articles appears in

Chew, D. *The New Corporate Finance: Where Theory Meets Practice* (New York: McGraw-Hill, 1993).

A particularly interesting article on capital structure is

Myers, S. "The Search for Optimal Capital Structure" in *The New Corporate Finance: Where Theory Meets Practice,* op. cit.

Merton Miller's Nobel lecture is reprinted as

Miller, M. "Leverage," *Journal of Finance* (June 1991).

An extremely influential set of articles arguing that bankruptcy costs are low are

Haugen, R. A., and L. Senbet. "The Insignificance of Bankruptcy Costs to the Theory of Optimal Capital Structure." *Journal of Finance* (May 1978).

Haugen, R. A., and L. Senbet. "New Perspectives on Informational Asymmetry and Agency Relationships." *Journal of Financial and Quantitative Analysis* (November 1979).

Haugen, R. A., and L. Senbet. "Bankruptcy and Agency Costs: Their Significance to the Theory of Optimal Capital Structure." *Journal of Financial and Quantitative Analysis* (March 1988).

The following excellent paper surveys the various capital-structure theories:

Harris, Milton, and A. Raviv. "The Theory of Capital Structure." *Journal of Finance* (March 1991).

Questions and Problems

Costs of Financial Distress

16.1 Good Time Co. is a regional chain department store. It will remain in business for one more year. The estimated probability of boom year is 60 percent and that of recession is 40 percent. It is projected that Good Time will have total cash flow of \$250 million in a boom year and \$100 million in recession. Its required debt payment is \$150 million per annum. Assume a one-period model.

Assume risk neutrality and an annual discount rate of 12 percent for both the stock and the bond.

a. What is the total stock value of the firm?

b. If the total value of bond outstanding of Good Time is \$108.93 million, what is the expected bankruptcy cost in case of recession?

c. What is the total value of the firm?

d. What is the promised return on the bond?

16.2 VanSant Corporation and Matta, Inc., are identical firms except that Matta, Inc., is more levered than VanSant. The companies' economists agree that the probability of a recession next year is 20 percent and the probability of a continuation of the current expansion is 80 percent. If the expansion continues, each firm will have EBIT of \$2 million. If a recession occurs, each firm will have EBIT of \$0.8 million. VanSant's debt obligation requires the firm to make \$750,000 in payments. Because Matta carries more debt, its debt payment obligations are \$1 million.

Assume that the investors in these firms are risk-neutral and that they discount the firms' cash flows at 15 percent. Assume a one-period example. Also assume there are no taxes.

a. Duane, the president of VanSant, commented to Matta's president, Deb, that his firm has a higher value than Matta, Inc., because VanSant has less debt and, therefore, less bankruptcy risk. Is Duane correct?

b. Using the data of the two firms, prove your answer to (*a*).

c. What might cause the firms to be valued differently?

Description of Costs

16.3 What are the direct and indirect costs of bankruptcy? Briefly explain each.

16.4 Chrysler's financial structure in August 1983 was as follows:

Security	*Number of units outstanding*	*Price per unit*	*Market value*
Common stock	115,000,000	$ 26.00	$2,990,000.000
Preferred stock	10,000,000	32.50	325,000,000
Warrants	14,400,000	13.50	194,400,000
Bonds	2,000,000	650.00	1,300,000.000

Due to large losses incurred during 1978–1981, Chrysler had $2 billion in tax-loss carryforwards; therefore, the next $2 billion of income was free from corporate income taxes. At the time, the consensus of security analysts was that Chrysler would not have cumulative profits in excess of $2 billion over the next five years.

Most of the preferred stock was held by banks. Chrysler had agreed to retire the preferred stock over the next few years. Chrysler had to decide whether to issue debt or sell common equity to raise the funds needed to retire the preferred stock.

If you were Lee Iacocca, what would you have done? Why?

16.5 Fountain Corporation economists estimate that the probability of a good business environment next year is equal to the probability of a bad environment. Knowing that, the managers of Fountain must choose between two mutually exclusive projects. Suppose the project that Fountain chooses will be the only business it does next year. Therefore, the payoff of the project will determine the value of the firm. Fountain is obliged to make a $500 payment to its bondholders. The first project is one of low risk.

Low-risk project

Economy	*Probability*	*Project payoff*	*Value of firm*		*Value of stock*		*Value of bonds*
Bad	0.5	$500	$500	=	0	+	$500
Good	0.5	$700	$700	=	$200	+	$500

If the firm does not undertake the low-risk project, it will choose the following high-risk project.

High-risk project

Economy	*Probability*	*Project payoff*	*Value of firm*		*Value of stock*		*Value of bonds*
Bad	0.5	$100	$100	=	0	+	$100
Good	0.5	$800	$800	=	$300	+	$500

Which project would the stockholders prefer? Why?

16.6 Do you agree or disagree with the following statement? Explain your answer.

> A firm's stockholders would never want the firm to invest in projects with negative NPVs.

16.7 Refer to the selfish strategy #1 in section 16.2. Suppose the bondholders are fully aware of the discrepancy between maximizing the firm value and the stock value. To minimize the agency costs, bondholders use a bond covenant to stipulate that when the firm takes on high-risk projects, bondholders can demand a higher debt payment. By how much would the bondholders need to raise the debt payment so that the stockholders would be indifferent between the two projects? What is the corporate finance implication of this postulated example?

Can Costs of Debt Be Reduced?

16.8 What measures do stockholders undertake to minimize the costs of debt?

Integration of Tax Effect and Financial Distress Costs

16.9 How would the consideration of financial distress costs and agency costs affect the MM proposition in a world where corporation pays taxes?

Shirking and Perquisites: A Note on Agency Cost of Equity

16.10 What are the sources of the agency costs of equity?

Personal Taxes

16.11 Fortune Enterprises (FE) is an all-equity firm that is considering issuing $13,500,000 in 10-percent debt. The firm will use the proceeds of the bond sale to repurchase equity. FE has a 100-percent payout policy. Because FE is a nongrowth firm, its earnings and debt would be perpetual. FE's income statement under each of the financial structures is shown below.

	All equity	*Debt*
EBIT	$3,000,000	$3,000,000
Interest	0	1,350,000
EBT	3,000,000	1,650,000
Taxes ($T_c = 0.4$)	1,200,000	660,000
Net income	$1,800,000	$990,000

a. If the personal tax rate is 30 percent, which plan offers the investors the higher cash flows? Why?

b. Which plan does the IRS prefer?

c. Suppose stockholders demand a 20-percent return after personal taxes. What is the value of the firm under each plan?

d. Suppose $T_S = 0.2$ and $T_B = 0.55$. What are the investors' returns under each plan?

16.12 The general expression for the value of a leveraged firm in a world in which $T_S = 0$ is

$$V_L = V_U + \left[\frac{1 - (1 - T_C)}{(1 - T_B)}\right] \times B - C(B)$$

where

V_U = Value of an unlevered firm
T_C = Effective corporate tax rate for the firm
T_B = Personal tax rate of the marginal bondholder
B = Debt level of the firm
$C(B)$ = Present value of the costs of financial distress for the firm as a function of its debt level. [Note: C(B) encompasses all non–tax-related effects of leverage on the firm's value.]

Assume all investors are risk-neutral.

a. In their no-tax model, what do Modigliani and Miller assume about T_C, T_B, and C(B)? What do these assumptions imply about a firm's optimal debt-equity ratio?

b. In their model that includes corporate taxes, what do Modigliani and Miller assume about T_C, T_B, and C(B)? What do these assumptions imply about a firm's optimal debt-equity ratio?

c. Assume that IBM is certain to be able to use its interest deductions to reduce its corporate tax bill. What would the change in the value of IBM be if the company issued $1 billion in debt and used the proceeds to repurchase equity? Assume that the personal tax rate on bond income is 20 percent, the corporate tax rate is 34 percent, and the costs of financial distress are zero.

d. Assume that USX is virtually certain not to be able to use interest deductions. What would the change in the value of the company be from adding $1 of perpetual debt rather than \$1 of equity? Assume that the personal tax rate on bond income is 20 percent, the corporate tax rate is 35 percent, and the costs of financial distress are zero.

e. For companies that may or may not be able to use the interest deduction, what would the change in the value of the company be from adding \$1 of perpetual debt rather than \$1 of equity? Assume that the personal tax rate on bond income is 20 percent, the corporate tax rate is 35 percent, and the costs of financial distress are zero. Also assume the probability of using the incremental deduction is 65 percent.

16.13 Because of the large cash inflows from the sales of its cookbook, *Fear of Frying,* the Overnight Publishing Company (OPC) has decided to retire all of its outstanding debt. The debt is made up of consul bonds; its maturity date is indefinitely far away. The debt is also considered risk-free. It carries a 10-percent coupon rate and has a book value of \$3 million. Because market rates on long-term bonds are 15 percent, the market value of the bonds is only \$2 million. All of the debt is held by one institution that will sell it back to OPC for \$2 million cash. The institution will not charge OPC any transaction costs, and there are no tax consequences from retiring the debt. Once OPC becomes an all-equity firm, it will remain unlevered forever.

If OPC does not retire the debt, the company will use the \$2 million in cash to buy back some of its stock on the open market. Repurchasing stock also has no transaction costs. Investors expect OPC to repurchase some stock, so they will be completely surprised when the debt-retirement plan is announced.

The required rate of return of the equity holders after OPC becomes all equity will be 20 percent. The expected annual earnings before interest and taxes for the firm are \$1,100,000; those earnings are expected to remain constant in perpetuity. OPC has no growth opportunities, and the company is subject to a 35-percent corporate tax rate. Assume that $T_B = 10\%$ and $T_S = 0$. Also assume that bankruptcy costs do not change for OPC as a result of this capital-structure change. How much does the market value of the company change?

16.14 The EXES Company is assessing its present capital structure and that structure's implications for the welfare of its investors. EXES is currently financed entirely with common stock, of which 1,000 shares are outstanding. Given the risk of the underlying cash flows (EBIT) generated by EXES, investors currently require a 20-percent return on the EXES common stock. The company pays out all earnings as dividends to common stockholders.

EXES estimates that operating income may be \$1,000, \$2,000, or \$4,200 with respective probabilities of 0.1, 0.4, and 0.5. Assume the firm's expectations about earnings will be met and that they will be unchanged in perpetuity. Also, assume that the corporate and personal tax rates are equal to zero.

a. What is the value of EXES Company?

b. The president of EXES has decided that shareholders would be better off if the company had equal proportions of debt and equity. He therefore proposes to issue \$7,500 of debt at an interest rate of 10 percent. He will use the proceeds to repurchase 500 shares of common stock.

i. What will the new value of the firm be?

ii. What will the value of EXES's debt be?

iii. What will the value of EXES's equity be?

c. Suppose the president's proposal is implemented.

i. What is the required rate of return on equity?

ii. What is the firm's overall required return?

d. Suppose the corporate tax rate is 40 percent.

i. Use the Modigliani-Miller framework that includes taxes to find the value of the firm.

ii. Does the presence of taxes increase or decrease the value of the firm? Why?

iii. Verbally explain how the presence of bankruptcy costs would change the effect of taxes on the value of the firm, if at all.

e. Suppose interest income is taxed at 40 percent while the effective tax on returns to equityholders is zero. Assume that the introduction of the personal tax rate does not affect the required return on equity.

i. What is the value of EXES in a world with personal taxes?

ii. Under the Miller model, what will happen to the value of the firm as the tax on interest income rises?

16.15 Mueller Brewing Company has been ordered by the EPA to stop polluting the Menomenie River. It must now spend $100 million on pollution-control equipment. The company has three alternatives for obtaining the needed $100 million.

1. Sell $100 million of perpetual, taxable corporate bonds with a 20-percent coupon rate.
2. Sell $100 million of perpetual pollution-control bonds with a 10-percent coupon rate. The interest on these bonds is not taxable to investors.
3. Sell $100 million of common stock with a 9.5-percent current dividend yield.

Mueller Brewing Company is in the 35-percent tax bracket.

The president of Mueller Brewing wants to sell the common stock because it has the lowest rate. Mr. Daniels, the company's treasurer, suggests bond financing because of the tax shield offered by the debt. His analysis shows that the value of the firm would increase $r_B B T_C / r_B$ = ($100 million) × (0.35) = $35 million if Mueller issues bonds instead of equity. A newly hired financial analyst, Ms. Harris, argues that it does not matter which type of bond is issued. She claims that the yields will be bid up to reflect taxes and, thus, the financing choice will not matter.

a. Comment on the analyses of the president, Mr. Daniels, and Ms. Harris.

b. Should Mueller be indifferent about which financing plan it chooses? If not, rank the three alternatives and give the benefits and costs of each.

16.16 Melvin Clark, CFO of the Matsushita Corp., is evaluating the value of the firm's current capital structure. Being conservative, he expects that Matsushita will have a perpetual EBIT of $800,000, with an after-tax discount rate of 10 percent if it is all-equity financed. Currently, the firm has $1.2 million debt. The Corporate tax rate is 35 percent. The uniform personal tax rate in the economy is 15 percent. Personal tax rates on equity income are effectively zero because of the possibility of infinite deferral of the realization of capital gains. The combined financial distress and agency costs associated with the debt are approximately 5 percent of the total debt value.

a. What is the added value of the debt?

b. What is the firm value of Matsushita?

The Miller Model and the Graduated Income Tax

16.17 Consider an economy with three investor groups with marginal personal tax rate of 10 percent, 20 percent, and 40 percent, respectively. The corporate tax rate is 35 percent. Assume zero personal tax rate on equity income. The required rate of return on all-equity financed project is 11 percent.

a. What is the prevailing equilibrium interest rate?

b. What is the investment pattern for each of the three investor groups?

c. If Quantex Corp. has an EBIT of $1 million in perpetuity, what is its firm value? Does the firm value vary with different capital structure choices?

16.18 Assume that there are three groups of investors with the following tax rates and investable funds:

Group	*Investable funds (in $ millions)*	*Tax rate (percent)*
A	375	50
B	220	32.5
C	105	10

Each group requires a minimum after-tax return of 8.1 percent on any security. The only types of securities available are common stock and perpetual corporate bonds. Income from corporate bonds is subject to a personal tax, but it is deductible for corporate tax purposes. Capital gains from common stock are untaxed at the personal level. In equilibrium, common stock yields an 8.1-percent pretax return; foreign real estate also earns this rate. All funds not invested in stocks or bonds will be invested in foreign real estate. Assume the common stock and the bonds are both risk-free.

Corporate earnings before interest and taxes total $85 million each year in perpetuity. The corporate tax rate is 35 percent.

a. What is the equilibrium market rate of interest on corporate bonds, r_B?
b. In equilibrium, what is the composition of each of the groups' portfolios?
c. What is the total market value of all companies?
d. What is the total tax bill?

16.19 Consider an economy in which there are four groups of people:

Group	*Marginal tax rate (percent)*	*Wealth (in $ millions)*
L	50	700
M	40	300
N	20	200
O	0	500

All investors can earn a tax-free return of 6 percent by investing in foreign real estate. Interest payments are taxable at the individual level, but equity income is untaxed at the personal level for all investors.

Corporations receive pretax cash flows of interest totalling $150 million. Interest payments are tax deductible at the corporate level. There are no depreciation deductions. Firms have no growth opportunities, and their plants are everlasting. The corporate tax rate is 40 percent.

a. What is the range of possible aggregate debt-equity ratios in the economy?
b. What would your answer to (*a*) be if the corporate tax rate is 30 percent?

APPENDIX 16A

SOME USEFUL FORMULAS OF FINANCIAL STRUCTURE

Definitions:

E(EBIT) = A perpetual expectation of cash operating income before interest and taxes

V_U = Value of an unlevered firm
V_L = Value of a levered firm
B = Present value of debt
S = Present value of equity
r_S = Cost of equity
r_B = Cost of debt capital
r_0 = Cost of capital to an all-equity firm. In a world of no corporate taxes, the weighted average cost of capital to a levered firm, r_{WACC}, is also equal to r_0. However, with corporate taxes, r_0 is above r_{WACC} for a levered firm.

Model I (No Tax)

$$V_L = V_U = \frac{\text{E(EBIT)}}{r_0}$$

$$r_S = r_0 + (r_0 - r_B) \times B/S$$

Model II (Corporate Tax, $T_C > 0$; No Personal Taxes, $T_S = T_B = 0$)

$$V_L = \frac{\text{E}[\text{EBIT} \times (1 - T_C)]}{r_0} + \frac{T_C r_B B}{r_B} = V_U + T_C B$$

$$r_S = r_0 + (1 - T_C) \times (r_0 - r_B) \times B/S$$

Model III (Corporate Tax, $T_C > 0$; Personal Tax, $T_B > 0$; $T_S > 0$)

$$V_L = V_U + \left[1 - \frac{(1 - T_C) \times (1 - T_S)}{(1 - T_B)}\right] \times B$$

APPENDIX 16B

THE MILLER MODEL AND THE GRADUATED INCOME TAX

In our previous discussion, we assumed a flat personal income tax on interest income. In other words, we assumed that all individuals are subject to the same personal tax rate on interest income. Merton Miller derived the results of the previous section in a classic paper.[32] However, the genius of his paper was to consider the implications of personal taxes when tax rates differ across individuals.

This *graduated* income tax is consistent with the real world. For example, individuals are currently taxed at rates of 0, 15, 28, 31, 36, and 39.6 percent in the United States, depending on income. In addition, other entities, such as corporate pension funds, individual retirement accounts (IRAs), and universities, are tax-exempt.

To illustrate Miller's model with graduated taxes, we consider a world where *all* firms initially only issue equity. We assume that $T_C = 35\%$ and $T_S = 0$.[33] The required return on stock, r_S, is 10 percent. In addition, we posit a graduated personal income tax, where tax rates vary between 0 and 50 percent. All individuals are risk-neutral.

Now consider a courageous firm contemplating a $1,000 issue of debt. What is the interest rate that the firm can pay and still be as well off as if it issued equity? Because debt is tax deductible, the after-corporate tax cost of debt is $(1 - T_C) \times r_B$. However, equity is not deductible at the corporate level, so the after-tax cost of equity is r_S. Thus, the firm is indifferent to whether it issues debt or equity when

$$(1 - T_C) \times r_B = r_S \tag{16.3}$$

Because $T_C = 35\%$ and $r_S = 10\%$, the firm could afford to pay a rate on debt as high as 15.38 percent.

Miller argues that those in the lowest tax brackets (tax-exempt in our example) will buy the debt because they pay the least personal tax on interest. These tax-exempt investors will be indifferent to whether they buy the stock or purchase bonds also yielding 10 percent. Thus, if this firm is the *only* one issuing debt, it can pay an interest rate well below its break-even rate of 15.38 percent.

[32] M. Miller, "Debt and Taxes," *Journal of Finance* (May 1977). Yes, this is the same Miller of MM.

[33] The assumption that $T_S = 0$ is perhaps an extreme one. However, it is commonly made in the literature, justified by the investor's ability to defer realization of capital gains indefinitely. Besides, the same qualitative conclusions hold if $T_S > 0$, though the explanation would be more involved.

Noticing the gain to the first firm, many other firms are likely to issue debt. However, if there are only a fixed number of tax-exempt investors, new debt issues must attract people in higher brackets. Because these individuals are taxed on interest at a higher rate than they are taxed on equity distributions, they will only buy debt if its yield is greater than 10 percent. For example, an individual in the 15-percent bracket has an interest rate after personal tax of $r_B \times (1 - 0.15)$. He will be indifferent to whether he buys bonds or stock if $r_B = 11.765\%$, because $0.11765 \times 0.85 = 10\%$. Because 11.765 percent is less than the 15.38 percent rate of equation (16.3), corporations gain by issuing debt to investors in the 15-percent bracket.

Now consider investors in the 35-percent bracket. A return on bonds of 15.38 percent provides them with a $10\% = 15.38\% \times (1 - 0.35)$ interest rate after personal tax. Thus, they are indifferent to whether they earn a 15.38-percent return on bonds or a 10-percent return on stock. Miller argues that, in equilibrium, corporations will issue enough debt so that investors with personal tax brackets up to and including 35 percent will hold debt.[34] Additional debt will not be issued because the interest rate needed to attract investors in higher tax brackets is above the 15.38-percent rate that corporations can afford to pay.

The beauty of competition is that other companies can so capitalize on someone's innovation that all value to the courageous first entrant is eliminated. According to the Miller model, firms will issue enough debt so that individuals up to and including the 35-percent bracket hold it. In order to induce these investors to hold bonds, the competitive interest rate becomes 15.38 percent. No firm profits from issuing debt in equilibrium. Rather, all firms are indifferent to whether they issue debt or equity in equilibrium.

Miller's work produces three results:

1. In aggregate, the corporate sector will issue just enough debt so that individuals with tax brackets equal to and below the corporate tax rate, T_C, will hold debt, and individuals with higher tax brackets will not hold debt. Thus, individuals in these higher brackets will hold stock.
2. Because people in tax brackets equal to the corporate rate hold debt, there is no gain or loss to corporate leverage. Therefore, the capital structure decision is a matter of indifference to an individual firm. Though the Miller model is quite sophisticated, this conclusion is identical to that reached by MM in a world without any taxes.
3. As given in (16.3), the return on bonds will be higher than the return on stocks of comparable risk. (An adjustment to (16.3) must be made to reflect the greater risk of stocks in the real world.)

• ***Example***

Consider an economy in which there are four groups of investors and no others:

Group	*Marginal Tax Rate (%) on Bonds* (T_B)	*Personal Wealth (in $ millions)*
Finance majors	50	1,200
Accounting majors	35	300
Marketing majors	20	150
Management majors	0	50

We assume that investors are risk-neutral and that equity income is untaxed at the personal level for all investors (i.e., $T_S = 0$). All investors can earn a tax-free return of 5.4 percent by investing in foreign real estate; therefore, this is the return on equity. The corporate tax rate is 35 percent. Interest payments are tax deductible at the corporate level and taxable at the individual level. Corporations receive a total of $120 million in cash flow before tax and interest. There are no growth opportunities, and every year is the same in perpetuity. What is the range of possible debt-equity ratios?

[34] All investors with $T_B < 35$ percent hold bonds. Because investors with $T_B = 35$ percent are indifferent to whether they hold stocks or bonds, only some of them are likely to choose bonds.

The return on equity, r_S, will be set equal to the return on foreign real estate, which is 0.054. In a Miller equilibrium, $r_S = (1 - T_C) \times r_B$. Therefore,

$$r_B = \frac{0.054}{1 - 0.35} = 0.0831$$

Given the tax brackets of the different groups of investors, we would expect that finance majors would hold equity and foreign real estate, and accounting majors would be indifferent to whether they held equity or debt. Marketing and management majors would hold bonds because their personal tax rates are below 0.35. Because accounting majors are indifferent to whether they hold bonds or stocks, we must learn what happens if they invest in bonds or equity. If accounting majors use their \$300 to buy bonds, $B = \$300 + \$150 + \$50 = \$500$. Then the following calculations can be made:

$$S = \frac{(\text{EBIT} - r_B B) \times (1 - T_C)}{r_S} = \frac{[\$120 - (0.0831 \times \$500)] \times (1 - 0.35)}{0.054}$$

$$= \$944$$

$$B = \frac{r_B B}{r_B} = \$500$$

$$V_L = S + B = \$944 + \$500 = \$1444$$

$$\frac{B}{S} = \frac{\$500}{\$944} = 0.530$$

If accounting majors buy stocks and foreign real estate ($B = \$150 + \$50 = \$200$),

$$S = \frac{(\text{EBIT} - r_B B) \times (1 - T_C)}{r_S} = \frac{[\$120 - (0.0831 \times \$200)] \times (1 - 0.35)}{0.054}$$

$$= \$1244$$

$$B = \$200$$

$$V_L = S + B = \$1244 + \$200 = \$1444$$

$$\frac{B}{S} = \frac{\$200}{\$1244} = 0.161$$

Thus, depending on the amount of bonds held by accounting majors, the debt-equity ratio in the economy can lie in the range of 0.161 to 0.530.•

CHAPTER 17 Valuation and Capital Budgeting for the Levered Firm

Instructors often structure the basic course in corporate finance around the two sides of the balance sheet. The left-hand side of the balance sheet contains assets. Chapters 4, 5, 6, 7, and 8 of this textbook treat the capital-budgeting decision, which is a decision concerning the assets of the firm. Chapters 9, 10, 11, and 12 treat the discount rate for a project, so those chapters also concern the left-hand side of the balance sheet. The right-hand side of the balance sheet contains liabilities and owner's equity. Chapters 13, 14, 15, and 16 of this textbook examine the debt-versus-equity decision, which is a decision about the right-hand side of the balance sheet.

While the preceding chapters of this textbook have, for the most part, treated the capital-budgeting decision separately from the capital-structure decision, the two decisions are actually related. As we will see, a project of an all-equity firm might be rejected, while the same project might be accepted for a levered but otherwise-identical firm. This occurs because the cost of capital frequently decreases with leverage, thereby turning some negative NPV projects into positive NPV projects.

Chapters 4 through 8 implicitly assumed that the firm is financed with only equity. The goal of this chapter is to value a project, or the firm itself, when leverage is employed. We point out that there are three standard approaches to valuation under leverage: the adjusted-present-value (APV) method, the flow-to-equity (FTE) method, and the weighted-average-cost-of-capital (WACC) method. These three approaches may seem, at first glance, to be quite different. However, we aim in this chapter to stress their similarities. For certain situations, the different approaches provide exactly the same answer. For other situations, the three approaches may provide somewhat different answers, and we discuss which method is preferred.

The three methods discussed below can be used to value either the firm as a whole or a project. The example below discusses project value, though everything we say applies to an entire firm as well.

17.1 Adjusted-Present-Value Approach

The **adjusted-present-value (APV)** method is best described by the following formula:

$$\text{APV} = \text{NPV} + \text{NPVF}$$

In words, the value of a project to a levered firm (APV) is equal to the value of the project to an unlevered firm (NPV) plus the net present value of the financing side effects (NPVF). One can generally think of four side effects:

1. *The Tax Subsidy to Debt.* This was discussed in Chapter 15, where we pointed out that, for perpetual debt, the value of the tax subsidy is $T_C B$. (T_C is the corporate tax rate, and B is the value of the debt.) The material on valuation under corporate taxes in Chapter 15 is actually an application of the APV approach.
2. *The Costs of Issuing New Securities.* As we will discuss in detail in Chapter 20, investment bankers participate in the public issuance of corporate debt. These bankers must be compensated for their time and effort, a cost that lowers the value of the project.
3. *The Costs of Financial Distress.* The possibility of financial distress, and bankruptcy in particular, arises with debt financing. As stated in the previous chapter, financial distress imposes costs, thereby lowering value.
4. *Subsidies to Debt Financing.* The interest on debt issued by state and local governments is not taxable to the investor. Because of this, the yield on tax-exempt debt is generally substantially below the yield on taxable debt. Frequently, corporations are able to obtain financing from a municipality at the tax-exempt rate because the municipality can borrow at that rate as well. As with any subsidy, this subsidy adds value.

While each of these four above side effects is important, the tax deduction to debt almost certainly has the highest dollar value in practice. For this reason, the following example considers the tax subsidy, but not the other three side effects.[1]

Consider a project of the P. B. Singer Co. with the following characteristics:

Sales: $500,000 per year for the indefinite future
Cash costs: 72% of sales
Initial investment: $475,000
$T_C = 34\%$
$r_0 = 20\%$, where r_0 is the cost of capital for a project of an all-equity firm.

If both the project and the firm are financed with only equity, the project's cash flow is

Sales	$500,000
Cash costs	−360,000
Operating income	140,000
Corporate tax (.34 tax rate)	−47,600
Unlevered cash flow (UCF)	$ 92,400

The distinction in Chapter 4 between present value and net present value is quite important for this example. As pointed out in Chapter 4, the *present value* of a project is determined before the initial investment at date 0 is subtracted. The initial investment is subtracted for the calculation of *net* present value.

Given a discount rate of 20 percent, the present value of the project is

$$\frac{\$92{,}400}{.20} = \$462{,}000$$

[1] The Bicksler Enterprises example of Section 17.6 handles both flotation costs and interest subsidies.

The net present value (NPV) of the project, that is, the value of the project to an all-equity firm, is

$$\$462{,}000 - \$475{,}000 = -\$13{,}000$$

Since the NPV is negative, the project would be rejected by an all-equity firm.

Now imagine that the firm finances the project with exactly \$126,229.50 in debt, so that the remaining investment of \$348,770.5 (\$475,000 − \$126,229.50) is financed with equity. The *net* present value of the project under leverage, which we call APV, is

$$\begin{aligned} \text{APV} &= \text{NPV} + T_C \times B \\ \$29{,}918 &= -13{,}000 + .34 \times \$126{,}229.50 \end{aligned}$$

That is, the value of the project when financed with some leverage is equal to the value of the project when financed with all equity plus the tax shield from the debt. Since this number is positive, the project should be accepted.

You may be wondering why we chose such a precise amount of debt. Actually, we chose it so that the ratio of debt to the present value of the project under leverage is 0.25.[2]

In this example, debt is a fixed proportion of the present value of the project, not a fixed proportion of the initial investment of \$475,000. This is consistent with the goal of a target debt-to-*market*-value ratio, which we find in the real world. For example, commercial banks typically lend to real estate developers a fixed percentage of the market value of a project, not a fixed percentage of the initial investment.

Concept Questions

- How is the APV method applied?
- What additional information beyond NPV does one need to calculate APV?

17.2 Flow-to-Equity Approach

The **flow-to-equity (FTE)** approach is an alternative capital-budgeting approach. The formula simply calls for discounting the cash flow from the project to the equityholders of the levered firm at the cost of equity capital, r_S. For a perpetuity, this becomes

$$\frac{\text{Cash flow from project to equityholders of the levered firm}}{r_S}$$

[2] That is, the present value of the project after the initial investment has been made is \$504,918 (\$29,918 + \$475,000). Thus, the debt-to-value ratio of the project is 0.25 (\$126,229.5/\$504,918). This level of debt can be calculated directly. Note that

$$\begin{aligned} \text{Present value of levered project} &= \text{Present value of unlevered project} + T_C \times B \\ V_{\text{With debt}} &= \$462{,}000 + 0.34 \times .25 \times V_{\text{With debt}} \end{aligned}$$

Rearranging the last line, we have

$$V_{\text{With debt}}(1 - 0.34 \times 0.25) = \$462{,}000$$

$$V_{\text{With debt}} = \$504{,}918$$

Since debt is 0.25 of value, debt is \$126,229.50 (0.25 × \$504,918).

There are three steps to the FTE approach.

Step 1: Calculating Levered Cash Flow (LCF)[3]

Assuming an interest rate of 10 percent, the perpetual cash flow to equityholders in our example is

Sales	$500,000.00
Cash costs	−360,000.00
Interest (10% × $126,229.50)	− 12,622.95
Income after interest	127,377.05
Corporate tax (.34 tax rate)	− 43,308.20
Levered cash flow (LCF)	$ 84,068.85

Alternatively, one can calculate levered cash flow (LCF) directly from unlevered cash flow (UCF). The key here is that the difference between the cash flow that equityholders receive in an unlevered firm and the cash flow that equityholders receive in a levered firm is the after-tax interest payment. (Repayment of principal does not appear in this example, since the debt is perpetual.) One writes this algebraically as

$$\text{UCF} - \text{LCF} = (1 - T_C)r_B B$$

The term on the right-hand side of this expression is the after-tax interest payment. Thus, since cash flow to the unlevered equityholders (UCF) is $92,400 and the after-tax interest payment is $8,331.15 [(.66).10 × $126,229.50], cash flow to the levered equityholders (LCF) is

$$\$92{,}400 - \$8{,}331.15 = \$84{,}068.85$$

which is exactly the number we calculated earlier.

Step 2: Calculating r_S

The next step is to calculate the discount rate, r_S. Note that we assumed that the discount rate on unlevered equity, r_0, is .20. As we saw in Chapter 15, the formula for r_S is

$$r_S = r_0 + \frac{B}{S}(1 - T_C)(r_0 - r_B)$$

Note that our target debt-to-value ratio of 1/4 implies a target debt-to-equity ratio of 1/3. Applying the above formula to this example, we have

$$r_S = .222 = .20 + \frac{1}{3}(.66)(.20 - .10)$$

Step 3: Valuation

The present value of the project's LCF is

$$\frac{\text{LCF}}{r_S} = \frac{\$84{,}068.85}{.222} = \$378{,}688.50$$

[3] We use the term *levered cash flow* (LCF) for simplicity. A more complete term would be *cash flow from the project to the equityholders of a levered firm.* Similarly, a more complete term for *unlevered cash flow* (UCF) would be *cash flow from the project to the equityholders of an unlevered firm.*

Since the initial investment is \$475,000 and \$126,229.50 is borrowed, the firm must advance the project \$348,770.50 (\$475,000 − \$126,229.50) out of its own cash reserves. The *net* present value of the project is simply the difference between the present value of the project's LCF and the investment not borrowed. Thus, the NPV is

$$\$378{,}688.50 - \$348.770.50 = \$29{,}918$$

which is identical to the result found with the APV approach.

Concept Questions

- How is the FTE method applied?
- What information is needed to calculate FTE?

17.3 Weighted-Average-Cost-of-Capital Method

Finally, one can value a project using the **weighted-average-cost-of-capital** (WACC) method. While this method was discussed in Chapters 12 and 15, it is worthwhile to review it here. The WACC approach begins with the insight that projects of levered firms are simultaneously financed with both debt and equity. The cost of capital is a weighted average of the cost of debt and the cost of equity. As seen in Chapters 12 and 15, the cost of equity is r_S. Ignoring taxes, the cost of debt is simply the borrowing rate, r_B. However, with corporate taxes, the appropriate cost of debt is $(1 - T_C)r_B$, the after-tax cost of debt.

The formula for determining the weighted average cost of capital, r_{WACC}, is

$$r_{\text{WACC}} = \frac{S}{S+B} r_S + \frac{B}{S+B} r_B(1 - T_C)$$

The weight for equity, $\frac{S}{S+B}$, and the weight for debt, $\frac{B}{S+B}$, are target ratios. Target ratios are generally expressed in terms of market values, not accounting values. (Another phrase for accounting value is *book value*.)

The formula calls for discounting the *unlevered* cash flow of the project (UCF) at the weighted average cost of capital, r_{WACC}. The net present value of the project can be written algebraically as

$$\sum_{t=1}^{\infty} \frac{\text{UCF}_t}{(1 + r_{\text{WACC}})^t} - \begin{matrix}\text{Initial}\\ \text{investment}\end{matrix}$$

If the project is a perpetuity, the net present value is

$$\frac{\text{UCF}}{r_{\text{WACC}}} - \begin{matrix}\text{Initial}\\ \text{investment}\end{matrix}$$

We previously stated that the target debt-to-value ratio of our project is 1/4 and the corporate tax rate is .34, implying that the weighted average cost of capital is

$$r_{\text{WACC}} = \frac{3}{4} \times .222 + \frac{1}{4} \times .10(.66) = .183$$

Note that r_{WACC}, .183, is lower than the cost of equity capital for an all-equity firm, .20. This must always be the case, since debt financing provides a tax subsidy that lowers the average cost of capital.

We previously determined the UCF of the project to be \$92,400, implying that the present value of the project is

$$\frac{\$92{,}400}{.183} = \$504{,}918$$

Since this initial investment is \$475,000, the NPV of the project is

$$\$504{,}918 - \$475{,}000 = \$29{,}918$$

In this example, all three approaches yield the same value.

Concept Question

- How is the WACC method applied?

17.4 A Comparison of the APV, FTE, and WACC Approaches

Capital-budgeting techniques in the early chapters of this text applied to all-equity firms. Capital budgeting for the levered firm could not be handled early in the book because the effects of debt on firm value were deferred until the previous two chapters. We learned there that debt increases firm value through tax benefits but decreases value through bankruptcy and related costs.

In the present chapter we provide three approaches to capital budgeting for the levered firm. The adjusted-present-value (APV) approach first values the project on an all-equity basis. That is, the project's after-tax cash flows under all-equity financing (UCF) are placed in the numerator of the capital-budgeting equation. The discount rate, assuming all-equity financing, appears in the denominator. At this point, the calculation is identical to that performed in the early chapters of this book. We then add the net present value of the debt. We point out that the net present value of the debt is likely to be the sum of four parameters: tax effects, flotation costs, bankruptcy costs, and interest subsidies.

The flow-to-equity (FTE) approach discounts the after-tax cash flow from a project going to the equityholders of a levered firm (LCF). LCF is the residual to equityholders after interest has been deducted. The discount rate is r_S, the cost of capital to the equityholders of a levered firm. For a firm with leverage, r_S must be greater than r_0, the cost of capital for an unlevered firm. This follows from our material in Chapter 15 showing that leverage raises the risk to the equityholders.

The last approach is the weighted-average-cost-of-capital (WACC) method. This technique calculates the project's after-tax cash flows assuming all-equity financing (UCF). The UCF is placed in the numerator of the capital-budgeting equation. The denominator, r_{WACC}, is a weighted average of the cost of equity capital and the cost of debt capital. The tax advantage of debt is reflected in the denominator because the cost of debt capital is determined net of corporate tax. The numerator does not reflect debt at all.

All three approaches attempt the same task: valuation in the presence of debt financing. However, as we saw above, the approaches are markedly different in technique. Because of this, it is worthwhile to stress two points.

1. *APV versus WACC.* As stated above, both the APV and the WACC approaches use unlevered cash flow (UCF). The APV discounts these flows

at r_0, yielding the value of the unlevered project. Adding the present value of the tax shield gives the value of the project under leverage. The WACC approach discounts UCF at r_{WACC}, which is lower than r_0. Thus, the APV and WACC approaches are different ways to determine the same value. While the APV approach adds a tax shield, the WACC approach lowers the denominator below r_0. Both approaches yield a value above that of the unlevered project.

2. *Entity Being Valued.* For both the APV and the WACC approaches, the initial investment is subtracted out in the final step ($475,000 in our example). However, for the FTE approach, only the firm's contribution to the initial investment ($348,770.50 = $475,000 − $126,229.50) is subtracted out. This occurs because, under the FTE approach, only the future cash flows to the levered equityholders (LCF) are included. Thus, since these future cash flows are reduced by interest payments, the initial investment is correspondingly reduced by debt financing.

A Suggested Guideline

The net present value of our project is exactly the same under each of the three methods. In theory, this should always be the case.[4] However, one method usually provides an easier computation than another, and, in many cases, one or more of the methods is virtually impossible computationally.

We first consider when it is best to use the WACC and FTE approaches. If the risk of a project stays constant throughout its life, it is plausible to assume that r_0 remains constant throughout the project's life. This assumption of constant risk appears to be reasonable for most real-world projects. In addition, if the debt-to-value ratio remains constant over the life of the project, both r_S and r_{WACC} will remain constant as well. Under this latter assumption, either the FTE or the WACC approach is easy to apply. However, if the debt-to-value ratio varies from year to year, both r_S and r_{WACC} vary from year to year as well. Using the FTE or the WACC approach when the denominator changes every year is computationally quite complex, and when computations become complex, the error rate rises. Thus, both the FTE and WACC approaches present difficulties when the debt-to-value *ratio* changes over time.

The APV approach is based on the *level* of debt in each future period. Consequently, when the debt level can be specified precisely for future periods, the APV approach is quite easy to use. However, when the debt level is uncertain, the APV approach becomes more problematic. For example, when the debt-to-value ratio is a constant, the debt level varies with the value of the project. Since the value of the project in a future year cannot be easily forecast, the level of debt cannot be easily forecast either.

Thus, we suggest the following guideline:

> Use WACC or FTE if the firm's target debt-to-value *ratio* applies to the project over its life.
> Use APV if the project's *level* of debt is known over the life of the project.

[4] See I. Inselbag and H. Kaufold, "A Comparison of Alternative Discounted Cash Flow Approaches to Firm Valuation," The Wharton School, University of Pennsylvania (June 1990), unpublished paper.

The Three Methods of Capital Budgeting with Leverage

1. Adjusted-Present-Value (APV) Method

$$\sum_{t=1}^{\infty} \frac{UCF_t}{(1 + r_0)^t} + \text{Additional effects of debt} - \text{Initial investment}$$

UCF_t = The project's cash flow at date t to the equityholders of an unlevered firm

r_0 = Cost of capital for project in an unlevered firm.

2. Flow-to-Equity (FTE) Method

$$\sum_{t=1}^{\infty} \frac{LCF_t}{(1 + r_S)^t} - \left(\text{Initial investment} - \text{Amount borrowed}\right)$$

LCF_t = The project's cash flow at date t to the equityholders of a levered firm

r_S = Cost of equity capital with leverage

3. Weighted-Average-Cost-of-Capital (WACC) Method

$$\sum_{t=1}^{\infty} \frac{UCF_t}{(1 + r_{WACC})^t} - \text{Initial investment}$$

r_{WACC} = Weighted average cost of capital

Notes:

1. The middle term in the APV formula implies that the value of a project with leverage is greater than the value of the project without leverage. Since $r_{WACC} < r_0$, the WACC formula implies that the value of a project with leverage is greater than the value of the project without leverage.
2. In the FTE method, cash flow *after interest* (LCF) is used. Initial investment is reduced by *amount borrowed* as well.

Guidelines:

1. Use WACC or FTE if the firm's target debt-to-value *ratio* applies to the project over its life.
2. Use APV if the project's *level* of debt is known over the life of the project.

There are a number of situations where the APV approach is preferred. For example, in a leveraged buyout (LBO) the firm begins with a large amount of debt but rapidly pays down the debt over a number of years. Since the schedule of debt reduction in the future is known when the LBO is arranged, tax shields in every future year can be easily forecast. Thus, the APV approach is easy to use here. (An illustration of the APV approach applied to LBOs is provided in the appendix to this chapter.) By contrast, the WACC and FTE approaches are virtually impossible to apply here, since the debt-to-equity ratio cannot be expected to be constant over time. In addition, situations involving interest subsidies and flotation costs are much easier to handle with the APV approach. (The Bicksler Enterprises example in Section 17.6 applies the APV approach to subsidies and flotation costs.) Finally, the APV approach handles the lease-versus-buy decision much more easily than does either the FTE or the WACC approach. (A full treatment of the lease-versus-buy decision appears in Chapter 23.)

The above examples are special situations. In order to see which approach is more appropriate for a typical capital-budgeting situation, we must answer the following question: When managers pursue debt policy, do they think of keeping the *level* of debt fairly constant through time, or do they think of keeping the debt-equity *ratio* fairly constant through time? This is ultimately an empirical question—and one that has not been rigorously investigated. However, we believe that managers *should* think in terms of an optimal debt-equity ratio. If a project does much better than expected, both its value and its debt capacity will likely rise. A shrewd financial manager will take advantage by increasing debt. Conversely, the firm should reduce debt if the value of a project were to decline unexpectedly. Because financing is a time-consuming task, the level of debt cannot be adjusted on a day-to-day or month-to-month basis. However, the adjustment should occur over the long run.

Because of this, we recommend that the WACC and the FTE approaches, rather than the APV approach, be used in most real-world situations. In addition, frequent discussions with business executives have convinced us that the WACC is the most widely used method in the real world, by far. Thus, practitioners seem to agree with us that, outside of the special situations mentioned above, the APV approach is a less important method of capital budgeting.

Concept Questions

- What is the main difference between APV and WACC?
- What is the main difference between the FTE approach and the other two approaches?
- When should the APV method be used?
- When should the FTE and WACC approaches be used?

17.5 Capital Budgeting for Projects that Are Not Scale-Enhancing

In Chapter 12, we covered scale-enhancing and non–scale-enhancing projects. A scale-enhancing project is one where the project is similar to the existing firm. For example, a project at General Motors to produce automobiles would be considered scale-enhancing. The analyses in Sections 17.1–17.3 can be used to value scale-enhancing projects. A somewhat different analysis is needed when a project is not scale-enhancing. This is best illustrated by an example.

- ***Example***

World-Wide Enterprises (WWE) is a large conglomerate thinking of entering the widget business, where it plans to finance projects with a debt-to-value ratio of 25 percent (or, alternatively, a debt-to-equity ratio of 1/3). There is currently one firm in the widget industry, American Widgets (AW). This firm is financed with 40-percent debt and 60-percent equity. The beta of AW's equity is 1.5. AW has a borrowing rate of 12 percent, and WWE expects to borrow for its widget venture at 10 percent. The corporate tax rate for both firms is .40, the market-risk premium is 8.5 percent, and the riskless interest rate is 8 percent. What is the appropriate discount rate for WWE to use for its widget venture?

As mentioned in Sections 17.1–17.3, a corporation may use one of three capital-budgeting approaches: APV, FTE, or WACC. The appropriate discount rates for these three approaches are r_0, r_S, and r_{WACC}, respectively. Since AW is WWE's only competitor in widgets, we look at AW's cost of capital to calculate r_0, r_S, and r_{WACC} for

WWE's widget venture. The four-step procedure below will allow us to calculate all three discount rates.

1. *Determining AW's Cost of Equity Capital.* First, we determine AW's cost of equity capital, using the security market line (SML) of Chapter 10:

AW's Cost of Equity Capital:

$$r_S = R_F + \beta \times (\overline{R}_M - R_F)$$
$$20.75\% = 8\% + 1.5 \times 8.5\%$$

Where $\overline{R}_M$ is the expected return on the market portfolio and R_F is the risk-free rate.

2. *Determining AW's Hypothetical All-Equity Cost of Capital.* However, we must standardize the above number in some way, since AW and WWE's widget ventures have different target debt-to-value ratios. The easiest approach is to calculate the hypothetical cost of equity capital for AW, assuming all-equity financing. This can be determined from MM's Proposition II under taxes (see Chapter 15):

AW's Cost of Capital If All-Equity:

$$r_S = r_0 + \frac{B}{S}(1 - T_C)(r_0 - r_B)$$

$$20.75\% = r_0 + \frac{.4}{.6}(.60)(r_0 - 12\%)$$

In the examples of Chapter 15, the unknown in this equation was r_S.[5] However, for this example, the unknown is r_0. By solving the equation, one finds that r_0 = .1825. Of course, r_0 is less than r_S because the cost of equity capital would be less when the firm employs no leverage.

At this point, firms in the real world generally make the assumption that the business risk of their venture is about equal to the business risk of the firms already in the business. Applying this assumption to our problem, we assert that the hypothetical discount rate of WWE's widget venture if all-equity financed is also .1825.[6] This discount rate would be employed if WWE uses the APV approach, since the APV approach calls for r_0, the project's cost of capital in a firm with no leverage.

3. *Determining* r_S *for WWE's Widget Venture.* Alternatively, WWE might use the FTE approach, where the discount rate for levered equity is determined from

Cost of Equity Capital for WWE's Widget Venture:

$$r_S = r_0 + \frac{B}{S}(1 - T_C)(r_0 - r_B)$$

$$19.9\% = 18.25\% + \frac{1}{3}(.60)(18.25\% - 10\%)$$

Note that the cost of equity capital for WWE's widget venture, .199, is less than the cost of equity capital for AW, .2075. This occurs because AW has a higher debt-to-equity ratio. (As mentioned above, both firms are assumed to have the same business risk.)

---

[5] In this example we are implicitly assuming that the debt betas for AW and WWE are not zero. This point is discussed in more detail in section 17.7.

[6] Alternatively, a firm might assume that its venture would be somewhat riskier since it is a new entrant. Thus, the firm might select a discount rate slightly higher than .1825. Of course, no exact formula exists for adjusting the discount rate upwards.

4. *Determining* r_{WACC} *for WWE's Widget Venture.* Finally, WWE might use the WACC approach. The appropriate calculation here is

r_{WACC} for WWE's Widget Venture:

$$r_{WACC} = \frac{B}{S+B} r_B(1 - T_C) + \frac{S}{S+B} r_S$$

$$16.425\% = \frac{1}{4}10\%(.60) + \frac{3}{4}19.9\% \bullet$$

17.6 APV Example

As mentioned above, the APV approach is effective in situations where flotation costs and subsidized financing arise. The FTE and the WACC approaches are less effective in these situations. The following is an example where the APV approach works well.

• **Example**
Bicksler Enterprises is considering a $10 million project that will last five years, implying straight-line depreciation per year of $2 million. The cash revenues less cash expenses per year are $3,500,000. The corporate tax bracket is 34 percent. The risk-free rate is 10 percent, and the cost of unlevered equity is 20 percent.

The cash flow projections each year are

	C_0	C_1	C_2	C_3	C_4	C_5
Initial outlay	−$10,000,000					
Depreciation tax shield		0.34 × $2,000,000 = $680,000	$680,000	$680,000	$680,000	$680,000
Revenue less expenses		(1 − 0.34) × $3,500,000 = $2,310,000	$2,310,000	$2,310,000	$2,310,000	$2,310,000

We stated above that the APV of a project is the sum of its all-equity value plus the additional effects of debt. We examine each in turn.

All-Equity Value

Assuming the project is financed with all equity, the value of the project is

$$\underbrace{-\$10{,}000{,}000}_{\text{Initial cost}} + \underbrace{\frac{\$680{,}000}{0.10} \times \left[1 - \left(\frac{1}{1.10}\right)^5\right]}_{\text{Depreciation tax shield}} +$$

$$\underbrace{\frac{\$2{,}310{,}000}{0.20} \times \left[1 - \left(\frac{1}{1.20}\right)^5\right]}_{\text{Present value of (Cash revenues − Cash expenses)}} = -\$513{,}951$$

This calculation uses the techniques of the early chapters of this book. Notice that the depreciation tax shield is discounted at the riskless rate of 10 percent. The revenues and expenses are discounted at the higher rate of 20 percent.

An all-equity firm would clearly *reject* this project, because the NPV is −$513,951. And equity-flotation costs (not mentioned in the example) would only make the NPV more negative. However, debt financing may add enough value to the project to justify acceptance. We consider the effects of debt below.

Additional Effects of Debt

Bicksler Enterprises can obtain a five-year, nonamortizing loan for \$7,500,000 after flotation costs at the risk-free rate of 10 percent. Flotation costs are fees paid when stock or debt is issued. These fees may go to printers, lawyers, and investment bankers, among others. Bicksler Enterprises is informed that flotation costs will be 1 percent of the gross proceeds of its loan. The previous chapter indicates that debt financing alters the NPV of a typical project. We look at the effects of debt below.

Flotation Costs

We represent the gross proceeds to be raised as *Gross proceeds.* Given that flotation costs are 1 percent of the gross proceeds, we have

$$\$7{,}500{,}000 = (1 - 0.01) \times \text{Gross proceeds} = 0.99 \times \text{Gross proceeds}$$

Thus, the gross proceeds are

$$\frac{\$7{,}500{,}000}{1 - 0.01} = \frac{\$7{,}500{,}000}{0.99} = \$7{,}575{,}758$$

This implies flotation costs of \$75,758 (1% × \$7,575,758). To check the calculation, note that net proceeds are \$7,500,000 (\$7,575,758 − \$75,758).

Flotation costs are paid immediately[7] but are deducted from taxes by amortizing on a straight-line basis over the life of the loan. The cash flows from flotation costs are

	Date 0	*Date 1*	*Date 2*	*Date 3*	*Date 4*	*Date 5*
Flotation costs	**−\$75,758**					
Deduction		$\$15{,}152 = \frac{\$75{,}758}{5}$	\$15,152	\$15,152	\$15,152	\$15,152
Tax shield from flotation costs		0.34 × \$15,152 = **\$5,152**	**\$5,152**	**\$5,152**	**\$5,152**	**\$5,152**

The relevant cash flows from flotation costs are in boldface. When discounting at 10 percent, the tax shield has a net present value of

$$\$5{,}152 \times A^{5}_{0.10} = \$19{,}530$$

This implies a net cost of flotation of

$$-\$75{,}758 + \$19{,}530 = -\$56{,}228$$

The net present value of the project after the flotation costs of debt but before the benefits of debt is

$$-\$513{,}951 - \$56{,}228 = -\$570{,}179$$

[7] In other words, Bicksler Enterprises receives only \$7,500,000. The flotation costs of \$75,758 are received by intermediaries, e.g., investment bankers.

Tax Subsidy

Interest must be paid on the gross proceeds of the loan, even though intermediaries receive the flotation costs. Since the gross proceeds of the loan are $7,575,578, annual interest is $757,576 ($7,575,758 × 0.10). The interest cost after taxes is $500,000 [$757,576 × (1 − 0.34)]. Because the loan is nonamortizing, the entire debt of $7,575,758 is repaid at date 5. These terms are indicated below:

	Date 0	*Date 1*	*Date 2*	*Date 3*	*Date 4*	*Date 5*
Loan (gross proceeds)	**$7,575,758**					
Interest paid		10% × $7,575,758 = $757,576	$757,576	$757,576	$757,576	$757,576
Interest cost after taxes		(1 − 0.34) × $757,576 = **$500,000**	**$500,000**	**$500,000**	**$500,000**	**$500,000**
Repayment of debt						**$7,575,758**

The relevant cash flows are listed in boldface in the above table. They are (1) loan received, (2) annual interest cost after taxes, and (3) repayment of debt. Note that we include the *gross* proceeds of the loan as an inflow, since the flotation costs have previously been subtracted.

In Chapter 15 we mentioned that the financing decision can be evaluated in terms of net present value. The net present value of the loan is simply the net present value of each of the three cash flows. This can be represented as

$$\text{NPV(Loan)} = +\ \begin{matrix}\text{Amount}\\\text{borrowed}\end{matrix} - \begin{matrix}\text{Present value}\\\text{of after-tax}\\\text{interest payments}\end{matrix} - \begin{matrix}\text{Present value}\\\text{of loan}\\\text{repayments}\end{matrix} \qquad (17.1)$$

The calculations for this example are

$$\$976{,}415 = +\$7{,}575{,}758 - \frac{\$500{,}000}{0.10} \times \left[1 - \left(\frac{1}{1.10}\right)^5\right] - \frac{\$7{,}575{,}758}{(1.10)^5} \qquad (17.1')$$

The NPV(Loan) is positive, reflecting the interest tax shield.[8]

The adjusted present value of the project with this financing is

$$\begin{aligned} \text{APV} &= \text{All-equity value} - \text{Flotation costs of debt} + \text{NPV(Loan)} \qquad &(17.2)\\ \$406{,}236 &= -\$513{,}951 - \$56{,}228 + \$976{,}415 \qquad &(17.2')\end{aligned}$$

Though we previously saw that an all-equity firm would reject the project, a firm would *accept* the project if a $7,500,000 (net) loan could be obtained.

Because the loan discussed above was at the market rate of 10 percent, we have considered only two of the three additional effects of debt (flotation costs and tax subsidy) so far. We now examine another loan where the third effect arises.

Non–Market-Rate Financing

A number of companies are fortunate enough to obtain subsidized financing from a governmental authority. Suppose that the project of Bicksler Enterprises is deemed

[8] The NPV(Loan) must be zero in a no-tax world, because interest provides no tax shield there. To check this intuition, we calculate

$$\text{No-tax case: } 0 = +\$7{,}575{,}758 - \frac{\$757{,}576}{0.10} \times \left[1 - \left(\frac{1}{1.10}\right)^5\right] - \frac{\$7{,}575{,}758}{(1.10)^5}$$

socially beneficial and the state of New Jersey grants the firm a $7,500,000 loan at 8-percent interest. In addition, all flotation costs are absorbed by the state. Clearly, the company will choose this loan over the one we previously calculated. The cash flows from the loan are

	Date 0	*Date 1*	*Date 2*	*Date 3*	*Date 4*	*Date 5*
Loan received	$7,500,000					
Interest paid		8% × $7,500,000 = $600,000	$600,000	$600,000	$600,000	$600,000
After-tax interest		(1 − 0.34) × $600,000 = $396,000	$396,000	$396,000	$396,000	$396,000
Repayment of debt						$7,500,000

Using (17.1), the NPV(Loan) is

$$\$1,341,939 = +\$7,500,000 - \frac{\$396,000}{0.10} \times \left[1 - \left(\frac{1}{1.10}\right)^5\right] - \frac{\$7,500,000}{(1.10)^5} \qquad (17.1'')$$

Why do we discount the cash flows in (17.1″) at 10 percent when the firm is borrowing at 8 percent? We discount at 10 percent because that is the fair or marketwide rate. That is, 10 percent is the rate at which one could borrow *without* benefit of subsidization. The net present value of the subsidized loan is larger than the net present value of the earlier loan because the firm is now borrowing at the below-market rate of 8 percent. Note that the NPV(Loan) calculation in equation (17.1″) captures both the tax effect *and* the non–market-rate effect.

The net present value of the project with subsidized debt financing is

$$\text{APV} = \begin{matrix}\text{All-equity}\\ \text{value}\end{matrix} - \begin{matrix}\text{Flotation}\\ \text{costs}\\ \text{of debt}\end{matrix} + \text{NPV(Loan)} \qquad (17.2)$$

$$+\$827,988 = -\$513,951 - 0 + \$1,341,939 \qquad (17.2'')$$

The above example illustrates the adjusted-present-value (APV) approach. The approach begins with the present value of a project for the all-equity firm. Next, the effects of debt are added in. The approach has much to recommend it. It is intuitively appealing because individual components are calculated separately and added together in a simple way. And, if the debt from the project can be specified precisely, the present value of the debt can be calculated precisely. •

17.7 Beta and Leverage

Chapter 12 provides the formula for the relationship between the beta of the common stock and the leverage of the firm in a world without taxes. We reproduce this formula here:

The No-Tax Case:

$$\beta_{\text{Equity}} = \beta_{\text{Asset}}\left(1 + \frac{\text{Debt}}{\text{Equity}}\right) \qquad (17.3)$$

As pointed out in Chapter 12, this relationship holds under the assumption that the beta of debt is zero.

Since firms must pay corporate taxes in practice, it is worthwhile to provide the relationship in a world with corporate taxes. It can be shown that the relationship between the beta of the unlevered firm and the beta of the levered equity is[9]

The Corporate-Tax Case:

$$\beta_{\text{Equity}} = \left(1 + \frac{(1 - T_C)\,\text{Debt}}{\text{Equity}}\right)\beta_{\text{Unlevered firm}} \tag{17.4}$$

when (1) the corporation is taxed at the rate of T_C and (2) the debt has a zero beta.

Because $[1 + (1 - T_C)\text{Debt/Equity}]$ must be more than 1 for a levered firm, it follows that $\beta_{\text{Unlevered firm}} < \beta_{\text{Equity}}$. The corporate-tax case of (17.4) is quite similar to the no-tax case of (17.3), because the beta of levered equity must be greater than the beta of the unlevered firm in either case. The intuition that leverage increases the risk of equity applies in both cases.

However, notice that the two equations are not equal. It can be shown that leverage increases the equity beta less rapidly under corporate taxes. This occurs because, under taxes, leverage creates a *riskless* tax shield, thereby lowering the risk of the entire firm.

• ***Example***

C. F. Lee Incorporated is considering a scale-enhancing project. The market value of the firm's debt is \$100 million, and the market value of the firm's equity is \$200 million. The debt is considered riskless. The corporate tax rate is 34 percent. Regression analysis indicates that the beta of the firm's equity is 2. The risk-free rate is 10 per-

---

[9] This result holds only if the beta of debt equals zero. To see this, note that

$$V_U + T_C B = V_L = B + S \tag{a}$$

where

V_U = Value of unlevered firm
V_L = Value of levered firm
B = Value of debt in a levered firm
S = Value of equity in a levered firm

As we stated in the text, the beta of the levered firm is a weighted average of the debt beta and the equity beta:

$$\frac{B}{B+S} \times \beta_B + \frac{S}{B+S} \times \beta_S$$

where β_B and β_S are the betas of the debt and the equity of the levered firm, respectively. Because $V_L = B + S$, we have

$$\frac{B}{V_L} \times \beta_B + \frac{S}{V_L} \times \beta_S \tag{b}$$

The beta of the levered firm can *also* be expressed as a weighted average of the beta of the unlevered firm and the beta of the tax shield:

$$\frac{V_U}{V_U + T_C B} \times \beta_U + \frac{T_C B}{V_U + T_C B} \times \beta_B$$

where β_U is the beta of the unlevered firm. This follows from equation (a). Because $V_L = V_U + T_C B$, we have

$$\frac{V_U}{V_L} \times \beta_U + \frac{T_C B}{V_L} \times \beta_B \tag{c}$$

We can equate (b) and (c) because both represent the beta of a levered firm. Equation (a) tells us that $V_U = S + (1 - T_C) \times B$. Under the assumption that $\beta_B = 0$, equating (b) and (c) and using equation (a) yields equation (17.4).

The generalized formula for the levered beta (where β_B is not zero) is:

$$\beta_S = \beta_U + (1 - T_C)(\beta_U - \beta_B)\frac{B}{S}$$

and

$$\beta_U = \frac{S}{B(1 - T_C) + S}\beta_S + \frac{B(1 - T_C)}{B(1 - T_C) + S}\beta_B$$

cent, and the expected market premium is 8.5 percent. What would the project's discount rate be in the hypothetical case that C. F. Lee, Inc., is all-equity? •

We can answer this question in two steps.

1. *Determining Beta of Hypothetical All-Equity Firm.* Rearranging equation (17.4), we have

Unlevered Beta:

$$\frac{\text{Equity}}{\text{Equity} + (1 - T_C) \times \text{Debt}} \times \beta_{\text{Equity}} = \beta_{\text{Unlevered firm}} \qquad (17.5)$$

$$\frac{\$200 \text{ million}}{\$200 \text{ million} + (1 - 0.34) \times \$100 \text{ million}} \times 2 = 1.50$$

2. *Determining Discount Rate.* We calculate the discount rate from the security market line (SML) as

Discount Rate:

$$r_S = R_F + \beta \times [\bar{R}_M - R_F]$$

$$22.75\% = 10\% + 1.50 \times 8.5\%$$

The Project Is Not Scale-Enhancing

Because the above example assumed that the project is scale-enhancing, we began with the beta of the firm's equity. If the project is not scale-enhancing, one could begin with the equity betas of firms in the industry of the project. For each firm, the hypothetical beta of the unlevered equity could be calculated by equation (17.5). The SML could then be used to determine the project's discount rate from the average of these betas.

17.8 Summary and Conclusions

Earlier chapters of this text showed how to calculate net present value for projects of all-equity firms. We pointed out in the last two chapters that the introduction of taxes and bankruptcy costs changes a firm's financing decisions. Rational corporations should employ some debt in a world of this type. Because of the benefits and costs associated with debt, the capital-budgeting decision is different for levered firms than for unlevered firms. The present chapter has discussed three methods for capital budgeting by levered firms: the adjusted-present-value (APV), flows-to-equity (FTE), and weighted-average-cost-of-capital (WACC) approaches.

1. The APV formula can be written as

$$\sum_{t=1}^{\infty} \frac{\text{UCF}_t}{(1 + r_0)^t} + \begin{matrix}\text{Additional} \\ \text{efects} \\ \text{of debt}\end{matrix} - \begin{matrix}\text{Initial} \\ \text{investment}\end{matrix}$$

There are four additional effects of debt:

- Tax shield from debt financing
- Flotation costs
- Bankruptcy costs
- Benefit of non-market-rate financing.

2. The FTE formula can be written as

$$\sum_{t=1}^{\infty} \frac{\text{LCF}_t}{(1 + r_S)^t} - \left(\begin{array}{c}\text{Initial}\\ \text{investment}\end{array} - \begin{array}{c}\text{Amount}\\ \text{borrowed}\end{array}\right)$$

3. The WACC formula can be written as

$$\sum_{t=1}^{\infty} \frac{\text{UCF}_t}{(1 + r_{\text{WACC}})^t} - \begin{array}{c}\text{Initial}\\ \text{investment}\end{array}$$

4. Corporations frequently follow the guideline:

   Use WACC or FTE if the firm's target debt-to-value *ratio* applies to the project over its life.

   Use APV if the project's *level* of debt is known over the life of the project.

5. The APV method is used frequently for special situations like interest subsidies, LBOs, and leases. The WACC and FTE methods are commonly used for more typical capital-budgeting situations. The APV approach is a rather unimportant method for typical capital-budgeting situations.
6. The beta of the equity of the firm is positively related to the leverage of the firm.

Key Terms

Adjusted present value (APV) 455
Flow to equity (FTE) 457
Weighted Average Cost of Capital 459

Suggested Readings

The following article contains a superb discussion of some of the subtleties of using WACC for project valuation:

Miles, J., and R. Ezzel. "The Weighted Average Cost of Capital, Perfect Capital Markets and Project Life: A Clarification." *Journal of Financial and Quantitative Analysis* 15 (September 1980).

This is an excellent article on how to use the SML in project valuation:

Weston, J. F. "Investment Decisions Using the Capital Asset Pricing Model," *Financial Management* (Spring 1973).

The following important article develops the adjusted-present-value approach:

Myers, S. "Interactions of Corporate Financing and Investment Decisions: Implications for Capital Budgeting." *Journal of Finance* (March 1974).

A fascinating article valuing levered buyouts in an APV framework is:

Inselbag, I., and H. Kaufold. "How to Value Recapitalizations and Leveraged Buyouts." *Journal of Applied Corporate Finance* (Summer 1989).

Questions and Problems

Adjusted Present-Value Approach

17.1 Honda and GM are competing to sell a fleet of cars to Hertz. Hertz's policies on its rental cars include use of straight-line depreciation and disposing of the cars after five years. Hertz expects that the autos will have no salvage value. Hertz expects a fleet of 25 cars to generate \$100,000 per year in pretax income. Hertz is in the 34-

percent tax bracket, and the firm's overall required return is 10 percent. The addition of the new fleet will not add to the risk of the firm. Treasury bills are priced to yield 6 percent.

a. What is the maximum price that Hertz should be willing to pay for the fleet of cars?

b. Suppose the price of the fleet (in U.S. dollars) is $325,000; both suppliers are charging this price. Hertz is able to issue $200,000 in debt to finance the project. The bonds can be issued at par and will carry an 8-percent interest rate. Hertz will incur no costs to issue the debt and no costs of financial distress. What is the APV of this project if Hertz uses debt to finance the auto purchase?

c. To entice Hertz to buy the cars from Honda, the Japanese government is willing to lend Hertz $200,000 at 5 percent. Now what is the maximum price that Hertz is willing to pay Honda for the fleet of cars?

17.2 Peatco, Inc., is considering a $2.1 million project that will be depreciated according to the straight-line method over the three-year life of the project. The project will generate pretax earnings of $900,000 per year, and it will not change the risk level of the firm. Peatco can obtain a three-year, 12.5-percent loan to finance the project; the bank will charge Peatco flotation fees of 1 percent of the gross proceeds of the loan. The fee must be paid up-front, not from the loan proceeds. If Peatco financed the project with all equity, its cost of capital would be 18 percent. The tax rate is 30 percent, and the risk-free rate is 6 percent.

a. Using the APV method, determine whether or not Peatco should undertake the project.

b. After hearing that Peatco would not be initiating the project in their town, the city council voted to subsidize Peatco's loan. Under the city's proposal, Peatco will pay the same flotation costs, but the rate on the loan will be 10 percent. Should Peatco accept the city's offer and begin the project?

17.3 MEO Foods, Inc., has made cat food for over 20 years. The company currently has a debt-equity ratio of 25 percent, borrows at a 10-percent interest rate, and is in the 40-percent tax bracket. Its shareholders require an 18-percent return.

MEO is planning to expand cat food production capacity. The equipment to be purchased would last three years and generate the following unlevered cash flows (UCF):

Unlevered Cash Flows by Year (in $ millions)

0	*1*	*2*	*3*	*4+*
−15	5	8	10	0

MEO has also arranged a $6 million debt issue to partially finance the expansion. Under the loan, the company would pay 10 percent annually on the outstanding balance. The firm would also make year-end principal payments of $2 million per year, completely retiring the issue at the end of the third year.

Ignoring costs of financial distress and issue costs, should MEO proceed with the expansion plan?

17.4 Roller and Decker Corp. have established a joint venture with Malaysia Road Construction Company to build a toll road in Malaysia. The initial investment in paving equipment is $20 million. Straight-line depreciation will be used, and the equipment has an economic life of five years with no salvage value. The annual construction costs are estimated to be $10 million. The project will be finished in two years. Net toll revenue collected from the usage of the road is projected to be $6 million per annum for 20 years starting from the end of the first year of usage. The local preferential corporate tax rate for joint ventures is 25 percent. There are no other taxes. The required rate of return for the project under all-equity financing is 12 percent. The prevailing market interest rate is 9 percent a year. To encourage foreign capital participation in infrastructure sector, the Malaysian government will subsidize the project with $10 million of 15-year, long-term loan, at an interest rate of 5 percent a year. What is the NPV of this project?

Flow-to-Equity Approach

17.5 Milano Pizza Club owns a chain of three identical restaurants popular for their Milan style pizza. Comparable stores have an equity value of $900,000 and debt-to-equity ratio of 30 percent. The prevailing market interest rate is 9.5 percent. An equivalent all-equity-financed store would have a discount rate of 15 percent. For each Milano store, the estimated annual sales is $1,000,000, costs of goods sold is $400,000, general and administrative costs is $300,000. (Every cash flow stream is assumed to be a perpetuity.) The marginal tax rate is 40 percent. What is the value of the Milano Pizza Club?

Weighted-Average-Cost-of-Capital Approach

17.6 The overall firm beta for Wild Widgets, Inc. (WWI) is 0.9. WWI has a target debt-equity ratio of 1/2. The expected return on the market is 16 percent, and Treasury bills are currently selling to yield 8 percent. WWI one-year bonds that carry a 7-percent coupon are selling for $972.72. The corporate tax rate is 34 percent.

a. What is WWI's cost of equity?
b. What is WWI's cost of debt?
c. What is WWI's weighted average cost of capital?

17.7 Value Company has compiled the following information on its financing costs:

Type of Financing	*Book Value*	*Market Value*	*Before-Tax Cost*
Long-term debt	$5,000,000	$2,000,000	10%
Short-term debt	5,000,000	5,000,000	8%
Common stock	10,000,000	13,000,000	15%
Total	$20,000,000	$20,000,000	

Value is in the 34-percent tax bracket and has a target debt-equity ratio of 100 percent. Value's managers would like to keep the market values of short-term and long-term debt equal.

a. Calculate the weighted average cost of capital for Value Company using
  i. Book-value weights
  ii. Market-value weights
  iii. Target weights.
b. Explain the differences between the WACCs. What are the correct weights to use in the WACC calculation?

17.8 Baber Corporation's stock returns have a covariance with the market of 0.031. The standard deviation of the market returns is 0.16, and the historical market premium is 8.5 percent. Baber bonds carry a 13-percent coupon rate and are priced to yield 11 percent. The market value of the bonds is $24 million. Baber stock, of which 4 million shares are outstanding, sells for $15 per share. Baber's CFO considers the firm's current debt-equity ratio optimal. The tax rate is 34 percent, and the Treasury bill rate is 7 percent.

Baber Corp. must decide whether or not to purchase additional capital equipment. The cost of the equipment is $27.5 million. The expected cash flows from the new equipment are $9 million a year for five years. Purchasing the equipment will not change the risk level of Baber Corp. Should Baber purchase the equipment?

17.9 National Electric Company (NEC) is considering a $20 million modernization expansion project in the power-systems division. Tom Edison, the company's chief financial officer, has evaluated the project; he determined that the project's after-tax cash flows will be $8 million in perpetuity. In addition, Mr. Edison has devised two possibilities for raising the necessary $20 million:

- Issue 10-year, 10-percent debt.
- Issue common stock.

NEC's cost of debt is 10 percent, and its cost of equity is 20 percent. The firm's target debt-equity ratio is 200 percent. The expansion project has the same risk as the existing business, and it will support the same amount of debt. NEC is in the 34-percent tax bracket.

Mr. Edison has advised the firm to undertake the expansion. He suggests they use debt to finance the project because it is cheaper and its issuance costs are lower.

a. Should NEC accept the project? Support your answer with the appropriate calculations.

b. Do you agree with Mr. Edison's opinion of the expense of the debt? Why or why not?

17.10 Refer to question **17.8.**

Baber Corporation has chosen to purchase the additional equipment. If Baber funds the project entirely with debt, what is the firm's weighted average cost of capital? Explain your answer.

A Comparison of the APV, FTE, and WACC Approaches

17.11 ABC, Inc., is an unlevered firm with expected perpetual annual before-tax cash flows of $30 million and required return on equity of 18 percent. It has 1 million shares outstanding. ABC is paying tax at a marginal rate of 34 percent. The firm is planning a recapitalization under which it will issue $50 million of perpetual debt bearing a 10-percent interest rate and use the proceeds to buy back shares. Calculate the post-recap share price, earnings per share, and required return on equity.

17.12 Kinedyne, Inc., has decided to divest one of its divisions. The assets of the group have the same operating risk characteristics as those of the parent firm. The capital structure for the parent has been stable at 40-percent debt/60-percent equity (in market-value terms), the level determined to be optimal given the firm's assets. The required return on Kinedyne's assets is 16 percent, and the firm (and the division) borrows at a rate of 10 percent.

Sales revenue for the division is expected to remain stable indefinitely at last year's level of $19,740,000. Variable costs amount to 60 percent of sales. Annual depreciation of $1.8 million is exactly matched each year by new investment in the division's equipment. The division would be taxed at the parent's current rate of 40 percent.

a. How much is the division worth in unleveraged form?

b. If the division had the same capital structure as the parent firm, how much would it be worth?

c. At this optimal capital structure, what return will the equityholders of the division require?

d. Show that the market value of the equity of the division would be justified by the earnings to shareholders and the required return on equity.

Capital Budgeting for Projects that Are Not Scale-Enhancing

17.13 Schwartz & Brothers Inc. is in the process of deciding whether or not to make an equity investment in a project of holiday gifts production and sales. Arron Buffet is in charge of the feasibility study of the project. To better assess the risk of the project, he used the average of 10 other firms in holiday gift industry with similar operational scale as the benchmark. The figures that he has are as follows:

	Project	Benchmark
Debt equity ratio	35%	30%
β	?	1.5
r_B	10%	10%

The expected market return is 17 percent, and the risk-free interest rate is 9 percent. Corporate tax rate is 40 percent. The initial investment in the project is estimated at $325,000, and the cash flow at the end of the first year is $55,000. Annual cash flow will grow at a constant rate of 5 percent till the end of the fifth year and remain constant forever thereafter. Should Schwartz & Brothers invest in this project (assume that the bond beta is zero)?

APV Example

17.14 Brenda Lynch, CFO of Hunter Enterprises, is evaluating a 10-year, 9-percent loan. The projected net proceeds after flotation costs to be raised by the loan is $4,250,000. The flotation costs are estimated to be 1.25 percent of the gross proceeds and will be amortized using a straight-line schedule over the life of the loan. The cost of similar debt is 9.4 percent. The applicable corporate tax is 40 percent. Suppose that the loan will not increase the financial distress cost of the firm. What is the net present value of this loan?

Beta and Leverage

17.15 North Pole Fishing Equipment Corp. and South Pole Fishing Equipment Corp. would have identical β of 1.2 if both of them were all-equity financed. The capital structures of the two firms are as follows:

	North Pole Fishing Equipment Corp.	South Pole Fishing Equipment Corp.
Debt	$1,000,000	$1,500,000
Equity	$1,500,000	$1,000,000

The expected market rate of return is 12.75 percent, and the three-month Treasury bill rate is 4.25 percent. Corporate tax rate is 35 percent (assume that bond beta is zero).

a. What are the βs of the two firms, respectively?

b. What are the required rate of returns on the two firms' equity?

c. Try to give an intuitive explanation of the different βs and the returns on equity obtained in parts *a* and *b*.

APPENDIX 17A

THE ADJUSTED-PRESENT-VALUE APPROACH TO VALUING LEVERAGED BUYOUTS[10]

Introduction

A leveraged buyout (LBO) is the acquisition by a small group of equity investors of a public or private company financed primarily with debt. The equityholders service the

[10] This appendix has been adapted by Isik Inselbag and Howard Kaufold, The Wharton School, University of Pennsylvania, from their unpublished manuscript entitled "Analyzing the RJR Nabisco Buyout: An Adjusted Present Value Approach."

heavy interest and principal payments with cash from operations and/or asset sales. The shareholders generally hope to reverse the LBO within three to seven years by way of a public offering or sale of the company to another firm. A buyout is therefore likely to be successful only if the firm generates enough cash to serve the debt in the early years, and if the company is attractive to other buyers as the buyout matures.

In a leveraged buyout, the equity investors are expected to pay off outstanding principal according to a specific timetable. The owners know that the firm's debt-equity ratio will fall and can forecast the dollar amount of debt needed to finance future operations. Under these circumstances, the adjusted-present-value (APV) approach is more practical than the weighted-average-cost-of-capital (WACC) approach because the capital structure is changing. In this appendix, we illustrate the use of this procedure in valuing the RJR Nabisco transaction, the largest LBO in history.

The RJR Nabisco Buyout

In the summer of 1988, the price of RJR stock was hovering around $55 a share. The firm had $5 billion of debt. The firm's CEO, acting in concert with some other senior managers of the firm, announced a bid of $75 per share to take the firm private in a management buyout. Within days of management's offer, Kohlberg Kravis and Roberts (KKR) entered the fray with a $90 bid of their own. By the end of November, KKR emerged from the ensuing bidding process with an offer of $109 a share, or $25 billion total. We now use the APV technique to analyze KKR's winning strategy.

The APV method as described in this chapter can be used to value companies as well as projects. Applied in this way, the maximum value of a levered firm (V_L) is its value as an all-equity entity (V_U) plus the discounted value of the interest tax shields from the debt its assets will support (PVTS).[11] This relation can be stated as

$$V_L = V_U + \text{PVTS}$$

$$= \sum_{t=1}^{\infty} \frac{\text{UCF}_t}{(1 + r_0)^t} + \sum_{t=1}^{\infty} \frac{T_C r_B B_{t-1}}{(1 + r_B)^t}$$

In the second part of this equation, UCF_t is the unlevered cash flow from operations for year t. Discounting these cash flows by the required return on assets, r_0, yields the all-equity value of the company. B_{t-1} represents the debt balance remaining at the end of year $(t - 1)$. Because interest in a given year is based on the debt balance remaining at the end of the previous year, the interest paid in year t is $r_B B_{t-1}$. The numerator of the second term, $T_C r_B B_{t-1}$, is therefore the tax shield for year t. We discount this series of annual tax shields using the rate at which the firm borrows, r_B.[12]

KKR planned to sell several of RJR's food divisions and operate the remaining parts of the firm more efficiently. Table 17A.1 presents KKR's projected unlevered

[11] One should also deduct from this value any costs of financial distress. However, we would expect these costs to be small in the case of RJR for two reasons. As a firm in the tobacco and food industries, its cash flows are relatively stable and recession resistant. Furthermore, the firm's assets are divisible and attractive to a number of potential buyers, allowing the firm to receive full value if disposition is required.

[12] The pretax borrowing rate, r_B, represents the appropriate discount rate for the interest tax shields when there is a precommitment to a specific debt repayment schedule under the terms of the LBO. If debt covenants require that the entire free cash flow be dedicated to debt service, the amount of debt outstanding and, therefore, the interest tax shield at any point in time are a direct function of the operating cash flows of the firm. Since the debt balance is then as risky as the cash flows, the required return on assets should be used to discount the interest tax shields.

TABLE 17A.1 RJR Operating Cash Flows (in $ millions)

	1989	1990	1991	1992	1993
Operating income	$2,620	$3,410	$3,645	$3,950	$4,310
Tax on operating income	891	1,142	1,222	1,326	1,448
After-tax operating income	1,729	2,268	2,423	2,624	2,862
Add back depreciation	449	475	475	475	475
Less capital expenditures	522	512	525	538	551
Less change in working capital	(203)	(275)	200	225	250
Add proceeds from asset sales	3,545	1,805			
Unlevered cash flow (UCF)	$5404	$4,311	$2,173	$2,336	$2,536

TABLE 17A.2 Projected Interest Expenses and Tax Shields (in $ millions)

	1989	1990	1991	1992	1993
Interest expenses	$3,384	$3,004	$3,111	$3,294	$3,483
Interest tax shields (T_C = 34%)	1,151	1,021	1,058	1,120	1,184

cash flows for RJR under the buyout, adjusting for planned asset sales and operational efficiencies.

With respect to financial strategy, KKR planned a significant increase in leverage with accompanying tax benefits. Specifically, KKR issued almost $24 billion of new debt to complete the buyout, raising annual interest costs to more than $3 billion.[13] Table 17A.2 presents the projected interest expense and tax shields for the transaction.

We now use the data from Tables 17A.1 and 17A.2 to calculate the APV of the RJR buyout. This valuation process is presented in Table 17A.3.

The valuation presented in Table 17A.3 involves four steps.

Step 1: Calculating the present value of unlevered cash flows for 1989–93. The unlevered cash flows for 1989–93 are shown in the last line of Table 17A.1 and the first line of Table 17A.3. These flows are discounted by the required asset return, r_0, which at the time of the buyout was approximately 14 percent. The value as of the end of 1988 of the unlevered cash flows expected from 1989 through 1993 is

$$\frac{5.404}{1.14} + \frac{4.311}{1.14^2} + \frac{2.173}{1.14^3} + \frac{2.336}{1.14^4} + \frac{2.536}{1.14^5} = \$12.224 \text{ billion}$$

Step 2: Calculating the present value of the unlevered cash flows beyond 1993 (unlevered terminal value). We assume the unlevered cash flows grow at the modest

[13] A significant portion of this debt was of the payment in kind (PIK) variety, which offers lenders additional bonds instead of cash interest. This PIK debt financing provided KKR with significant tax shields while allowing it to postpone the cash burden of debt service to future years. For simplicity of presentation, Table 17A.2 does not separately show cash versus noncash interest charges.

TABLE 17A.3 RJR LBO Valuation (in $ millions except share data)

	1989	1990	1991	1992	1993
Unlevered cash flow (UCF)	$ 5,404	$4,311	$2,173	$2,336	$ 2,536
Terminal value: (3% growth after 1993)					
Unlevered terminal value (UTV)					23,746
Terminal value at target debt					26,654
Tax shield in terminal value					2,908
Interest tax shields	1,151	1,021	1,058	1,120	1,184
PV of UCF 1989–93 at 14%	12,224				
PV of UTV at 14%	12,333				
Total unlevered value	24,557				
PV of tax shields 1989–93 at 13.5%	3,877				
PV of tax shield in TV at 13.5%	1,544				
Total value of tax shields	5,421				
Total value	29,978				
Less value of assumed debt	5,000				
Value of equity	$24,978				
Number of shares	229 million				
Value per share	$109.07				

annual rate of 3 percent after 1993. The value, as of the end of 1993, of these cash flows is equal to the following discounted value of a growing perpetuity:

$$\frac{2.536(1.03)}{0.14 - 0.03} = \$23.746 \text{ billion}$$

This translates to a 1988 value of

$$\frac{23.746}{1.14^5} = \$12.333 \text{ billion}$$

As in Step 1, the discount rate is the required asset rate of 14 percent.

The total unlevered value of the firm is therefore ($12.224 + $12.333 =) $24.557 billion.

To calculate the total buyout value, we must add the interest tax shields expected to be realized by debt financing.

Step 3: Calculating the present value of interest tax shields for 1989–93. Under the prevailing U.S. tax laws in 1989, every dollar of interest reduces taxes by 34 cents. The present value of the interest tax shields for the period from 1989–93 can be calculated by discounting the annual tax savings at the pretax average cost of debt, which was approximately 13.5 percent. Using the tax shields from Table 17A.2, the discounted value of these tax shields is calculated as

$$\frac{1.151}{1.135} + \frac{1.021}{1.135^2} + \frac{1.058}{1.135^3} + \frac{1.120}{1.135^4} + \frac{1.184}{1.135^5} = \$3.877 \text{ billion}$$

Step 4: Calculating the present value of interest tax shields beyond 1993. Finally, we must calculate the value of tax shields associated with debt used to finance the operations of the company after 1993. We assume that debt will be reduced and maintained at 25 percent of the value of the firm from that date forward.[14] Under this assumption it is appropriate to use the WACC method to calculate a terminal value for the firm at the target capital structure. This in turn can be decomposed into an all-equity value and a value from tax shields.

If, after 1993, RJR uses 25-percent debt in its capital structure, its WACC at this target capital structure would be approximately 12.8 percent.[15] Then the levered terminal value as of the end of 1993 can be estimated as

$$\frac{2.536(1.03)}{0.128 - 0.03} = \$26{,}654 \text{ billion}$$

Since the levered value of the company is the sum of the unlevered value plus the value of interest tax shields, it is the case that

$$\begin{aligned}\text{Value of tax shields (end 1993)} &= V_L \text{ (end 1993)} - V_U \text{ (end 1993)}\\ &= \$26.654 \text{ billion} - 23.746 \text{ billion}\\ &= 2.908 \text{ billion}\end{aligned}$$

To calculate the value, as of the end of 1988, of these future tax shields, we again discount by the borrowing rate of 13.5 percent to get[16]

$$\frac{2.908}{1.135^5} = \$1.544 \text{ billion}$$

The total value of interest tax shields therefore equals (\$3.877 + \$1.544) \$5.421 billion.

Adding all of these components together, the total value of RJR under the buyout

[14] This 25-percent figure is consistent with the debt utilization in industries in which RJR Nabisco is involved. In fact, that was the debt-to-total-market-value ratio for RJR immediately before management's initial buyout proposal. The firm can achieve this target by 1993 if a significant portion of the convertible debt used to finance the buyout is exchanged for equity by that time. Alternatively, KKR could issue new equity (as would occur, for example, if the firm were taken public) and use the proceeds to retire some of the outstanding debt.

[15] To calculate this rate, use the weighted average cost of capital from this chapter:

$$r_{\text{WACC}} = \frac{S}{S+B} r_S + \frac{B}{S+B} r_B (1 - T_C)$$

and substitute the appropriate values for the proportions of debt and equity used, as well as their respective costs. Specifically, at the target debt-value ratio, $\frac{B}{S+B} = 25\%$, and $\frac{S}{S+B} = \left(1 - \frac{B}{S+B}\right) = 75\%$. Given this blend,

$$\begin{aligned}r_S &= r_0 + \frac{B}{S}(1 - T_C)(r_0 - r_B)\\ &= .14 + \frac{.25}{.75}(1 - .34)(.14 - .135) = .141\end{aligned}$$

Using these findings plus the borrowing rate of 13.5 percent in r_{WACC}, we find

$$r_{\text{WACC}} = .75(.141) + .25\,(.135)(1 - .34) = .128$$

In fact, this value is an approximation to the true weighted average cost of capital when the market debt-value blend is constant, or when the cash flows are growing. For a detailed discussion of this issue, see Isik Inselbag and Howard Kaufold, "A Comparison of Alternative Discounted Cash Flow Approaches to Firm Valuation," The Wharton School, University of Pennsylvania (June 1990), unpublished paper.

[16] A good argument can be made that since post-1993 debt levels are proportional to firm value, the tax shields are as risky as the firm and should be discounted at the rate *e*.

proposal is $29.978 billion. Deducting the $5 billion market value of assumed debt yields a value for equity of $24.978 billion, or $109.07 per share.

Concluding Comments on LBO Valuation Methods

As mentioned earlier in this chapter, the WACC method is by far the most widely applied approach to capital budgeting. One could analyze an LBO and generate the results of the second section of this appendix using this technique, but it would be a much more difficult process. We have tried to show that the APV approach is the preferred way to analyze a transaction in which the capital structure is not stable over time.

Consider the WACC approach to valuing the KKR bid for RJR. One could discount the operating cash flows of RJR by a set of weighted average costs of capital and arrive at the same $30 billion total value for the company. To do this, one would need to calculate the appropriate rate for each year since the WACC rises as the buyout proceeds. This occurs because the value of the tax subsidy declines as debt principal is repaid. In other words, there is no single return that represents the cost of capital when the firm's capital structure is changing.

There is also a theoretical problem with the WACC approach to valuing a buyout. To calculate the changing WACC, one must know the market value of a firm's debt and equity. But if the debt and equity values are already known, the total market value of the company is also known. That is, one must know the value of the company to calculate the WACC. One must therefore resort to using book-value measures for debt and equity, or make assumptions about the evolution of their market values, in order to implement the WACC method.

Chapter 19 Issuing Equity Securities to the Public

This chapter looks at how corporations issue equity securities to the investing public. The general procedures for debt, which are quite similar, are presented in the next chapter.

Before securities can be traded on a securities market, they must be issued to the public. A firm making an issue to the public must satisfy requirements set out in various federal legislation and statutes and enforced by the Securities and Exchange Commission (SEC). In general, investors must be given all material information in the form of a registration statement and prospectus. In the first part of this chapter we discuss what this entails.

A public issue of equity can be sold directly to the public with the help of underwriters. This is called a *general cash offer.* Alternatively, a public equity issue can be sold to the firm's existing stockholders by what is called a *rights offer.* This chapter examines the differences between a general cash offer and a rights offer.

Stock of companies going public for the first time is typically underpriced. We describe this unusual phenomenon and provide a possible explanation.

19.1 The Public Issue

The basic steps in a public offering are depicted in Table 19.1. The Securities Act of 1933 sets forth the federal regulation for all new interstate securities issues. The Securities Exchange Act of 1934 is the basis for regulating securities already outstanding. The SEC administers both acts.

The Basic Procedure for a New Issue

1. Management's first step in any issue of securities to the public is to obtain approval from the board of directors.

2. Next, the firm must prepare and file a **registration statement** with the SEC. This statement contains a great deal of financial information, including a financial history, details of the existing business, proposed financing, and plans for the future. It can easily run to 50 or more pages. The document is required for all public issues of securities with two principal exceptions:

a. Loans that mature within nine months.

b. Issues that involve less than $5.0 million.

TABLE 19.1 The Process of Raising Capital

Steps in Public Offering	*Time*	*Activities*
1. Preunderwriting conferences	Several months	Discuss the amount of money to be raised and the type of security to be issued. The underwriting syndicate and selling group are put together. The underwriting contract is negotiated. Board approval is obtained.
2. Registration statements filed and approved	A 20-day waiting period	The registration statement contains all relevant financial and business information.
3. Pricing the issue	Usually not before the last day of the registration period	For seasoned offerings the price is set close to the prevailing market price. For initial public offerings intensive research and analysis are required.
4. Public offering and sale	Shortly after the last day of the registration period	In a typical firm commitment contract, the underwriter buys a stipulated amount of stock from the firm and sells it at a higher price. The selling group assists in the sale.
5. Market stabilization	Usually 30 days after the offering	The underwriter stands ready to place orders to buy at a specified price on the market.

The second exception is known as the *small-issues exemption.* Issues of less than \$5.0 million are governed by **Regulation A,** for which only a brief offering statement—rather than the above registration statement—is needed. For Regulation A to be operative, no more than \$1.5 million may be sold by insiders.

3. The SEC studies the registration statement during a *waiting period.* During this time, the firm may distribute copies of a preliminary **prospectus.** The preliminary prospectus is called a **red herring** because bold red letters are printed on the cover. A prospectus contains much of the information put into the registration statement, and it is given to potential investors by the firm. The company cannot sell the securities during the waiting period. However, oral offers can be made.

A registration statement will become effective on the 20th day after its filing unless the SEC sends a *letter of comment* suggesting changes. After the changes are made, the 20-day waiting period starts anew.

4. The registration statement does not initially contain the price of the new issue. On the effective date of the registration statement, a price is determined and a full-fledged selling effort gets under way. A final prospectus must accompany the delivery of securities or confirmation of sale, whichever comes first.

5. **Tombstone** advertisements are used during and after the waiting period. An example is reproduced in Figure 19.1.

Concept Questions

- Describe the basic procedures in a new issue.
- What is a registration statement?

19.2 Alternative Issue Methods

When a company decides to issue a new security, it can sell it as a public issue or a private issue. If it is a public issue, the firm is required to register the issue with the

FIGURE 19.1 An Example of a Tombstone Advertisement

58,750,000 Shares

Consolidated Rail Corporation

Common Stock

(par value $1.00 per share)

Price $28 Per Share

The shares are being sold by the United States Govemment pursuant to the Conrail Privatization Act. The Company will not receive any prceeds from the sale of the shares.

Upon request, a copy of the Prospectus desrcibing these securities and the business of the Company may be obtained within any state from any Underwriter who may legally distribute it within such State. The securities are offered only by means of the Prospectus,and this announcement is neither an offer to sell nor a solicitation of any offer to buy.

52,000,000 Shares

This portion of the offering is being offered in the United States and Canada by the undersigned.

Goldman, Sachs & Co.

The First Boston Corporation

Merrill Lynch Capital Markets

Morgan Stanley & Co. Incorporated

Salomon Brothers Inc.

Shearson Lehman Brothers Inc.

Alex. Brown & Sons Incorporated   Dillion, Read & Co. Inc.   Donaldson, Lufkin & Jenrette Securities Corporation   Drexel Burnham Lambert Incorporated   Hambrecht & Quist Incorporated   E.F. Hutton & Compnay Inc.

Kidder, Peabody & Co. Incorporated   Lazard Freres & Co.   Montgomery Securities   Prudential-Bache Capital Funding   Robertson, Colman & Stephens

L.F. Rothschild, Unterberg, Towbin, Inc.   Smith Barney, Harris Upham & Co. Incorporated   Wertheim Schroder & Co. Incorporated   Dean Witter Reynolds Inc.

Wiliam Blair & Company   J.C. Bradford & Co. Incorporated   Dain Bosworth Incorporated   A.G. Edwards & Sons, Inc.   McDonald & Co. Securities, Inc.   Oppenheimer & Co., Inc.

Piper, Jaffray & Hopwood Incorporated   Prescott, Ball & Turben, Inc.   Thomson McKinnon Securities Inc.   Wheat, First Securities, Inc.

Advest, Inc.   American Securities Corporation   Arnhold and S. Bleichroeder, Inc.   Robert W. Baird & Co. Incorporated   Bateman Eichier, Hill Richards Incorporated

Sanford C. Bernstein & Co., Inc.   Blunt Ellis & Loewi Incorporated   Boettcher & Company, Inc.   Burns Fry and Timmins Inc.   Butcher & Singer Inc.   Cowen & Company

Dominion Securities Corporation   Eberstadt Fleming Inc.   Eppler, Guerin & Tuner, Inc.   First of Michigan Corporation   First Southwest Company

Furman Seiz Mager Dietz & Birney Incorporated   Gruntal & Co., Incorporated   Howard, Weil, Labouisse, Friedrichs Incorporated   Interstate Securities Corporation

Janney Montgomery Scott Inc.   Johnson, Lane, Space, Smith & Co., Inc.   Jonston , Lemon & Co. Incorporated   Josephthal & Co. Incorporated   Ladenburg , Thalman & Co.

Cyrus J Lawrence Incorporated   Legg Mason Wood Walker Incorporated   Morgan Keegan & Company, Inc.   Moseley Securities Corporation   Needham & Company, Inc.

Neuberger & Berman   The Ohio Company   Rauscher Pierce Refsnes, Inc.   The Robinson-Humphrey Company, Inc.   Rothschild Inc.   Stephens Inc.

Stifel, Nicolaus & Company Incorporated   Sutro & Co. Incorporated   Tucker, Anthony & R. L. Day, Inc.   Underwood, Neuhaus & Co. Incorporated   Wood Gundy Corp.

This special bracket of minority-owned and controlled firms assisted the Co-Lead Managers in the Unted States Offering pursuant to the Conrail Privatization Act:

AIBC Investment Services Corporation   **Daniels & Bell, Inc.**   **Doley Securities, Inc.**

WR Lazard Securities Corporation   **Pryor, Govan, Counts & Co., Inc.**   **Muriel Siebert & Co., Inc.**

6,750,000 Shares

This Portion of the offering is being offered outside the United States and Canada by the undersigned.

Goldman Sachs International Corp.

First Boston International Limited

Merril Lynch Capital Markets

Morgan Stanley International

Salomon Brothers International Limited

Shearson Lehman Brothers International

Algemene Bank Nederland N.V.   Banque Bruxelles Lambert S.A.   Banque Nationale de Paris   Cazenove & Co.   The Nikko Securities Co., (Europe) Ltd.

Nomura International Limited   N.M. Rothschild & Sons Limited   J. Henery Schroder Wagg & Co. Limited   Soclété Générate   S. G. Warburg Securities

ABC International Ltd.   Banque Paribas Capital Markets Limited   Caisse Nationale de Credit Agricole   Campagnie de Banque et d'investissements, CBI

Criédit Lyonnais   Daiwa Europe Limited   IMI Capital Markets (UK) Ltd.   Joh. Berenberg, Gossler & Co.   Leu Securities Limited

Morgan Grenfell & Co. Limited   Peterbroeck, van Campenhout & Cie SCS   Swiss Volksbank   Vereins- und Westbank Aktiengesellschaft

J. Vontobel & Co. Ltd   M.M.Warburg- Brinckmann, Wirtz & Co.   Westdeutsche Landesbank Girozentrale   Yamaichi International (Europe) Limited

March 27, 1987

TABLE 19.2 The Methods of Issuing New Securities

Method	Type	Definition
Public		
Traditional negotiated cash offer	Firm-commitment cash offer	Company negotiates an agreement with an investment banker to underwrite and distribute the new stocks or bonds. A specified number of shares is bought by underwriters and sold at a higher price.
	Best-efforts cash offer	Company has investment bankers sell as many of the new shares as possible at the agreed-upon price. There is no guarantee concerning how much cash will be raised.
Privileged subscription	Direct rights offer	Company offers new stock directly to its existing shareholders.
	Standby rights offer	Like the direct rights offer, this contains a privileged subscription arrangement with existing shareholders. The net proceeds are guaranteed by the underwriters.
Nontraditional cash offer	Shelf cash offer	Qualifying companies can authorize all shares they expect to sell over a two-year period and sell them when needed.
	Competitive firm cash offer	Company can elect to award underwriting contract through a public auction instead of negotiation.
Private	Direct placement	Securities are sold directly to purchaser, who cannot resell securities for at least two years.

SEC. If the issue is sold to fewer than 35 investors, it can be treated as a private issue. A registration statement is not required in this case.[1]

There are two kinds of public issues: the *general cash offer* and the *rights offer.* Cash offers are sold to all interested investors, and rights offers are sold to existing shareholders. Equity is sold by both the cash offer and the rights offer, though almost all debt is sold by cash offer.

The first public equity issue that is made by a company is referred to as an **initial public offering (IPO)** or an **unseasoned new issue.** All initial public offerings are cash offers because, if the firm's existing shareholders wanted to buy the shares, the firm would not need to sell them publicly. More than $5 billion was raised in 116 IPOs in 1994. A **seasoned new issue** refers to a new issue where the company's securities have been previously issued. A seasoned new issue of common stock may be made by using a cash offer or a rights offer.

These methods of issuing new securities are shown in Table 19.2 and discussed in the next few sections.

19.3 The Cash Offer

As mentioned above, stock is sold to all interested investors in a **cash offer.** If the cash offer is a public one, **investment bankers** are usually involved. Investment bankers are financial intermediaries who perform a wide variety of services. In addition to aiding in the sale of securities, they may facilitate mergers and other corporate reorganizations, act as brokers to both individual and institutional clients, and trade for their

[1] However, regulation significantly restricts the resale of unregistered securities. The purchaser must hold the securities at least two years.

TABLE 19.3 The Leading U.S. Underwriters in 1994

Top Underwriters of U.S. Debt and Equity

	1994		1993		
Manager	*Amount (in billions)*	*Market Share (%)*	*Amount (in billions)*	*Rank*	*Market Share (%)*
Merrill Lynch	$117.0	16.5%	$173.4	1	16.4%
Lehman Brothers	78.7	11.1	115.2	3	10.9
CS First Boston	73.5	10.4	89.3	6	8.4
Goldman Sachs	64.4	9.1	126.8	2	12.0
Morgan Stanley	58.7	8.3	67.4	7	6.4
Salomon Brothers	57.2	8.1	90.6	5	8.6
Kidder Peabody	48.8	6.9	94.0	4	11.7
Bear, Stearns	34.0	4.8	55.6	8	5.3
J.P. Morgan	26.5	3.7	23.6	11	2.2
Donaldson, Lufkin & Jenrette	23.1	3.3	36.2	9	3.4
TOP 10	$582.1	82.2%	$872.2	—	85.3%
INDUSTRY TOTAL	$709.8	100.0%	$1,058.2	—	100.0%

Disclosed Fees from New Issue Underwriting

	1994			1993	
Manager	*Amount (in millions)*	*Market Share (%)*	*Number of Issues*	*Amount (in millions)*	*Rank*
Merrill Lynch	$944.2	16.9%	691	$1,784.6	1
Goldman Sachs	666.3	12.0	396	1,121.9	2
Morgan Stanley	564.6	10.1	435	653.9	4
Lehman Brothers	361.1	6.5	573	741.5	3
Salomon Brothers	331.2	5.9	482	590.9	5
CS First Boston	329.7	5.9	526	526.6	6
Donaldson, Lufkin & Jenrette	277.7	5.0	220	484.0	7
Smith Barney	268.4	4.8	172	323.9	8
Kidder Peabody	192.3	3.5	214	278.5	9
Bear, Stearns	145.2	2.6	197	265.5	11
Top 10	$4,080.7	73.2%	3,906	$6,771.3	—
Industry Total	$5,571.5	100.0%	6,251	$9,171.4	—

Source: *The Wall Street Journal,* January 2, 1995.

own accounts. You may very well have heard of large Wall Street investment banking houses such as Goldman Sachs, Merrill Lynch, and Salomon Brothers. Table 19.3 lists the leading investment bankers for public security offerings in 1990.

For corporate issuers, investment bankers perform services such as the following:

Formulating the method used to issue the securities.

Pricing the new securities.

Selling the new securities.

There are two basic methods of issuing securities for cash.

1. **Firm commitment.** Under this method, the investment banker buys the securities for less than the offering price and accepts the risk of not being able to sell them. Because this function involves risk, we say that the investment banker *underwrites* the securities in a firm commitment. In other words, when participating in a firm-com-

TABLE 19.4 Initial Public Offerings of Stock Categorized by Gross Proceeds: 1977–1982

Gross proceeds ($)	*All Offerings*	*Firm Commitment*	*Best Efforts*	*Fraction Best Efforts*
100,000–1,999,999	243	68	175	0.720
2,000,000–3,999,999	311	165	146	0.469
4,000,000–5,999,999	156	133	23	0.147
6,000,000–9,999,999	137	122	15	0.109
10,000,000–120,174,195	180	176	4	0.022
All offerings	1,027	664	363	0.353

From J. R. Ritter, "The Costs of Going Public," *Journal of Financial Economics* 19 (1987). © Elsevier Science Publishers B. V. (North-Holland).

mitment offering, the investment banker acts as an *underwriter.* (Because firm commitments are so prevalent, we will use *investment banker* and *underwriter* interchangeably in this chapter.)

To minimize the risks here, investment bankers combine to form an underwriting group (**syndicate**) to share the risk and to help sell the issue. In such a group, one or more managers arrange or co-manage the deal. The manager is designated as the lead manager or principal manager. The lead manager typically has responsibility for all aspects of the issue. The other investment bankers in the syndicate serve primarily to sell the issue to their clients.

The difference between the underwriter's buying price and the offering price is called the *spread* or *discount.* It is the basic compensation received by the underwriter. Sometimes the underwriter will get noncash compensation in the form of warrants or stock in addition to the spread.

Firm-commitment underwriting is really just a purchase-sale arrangement, and the investment banker's fee is the spread. The issuer receives the full amount of the proceeds less the spread, and all the risk is transferred to the underwriter. If the underwriter cannot sell all of the issue at the agreed-upon offering price, it may need to lower the price on the unsold shares. However, because the offering price usually is not set until the underwriters have investigated how receptive the market is to the issue, this risk is usually minimal. This is particularly true with seasoned new issues because the price of the new issue can be based on prior trades in the security.

2. **Best efforts.** The underwriter bears risk with a firm commitment because it buys the entire issue. Conversely, the investment banker avoids this risk under a best-efforts offering because it does not purchase the shares. Instead, it merely acts as an agent, receiving a commission for each share sold. The investment banker is legally bound to use its best efforts to sell the securities at the agreed-upon offering price. If the issue cannot be sold at the offering price, it is usually withdrawn.

This form is more common for initial public offerings than for seasoned new issues. In addition, a recent study by Jay Ritter shows that best-efforts offerings are generally used for small IPOs and firm-commitment offerings are generally used for large IPOs. His results are reproduced in our Table 19.4. The last column in the table best illustrates his finding.

For either firm-commitment or best-efforts issues, the principal underwriter is permitted to buy shares if the market price falls below the offering price. The purpose is to *support* the market and *stabilize* the price from temporary downward pressure. If the issue remains unsold after a time (for example, 30 days), members may leave the group and sell their shares at whatever price the market will allow.

Many underwriting contracts contain a **Green Shoe provision,** which gives the members of the underwriting group the option to purchase additional shares at the offering price.[2] The stated reason for the Green Shoe option is to cover excess demand and oversubscription. Green Shoe options usually last for about 30 days and involve no more than 15 percent of the newly issued shares. The Green Shoe option is a benefit to the underwriting syndicate and a cost to the issuer. If the market price of the new issue goes above the offering price within 30 days, the underwriters can buy shares from the issuer and immediately resell the shares to the public.

Investment Bankers

Investment bankers are at the heart of new security issues. They provide advice, market the securities (after investigating the market's receptiveness to the issue), and underwrite the amount an issue will raise. They accept the risk that the market price may change between the date the offering price is set and the time the issue is sold.

In addition, investment bankers have the responsibility of pricing fairly. When a firm goes public, particularly for the first time, the buyers know relatively little about the firm's operations. After all, it is not rational for a buyer of, say, only 1,000 shares of stock to study the company at length. Instead, the buyer must rely on the judgment of the investment banker, who has presumably examined the firm in detail. Given this asymmetry of information, what prevents the investment banker from pricing the issued securities too high? While the underwriter has a short-run incentive to price high, it has a long-run incentive to make sure that its customers do not pay too much; they might desert the underwriter in future deals if they lose money on this one. Thus, as long as investment bankers plan to stay in business over time, it is in their self-interest to price fairly.

In other words, financial economists argue that each investment bank has a reservoir of "reputation capital."[3] Mispricing of new issues, as well as unethical dealings, is likely to reduce this reputation capital.

One measure of this capital is the pecking order among the investment banks. MBA students are aware of this order because they know that accepting a job with a top-tier firm is universally regarded as more prestigious than accepting a job with a lower-tier firm. This pecking order can be seen in Figure 19.1. The investment banks listed diagonally in the figure are considered the most prestigious. These appear alphabetically so that one cannot distinguish the relative status of these firms from the figure. The next set of firms, running from Alex. Browns & Sons to Dean Witter Reynolds, is also in alphabetical order. By noting when the alphabetical order begins anew, one can determine the number of firms in each tier.

Investment banks put great importance in their relative rankings and view downward movement in their placement with much distaste. While this jockeying for position may seem as unimportant as the currying of royal favor in the court of Louis XVI, it is explained by the above discussion. In any industry where reputation is so important, the firms in the industry must guard theirs with great vigilance.

---

[2] The Green Shoe Corp. was the first firm to allow this provision.

[3] For example, see R. Carter and S. Manaster, "Initial Public Offerings and Underwriter Reputation," unpublished Iowa State and University of Utah working paper (1988); and R. Beatty and J. Ritter, "Investment Banking, Reputation and the Underpricing of Initial Public Offerings," *Journal of Financial Economics* (1986).

There are two basic methods for selecting the investment banker. In a **competitive offer,** the issuing firm can offer its securities to the underwriter bidding highest. In a **negotiated offer,** the issuing firm works with one underwriter. Because the firm generally does not negotiate with many underwriters concurrently, negotiated deals may suffer from lack of competition.

While competitive bidding occurs frequently in other areas of commerce, it may surprise you that negotiated deals in investment banking occur with all but the largest issuing firms. Investment bankers argue that they must expend much time and effort learning about the issuer before setting an issue price and a fee schedule. Except in the case of large issues, these underwriters could not expend the time and effort without the near certainty of receiving the contract.

Studies generally show that issuing costs are higher in negotiated deals than in competitive ones. However, many financial economists argue that issuing firms are not necessarily hurt by negotiated deals. They point out that the underwriter gains much information about the issuing firm through negotiation, information likely to increase the probability of a successful offering.[4]

The Offering Price

Determining the correct offering price is the most difficult thing an investment banker must do for an initial public offering. The issuing firm faces a potential cost if the offering price is set too high or too low. If the issue is priced too high, it may be unsuccessful and be withdrawn. If the issue is priced below the true market price, the issuer's existing shareholders will experience an opportunity loss.

Ibbotson has found that unseasoned new equity issues typically have been offered at 11 percent below their true market price.[5] Underpricing helps new shareholders earn a higher return on the shares they buy. However, the existing shareholders of the issuing firm are not helped by underpricing. To them it is an indirect cost of issuing new securities.

Several studies have confirmed the early research of Ibbotson. For example, Ritter examined approximately 1,030 firms that went public from 1977 through 1982 in the United States.[6] He finds that the average firm-commitment IPO rose in price 14.8 percent in the first day of trading following issuance. The comparable figure is 47.8 percent for best-efforts IPOs. These figures are not annualized! Both of these results are clearly consistent with substantial underpricing.

Underpricing: The Case of Conrail and Shiva

The sale on March 26, 1987, of more than 58 million shares of Conrail, the previously U.S. government–owned railroad company, was the largest new issue (IPO) of stock in U.S. history. A total of $1.65 billion was raised. This is more than the $1.5 billion

[4] This choice has been studied recently by S. Bhagat, "The Effect of Management's Choice between Negotiated and Competitive Equity Offerings on Shareholder Wealth," *Journal of Financial and Quantitative Analysis* (1986); and D. Logue and R. Jarrow, "Negotiation vs. Competitive Bidding in the Sales of Securities by Public Utilities," *Financial Management* 7 (1978).

[5] R. Ibbotson, "Price Performance of Common Stock New Issues," *Journal of Financial Economics* 2 (1975).

[6] J. R. Ritter, "The Costs of Going Public," *Journal of Financial Economics* (1987). Underpricing also exists for new issues of seasoned stock, but to a much smaller extent. See J. Parsons and A. Raviv, "Underpricing of Seasoned Issues," *Journal of Financial Economics* 14 (1985).

that AT&T obtained in 1983 in what had previously been the largest U.S. stock offering, but less than the $4.76 billion raised when Telecom (the British government-owned telephone company) went public in 1984.

At the end of the first day after the Conrail offering, the shares were more than 10 percent above their initial offering price. This is a good example of underpricing. Two opposing views of the sale were prominent in the press after the offering:

1. The issue was hailed as a great success by underwriters and the U.S. Congress. By selling 100 percent of the railroad company, the government achieved its largest divestiture of state assets yet.
2. Others saw the sale as the largest commercial giveaway in U.S. government history. They asked how the government could set the price so low.

A recent dramatic example of underpricing came with the IPO of Shiva Corporation. Shiva makes hardware and software that allows desktop and laptop computers to hook directly into a local area network from outside the office. The initial offering, on November 18, 1994, of 2.76 million shares priced at $15 rose $16½ to $31½ by the end of the first trading day. Goldman Sachs, head of the underwriting syndicate that underwrote the issue, was quoted as saying that pricing an IPO is not just about what the market will bear at the time, but "we are trying to get the company launched for the long term and build a good investor base."[7]

Underpricing: A Possible Explanation

When the price of a new issue is too low, the issue is often *oversubscribed.* This means investors will not be able to buy all of the shares they want, and the underwriters will allocate the shares among investors. The average investor will find it difficult to get shares in an oversubscribed offering because there will not be enough shares to go around. While initial public offerings have positive initial returns on average, a significant fraction of them have price drops. An investor submitting an order for all new issues may well find that he or she will be allocated more shares in issues that go down in price.

Consider this tale of two investors. Ms. Smarts knows precisely what companies are worth when their shares are offered. Mr. Average knows only that prices usually rise one month after the IPO. Armed with this information, Mr. Average decides to buy 1,000 shares of every IPO. Does Mr. Average actually earn an abnormally high average return across all initial offerings?

The answer is no, and at least one reason is Ms. Smarts. For example, because Ms. Smarts knows that company *XYZ* is underpriced, she invests all her money in its IPO. When the issue is oversubscribed, the underwriters must allocate the shares between Ms. Smarts and Mr. Average. If they do it on a pro rata basis and if Ms. Smarts has bid for twice as many shares as Mr. Average, she will get two shares for each one Mr. Average receives. The net result is that when an issue is underpriced, Mr. Average cannot buy as much of it as he wanted.

Ms. Smarts also knows that company *ABC* is overpriced. In this case she avoids its IPO altogether, and Mr. Average ends up with a full 1,000 shares. To summarize, Mr. Average receives fewer shares when more knowledgeable investors swarm to buy an underpriced issue, but he gets all he wants when the smart money avoids the issue.

---

[7] *The New York Times,* February 19, 1995, "Anatomy of a High Flying IPO, Problems and All," p. 7.

IN THEIR OWN WORDS . . . Jay R. Ritter on IPO Underpricing around the World

The United States is not the only country in which initial public offerings of common stock (IPOs) are underpriced. The phenomenon exists in every country with a stock market, although the amount of underpricing varies from country to country.

Many countries have government regulators who force issuing companies to sell shares at a lower price than they otherwise would. Sometimes the purpose is to protect unsophisticated investors. However, in some denationalizations, or privatizations, there has been another motive for underpricing.

For example, in 1979, when Margaret Thatcher became Prime Minister of Britain amid a wave of strikes and a declining economy, there were more union members than stockholders in Britain. To give British voters a positive experience with capitalism, as the government denationalized several government-owned businesses, it intentionally sought to both underprice the shares and to allow as many voters as possible to buy them. As a result of this strategy, by the mid-1980s there were more shareholders than union members. As a by-product of the denationalizations, the British government ran a budget surplus, because of the cash raised as the asset sales continued.

The table below gives a summary of the average initial returns on IPOs in a number of countries around the world, with the figures collected from a number of studies by various authors.

Country	*Sample Size*	*Time Period*	*Average Initial Return*
Australia	266	1976–89	11.9%
Belgium	28	1984–90	10.1
Brazil	62	1979–90	78.5
Canada	258	1971–92	5.4
Chile	19	1982–90	16.3
Finland	85	1984–92	9.6
France	187	1983–92	4.2
Germany	170	1978–92	10.9
Hong Kong	80	1980–90	17.6
Italy	75	1985–91	27.1
Japan	472	1970–91	32.5
Korea	347	1980–90	78.1
Malaysia	132	1980–91	80.3
Mexico	37	1987–90	33.0
Netherlands	72	1982–91	7.2
New Zealand	149	1979–91	28.8
Portugal	62	1986–87	54.4
Singapore	66	1973–87	27.0
Spain	71	1985–90	35.0
Sweden	213	1970–91	39.0
Switzerland	42	1983–89	35.8
Taiwan	168	1971–90	45.0
Thailand	32	1988–89	58.1
United Kingdom	2,133	1959–90	12.0
United States	10,626	1960–92	15.3

Jay R. Ritter is professor of finance at the University of Illinois. An outstanding scholar, he is well respected for his insightful analyses of new issues and going public.

This is called the *winner's curse,* and it explains much of the reason why IPOs have such a large average return. When the average investor wins and gets his allocation, it is because those who knew better avoided the issue. To counteract the winner's curse and attract the average investor, underwriters underprice issues.[8]

[8] This explanation was first suggested in K. Rock, "Why New Issues Are Underpriced," *Journal of Financial Economics* 15 (1986).

Concept Questions

- Describe a firm-commitment underwriting and a best-efforts underwriting.
- Suppose that a stockbroker calls you up out of the blue and offers to sell you some shares of a new issue. Do you think the issue will do better or worse than average?

19.4 The Announcement of New Equity and the Value of the Firm

It seems reasonable to believe that new long-term financing is arranged by firms after positive net-present-value projects are put together. As a consequence, when the announcement of external financing is made, the firm's market value should go up. As we mentioned in an earlier chapter, this is precisely the opposite of what actually happens in the case of new equity financing. Asquith and Mullins, Masulis and Korwar, and Mikkelson and Partch have all found that the market value of existing equity drops on the announcement of a new issue of common stock.[9] Plausible reasons for this strange result include:

1. *Managerial Information.* If managers have superior information about the market value of the firm, they may know when the firm is overvalued. If they do, they might attempt to issue new shares of stock when the market value exceeds the correct value. This will benefit existing shareholders. However, the potential new shareholders are not stupid. They will infer overvaluation from the new issue, thereby bidding down the stock price on the announcement date of the issue.
2. *Debt Capacity.* The stereotypical firm chooses a debt-to-equity ratio that balances the tax shield from debt with the cost of financial distress. When the managers of a firm have special information that the probability of financial distress has risen, the firm is more likely to raise capital through stock than through debt. If the market infers this chain of events, the stock price should fall on the announcement date of an equity issue.

Concept Question

- What are some reasons that the price of stock drops on the announcement of a new equity issue?

19.5 The Cost of New Issues

Issuing securities to the public is not free, and the costs of different issuing methods are important determinants of which is used. The costs fall into six categories.

1. Spread or underwriting discount	The spread is the difference between the price the issue receives and the price offered to the public.

[9] P. Asquith and D. Mullins, "Equity Issues and Offering Dilution," *Journal of Financial Economics* 15 (1986); R. Masulis and A. N. Korwar, "Seasoned Equity Offerings: An Empirical Investigation," *Journal of Financial Economics* 15 (1986); and W. H. Mikkelson and M. M. Partch, "The Valuation Effects of Security Offerings and the Issuance Process," *Journal of Financial Economics* 15 (1986).

2. Other direct expenses	These are costs incurred by the issuer that are not part of the compensation to underwriters. They include filing fees, legal fees, and taxes—all reported in the prospectus.
3. Indirect expenses	These costs are not reported in the prospectus and include management time on the new issue.
4. Abnormal returns	In a seasoned issue of stock, the price drops by 1 percent to 2 percent upon the announcement of the issue. The drop protects shareholders against the firm's selling overpriced stock to new shareholders.
5. Underpricing	For initial public offerings, the stock typically rises substantially after the issue date. This is a cost to the firm because the stock is sold for less than its efficient price in the aftermarket.[10]
6. Green-Shoe option	The Green-Shoe option gives the underwriters the right to buy additional shares at the offer price to cover overallotments. This is a cost to the firm because the underwriter will only buy additional shares when the offer price is below the price in the aftermarket.

An interesting study by Ritter estimated three of these six costs: underwriting discount, other direct expenses, and underpricing. His findings for both firm-commitment offerings and best-efforts offerings are reproduced in Table 19.5. Five conclusions emerge from the table.

1. The costs in each category, for both firm-commitment offerings and best-efforts offerings, decline as the gross proceeds of the offering increase. Thus, it appears that issuance costs are subject to substantial economies of scale.
2. The bottom line of Table 19.5 indicates that, across all offerings, direct expenses are higher for best-efforts offers than for firm-commitment offers. However, for a given size offering, the direct expenses of best-efforts underwriting and firm-commitment underwriting are of the same magnitude.
3. For almost all size classes, underpricing is higher for best-efforts offers than for firm-commitment offers.
4. On average, underpricing is greater than total direct discount for both firm-commitment offers and best-efforts offers. Thus, underpricing is a significant cost to the issuer. However, because underpricing is a subtle and indirect cost, many issuers

[10] Some people have argued that the price in the aftermarket is not efficient after all. However, R. Ibbotson, "Price Performance of Common Stock New Issues," *Journal of Financial Economics* 2 (1975), shows that, on average, new issues exhibit no abnormal price performance over the first five years following issuance. This result is generally viewed as being consistent with market efficiency. That is, the stock obtains an efficient price immediately following issuance and remains at an efficient price.

TABLE 19.5 Direct and Indirect Costs of Going Public

Total Transactions Costs as a Percentage of Gross Proceeds, 1977–1982

	Firm-Commitment Offerings					Best-Efforts Offerings				
Gross Proceeds ($)	*(1) Spread or Underwriting Discount (%)*	*(2) Other Direct Expenses (%)*	*(3) Total Direct Discount (%) (1) + (2)*	*(4) Underpricing (%)*	*(5) Total Expenses (%)*	*(6) Spread or Underwriting Discount (%)*	*(7) Other Direct Expenses (%)*	*(8) Total Direct Discount (%) (6) + (7)*	*(9) Underpricing (%)*	*(10) Total Expenses (%)*
1,000,000–1,999,999	9.84	9.64	19.48	26.92	31.73	10.63	9.52	20.15	39.62	31.89
2,000,000–3,999,999	9.83	7.60	17.43	20.70	24.93	10.00	6.21	16.21	63.41	36.28
4,000,000–5,999,999	9.10	5.67	14.77	12.57	20.90	9.86*	3.71*	13.57*	26.82*	14.49*
6,000,000–9,999,999	8.03	4.31	12.34	8.99	17.85	9.80*	3.42*	13.22*	40.79*	25.97*
10,000,000–120,174,195	7.24	2.10	9.34	10.32	16.27	8.03*	2.40*	10.43*	−5.42*	−0.17*
All offerings	8.67	5.36	14.03	14.80	21.22	10.26	7.48	17.74	47.78	31.87

Underpricing is computed as (p − OP) OP, multiplied by 100 percent, where p is the closing bid price on the first day of trading and OP is the offering price. These are not annualized returns. Total expenses are computed as 100 percent minus the net proceeds as a percentage of the market value of securities in the aftermarket. Consequently, total expenses are not the sum of underwriting expenses and the average underpricing. The underwriting discount is the commission paid by the issuing firm; this is listed on the front page of the firm's prospectus.

The other expense figure is comprised of accountable and nonaccountable fees of the underwriters and cash expenses of the issuing firm for legal, printing, and auditing fees and other out-of-pocket costs. These other expenses are described in footnotes on the front page of the issuing firm's prospectus. None of the expense categories includes the value of warrants granted to the underwriter, a practice that is common with best-efforts offerings.

Gross-proceeds categories are nominal; no price-level adjustments have been made.

Also note that the −0.17-percent figure for the total expenses for best-efforts offerings raising $10 million or more means that, on the average, these firms received net proceeds larger than the market value of the securities after the offering. It should be mentioned that there was less than one offering per year in the category.

*Based on fewer than 25 firms.

Modified from J. R. Ritter, "The Costs of Going Public," *Journal of Financial Economics* 19 (1987), © Elsevier Science Publishers B.V. (North-Holland).

do not view it as a cost at all. In fact, we have found many investment bankers who advise the issuer to underprice an issue to get a well-received offering.

5. Last, and perhaps most important, the costs of going public are quite large. For example, total expenses are greater than 30 percent for an offering of less than \$2,000,000. This implies that going public for the first time is a weighty decision. While there are many benefits, such as raising needed capital and spreading ownership, the costs cannot be ignored.

Concept Questions

- Describe the costs of a new issue of common stock.
- What conclusions emerge from an analysis of Table 19.5?

19.6 Rights

When new shares of common stock are offered to the general public, the proportionate ownership of existing shareholders is likely to be reduced. However, if a preemptive right is contained in the firm's articles of incorporation, the firm must first offer any new issue of common stock to existing shareholders.

An issue of common stock to existing stockholders is called a *rights offering.* Here, each shareholder is issued an *option* to buy a specified number of new shares from the firm at a specified price within a specified time, after which the rights expire. For example, a firm whose stock is selling at \$30 may let current stockholders buy a fixed number of shares at \$10 per share within two months. The terms of the option are evidenced by certificates known as *share warrants* or *rights.* Such rights are often traded on securities exchanges or over the counter.

The Mechanics of a Rights Offering

The various considerations confronting a financial manager in a rights offering are illustrated by the situation of the National Power Company, whose initial financial statements are given in Table 19.6.

National Power earns \$2 million after taxes and has 1 million shares outstanding. Earnings per share are \$2, and the stock sells at 10 times earnings (that is, its price-earnings ratio is 10). The market price of each share is therefore \$20. The company plans to raise \$5 million of new equity funds by a rights offering.

The process of issuing rights differs from the process of issuing shares of stock for cash. Existing stockholders are notified that they have been given one right for each share of stock they own. Exercise occurs when a shareholder sends payment to the firm's subscription agent (usually a bank). Shareholders of National Power will have several choices: (1) subscribe for the full number of entitled shares, (2) order all the rights sold, or (3) do nothing and let the rights expire.

The financial management of National Power must answer the following questions:

1. What price should the existing shareholders be allowed to pay for a share of new stock?
2. How many rights will be required to purchase one share of stock?
3. What effect will the rights offering have on the existing price of the stock?

Table 19.6 Financial Statement before Rights Offering

NATIONAL POWER COMPANY
Balance Sheet and Income Statement

Balance Sheet

Assets	Shareholder Equity	
	Common stock	$10,000,000
	Retained earnings	10,000,000
Total $20,000,000	Total	$20,000,000

Income Statement

Earnings before taxes	$ 3,030,303
Taxes (34%)	1,030,303
Net income	$ 2,000,000
Earnings per share	$ 2
Shares outstanding	1,000,000
Market price per share	$ 20
Total market value	$20,000,000

Subscription Price

In a rights offering, the **subscription price** is the price that existing shareholders are allowed to pay for a share of stock. A rational shareholder will only subscribe to the rights offering if the subscription price is below the market price of the stock on the offer's expiration date. For example, if the stock price at expiration is $13 and the subscription price is $15, no rational shareholder will subscribe. Why pay $15 for something worth $13? National Power chooses a price of $10, which is well below the current market price of $20. As long as the market price does not fall by half before expiration, the rights offering will succeed.

Number of Rights Needed to Purchase a Share

National Power wants to raise $5 million in new equity. With a subscription price of $10, it must issue 500,000 new shares. This can be determined by dividing the total amount to be raised by the subscription price:

$$\text{Number of new shares} = \frac{\text{Funds to be raised}}{\text{Subscription price}} = \frac{\$5{,}000{,}000}{\$10} = 500{,}000 \text{ shares}$$

Because stockholders always get one right for each share of stock they own, 1 million rights will be issued by National Power. To determine how many rights must be exercised to get one share of stock, we can divide the number of existing outstanding shares of stock by the number of new shares:

$$\begin{array}{c}\text{Number of rights}\\ \text{needed to buy a}\\ \text{share of stock}\end{array} = \frac{\text{“Old” shares}}{\text{"New" shares}} = \frac{1{,}000{,}000}{500{,}000} = 2 \text{ rights}$$

Thus, a shareholder must give up two rights plus $10 to receive a share of new stock. If all the stockholders do this, National Power will raise the required $5 million.

It should be clear that the subscription price, the number of new shares, and the number of rights needed to buy a new share of stock are interrelated. If National

TABLE 19.7 The Value to the Individual Shareholder of National Power's Rights

	The Shareholder
Initial position	
Number of shares	2
Share price	\$20
Value of holding	\$40
Terms of offer	
Subscription price	\$10
Number of rights issued	2
Number of rights for a share	2
After offer	
Number of shares	3
Value of holdings	\$50
Share price	\$16.67
Value of a right	
Old price − New price	\$20 − \$16.67 = \$3.33
(New price − Subscription price) / Number of rights for a share	(\$16.67 − \$10)/2 = \$3.33

Power lowers the subscription price, it must issue more new shares to raise \$5 million in new equity. Several alternatives appear here:

Subscription Price	*Number of New Shares*	*Number of Rights Needed to Buy a Share of Stock*
\$20	250,000	4
10	500,000	2
5	1,000,000	1

Effect of Rights Offering on Price of Stock

Rights clearly have value. In the case of National Power, the right to be able to buy a share of stock worth \$20 for \$10 is valuable.

Suppose a shareholder of National Power owns two shares of stock just before the rights offering. This situation is depicted in Table 19.7. Initially, the price of National Power is \$20 per share, so the shareholder's total holding is worth 2 × \$20 = \$40. The stockholder who has two shares will receive two rights. The National Power rights offer gives shareholders with two rights the opportunity to purchase one additional share for \$10. The holding of the shareholder who exercises these rights and buys the new share would increase to three shares. The value of the new holding would be \$40 + \$10 = \$50 (the \$40 initial value plus the \$10 paid to the company). Because the stockholder now holds three shares, the price per share would drop to \$50/3 = \$16.67 (rounded to two decimal places).

The difference between the old share price of \$20 and the new share price of \$16.67 reflects the fact that the old shares carried rights to subscribe to the new issue. The difference must be equal to the value of one right, that is, \$20 − \$16.67 = \$3.33.

Just as we learned of an ex-dividend date in the previous chapter, there is an **ex-rights** date here. An individual buying the stock prior to the ex-rights date will receive the rights when distributed. An individual buying the stock on or after the ex-rights date will not receive the rights. In our example, the price of the stock prior to the ex-

TABLE 19.8 National Power Company Rights Offering

Initial position	
Number of shares	1 million
Share price	$20
Value of firm	$20 million
Terms of offer	
Subscription price	$10
Number of rights issued	1 million
Number of rights for a share	2
After offer	
Number of shares	1.5 million
Share price	$16.67
Value of firm	$25 million
Value of one right	$20 − $16.67 = $3.33
	or ($16.67 − $10)/2 = $3.33

rights date is $20. An individual buying on or after the ex-rights date is not entitled to the rights. The price on or after the ex-rights date is $16.67.

Table 19.8 shows what happens to National Power. If all shareholders exercise their rights, the number of shares will increase to 1.5 million and the value of the firm will increase to $25 million. After the rights offering the value of each share will drop to $16.67 (= $25 million/1.5 million).

An investor holding no shares of National Power stock who wants to subscribe to the new issue can do so by buying rights. An outside investor buying two rights will pay $3.33 × 2 = $6.67 (to account for previous rounding). If the investor exercises the rights at a subscription cost of $10, the total cost would be $10 + $6.67 = $16.67. In return for this expenditure, the investor will receive a share of the new stock, which is worth $16.67.

Of course, outside investors can also buy National Power stock directly at $16.67 per share. In an efficient stock market it will make no difference whether new stock is obtained via rights or via direct purchase.

Effects on Shareholders

Shareholders can exercise their rights or sell them. In either case, the stockholder will neither win nor lose by the rights offering. The hypothetical holder of two shares of National Power has a portfolio worth $40. On the one hand, if the shareholder exercises the rights, he or she ends up with three shares worth a total of $50. In other words, by spending $10, the investor increases the value of the holding by $10, which means that he or she is neither better nor worse off.

On the other hand, a shareholder who sells the two rights for $3.33 each obtains $3.33 × 2 = $6.67 in cash. Because the two shares are each worth $16.67, the holdings are valued at

$$\begin{aligned} \text{Shares} &= \quad 2 \times \$16.67 = \$33.33 \\ \text{Sold rights} &= 2 \times \$\ 3.33 = \underline{\$\ 6.67} \\ \text{Total} &= \qquad\qquad\qquad \$40.00 \end{aligned}$$

The new $33.33 market value plus $6.67 in cash is exactly the same as the original holding of $40. Thus, stockholders can neither lose nor gain from exercising or selling rights.

It is obvious that the new market price of the firm's stock will be lower after the rights offering than it was before the rights offering. The lower the subscription price, the greater the price decline of a rights offering. However, our analysis shows that the stockholders have suffered no loss because of the rights offering.

The Underwriting Arrangements

Undersubscription can occur if investors throw away rights or if bad news causes the market price of the stock to fall below the subscription price. To ensure against these possibilities, rights offerings are typically arranged by **standby underwriting**. Here, the underwriter makes a firm commitment to purchase the unsubscribed portion of the issue at the subscription price less a small take-up fee. The underwriter usually receives a **standby fee** as compensation for his risk-bearing function.

In practice, the subscription price is usually set well below the current market price, making the probability of a rights failure quite small. Though a small percentage (less than 10 percent) of shareholders fail to exercise valuable rights, shareholders are usually allowed to purchase unsubscribed shares at the subscription price. This **oversubscription privilege** makes it unlikely that the corporate issuer would need to turn to its underwriter for help.

Concept Questions

- Describe the details of a rights offering.
- What are the questions that financial management must answer in a rights offering?
- How is the value of a right determined?

19.7 The New-Issues Puzzle

Smith calculated the issuance costs from three alternative methods: an equity issue with underwriting, a rights issue with standby underwriting, and a pure rights issue.[11] The results of his study, which appear in Table 19.9, suggest that a pure rights issue is the cheapest of the three alternatives. The bottom line of the table shows that total costs as a percentage of proceeds is 6.17 percent, 6.05 percent, and 2.45 percent for the three alternatives, respectively. As the body of the table indicates, this disparity holds when issues of different sizes are separated.

If corporate executives are rational, they will raise equity in the cheapest manner. Thus, the above evidence suggests that issues of pure rights should dominate. Surprisingly, Smith points out that over 90 percent of new issues are underwritten. This is generally viewed as an anomaly in the finance profession, though a few explanations have been advanced.

1. Underwriters increase the stock price. This is supposedly accomplished because of increased public confidence or by the selling effort of the underwriting group. However, Smith could find no evidence of this in an examination of 52 rights offerings and 344 underwritten offerings.

[11] C. W. Smith, Jr., "Alternative Methods for Raising Capital: Rights versus Underwritten Offerings," *Journal of Financial Economics* 5 (December 1977).

Table 19.9 Costs of Flotation as a Percentage of Proceeds*

	Underwriting				Rights with Standby Underwriting				Pure rights	
Size of Issue (in $ millions)	*Number*	*Compensation as a Percentage of Proceeds*	*Other Expenses as a Percentage of Proceeds*	*Total Cost as a Percentage of Proceeds*	*Number*	*Compensation as a Percentage of Proceeds*	*Other Expenses as a Percentage of Proceeds*	*Total Cost as a Percentage of Proceeds*	*Number*	*Total Cost as a Percentage of Proceeds*
Under 0.50 0	—	—	—	0	—	—	—	3	8.99	
0.50 to 0.99	6	6.96	6.78	13.74	2	3.43	4.80	8.24	2	4.59
1.00 to 1.99	18	10.40	4.89	15.29	5	6.36	4.15	10.51	5	4.90
2.00 to 4.99	61	6.59	2.87	9.47	9	5.20	2.85	8.06	7	2.85
5.00 to 9.99	66	5.50	1.53	7.03	4	3.92	2.18	6.10	6	1.39
10.00 to 19.99	91	4.84	0.71	5.55	10	4.14	1.21	5.35	3	0.72
20.00 to 49.99	156	4.30	0.37	4.67	12	3.84	0.90	4.74	1	0.52
50.00 to 99.99	70	3.97	0.21	4.18	9	3.96	0.74	4.70	2	0.21
100.00 to 500.00	16	3.81	0.14	3.95	5	3.50	0.50	4.00	9	0.13
Total/average	484	5.02	1.15	6.17	56	4.32	1.73	6.05	38	2.45

*Based on 578 common stock issues registered under the Securities Act of 1933 during 1971–1975. The issues are subdivided by size of issue and method of financing: underwriting, rights with standby underwriting, and pure rights offering.

Issues are included only if the company's stock was listed on the NYSE, AMEX, or regional exchanges before the offering; any associated secondary distribution represents less than 10 percent of the total proceeds of the issue, and the offering contains no other types of securities. The costs reported are: (1) compensation received by investment bankers for underwriting services rendered, (2) legal fees, (3) accounting fees, (4) engineering fees, (5) trustees' fees, (6) printing and engraving expenses, (7) SEC registration fees, (8) federal revenue stamps, and (9) state taxes.

Modified from C. W. Smith, Jr., "Costs of Underwritten versus Rights Issues," *Journal of Financial Economics* 5 (December 1977), p. 277 (Table 1).

2. Because the underwriter buys the shares at the agreed-upon price, it is providing insurance to the firm. That is, the underwriter loses if it is unable to sell all the shares to the public. This potential loss might mean that the underwriter's effective compensation is less than that measured in Table 19.9. However, the potential economic loss is probably not large. In most cases, the offer price is set within 24 hours of the offering, by which time the underwriter has usually made a careful assessment of the market for the shares.

3. Other arguments include (*a*) the proceeds of underwritten issues are available sooner than are the proceeds from a rights offer, (*b*) underwriters provide a wider distribution of ownership than would be true with a rights offering, (*c*) consulting advice from investment bankers may be beneficial, and (*d*) stockholders find exercising rights a nuisance.

All of the preceding arguments are pieces of the puzzle, but none seems very convincing. Recently, Booth and Smith identified a function of the underwriter that had not been taken into account in previous cost studies.[12] They argue that the underwriter *certifies* that the offering price is consistent with the true value of the issue. This certification is implied in the underwriting relationship and is provided when the underwriting firm gets access to inside information and puts its reputation for correct pricing on the line.

Concept Questions

- What are the several kinds of dilution?
- Is dilution important?
- Why might a firm prefer a general cash offering to a rights offering?

19.8 Shelf Registration

To simplify the procedures for issuing securities, the SEC currently allows **shelf registration.** Shelf registration permits a corporation to register an offering that it reasonably expects to sell within the next two years. A master registration statement is filed at the time of registration. The company is permitted to sell the issue whenever it wants over those two years as long as it distributes a short-form statement.

Not all companies are allowed shelf registration. The major qualifications are as follows:

1. The company must be rated *investment* grade.
2. The firm cannot have defaulted on its debt in the past twelve months.
3. The aggregate market value of the firm's outstanding stock must be more than $75 million.
4. The firm must not have violated the Securities Act of 1934 in the past twelve months.

Casual observation indicates that shelf registration is changing the basic procedures for issuing new securities. Hershman reports on the use of the *dribble* method of new equity issuance.[13] With dribbling, a company registers the issue and hires an

[12] J. Booth and R. Smith, "The Certification Role of the Investment Banker in New Issue Pricing," *Midland Corporate Finance Journal* (Spring 1986).

[13] A. Hershman, "New Strategies in Equity Financing," *Dunn's Business Monthly* (June 1983).

underwriter to be its selling agent. The company sells shares in small amounts from time to time via a stock exchange. Companies that have dribble programs include Middle South Utilities, Niagara Mohawk, Pacific Gas and Electric, and the Southern Company.

The rule has been very controversial. Several arguments have been made against shelf registration.

1. The timeliness of disclosure is reduced with shelf registration, because the master registration statement may have been prepared up to two years before the actual issue occurs.

2. Some investment bankers have argued that shelf registration will cause a market overhang, because registration informs the market of future issues. It has been suggested that this overhang will depress market prices. However, a careful empirical analysis by Bhagat, Marr, and Thompson found that shelf registration is less costly than conventional underwriting and found no evidence to suggest a market-overhang effect.[14] Surprisingly, few eligible companies are currently selling equity by using shelf registration.[15]

Concept Questions

- Describe shelf registration.
- What are the arguments against shelf registration?

19.9 Venture Capital

The previous sections of this chapter assume that a company is big enough and old enough to raise capital in the public equity markets. Of course, there are many firms that have not reached this stage. These small and young firms often find it more convenient to raise funds in that part of the private financial marketplace known as the market for venture capital. Venture capital can be viewed as "early-stage financing of new and young companies seeking to grow rapidly."[16]

Suppliers of Venture Capital

There are at least four types of suppliers of venture capital. First, a few old-line, wealthy families have traditionally provided start-up capital to promising businesses. For example, over the years, the Rockefeller family has made the initial capital contribution to a number of successful businesses. These families have been involved in venture capital for the better part of this century, if not longer.

Second, a number of private partnerships and corporations have been formed to provide investment funds. The organizer behind the partnership might raise capital from institutional investors, such as insurance companies and pension funds. Alternatively, a group of individuals might provide the funds to be ultimately invested with budding entrepreneurs.

[14] S. Bhagat, M. W. Marr, and G. R. Thompson, "The Rule 415 Experiment: Equity Markets," *Journal of Finance* 19 (December 1985).

[15] R. Rogowski and E. Sorenson, "Deregulation in Investment Banking: Shelf Registration, Structure, and Performance," *Financial Management* (Spring 1985).

[16] S. E. Pratt, "Overview and Introduction to the Venture Capital Industry," *Guide to Venture Capital Sources,* 10th ed., 1987 (Venture Economics. Laurel Avenue, Box 348, Wellesley Hills, MA 02181).

Of the early partnerships, the most well-known is clearly American Research and Development (ARD), which was formed in 1946. Though ARD invested in many companies, its success was largely due to its investment in Digital Equipment Company (DEC). When Textron acquired ARD in 1972, over 85 percent of the shareholders' distribution was due to the investment in DEC.[17] Among the more recent venture capitalists, Arthur Rock & Co. of San Francisco may very well be the best known. Because of its huge success with Apple Computer and other high-tech firms, it has achieved near mythic stature in the venture-capital industry.

Recent estimates put the number of venture-capital firms at about 2,000. Pratt's *Guide to Venture Capital* (Venture Economics) provides a list of the names of many of these firms.[18] The average amount invested per venture has been estimated to be between $1 million and $2 million. However, one should not make too much of this figure, because the amount of financing varies considerably with the venture to be funded.

Stories used to abound about how easily an individual could obtain venture capital. Though that may have been the case in an earlier era, it is certainly not the case today. Venture-capital firms employ various screening procedures to prevent inappropriate funding. For example, because of the large demand for funds, many venture capitalists have at least one employee whose full-time job consists of reading business plans. Only the very best plans can expect to attract funds. Maier and Walker indicate that only about 2 percent of requests actually receive financing.[19]

Third, large industrial or financial corporations have established venture-capital subsidiaries. The Lambda Fund of Drexel Burnham Lambert, Manufacturers Hanover Venture Capital Corp., Citicorp Venture Capital, and Chemical Venture Capital Corporation of Chemical Bank are examples of this type. However, subsidiaries of this type appear to make up only a small portion of the venture-capital market.

Fourth, participants in an informal venture-capital market have recently been identified.[20] Rather than belonging to any venture-capital firm, these investors (often referred to as *angels*) act as individuals when providing financing. However, they should not, by any means, be viewed as isolated. Wetzel and others indicate that there is a rich network of angels, continually relying on each other for advice. A number of researchers have stressed that, in any informal network, there is likely one knowledgeable and trustworthy individual who, when backing a venture, brings a few less experienced investors in with him.

The venture-capital community has unfortunately chosen to refer to these individuals as "dumb dentists." Although a number indeed may be dentists, their lack of intelligence should not be called into question. Wetzel argues that the prototypical angel has income over $100,000, net worth over $1,000,000, and substantial business experience and knowledge. As one might expect, the informal venture capitalist is able to tolerate high risks.

Though this informal market may seem small and unimportant, it is perhaps the largest of all sources of venture capital. Wetzel argues that aggregate investments from this source total around $50 billion, about twice the amount invested by more profes-

[17] H. Stevenson, D. Muzka, and J. Timmons, "Venture Capital in Transition: A Monte-Carlo Simulation of Changes in Investment Patterns," *Journal of Business Venturing* (Spring 1987).

[18] Pratt, "Overview and Introduction to the Venture Capital Industry."

[19] J. B. Maier and D. Walker, "The Role of Venture Capital in Financing Small Business," *Journal of Business Venturing* (Summer 1987).

[20] See W. E. Wetzel, "The Informal Venture Capital Market: Aspects of Scale and Market Efficiency," *Journal of Business Venturing* (Fall 1987).

sional venture capitalists. The size of each contribution is smaller here. Perhaps, on average, only $250,000 per venture is raised when the informal market is tapped.

Stages of Financing

A. V. Bruno and T. T. Tyebjee identify six stages in venture-capital financing:[21]

1. *Seed-Money Stage.* A small amount of financing needed to prove a concept or develop a product. Marketing is not included in this stage.
2. *Start-Up.* Financing for firms that started within the past year. Funds are likely to pay for marketing and product development expenditures.
3. *First-Round Financing.* Additional money to begin sales and manufacturing after a firm has spent its start-up funds.
4. *Second-Round Financing.* Funds earmarked for working capital for a firm that is currently selling its product but still losing money.
5. *Third-Round Financing.* Financing for a company that is at least breaking even and is contemplating an expansion. This is also known as mezzanine financing.
6. *Fourth-Round Financing.* Money provided for firms that are likely to go public within half a year. This round is also known as bridge financing.

Although these categories may seem vague to the reader, we have found that the terms are well-accepted within the industry. For example, the venture-capital firms listed in Pratt's *Guide to Venture Capital* indicate which of the above stages they are interested in financing.

The penultimate stage in venture capital finance is the initial public offering.[22] Venture capitalists are very important participants in initial public offerings. Venture capitalists rarely sell all of the shares they own at the time of the initial public offering. Instead, they usually sell out in subsequent public offerings. However, there is considerable evidence that venture capitalists can successfully time IPOs by taking firms public when the market values are at the highest. This is illustrated in Figure 19.2. Figure 19.2. shows the number of IPOs of privately held venture-capital-backed biotechnology companies in each month from 1978 to 1992. The venture-capital-backed IPOs clearly coincide with the ups and downs in the biotech market index in the top panel.

Concept Questions

- What are the different sources of venture-capital financing?
- What are the different stages for companies seeking venture-capital financing?

[21] A. V. Bruno and T. T. Tyebjee, "The Entrepreneur's Search for Capital," *Journal of Business Venturing* (Winter 1985).

[22] A very influential paper by Christopher Barry, Chris J. Muscarella, John W. Peavey III, and Michael R. Vetsuypens, "The Role of Venture Capital in the Creation of Public Companies: Evidence from the Going Public Process," *Journal of Financial Economics* 27 (1990), shows that venture capitalists do not usually sell shares at the time of the initial public offering, but they usually have board seats and act as advisors to managers.

FIGURE 19.2 Initial Public Offerings by Venture-Capital-Backed Biotechnology Firms, January 1978 to September 1992

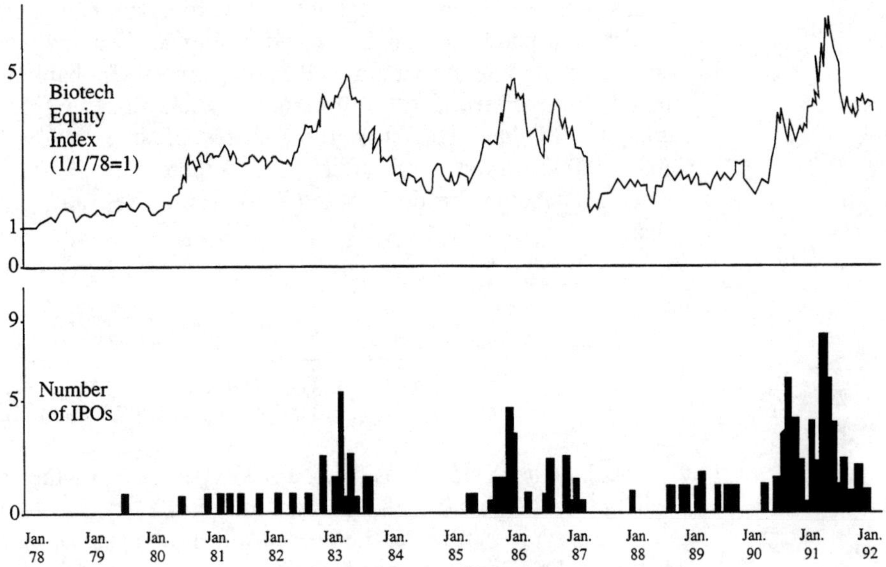

Source: Joshua Lerner, "Venture Capitalists and the Decision to Go Public," 35, *Journal of Financial Economics* (June 1994).

19.10 The Decision to Do an Initial Public Offering (IPO): The Case of Medstone International, Inc.

Most firms initially raise equity financing with private placements in the venture-capital market from a small number of investor capitalists. If a firm does well and needs to raise more equity financing, it may decide to sell stock with an initial public offering. We see how this occurs with the case of Medstone International, Inc.

Medstone International, Inc., was created in 1984 to manufacture and sell medical products using the new technology of shockwave lithotripsy. Initially, Medstone raised its cash from contributions from its founders and from banks. From 1984 to 1986 Medstone spent most of its available cash on research and development of the technology of shockwave lithotripsy. Eventually, in 1986 the company developed a product called the Medstone 1050 ST. The purpose of the Medstone 1050 ST was for nonsurgical disintegration of kidney stones and gallstones.

However, it wasn't until 1987 that the company actually generated profits from the Medstone 1050 ST (see below).

	Summary of Financial Information (in thousands)	
	1986	*1987*
Revenues	$25	$6,562
Income	(1,698)	680
Assets	865	3,205
Liabilities	6,062	5,517
Equity	(5,197)	(2,312)

By January 1988 Medstone International had obtained an investigative new drug permit from the Food and Drug Administration (FDA) and had entered into an agreement to sell and install the Medstone System in seven U.S. states. In early 1988 the firm's prospects seemed excellent and its founders had reason to be optimistic. But Medstone needed additional cash and its founders wanted the opportunity to cash out, so it hired the Weeden Co., a well-known investment banking firm, to arrange for an initial public offering (IPO) of common stock. In June 1988, Medstone went public with an IPO and sold 1 million shares of stock at $13 per share and raised $11,700,000. Immediately after the IPO there were 4,500,000 shares of Medstone stock outstanding. Insiders owned 3,500,000 shares, and outsiders owned 1,000,000 shares.

	Price to public	*Underwriting discount*	*Proceeds to company*
Per share	$13,000,000	$1,300,000	$11,700,000
Total	13,000,000	1,300,000	11,700,000

Although the stock was offered at $13 per share, by the end of the first day, it was selling for $18 (this is a 38.5 percent increase).

As is typical in IPOs, the proceeds from the sale of stock had two purposes: to reduce indebtedness to banks and to cash out insiders, and to finance present and future operations and growth opportunities.

In 1984 when Medstone was formed, it was a "startup" with no operating history and virtually no manufacturing and marketing experience. Moreover, when Medstone did its IPO, its product had not yet received final FDA approval. The company's potential was great and so were its risks of failure. The company's ultimate success depended upon its ability to form a new business, introduce new products, and successfully compete in the marketplace. However, in the case of medical products, success depends on obtaining FDA approval. Obtaining FDA approval for a new product can be a time-consuming process, and there is no guarantee that final clearance will ever be granted. Unfortunately, Medstone was never able to obtain final FDA approval.

When the company announced that it would no longer try to sell the Medstone 1050 ST, the market for its stock collapsed and the firm was forced to reorganize.

Every IPO is unique but there are some familiar themes.

1. *Underpricing.* Firms going through an IPO usually have their shares underpriced. This means that the initial market price is usually significantly less than their market price prevailing at the end of the first trading day. This is one of the indirect costs of IPOs, and Medstone's underpricing was typical.
2. *Underperformance.* The Medstone IPO did not work out very well for many of the outside investors because the firm ultimately could not sell its Medstone 1050 ST. The Medstone IPO is typical in that the average firm performs very poorly after an IPO. Three years after an IPO, the stock price of firms doing IPOs has typically fallen below the initial price. This is a puzzle and several reasons have been put forth to explain it.[23] It is consistent

[23] J. R. Ritter "The Long-Run Performance of Initial Public Offerings," *Journal of Finance* (March 1991).

3. *Going Public.* Many IPOs such as Medstone are to give inside equity investors an opportunity to exchange their private equity for public equity and cash out their stakes in the firm. Usually only a fraction of the inside equity is sold in the IPO. Later in subsequent common stock sales, the rest of the inside ownership is sold.

19.11 Summary and Conclusions

This chapter looks closely at how equity is issued. The main points follow.

1. Large issues have proportionately much lower costs of issuing equity than small ones.
2. Firm-commitment underwriting is far more prevalent for large issues than is best-efforts underwriting. Smaller issues probably primarily use best efforts because of the greater uncertainty of these issues. For an offering of a given size, the direct expenses of best-efforts underwriting and firm-commitment underwriting are of the same magnitude.
3. Rights offerings are cheaper than general cash offers and eliminate the problem of underpricing. Yet, most new equity issues are underwritten general cash offers.
4. Shelf registration is a new method of issuing new debt and equity. The direct costs of shelf issues seem to be substantially lower than those of traditional issues.
5. Venture capitalists are an increasingly important influence in start-up firms and subsequent financing.

Key Terms

Registration statement 520
Regulation A 521
Prospectus 521
Red herring 521
Tombstone 521
Initial public offering (IPO) 523
Unseasoned new issue 523
Seasoned new issue 523
Cash offer 523
Investment bankers 523
Firm commitment 524
Syndicate 525
Best efforts 525
Green Shoe provision 526
Competitive offer 527
Negotiated offer 527
Subscription price 534
Ex-rights 535
Standby underwriting 537
Standby fee 537
Oversubscription privilege 537
Shelf registration 539

Suggested Readings

The costs of issuing new equity are documented in

Ritter, J. R. "The Costs of Going Public." *Journal of Financial Economics* 19 (1987).
Smith, C. W., Jr. "Alternative Methods for Raising Capital: Rights versus Underwritten Offerings." *Journal of Financial Economics* 5 (December 1977).
Several articles that examine the puzzle of underpricing:
Ibbotson, R. G. "Price Performance of Common Stock New Issues." *Journal of Financial Economics* 2 (1975).
Ritter, J. R. "The 'Hot Issue' Market of 1980." *Journal of Business* 32 (1984).
Rock, K. "Why New Issues Are Underpriced." *Journal of Financial Economics* 15 (1986).

Rock, K. "Why New Issues Are Underpriced." *Journal of Financial Economics* 15 (1986).
Discussions of Rule 415:
Bhagat, S.; M. W. Marr; and G. R. Thompson. "The Rule 415 Experiment: Equity Markets." *Journal of Finance* 19 (December 1985).
Hershman, A. "New Strategies in Equity Financing." *Dunn's Business Monthly* (June 1983).
The effect of seasoned new equity on stock prices is discussed in
Asquith, P., and D. Mullins. "Equity Issues and Offering Dilution." *Journal of Financial Economics* 15 (1986).
Masulis, R., and A. N. Korwar. "Seasoned Equity Offerings: An Empirical Investigation." *Journal of Financial Economics* 15 (1986).
Mikkelson, W. H., and M. M. Partch. "The Valuation Effects of Security Offerings and the Issuance Process." *Journal of Financial Economics* 15 (1986).
A summary of much of the most recent research:
Hansen, R. "Evaluating the Costs of a New Equity Issue." *Midland Corporate Finance Journal* (Spring 1986).
Ibbotson, R. G.; J. L. Sindelar; and J. R. Ritter. "Initial Public Offerings." *Journal of Applied Corporate Finance* 1 (Summer 1988).
The long-run performance of IPOs is discussed in
Ritter, J. R. "The Long-Run Performance of Initial Public Offerings." *Journal of Finance* (March 1991) pp. 3–27.

Questions and Problems

The Public Issue

19.1 Define the following terms related to the issuance of public securities.
a. General cash offer
b. Rights offer
c. Registration statement
d. Prospectus
e. Initial public offering
f. Seasoned new issue
g. Shelf registration

19.2 *a.* What does the Securities Exchange Act of 1933 regulate?
b. What does the Securities Exchange Act of 1934 regulate?

The Cash Offer

19.3 What are the comparative advantages of competitive offer and negotiated offer respectively?

19.4 Define the following terms related to underwriting.
a. Firm commitment
b. Syndicate
c. Spread
d. Best efforts

19.5 *a.* Who bears the risk in firm-commitment underwriting? Explain.
b. Who bears the risk in best-efforts underwriting? Explain.

19.6 Suppose the Newton Company has 10,000 shares of stock. Each share is worth $40, and the company's market value of equity is $400,000. Suppose the firm issues 5,000 shares of new stock at the following prices: $40, $20, and $10. What will be the effect of each of the alternative offering prices on the existing price per share?

19.7 In 1980 a certain assistant professor of finance bought 12 initial public offerings of common stock. He held each of these for approximately one month and then sold them. The investment rule he followed was to submit a purchase order for every firm-commitment initial public offering of oil- and gas-exploration companies. There were

22 such offerings, and he submitted a purchase order for approximately $1,000 of stock for each one. With 10 of these, no shares were allocated to this assistant professor. With five of the 12 offerings that were purchased, fewer than the requested number of shares were allocated.

The year 1980 was very good for oil- and gas-exploration company owners: For the 22 stocks that went public, the stock was selling on average for 80 percent above the offering price within a month. Yet, this assistant professor looked at his performance record and found the $8,400 invested in the 12 companies had grown to only $10,100, a return of only about 20 percent. (Commissions were negligible.) Did he have bad luck, or should he have expected to do worse than the average initial-public-offering investor? Explain.

The Announcement of New Equity and the Value of the Firm

19.8 What are the possible reasons for why the stock price typically drops on the announcement of a seasoned new equity issue?

The Cost of New Issues

19.9 What are the costs of new issues?

Rights

19.10 Bountiful Beef Processors (BBP) wants to raise equity through a rights offering. BBP has 2,400,000 shares of common stock outstanding, and must raise $12,000,000. The subscription price of the rights will be $15.

a. How many new shares of stock must BBP issue?
b. How many rights will be necessary to purchase one share of stock?
c. What must a shareholder remit to receive one share of stock?

19.11 Jelly Beans, Inc., is proposing a rights offering. There are 100,000 outstanding shares at $25 each. There will be 10,000 new shares issued at a $20 subscription price.

a. What is the value of a right?
b. What is the ex-rights price?
c. What is the new market value of the company?
d. Why might a company have a rights offering rather than a common stock offering?

19.12 Superior, Inc., is a manufacturer of beta-blockers. Management has concluded that additional equity financing is required to increase production capacity, and that these funds are best attained through a rights offering. It has correctly concluded that, as a result of the rights offering, share price will fall from $50 to $45 ($50 is the rights-on price; $45 is the ex-rights price, also known as the *when-issued* price). The company is seeking $5 million in additional funds with a per-share subscription price equal to $25.

How many shares were there before the offering?

19.13 A company's stock currently sells for $45 per share. Last week the firm issued rights to raise new equity. To purchase a new share, a stockholder must remit $10 and three rights.

a. What is the ex-rights stock price?
b. What is the price of one right?
c. When will the price drop occur? Why will it occur then?

19.14 Summit Corp.'s stock is currently selling at $13 per share. There are 1 million shares outstanding. The firm is planning to raise $2 million to finance a new project. What is the ex-right stock price, the value of a right and the appropriate subscription prices, if

a. Two shares of outstanding stock are entitled to purchase one additional share of the new issue.
b. Four shares of outstanding stock are entitled to purchase one additional share of the new issue.
c. How does the stockholders' wealth change from *a* to *b?*

The New Issue Puzzle

19.15 Megabucks Industries is planning to raise fresh equity capital by selling a large new issue of common stock. Megabucks is a publicly traded corporation, and is trying to choose between an underwritten cash offer and a rights offering (not underwritten) to current shareholders. Megabucks management is interested in maximizing the wealth of current shareholders and has asked you for advice on the choice of issue methods. What is your recommendation? Why?

Shelf Registration

19.16 Explain why shelf registration has been used by many firms instead of syndication.

Venture Capital

19.17 Who are the different suppliers of venture capital?

The Decision to Do an Initial Public Offering (IPO): The Case of Medstone International, Inc.

19.18 What are the uses for the proceeds from an IPO?

19.19 Every IPO is unique, but what are the basic empirical regularities in IPOs?

CHAPTER

22 Warrants and Convertibles

We study two financing instruments in this chapter, warrants and convertibles. A warrant gives the holder the right to buy common stock for cash. In this sense, it is very much like a call. Warrants are generally issued with privately placed bonds, though they are also combined with new issues of common stock and preferred stock. In the case of new issues of common stock, warrants are sometimes given to investment bankers as compensation for underwriting services.

A convertible bond gives the holder the right to exchange the bond for common stock. Therefore, it is a mixed security blurring the traditional line between stocks and bonds. There is also convertible preferred stock.

The chapter describes the basic features of warrants and convertibles. Here are some of the most important questions concerning warrants and convertibles:

1. How can warrants and convertibles be valued?
2. What impact do warrants and convertibles have on the value of the firm?
3. What are the differences between warrants, convertibles, and call options?
4. Why do some companies issue bonds with warrants and convertible bonds?
5. Under what circumstances are warrants and convertibles converted into common stock?

22.1 Warrants

Warrants are securities that give holders the right, but not the obligation, to buy shares of common stock directly from a company at a fixed price for a given period of time. Each warrant specifies the number of shares of stock that the holder can buy, the exercise price, and the expiration date.

From the preceding description of warrants, it is clear that they are similar to call options. The differences in contractual features between warrants and the call options that trade on the Chicago Board Options Exchange are small. For example, warrants have longer maturity periods.[1] Some warrants are actually perpetual, meaning that they never expire at all.

[1] Warrants are usually protected against stock splits and dividends in the same way that call options are.

FIGURE 22.1 Safeway Warrants on April 26, 1990

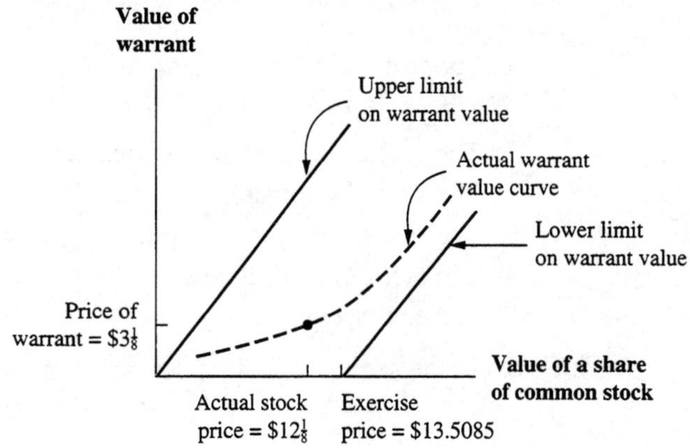

Warrants are referred to as *equity kickers* because they are usually issued in combination with privately placed bonds.[2] In most cases, warrants are attached to the bonds when issued. The loan agreement will state whether the warrants are detachable from the bond, that is, whether they can be sold separately. Usually the warrant can be detached immediately.

• ***Example***
Safeway, Inc., is one of the nation's largest supermarket chains. On November 24, 1986, Safeway was acquired in a levered buyout by the private investment firm Kohlberg Kravis Roberts and Co. (KKR). Each share of old common stock was converted into a junior subordinated debenture (i.e., junk bond) and a "merger" warrant. Each warrant gives the holder the right to purchase .279 shares of new common stock for $1.052 per warrant. To purchase one share of common stock, a holder must give up 3.584 warrants and pay an amount of $3.7691 per warrant. This makes the exercise price of the Safeway warrants equal to $13.5085 ($3.584 \times \$3.7691 = \$13.5085$). The warrants expire on November 24, 1996. They are called *merger warrants* because Safeway issued the warrants in a buyout of old shares.

When Safeway was acquired by KKR, it was a private firm with no publicly traded common stock or warrants. However, KKR took Safeway public on April 26, 1990, by issuing 10 million shares in a new issue of common stock. The stock was listed on the New York Stock Exchange. On that day, several thousand warrants were traded at a closing price of 3⅛. The price of Safeway common stock was 12⅛. •

The relationship between the value of Safeway's warrants and its stock price can be viewed like the relationship between a call option and its stock price, described in a previous chapter. Figure 22.1 depicts the relationship for Safeway warrants. The lower limit on the value of the warrants is zero if Safeway's stock price is below $13.5085 per share. If the price of Safeway's common stock rises above $13.5085 per share, the lower limit is the stock price minus $13.5085 divided by 3.584.[3] The upper

[2] Warrants are also issued with publicly distributed bonds and new issues of common stock.
[3] We need to divide by 3.584 because it takes 3.584 warrants to purchase one share of stock.

limit is the price of Safeway's common stock divided by 3.584. A warrant to buy one share of common stock cannot sell at a price above the price of the underlying common stock.

The price of Safeway warrants on April 26, 1990, was higher than the lower limit. The height of the warrant price above the lower limit will depend on the following:

1. The variance of Safeway's stock returns.
2. The time to expiration date.
3. The risk-free rate of interest.
4. The stock price of Safeway.
5. The exercise price.

These are the same factors that determine the value of a call option.

22.2 The Difference between Warrants and Call Options

From the holder's point of view, warrants are similar to call options on common stock. A warrant, like a call option, gives its holder the right to buy common stock at a specified price. Warrants usually have an expiration date, though in most cases they are issued with longer lives than call options. From the firm's point of view, however, a warrant is very different from a call option on the company's common stock.

The most important difference between call options and warrants is that call options are issued by individuals and warrants are issued by firms. When a warrant is exercised, a firm must issue new shares of stock. Each time a warrant is exercised, then, the number of shares outstanding increases.

To illustrate, suppose the Endrun Company issues a warrant giving holders the right to buy one share of common stock at $25. Further suppose the warrant is exercised. Endrun must print one new stock certificate. In exchange for the stock certificate, it receives $25 from the holder.

In contrast, when a call option is exercised, there is no change in the number of shares outstanding. Suppose Ms. Eager holds a call option on the common stock of the Endrun Company. The call option gives Ms. Eager the right to buy one share of the common stock of the Endrun Company for $25. If Ms. Eager chooses to exercise the call option, a seller, say Mr. Swift, is obligated to give her one share of Endrun's common stock in exchange for $25. If Mr. Swift does not already own a share, he must enter the stock market and buy one. The call option is a side bet between buyers and sellers on the value of the Endrun Company's common stock. When a call option is exercised, one investor gains and the other loses. The total number of shares outstanding of the Endrun Company remains constant, and no new funds are made available to the company.

• ***Example***

To see how warrants affect the value of the firm, imagine that Mr. Gould and Ms. Rockefeller are two investors who have together purchased six ounces of platinum. At the time they bought the platinum, Mr. Gould and Ms. Rockefeller each contributed one half of the cost, which we will assume was $3,000 for six ounces, or $500 an ounce (they each contributed $1,500). They incorporated, printed two stock certificates, and named the firm the GR Company. Each certificate represents a one-half claim to the platinum. Mr. Gould and Ms. Rockefeller each own one certificate. Mr. Gould and Ms. Rockefeller have formed a company with platinum as its only asset.

A Call Is Issued Suppose Mr. Gould later decides to sell to Mrs. Fiske a call option issued on Mr. Gould's share. The call option gives Mrs. Fiske the right to buy Mr. Gould's share for $1,800 within the next year. If the price of platinum rises above $600 per ounce, the firm will be worth more than $3,600 and each share will be worth more than $1,800. If Mrs. Fiske decides to exercise her option, Mr. Gould must turn over his stock certificate and receive $1,800.

How would the firm be affected by the exercise? The number of shares will remain the same. There will still be two shares, now owned by Ms. Rockefeller and Mrs. Fiske. If the price of platinum rises to $700 an ounce, each share will be worth $2,100 ($4,200/2). If Mrs. Fiske exercises her option at this price, she will profit by $300.

A Warrant Is Issued Instead This story changes if a warrant is issued. Suppose that Mr. Gould does not sell a call option to Mrs. Fiske. Instead, Mr. Gould and Ms. Rockefeller have a stockholders' meeting. They vote that GR Company will issue a warrant and sell it to Mrs. Fiske. The warrant will give Mrs. Fiske the right to receive a share of the company at an exercise price of $1,800.[4] If Mrs. Fiske decides to exercise the warrant, the firm will issue another stock certificate and give it to Mrs. Fiske in exchange for $1,800.

From Mrs. Fiske's perspective, the call option and the warrant *seem* to be the same. The exercise prices of the warrant and the call are the same: $1,800. It is still advantageous for Mrs. Fiske to exercise the option when the price of platinum exceeds $600 per ounce. However, we will show that Mrs. Fiske actually makes less in the warrant situation due to dilution.

The GR Company must also consider dilution. Suppose the price of platinum increases to $700 an ounce and Mrs. Fiske exercises her warrant. Two things will occur:

1. Mrs. Fiske will pay $1,800 to the firm.
2. The firm will print one stock certificate and give it to Mrs. Fiske. The stock certificate will represent a one-third claim on the platinum of the firm.

Because Mrs. Fiske contributes $1,800 to the firm, the value of the firm increases. It is now worth

$$\begin{aligned}\text{New value of firm} &= \text{Value of platinum} + \text{Contribution to the firm by Mrs. Fiske}\\ &= \$4{,}200 + \$1{,}800\\ &= \$6{,}000\end{aligned}$$

Because Mrs. Fiske has a one-third claim on the firm's value, her share is worth $2,000 ($6,000/3). By exercising the warrant, Mrs. Fiske gains $2,000 − $1,800 = $200. This is illustrated in Table 22.1.

Dilution Why does Mrs. Fiske only gain $200 in the warrant case while gaining $300 in the call option case? The key is dilution, that is, the creation of another share. In the call option case, she contributes $1,800 and receives one of the two outstand-

---

[4] The sale of the warrant brings cash into the firm. We assume that the sale proceeds immediately leave the firm through a cash dividend to Mr. Gould and Ms. Rockefeller. This simplifies the analysis, because the firm with warrants then has the same total value as the firm without warrants.

TABLE 22.1 Effect of Call Option and Warrant on the GR Company*

	Price of Platinum per Share	
Value of Firm if:	*$700*	*$600*
No warrant		
Mr. Gould's share	$2,100	$1,800
Ms. Rockefeller's share	2,100	1,800
Firm	$4,200	$3,600
Call option		
Mr. Gould's claim	$ 0	$1,800
Ms. Rockefeller's claim	2,100	1,800
Mrs. Fiske's claim	2,100	0
Firm	$4,200	$3,600
Warrant		
Mr. Gould's share	$2,000	$1,800
Ms. Rockefeller's share	2,000	1,800
Mrs. Fiske's share	2,000	0
Firm	$6,000	$3,600

*If the price of platinum is $700, the value of the firm is equal to the value of six ounces of platinum plus the excess dollars paid into the firm by Mrs. Fiske. This amount is $4,200 + $1,800 = $6,000.

ing shares. That is, she receives a share worth $2,100(½ × $4,200). Her gain is $300 ($2,100 − $1,800). We rewrite this gain as

Gain on Exercise of Call:

$$\frac{\$4{,}200}{2} - \$1{,}800 = \$300 \qquad (22.1)$$

In the warrant case, she contributes $1,800 and receives a newly created share. She now owns one of the three outstanding shares. Because the $1,800 remains in the firm, her share is worth $2,000 ($4,200 + $1,800)/3. Her gain is $200 ($2,000 − $1,800). We rewrite this gain as

Gain on Exercise of Warrant:

$$\frac{\$4{,}200 + \$1{,}800}{2 + 1} - \$1{,}800 = \$200 \qquad (22.2)$$

Warrants also affect accounting numbers. Warrants and (as we shall see) convertible bonds cause the number of shares to increase. This causes the firm's net income to be spread over a larger number of shares, thereby decreasing earnings per share. Firms with significant amounts of warrants and convertible issues must report earnings on a *primary* basis and a *fully diluted* basis. •

How the Firm Can Hurt Warrant Holders

The platinum firm owned by Mr. Gould and Ms. Rockefeller has issued a warrant to Mrs. Fiske that is *in the money* and about to expire. One way that Mr. Gould and Ms. Rockefeller can hurt Mrs. Fiske is to pay themselves a large dividend. This could be funded by selling a substantial amount of platinum. The value of the firm would fall, and the warrant would be worth much less.

Concept Questions

- What is the key difference between a warrant and a traded call option?
- Why does dilution occur when warrants are exercised?
- How can the firm hurt warrant holders?

22.3 Warrant Pricing and the Black-Scholes Model (Advanced)

We now wish to express the gains from exercising a call and a warrant in more general terms. The gain on a call can be written as

Gain from Exercising a Single Call:

$$\underbrace{\frac{\text{Firm's value net of debt}}{\#}}_{\text{(Value of a share of stock)}} - \text{Exercise price} \tag{22.3}$$

Equation (22.3) generalizes equation (22.1). We define the *firm's value net of debt* to be the total firm value less the value of the debt. The total firm value is $4,200 in our example and there is no debt. The # stands for the number of shares outstanding, which is 2 in our example. The ratio on the left is the value of a share of stock. The gain on a warrant can be written as

Gain from Exercising a Single Warrant:

$$\underbrace{\frac{\text{Firm's value net of debt} + \text{Exercise price} \times \#_w}{\# + \#_w}}_{\text{(Value of a share of stock after warrant is exercised)}} - \text{Exercise price} \tag{22.4}$$

Equation (22.4) generalizes (22.2). The numerator on the left-hand term is the firm's value net of debt *after* the warrant is exercised. It is the sum of the firm's value net of debt *prior* to the warrant's exercise plus the proceeds the firm receives from the exercise. The proceeds equal the product of the exercise price multiplied by the number of warrants. The number of warrants appears as $\#_w$. (Our analysis uses the plausible assumption that all warrants in the money will be exercised.) Note that $\#_w = 1$ in our numerical example. The denominator, $\# + \#_w$, is the number of shares outstanding *after* the exercise of the warrants. The ratio on the left is the value of a share of stock after exercise. By rearranging terms, (22.4) can be rewritten as[5]

Gain from Exercising a Single Warrant:

$$\frac{\#}{\# + \#_w} \times \underbrace{\left(\frac{\text{Firm's value net of debt}}{\#} - \text{Exercise price}\right)}_{\text{(Gain from a call on a firm with no warrants)}} \tag{22.5}$$

Formula (22.5) relates the gain on a warrant to the gain on a call. Note that the term within parentheses is (22.3). Thus, the gain from exercising a warrant is a proportion of the gain from exercising a call in a firm without warrants. The proportion #/(# +

[5] To derive (22.5), one should separate "Exercise price" in (22.4). This yields

$$\frac{\text{Firm's value net of debt}}{\# + \#_w} - \frac{\#}{\# + \#_w} \times \text{Exercise price}$$

By rearranging terms, one can obtain (22.5).

$\#_w$) is the ratio of the number of shares in the firm without warrants to the number of shares after all the warrants have been exercised. This ratio must always be less than 1. Thus, the gain on a warrant must be less than the gain on an identical call in a firm without warrants. Note that $\#/(\# + \#_w) = 200/300 = 2/3$ in our example, which explains why Mrs. Fiske gains $300 on her call yet gains only $200 on her warrant.

The above implies that the Black-Scholes model must be adjusted for warrants. When a call option is issued to Mrs. Fiske, we know that the exercise price is $1,800 and the time to expiration is one year. Though we have posited neither the price of the stock, the variance of the stock, nor the interest rate, we could easily provide these data for a real-world situation. Thus, we could use the Black-Scholes model to value Mrs. Fiske's call.

Suppose that the warrant is to be issued tomorrow to Mrs. Fiske. We know the number of warrants to be issued, the warrant's expiration date, and the exercise price. Using our assumption that the warrant proceeds are immediately paid out as a dividend, we could use the Black-Scholes model to value the warrant. We would first calculate the value of an identical call. The warrant price is the call price multiplied by the ratio $\#/(\# + \#_w)$. As mentioned earlier, this ratio is 2/3 in our example.

22.4 Convertible Bonds

A **convertible bond** is similar to a bond with warrants. The most important difference is that a bond with warrants can be separated into distinct securities and a convertible bond cannot. A convertible bond gives the holder the right to exchange it for a given number of shares of stock anytime up to and including the maturity date of the bond.

Preferred stock can frequently be converted into common stock. A convertible preferred stock is the same as a convertible bond except that it has an infinite maturity date.

- ***Example***

Crazy Eddie was a New York retailer of home entertainment and consumer electronic products. Its stock was traded over the counter (OTC). On June 21, 1989, Crazy Eddie filed for bankruptcy under Chapter 11 of the federal bankruptcy code. Several months later it closed all of its remaining stores.

On June 24, 1986, Crazy Eddie raised $72 million by issuing 6-percent convertible subordinated debentures due in 2011. It planned to use the proceeds to add new stores to its chain. Like typical debentures, they had a sinking fund and were callable after two years. Crazy Eddie bonds differed from other debentures in their convertible feature: Each bond was convertible into 21.62 shares of the common stock of Crazy Eddie anytime before maturity. The number of shares received for each bond (21.62 in this example) is called the **conversion ratio.**

Bond traders also speak of the **conversion price** of the bond. This is calculated as the ratio of the face value of the bond to the conversion ratio. Because the face value of each Crazy Eddie bond was $1,000, the conversion ratio was $46.25 ($1,000/21.62). The bondholders of Crazy Eddie could give up bonds with a face value of $1,000 and receive 21.62 shares of Crazy Eddie common stock. This was equivalent to paying $46.25 ($1,000/21.62) for each share of Crazy Eddie common stock received.

When Crazy Eddie issued its convertible bonds, its common stock was trading at $38 per share. The conversion price of $46.25 was 22 percent higher than the actual common-stock price. This 22 percent is referred to as the **conversion premium.** It reflects the fact that the conversion option in Crazy Eddie convertible bonds was *out of the money.* This conversion premium is typical.

Convertibles are almost always protected against stock splits and stock dividends. If Crazy Eddie's common stock had been split two for one, the conversion ratio would have been increased from 21.62 to 43.24. •

Conversion ratio, conversion price, and conversion premium are well-known terms in the real world. For that reason alone, the student should master the concepts. However, conversion price and conversion premium implicitly assume that the bond is selling at par. If the bond is selling at another price, the terms have little meaning. By contrast, conversion ratio can have a meaningful interpretation regardless of the price of the bond.

Concept Question

- What are the conversion ratio, the conversion price, and the conversion premium?

22.5 The Value of Convertible Bonds

The value of a convertible bond can be described in terms of three components: straight bond value, conversion value, and option value.[6] We examine these three components below.

Straight Bond Value

The straight bond value is what the convertible bonds would sell for if they could not be converted into common stock. It will depend on the general level of interest rates and on the default risk. Suppose that straight debentures issued by Crazy Eddie had been rated A, and A-rated bonds were priced to yield 10 percent on June 24, 1986. The straight bond value of Crazy Eddie convertible bonds can be determined by discounting the coupon payment and principal amount at 10 percent:[7]

$$\begin{aligned}\text{Straight bond} &= \sum_{t=1}^{25} \frac{\$60}{(1.1)^t} + \frac{\$1{,}000}{(1.1)^{25}} \\ &= \$60 \times A_{0.10}^{25} + \frac{\$1{,}000}{(1.1)^{25}} \\ &= \$544.6 + \$92.3 \\ &= \$636.9\end{aligned}$$

The straight bond value of a convertible bond is a minimum value. The price of Crazy Eddie's convertible could not have gone lower than the straight bond value. The straight-bond-value portion of a convertible will depend on the market's assessment of default risk.

When Crazy Eddie experienced poor economic results, its bond value declined. We know from previous discussions that the value of straight bonds is related to the

[6] For a similar treatment see Richard Brealey and Stewart Myers, *Principles of Corporate Finance,* 2nd ed. (New York: McGraw-Hill, 1984), chapter 23; and James C. Van Horne, *Financial Markets and Flows,* 2nd ed. (Engelwood Cliffs, N.J.: Prentice Hall, 1987), chapter 11.

[7] This formula assumes that coupons are paid annually.

FIGURE 22.2 The Market Value of Convertible Bonds

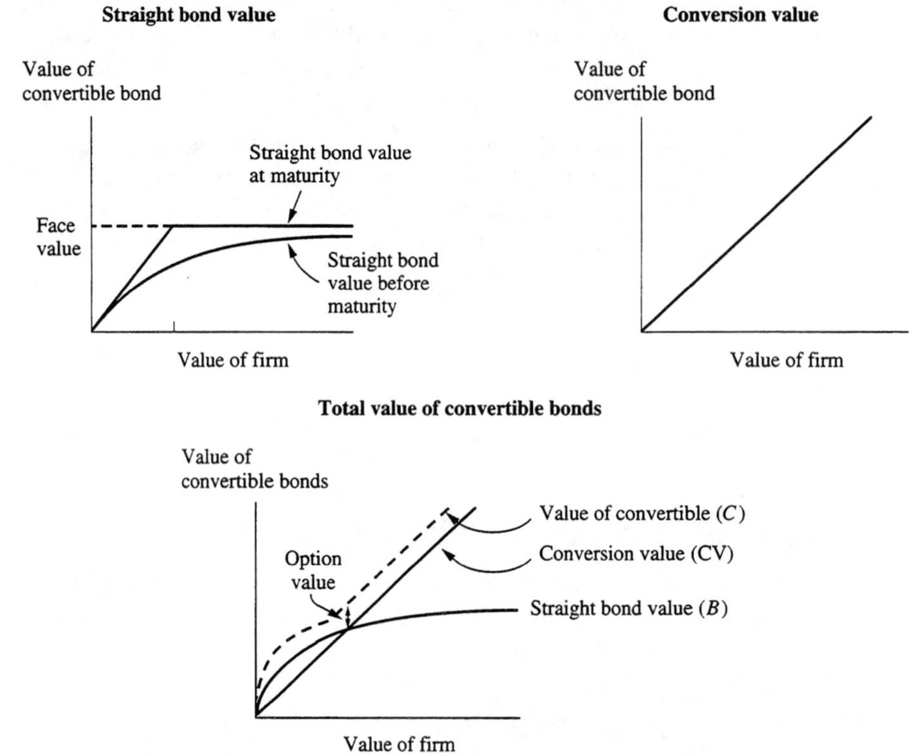

See Richard Brealey and Stewart Myers, *Principles of Corporate Finance,* 2nd ed. (New York: McGraw-Hill, 1984); and James C. Van Horne, *Financial Rates and Flows,* 3rd ed. (Englewood Cliffs, N.J.: Prentice Hall, 1987), chapter 11.

The actual value of a convertible is always higher than either its straight bond value or its conversion value.

value of the firm. The upper left-hand corner of Figure 22.2 illustrates the relationship between straight bond value and firm value. If the value of Crazy Eddie's retail stores became zero, the value of the Crazy Eddie bonds would be zero. Conversely, Crazy Eddie's straight debt could be worth, at most, only the value of an equivalent risk-free bond.

Conversion Value

The value of convertible bonds depends on conversion value. **Conversion value** is what the bonds would be worth if they were immediately converted into the common stock at current prices. Typically, conversion value is computed by multiplying the number of shares of common stock that will be received when the bond is converted by the current price of the common stock.

On June 24, 1986, each Crazy Eddie convertible bond could have been converted into 21.62 shares of Crazy Eddie common stock. Crazy Eddie common was selling for \$38. Thus, the conversion value was 21.62 × \$38 = \$821.56. A convertible cannot sell for less than its conversion value. Arbitrage prevents this from happening. If

Crazy Eddie's convertible sold for less than $821.56, investors would have bought the bonds and converted them into common stock and sold the stock. The profit would have been the difference between the value of the stock sold and the bond's conversion value.

Thus, convertible bonds have two minimum values: the straight bond value and the conversion value. The conversion value is determined by the value of the firm's underlying common stock. This is illustrated in the upper right-hand corner of Figure 22.2. As the value of common stock rises and falls, the conversion price rises and falls with it. When the value of Crazy Eddie's common stock increased by $1, the conversion value of its convertible bonds increased by $21.62.

Option Value

The value of a convertible bond will generally exceed both the straight bond value and the conversion value.[8] This occurs because holders of convertibles need not convert immediately. Instead, by waiting they can take advantage of whichever is greater in the future, the straight bond value or the conversion value. This option to wait has value, and it raises the value over both the straight bond value and the conversion value.

When the value of the firm is low, the value of convertible bonds is most significantly influenced by their underlying value as straight debt. However, when the value of the firm is very high, the value of convertible bonds is mostly determined by their underlying conversion value. This is illustrated in the bottom portion of Figure 22.2.

The bottom portion of the figure implies that the value of a convertible bond is the maximum of its straight bond value and its conversion value, plus its option value:

$$\text{Value of convertible bond} = \text{The greater of (Straight bond value, Conversion value)} + \text{Option value}$$

• ***Example***

Suppose the Moulton Company has outstanding 1,000 shares of common stock and 100 bonds. Each bond has a face value of $1,000 at maturity. They are discount bonds and pay no coupons. At maturity each bond can be converted into 10 shares of newly issued common stock.

What are the circumstances that will make it advantageous for the holders of Moulton convertible bonds to convert to common stock at maturity?

If the holders of the convertible bonds convert, they will receive $100 \times 10 =$ 1,000 shares of common stock. Because there were already 1,000 shares, the total number of shares outstanding becomes 2,000 upon conversion. Thus, converting bondholders own 50 percent of the value of the firm, V. If they do not convert, they will receive $100,000 or V, whichever is less. The choice for the holders of the Moulton bonds is obvious. They should convert if 50 percent of V is greater than $100,000. This will be true whenever V is greater than $200,000. This is illustrated as follows:

[8] The most plausible exception is when conversion would provide the investor with a dividend much greater than the interest available prior to conversion. The optimal strategy here could very well be to convert immediately, implying that the market value of the bond would exactly equal the conversion value. Other exceptions occur when the firm is in default or the bondholders are forced to convert.

Payoff to Convertible Bondholders and Stockholders of the Moulton Company

	(1) $V \leq \$100,000$	(2) $\$100,000 < V \leq \$200,000$	(3) $V > \$200,000$
Decision:	Bondholder Will Not Convert	Bondholders Will Not Convert	Bondholders Will Convert
Convertible bondholders	V	\$100,000	$0.5V$
Stockholders	0	$V - \$100,000$	$0.5V$

Concept Questions

- What three elements make up the value of a convertible bond?
- Describe the payoff structure of convertible bonds.

22.6 Reasons for Issuing Warrants and Convertibles

Probably there is no other area of corporate finance where real-world practitioners get as confused as they do on the reasons for issuing convertible debt. In order to separate fact from fantasy, we present a rather structured argument. We first compare convertible debt with straight debt. Then we compare convertible debt with equity. For each comparison, we ask in what situations is the firm better off with convertible debt and in what situations is it worse off.

Convertible Debt versus Straight Debt

Convertible debt pays a lower interest rate than does otherwise-identical straight debt. For example, if the interest rate is 10 percent on straight debt, the interest rate on convertible debt might be 9 percent. Investors will accept a lower interest rate on a convertible because of the potential gain from conversion.

Imagine a firm that seriously considers both convertible debt and straight debt finally deciding to issue convertibles. When would this decision have benefited the firm and when would it have hurt the firm? We consider two situations.

The Stock Price Later Rises so that Conversion Is Indicated
The firm clearly likes to see the stock price rise. However, it would have benefited even more had it previously issued straight debt instead of a convertible. While the firm paid out a lower interest rate than it would have with straight debt, it was obligated to sell the convertible holders a chunk of the equity at a below-market price.

The Stock Price Later Falls or Does Not Rise Enough to Justify Conversion
The firm hates to see the stock price fall. However, as long as the stock price does fall, it is glad that it had previously issued convertible debt instead of straight debt. This is because the interest rate on convertible debt is lower. Because conversion does not take place, our comparison of interest rates is all that is needed.

Summary
Compared to straight debt, the firm is worse off having issued convertible debt if the underlying stock subsequently does well. The firm is better off having issued convertible debt if the underlying stock subsequently does poorly. In an efficient market, one cannot predict future stock price. Thus, we cannot argue that convertibles either dominate or are dominated by straight debt.

Convertible Debt versus Common Stock

Next, imagine a firm that seriously considers both convertible debt and common stock finally deciding to issue convertibles. When would this decision have benefited the firm and when would it have hurt the firm? We consider our two situations.

The Stock Price Later Rises so that Conversion Is Indicated

The firm is better off having previously issued a convertible instead of equity. To see this, consider the Crazy Eddie case. The firm could have issued stock for $38. Instead, by issuing a convertible, the firm effectively received $46.25 for a share upon conversion.

The Stock Price Later Falls or Does Not Rise Enough to Justify Conversion

No firm wants to see the stock price fall. However, given that the price did fall, the firm would have been better off if it had previously issued stock instead of a convertible. The firm would have benefited by issuing stock above its later market price. That is, the firm would have received more than the subsequent worth of the stock. However, the drop in stock price did not affect the value of the convertible much because the straight bond value serves as a floor.

Summary

Compared with equity, the firm is better off having issued convertible debt if the underlying stock subsequently does well. The firm is worse off having issued convertible debt if the underlying stock subsequently does poorly. One cannot predict future stock price in an efficient market. Thus, we cannot argue that issuing convertibles is better or worse than issuing equity. The above analysis is summarized in Table 22.2.

Modigliani-Miller (MM) pointed out that, abstracting from taxes and bankruptcy costs, the firm is indifferent to whether it issues stock or issues debt. The MM relationship is a quite general one. Their pedagogy could be adjusted to show that the firm is indifferent to whether it issues convertibles or issues other instruments. To save space (and the patience of students), we have omitted a full-blown proof of MM in a world with convertibles. However, the above results are perfectly consistent with MM. Now we turn to the real-world view of convertibles.

TABLE 22.2 The Case for and against Convertible Bonds (CBs)

	If Firm Subsequently Does Poorly	*If Firm Subsequently Prospers*
Convertible bonds (CBs)	No conversion because of low stock price	Conversion because of high stock price
Compared to:		
Straight bonds	CBs provide cheap financing because coupon rate is lower.	CBs provide expensive financing because bonds are converted, which dilutes existing equity.
Common stock	CBs provide expensive financing because firm could have issued common stock at high prices.	CBs provide cheap financing because firm issues stock at high prices when bonds are converted.

The "Free Lunch" Story

The above discussion suggests that issuing a convertible bond is no better and no worse than issuing other instruments. Unfortunately, many corporate executives fall into the trap of arguing that issuing convertible debt is actually better than issuing alternative instruments. This is a free lunch type of explanation, of which we are quite critical.

• ***Example***

The stock price of RW Company is $20. Suppose this company can issue subordinated debentures at 10 percent. It can also issue convertible bonds at 6 percent with a conversion value of $800. The conversion value means that the holders can convert a convertible bond into 40 ($800/$20) shares of common stock.

A company treasurer who believes in free lunches might argue that convertible bonds should be issued because they represent a cheaper source of financing than either subordinated bonds or common stock. The treasurer will point out that if the company does poorly and the price does not rise above $20, the convertible bondholders will not convert the bonds into common stock. In this case, the company will have obtained debt financing at below-market rates by attaching worthless equity kickers. On the other hand, if the firm does well and the price of its common stock rises to $25 or above, convertible holders will convert. The company will issue 40 shares. The company will receive a bond with face value of $1,000 in exchange for issuing 40 shares of common stock, implying a conversion price of $25. The company will have issued common stock *de facto* at $25 per share, or 20 percent above the $20 common-stock price prevailing when the convertible bonds were issued. This enables it to lower its cost of equity capital. Thus, the treasurer happily points out, regardless of whether the company does well or poorly, convertible bonds are the cheapest form of financing.

Although this argument may sound quite plausible at first glance, there is a flaw. The treasurer is comparing convertible financing *with straight debt* when the stock subsequently falls. However, the treasurer compares convertible financing *with common stock* when the stock subsequently rises. This is an unfair mixing of comparisons. By contrast, our analysis of Table 22.2 was fair, because we examined both stock increases and decreases when comparing a convertible with each alternative instrument. We found that no single alternative dominated convertible bonds in *both* up and down markets. •

The "Expensive Lunch" Story

Suppose we stand the treasurer's argument on its head by comparing (1) convertible financing with straight debt when the stock rises and (2) convertible financing with equity when the stock falls.

From Table 22.2, we see that convertible debt is more expensive than straight debt when the stock subsequently rises. The firm's obligation to sell convertible holders a chunk of the equity at a below-market price more than offsets the lower interest rate on a convertible.

Also from Table 22.2, we see that convertible debt is more expensive than equity when the stock subsequently falls. Had the firm issued stock, it would have received a price higher than its subsequent worth. Therefore, the expensive lunch story implies that convertible debt is an inferior form of financing. Of course, we dismiss both the free lunch and the expensive lunch arguments.

A Reconciliation

In an efficient financial market there is neither a free lunch nor an expensive lunch. Convertible bonds can be neither cheaper nor more expensive than other instruments. A convertible bond is a package of straight debt and an option to buy common stock. The difference between the market value of a convertible bond and the value of a straight bond is the price investors pay for the call-option feature. In an efficient market this is a fair price.

In general, if a company prospers, issuing convertible bonds will turn out to be worse than issuing straight bonds and better than issuing common stock. In contrast, if a company does poorly, convertible bonds will turn out to be better than issuing straight bonds and worse than issuing common stock.

Concept Questions

- What is wrong with the simple view that it is cheaper to issue a bond with a warrant or a convertible feature because the required coupon is lower?
- What is wrong with the Free Lunch story?
- What is wrong with the Expensive Lunch story?

22.7 Why Are Warrants and Convertibles Issued?

From studies it is known that firms that issue convertible bonds are different from other firms. Here are some of the differences:

1. The bond ratings of firms using convertibles are lower than those of other firms.[9]
2. Convertibles tend to be used by smaller firms with high growth rates and more financial leverage.[10]
3. Convertibles are usually subordinated and unsecured.

The kind of company that uses convertibles provides clues to why they are issued. Here are some explanations that make sense.

Matching Cash Flows

If financing is costly, it makes sense to issue securities whose cash flows match those of the firm. A young, risky, and, it hopes, growing firm might prefer to issue convertibles or bonds with warrants because these will have lower initial interest costs. When the firm is successful, the convertibles (or warrants) will be converted. This causes expensive dilution, but it occurs when the firm can most afford it.

Risk Synergy

Another argument for convertible bonds and bonds with warrants is that they are useful when it is very costly to assess the risk of the issuing company. Suppose you are

[9] E. F. Brigham, "An Analysis of Convertible Debentures," *Journal of Finance* 21 (1966).

[10] W. H. Mikkelson, "Convertible Calls and Security Returns," *Journal of Financial Economics* 9 (September 1981), p. 3.

TABLE 22.3 A Hypothetical Case of the Yields on Convertible Bonds*

	Firm Risk	
	Low	*High*
Straight bond yield	10%	15%
Convertible bond yield	6	7

*The yields on straight bonds reflect the risk of default. The yields on convertibles are not sensitive to default risk.

evaluating a new product by a start-up company. The new product is a biogenetic virus that may increase the yields of corn crops in northern climates. It may also cause cancer. This type of product is difficult to value properly. Thus, the risk of the company is very hard to determine: it may be high, or it may be low. If you could be sure the risk of the company was high, you would price the bonds for a high yield, say 15 percent. If it was low, you would price them at a lower yield, say 10 percent.

Convertible bonds and bonds with warrants can protect somewhat against mistakes of risk evaluation. Convertible bonds and bonds with warrants have two components: straight bonds and call options on the company's underlying stock. If the company turns out to be a low-risk company, the straight bond component will have high value and the call option will have low value. However, if the company turns out to be a high-risk company, the straight bond component will have low value and the call option will have high value. This is illustrated in Table 22.3.

However, although risk has effects on value that cancel each other out in convertibles and bonds with warrants, the market and the buyer nevertheless must make an assessment of the firm's potential to value securities, and it is not clear that the effort involved is that much less than is required for a straight bond.

Agency Costs

Convertible bonds can resolve agency problems associated with raising money. In a previous chapter we showed that straight bonds are like risk-free bonds minus a put option on the assets of the firm. This creates an incentive for creditors to force the firm into low-risk activities. In contrast, holders of common stock have incentives to adopt high-risk projects. High-risk projects with negative NPV transfer wealth from bondholders to stockholders. If these conflicts cannot be resolved, the firm may be forced to pass up profitable investment opportunities. However, because convertible bonds have an equity component, less expropriation of wealth can occur when convertible debt is issued instead of straight debt.[11] In other words, convertible bonds mitigate agency costs. One implication is that convertible bonds have less-restrictive debt covenants than do straight bonds in the real world. Casual empirical evidence seems to bear this out.

[11] A. Barnea, R. A. Haugen, and L. Senbet, *Agency Problems and Financial Contracting,* Prentice Hall Foundations of Science Series (New York: Prentice Hall, 1985), chapter VI.

Concept Question

- Why do firms issue convertible bonds and bonds with warrants?

22.8 Conversion Policy

There is one aspect of convertible bonds that we have omitted so far. Firms are frequently granted a call option on the bond. The typical arrangements for calling a convertible bond are simple. When the bond is called, the holder has about 30 days to choose between the following:

1. Converting the bond to common stock at the conversion ratio.
2. Surrendering the bond and receiving the call price in cash.

What should bondholders do? It should be obvious that if the conversion value of the bond is greater than the call price, conversion is better than surrender; and if the conversion value is less than the call price, surrender is better than conversion. If the conversion value is greater than the call price, the call is said to **force conversion.**

What should financial managers do? Calling the bonds does not change the value of the firm as a whole. However, an optimal call policy can benefit the stockholders at the expense of the bondholders. Because we are speaking of dividing a pie of fixed size, the optimal call policy is very simple: Do whatever the bondholders do not want you to do.

Bondholders would love the stockholders to call the bonds when the bond's market value is below the call price. Shareholders would be giving bondholders extra value. Alternatively, should the value of the bonds rise above the call price, the bondholders would love the stockholders not to call the bonds, because bondholders would be allowed to hold onto a valuable asset.

There is only one policy left. This is the policy that maximizes shareholder value and minimizes bondholder value. This policy is

> Call the bond when its value is equal to the call price.

It is a puzzle that firms do not always call convertible bonds when the conversion value reaches the call price. Ingersoll examined the call policies of 124 firms between 1968 and 1975.[12] In most cases he found that the company waited to call the bonds until the conversion value was much higher than the call price. The median company waited until the conversion value of its bonds was 44 percent higher than the call price. This is not even close to the optimal strategy.

[12] J. Ingersoll, "An Examination of Corporate Call Policies on Convertible Bonds," *Journal of Finance* (May 1977). See also M. Harris and A. Raviv, "A Sequential Signalling Model of Convertible Debt Policy," *Journal of Finance* (December 1985). Harris and Raviv describe a signal equilibrium that is consistent with Ingersoll's result. They show that managers with favorable information will delay calls to avoid depressing stock prices.

Concept Questions

- Why will convertible bonds not be voluntarily converted to stock before expiration?
- When should firms force conversion of convertibles? Why?

22.9 Summary and Conclusions

1. A warrant gives the holder the right to buy shares of common stock at an exercise price for a given period of time. Typically, warrants are issued in a package with privately placed bonds. Afterward they become detached and trade separately.
2. A convertible bond is a combination of a straight bond and a call option. The holder can give up the bond in exchange for shares of stock.
3. Convertible bonds and warrants are like call options. However, there are some important differences:
   a. Warrants and convertible securities are issued by corporations. Call options are traded between individual investors.
      i. Warrants are usually issued privately and are combined with a bond. In most cases the warrants can be detached immediately after the issue. In some cases warrants are issued with preferred stock, with common stock, or in executive compensation programs.
      ii. Convertibles are usually bonds that can be converted into common stock.
      iii. Call options are sold separately by individual investors (called *writers* of call options).
   b. Warrants and call options are exercised for cash. The holder of a warrant gives the company cash and receives new shares of the company's stock. The holder of a call option gives another individual cash in exchange for shares of stock. When someone converts a bond, it is exchanged for common stock. As a consequence, bonds with warrants and convertible bonds have different effects on corporate cash flow and capital structure.
   c. Warrants and convertibles cause dilution to the existing shareholders. When warrants are exercised and convertible bonds converted, the company must issue new shares of common stock. The percentage ownership of the existing shareholders will decline. New shares are not issued when call options are exercised.
4. Many arguments, both plausible and implausible, are given for issuing convertible bonds and bonds with warrants. One plausible rationale for such bonds has to do with risk. Convertibles and bonds with warrants are associated with risky companies. Lenders can do several things to protect themselves from high-risk companies:
   a. They can require high yields.
   b. They can lend less or not at all to firms whose risk is difficult to assess.
   c. They can impose severe restrictions on such debt.
   Another useful way to protect against risk is to issue bonds with equity kickers. This gives the lenders the chance to benefit from risks and reduces the conflicts between bondholders and stockholders concerning risk.
5. A puzzle particularly vexes financial researchers: Convertible bonds usually have call provisions. Companies appear to delay calling convertibles until the conversion value greatly exceeds the call price. From the shareholders' standpoint, the optimal call policy would be to call the convertibles when the conversion value equals the call price.

Key Terms

Warrants 606	Conversion premium 612
Convertible bond 612	Conversion value 614
Conversion ratio 612	Force conversion 621
Conversion price 612	

Suggested Readings

The following article analyzes when it is optimal to force conversion of convertible bonds:
Brennan, M., and E. Schwartz. "Convertible Bonds: Valuation and Optimal Strategies for Call Conversion." *Journal of Finance* (December 1977).

Michael Brennan examines the conventional arguments for and against convertible bonds and offers a new "risk synergy" rationale:
Brennan, M. "The Case for Convertibles." In J. M. Stern and D. H. Crew, eds. *The Revolution in Corporate Finance.* New York: Basil Blackwell, 1986.

Courtadon and Merrick outline the basic elements of the option-pricing model and then identify some applications to the design and pricing of corporate securities:
Courtadon, G. R., and J. J. Merrick. "The Option Pricing Model and the Valuation of Corporate Securities." *Midland Corporate Finance Journal* (Fall 1983).

Questions and Problems

22.1 Define:
a. Warrants
b. Convertibles

Warrants

22.2 Explain why the following limits on warrant prices exist.
a. The lower limit is zero if the stock price is below the exercise price.
b. The lower limit is stock price less exercise price if the stock price is above the exercise price.
c. The upper limit is the price of the stock.

22.3 *a.* What is the primary difference between warrants and calls?
b. What is the implication of that difference?

22.4 Suppose the GR Company, which was discussed in the text, sells Mrs. Fiske a warrant. Prior to the sale, the company had two shares outstanding. Mr. Gould owns one share and Ms. Rockefeller owns the other share. The assets of the firm are seven ounces of platinum, which was purchased at $500 per ounce. The exercise price of the warrant is $1,800. All funds that enter the firm are used to purchase more platinum. Mrs. Fiske is sold the warrant moments after incorporation for $500.
a. What is the price of GR stock before the warrant is sold?
b. At what price for platinum will Mrs. Fiske exercise her warrant?
c. Suppose the price of platinum suddenly rises to $520 per ounce.
i. What is the value of GR?
ii. What will Mrs. Fiske do?

iii. What is the new price per share of GR stock?
iv. What was Mrs. Fiske's gain from exercise?
d. What would Mrs. Fiske's gain have been if Mr. Gould had sold her a call?
e. Why are Mrs. Fiske's gains different?

22.5 General Autos has its warrants traded in the market and will expire five years from today. Each warrant is entitled to purchase 0.25 shares of General Autos common stock at $10 per share.
a. Suppose General Autos stock is currently selling for $8, what is the lower limit on the warrant value? What is the upper limit?
b. Suppose General Autos stock is currently selling for $12, what is the lower limit on the warrant value? What is the upper limit?

22.6 Pace Western Crystal, Inc., has outstanding 10 million common shares and 200,000 warrants. Each warrant can purchase five shares of common stock at $15 per share. Warrant holders exercised all of their warrants today. Pace Western's stock price before the exercise was $17. What should the new stock price be after the exercise? Assume there is no information content on the exercise of the warrants.

22.7 A warrant entitles the holder to buy 10 shares of common stock at $21 per share. When the market price of the stock is $15, will the market price of the warrant equal zero? Why or why not?

22.8 Grand Mills Corporation has 4 million shares of common stock outstanding. The company has 500,000 warrants being traded in the market. Each warrant has the right to buy one share of common stock at $20 per share. The warrant will expire one year from today. Grand Mills stock is selling for $22 per share and the variance of the return on the stock is 0.005. The risk-free rate is 5 percent. Use the Black-Scholes model to price the warrant.

22.9 Express Transportation's current market-balance sheet shows assets of the firm are $150 million. The market value of the debt Express has issued is $47 million. Express has 1.5 million shares of common stock outstanding. Tomorrow, Express will issue 100,000 warrants. Each warrant has the option to buy five shares of Express common stock for one year. The proceeds of the issue will be used to pay the dividend that is due tomorrow. Call options on the firm's stock with similar terms are currently selling for $4.70.

22.10 Consider the following warrants.

Warrant X: For each warrant held, three shares of common stock can be purchased at an exercise price of $20 per share.

Warrant Y: For each warrant held, two shares of common stock can be purchased at an exercise price of $30 per share.

The current market price of stock X is $30 per share. The current market price of stock Y is $40 per share.
a. What is the minimum value of warrant X?
b. What is the minimum value of warrant Y?

Convertibles

22.11 At issuance of McArthur Corp.'s convertible bonds, one of the two following sets of characteristics were true.

	A	*B*
Offering price of bond	$900	$1,000
Bond value (straight debt)	$900	$950
Stock price	$20	$30
Conversion ratio	50	30

Which of the relationships do you believe was more likely to have prevailed? Why?

22.12 The following facts apply to a convertible security:

Conversion price	$25/share
Coupon rate	6%
Par value	$1,000
Yield on nonconvertible debenture of same quality	10%
Market value of straight bond of same quality with coupon rate of 10%	$950
Stock price	$24/share

a. What is the minimum price at which the convertible should sell?

b. What accounts for any premium in the market price of the convertible over the value of the common stock into which it can be converted?

22.13 Ms. Mary Malone is a CEO of Malone, Inc, and owns 500,000 shares of the common stock. The company's total number of common shares outstanding is 4 million. The company also has $20 million of convertible bond outstanding. The face value of the bond is $1,000 and its conversion price is $20. Malone's common stock is currently selling for $25, and the company has decided to call the bond to force conversion. Calculate Ms. Malone's ownership changes between before and after the call. Assume that Ms. Malone does not hold any of the company's convertible bond.

22.14 Ryan Home Products, Inc., issued $430,000 of 8-percent convertible debentures. Each bond is convertible into 28 shares of common stock anytime before maturity.

a. Suppose the current price of the bonds is $1,000 and the current price of Ryan common is $31.25.

i. What is the conversion ratio?

ii. What is the conversion price?

iii. What is the conversion premium?

b. Suppose the current price of the bonds is $1,180 and the current price of Ryan common is $31.25.

i. What is the conversion ratio?

ii. What is the conversion price?

iii. What is the conversion premium?

c. What is the conversion value of the debentures?

d. If the value of Ryan common increases by $2, what will the conversion value be?

22.15 Acme Medical Supplies, Inc., issued a zero coupon convertible bond due 10 years from today. The bond has a face value of $1,000 at maturity. Each bond can be converted into 25 shares of Acme's common stock. The appropriate interest rate is 10 percent. The company's stock is selling for $12 per share. Each convertible bond is traded at $400 in the market.

a. What is the straight bond value?

b. What is the conversion value?

c. What is the option value of the bond?

22.16 A $1,000 par convertible debenture has a conversion price for common stock of $180 per share. With the common stock selling at $60, what is the conversion value of the bond?

CHAPTER 24 Derivatives and Hedging Risk

In China, 1994 was the year of the dog and 1995 the year of the pig. In the world of finance we usually remember years for their catastrophic events. Both 1929 and 1987 are years of great stock market crashes. In the international world of finance, 1994 will be remembered as the year of the derivative. Hardly a day went by without a story in the popular press about some firm that had taken a major hit to its bottom line from its activities in the derivatives markets. It begins with Procter and Gamble and Gibson Greeting Cards who allegedly lost hundreds of millions of dollars in trading derivatives. It ends with Nicholas Leeson, whose activities trading derivatives are widely credited with having brought down the venerable international merchant bank of Barings. In between, we have the Piper Jaffrey funds in which investors in a supposedly secure medium-term government bond fund lost 50 percent of their value, and Orange County (California), whose investments lost so much that there was concern about whether basic public services will be disrupted. Whether all of these really happened because of the use or misuse of derivatives will probably be settled years later in the courts, but in the court of public opinion, the culprit has been named—derivatives—and regulators and politicians are deciding on the sentence.

But, despite all of the unfavorable attention showered on derivatives, the one thing we know about them is that they are not going to go away. They are the essence of modern finance, and they are too useful and too important to disappear. Table 24.1 displays some estimates of the size of the exchange traded and the over-the-counter (dealer markets) derivatives markets by categories. You will learn below what these different categories stand for, but for now just look at the totals at the bottom of the columns. The estimate for the end of 1994 was $35 *trillion*. By contrast, the estimated size of the traditional market for bonds, cash, and stock is about $48 trillion. Clearly the derivatives business is a big business, and if we are going to argue for changing it we had better understand it very well indeed. Changes in multitrillion dollar markets have a way of rippling through the rest of the economy.

In this chapter we take a close look at derivatives—what they are, how they work, and the uses to which they can be put. When we are done, you will understand how financial derivatives are designed, and you will be able to decide for yourself in an informed fashion what is happening when the next derivatives scandal erupts.

TABLE 24.1 The Size of the World Derivatives Market

Type of Derivative	*Current Amount (billions)*
Exchange Trader Derivatives	
Forwards	
Interest-rate futures	$6,440
Stock-index futures	150
Currency futures	28
Options	
Interest-rate options	3,390
Currency options	390
Stock-index options	250
Individual stock options	50
Over-the-Counter Derivatives	
Forwards	
Currency contracts	9.000*
Interest-rate contracts	3,500*
Options	
OTC Interest-rate options	2,000*
OTC currency options	800*
Swaps	
Interest-rate swaps	8,000*
Currency swaps	1,100*
Derivative Securities	
Mortgage derivatives	710
Structured Notes	250
Total Derivatives (excl. derivatives securities)	35,078
Traditional Securities	
Bonds	18,600
Cash	15,500
Stocks	13,700
Total Bonds, Cash, Stocks	**47,800**

N.A. = Not Available
* Estimate for year-end 1993
Source: *The Wall Street Journal,* Thursday, August 25, 1994.

Derivatives, Hedging, and Risk

The name *derivatives* is self-explanatory. A derivative is a financial instrument whose payoffs and values are derived from, or depend on, something else. Often we speak of the thing that the derivative depends on as the *primitive* or the *underlying.* For example, in Chapter 21 we studied how options work. An option is a derivative. The value of a call option depends on the value of the underlying stock on which it is written. Actually, call options are quite complicated examples of derivatives. The vast majority of derivatives are simpler than call options. Most derivatives are forward or futures agreements or what are called swaps, and we will study each of these in some detail.

Why do firms use derivatives? The answer is that derivatives are tools for changing the firm's risk exposure. Derivatives are to finance what scalpels are to surgery. By using derivatives, the firm can cut away unwanted portions of risk exposure and even transform the exposures into quite different forms. A central point in finance is that risk is undesirable. In our chapters on risk and return, we pointed out that individuals would choose risky securities only if the expected return compensated for the risk. Similarly, a firm will accept a project with high risk only if the return on the project compensates for this risk. Not surprisingly, then, firms are usually looking for ways to reduce their risk. When the firm reduces its risk exposure, it is said to be **hedging.** Hedging offsets the firm's risk, such as the risk in a project, by one or more transactions in the financial markets.

Derivatives can also be used to merely change or even increase the firm's risk exposure. When this occurs, the firm is **speculating** on the movement of some economic variables—those that underlie the derivative. For example, if a derivative is purchased that will rise in value if interest rates rise, and if the firm has no offsetting exposure to interest rate changes, then the firm is speculating that interest rates will rise and give it a profit on its derivatives position. Using derivatives to translate an opinion about whether interest rates or some other economic variable will rise or fall is the opposite of hedging—it is risk enhancing. Speculating on your views on the economy and using derivatives to profit if that view turns out to be correct is not necessarily wrong, but the speculator should always remember that sharp tools cut deep, and if the opinions on which the derivatives position is based turn out to be incorrect, then the consequences can prove costly. Efficient market theory teaches how difficult it is to predict what markets will do. Most of the sad experiences with derivatives occurred not from their use as instruments for hedging and offsetting risk, but, rather, from speculation.

24.1 Forward Contracts

We can begin our discussion of hedging by considering forward contracts. One frequently hears the one-liner about the gentleman who was shocked to find he had been speaking prose all his life. Forward contracts are a lot like that; you have probably been dealing in them your whole life without knowing it. Suppose you walk into a bookstore on, say, February 1 to buy the best-seller *Eating Habits of the Rich and Famous.* The cashier tells you that the book is currently sold out, but he takes your phone number, saying that he will reorder it for you. He says the book will cost \$10.00. If you agree on February 1 to pick up and pay \$10.00 for the book when called, you and the cashier have engaged in a **forward contract.** That is, you have agreed both to pay for the book and to pick it up when the bookstore notifies you. Since you are agreeing to buy the book at a later date, you are *buying* a forward contract on February 1. In commodity parlance, you will be **taking delivery** when you pick up the book. The book is called the **deliverable instrument.**

The cashier, acting on behalf of the bookstore, is selling a forward contract. (Alternatively, we say that he is writing a forward contract.) The bookstore has agreed to turn the book over to you at the predetermined price of \$10.00 as soon as the book arrives. The act of turning the book over to you is called **making delivery.** Table 24.2 illustrates the book purchase. Note that the agreement takes place on February 1. The price is set and the conditions for sale are set at that time. In this case, the sale will occur when the book arrives. In other cases, an exact date of sale would be given.

TABLE 24.2 Illustration of Book Purchase as a Forward Contract

	February 1	*Date when Book Arrives*
Buyer	Buyer agrees to: 1. Pay the purchase price of $10.00. 2. Receive book when book arrives.	Buyer: 1. Pays purchase price of $10.00. 2. Receives book.
Seller	Seller agrees to: 1. Give up book. 2. Accept payment of $10.00 when book arrives.	Seller: 1. Gives up book. 2. Accepts payment of $10.00.

Note that cash does not change hands on February 1. Cash changes hands when the book arrives.

However, *no* cash changes hands on February 1; cash changes hands only when the book arrives.

Though forward contracts may have seemed exotic to you before you began this chapter, you can see that they are quite commonplace. Dealings in your personal life probably have involved forward contracts. Similarly, forward contracts occur all the time in business. Every time a firm orders an item that cannot be delivered immediately, a forward contract takes place. Sometimes, particularly when the order is small, an oral agreement will suffice. Other times, particularly when the order is larger, a written agreement is necessary.

Note that a forward contract is not an option. Both the buyer and the seller are obligated to perform under the terms of the contract. Conversely, the buyer of an option *chooses* whether or not to exercise the option.

A forward contract should be contrasted with a **cash transaction,** that is, a transaction where exchange is immediate. Had the book been on the bookstore's shelf, your purchase of it would constitute a cash transaction.

Concept Questions

- What is a forward contract?
- Give examples of forward contracts in your life.

24.2 Futures Contracts

A variant of the forward contract takes place on financial exchanges. Contracts on exchanges are usually called **futures contracts.** For example, consider Table 24.3, which provides data on trading in wheat for Thursday, September 15, 19X1. Let us focus on the September futures contract, which is illustrated in the first row of the table. The first trade of the day in the contract was for $4.11 per bushel. The price reached a high of $4.16½ during the day and reached a low of $4.07. The last trade was also at $4.07. In other words, the contract *closed* or *settled* at $4.07. The price dropped 6¼ cents per bushel during the day, indicating that the price closed the previous day at $4.13¼ ($4.07 + $0.0625). The contract had been trading for slightly less than a year. During that time, the price reached a high of $4.21 per bushel and a low of $2.72 per bushel. The open interest indicates the number of *contracts outstanding.* The number of contracts outstanding at the close of September 15 was 423.

TABLE 24.3 Data on Wheat Futures Contracts, Thursday, September 15, 19X1

						Lifetime		
	Open	*High*	*Low*	*Settle*	*Change*	*High*	*Open Low*	*Interest*
Sept	411	416¼	407	407	−6¼	421	272	423
Oct	427	432¼	422	423¼	−5½	432¼	289	47,454
Mar X2	430½	436	426½	427	−4¼	436	323	42,823
May	409	443½	404	405	−5½	420	330	3,422
July	375	376½	369	370¾	−6¾	395	327	4,805

Though we are discussing a futures contract, let us work with a forward contract first. Suppose you wrote a *forward* contract for September wheat at $4.07. From our discussion on forward contracts, this would mean that you would agree to turn over an agreed-upon number of wheat bushels for $4.07 per bushel on some specified date in the remainder of the month of September.

A futures contract differs somewhat from a forward contract. First, the seller can choose to deliver the wheat on any day during the delivery month, that is, the month of September. This gives the seller leeway that he would not have with a forward contract. When the seller decides to deliver, he notifies the exchange clearinghouse that he wants to do so. The clearinghouse then notifies an individual who bought a September wheat contract that she must stand ready to accept delivery within the next few days. Though each exchange selects the buyer in a different way, the buyer is generally chosen in a random fashion. Because there are so many buyers at any one time, the buyer selected by the clearinghouse to take delivery almost certainly did not originally buy the contract from the seller now making delivery.

Second, futures contracts are traded on an exchange whereas forward contracts are generally traded off an exchange. Because of this, there is generally a liquid market in futures contracts. A buyer can net out her futures position with a sale. A seller can net out his futures position with a purchase. This procedure is analogous to the *netting-out* process in the options markets. However, the buyer of an options contract can also walk away from the contract by not exercising it. If a buyer of a futures contract does not subsequently sell her contract, she must take delivery.

Third, and most important, the prices of futures contracts are **marked to the market** on a daily basis. That is, suppose that the price falls to $4.05 on Friday's close. Because all buyers lost two cents per bushel on that day, they each must turn over the two cents per bushel to their brokers within 24 hours, who subsequently remit the proceeds to the clearinghouse. Because all sellers gained two cents per bushel on that day, they each receive two cents per bushel from their brokers. Their brokers are subsequently compensated by the clearinghouse. Because there is a buyer for every seller, the clearinghouse must break even every day.

Now suppose that the price rises to $4.12 on the close of the following Monday. Each buyer receives seven cents ($4.12 − $4.05) per bushel and each seller must pay seven cents per bushel. Finally, suppose that, on Monday, a seller notifies his broker of his intention to deliver.[1] The delivery price will be $4.12, which is Monday's close.

There are clearly many cash flows in futures contracts. However, after all the dust settles, the *net price* to the buyer must be the price at which she bought originally. That

[1] He will deliver on Wednesday, two days later.

Illustration of Example Involving Marking to Market in Futures Contracts

Both buyer and seller originally transact at Thursday's closing price. Delivery takes place at Monday's closing price.*

	Thursday, September 19	*Friday, September 20*	*Monday, September 23*	*Delivery (Notification given by seller on Monday)*
Closing price:	\$4.07	\$4.05	\$4.12	
BUYER	Buyer purchases futures contract at closing price of \$4.07/bushel.	Buyer must pay two cents/bushel to clearinghouse within one business day.	Buyer receives seven cents/bushel from clearinghouse within one business day.	Buyer pays \$4.12 per bushel and receives grain.

Buyer's net payment of −\$4.07 (−\$0.02 + \$0.07 − \$4.12) is the same as if buyer purchased a forward contract for \$4.07/bushel.

SELLER	Seller sells futures contract at closing price of \$4.07/bushel.	Seller receives two cents/bushel from clearinghouse within one business day.	Seller pays seven cents/bushel to clearinghouse within one business day.	Seller receives \$4.12 per bushel and delivers grain within one business day.

Seller's net receipts of \$4.07 (\$0.02 − \$0.07 + \$4.12) are the same as if seller sold a forward contract for \$4.07/bushel.

*For simplicity, we assume that buyer and seller both (1) initially transact at the same time and (2) meet in delivery process. This is actually very unlikely to occur in the real world because the clearinghouse assigns the buyer to take delivery in a random manner.

is, an individual buying at Thursday's closing price of \$4.07 and being called to take delivery on Monday pays two cents per bushel on Friday, receives seven cents per bushel on Monday, and takes delivery at \$4.12. Her net outflow per bushel is −\$4.07 (−\$0.02 + \$0.07 − \$4.12), which is the price at which she contracted on Thursday. (Our analysis ignores the time value of money.) Conversely, an individual selling at Thursday's closing price of \$4.07 and notifying his broker concerning delivery the following Monday, receives two cents per bushel on Friday, pays seven cents per bushel on Monday, and makes delivery at \$4.12. His net inflow per bushel is \$4.07 (\$0.02 − \$0.07 + \$4.12), which is the price at which he contracted on Thursday.

These details are presented in the adjacent box. For simplicity, we assumed that the buyer and seller who initially transact on Thursday's close meet in the delivery process.[2] The point in the example is that the buyer's net payment of \$4.07 per bushel is the same as if she purchased a forward contract for \$4.07. Similarly, the seller's net receipt of \$4.07 per bushel is the same as if he sold a forward contract for \$4.07 per

[2] As pointed out earlier, this is actually very unlikely to occur in the real world.

bushel. The only difference is the timing of the cash flows. The buyer of a forward contract knows that he will make a single payment of \$4.07 on the expiration date. He will not need to worry about any other cash flows in the interim. Conversely, though the cash flows to the buyer of a futures contract will net to exactly \$4.07 as well, the pattern of cash flows is not known ahead of time.

The mark-to-the-market provision on futures contracts has two related effects. The first concerns differences in net present value. For example, a large price drop immediately following purchase means an immediate outpayment for the buyer of a futures contract. Though the net outflow of \$4.07 is still the same as under a forward contract, the present value of the cash outflows is greater to the buyer of a futures contract. Of course, the present value of the cash outflows is less to the buyer of a futures contract if a price rise followed purchase.[3] Though this effect could be substantial in certain theoretical circumstances, it appears to be of quite limited importance in the real world.[4]

Second, the firm must have extra liquidity to handle a sudden outflow prior to expiration. This added risk may make the futures contract less attractive.

Students frequently ask, "Why in the world would managers of the commodity exchanges ruin perfectly good contracts with these bizarre mark-to-the-market provisions?" Actually, the reason is a very good one. Consider the forward contract of Table 24.2 concerning the bookstore. Suppose that the public quickly loses interest in *Eating Habits of the Rich and Famous.* By the time the bookstore calls the buyer, other stores may have dropped the price of the book to \$6.00. Because the forward contract was for \$10.00, the buyer has an incentive not to take delivery on the forward contract. Conversely, should the book become a hot item selling at \$15.00, the bookstore may simply not call the buyer.

As indicated, forward contracts have a very big flaw. Whichever way the price of the deliverable instrument moves, one party has an incentive to default. There are many cases where defaults occurred in the real world. One famous case concerned Coca-Cola. When the company began in the early 20th century, Coca-Cola made an agreement to supply its bottlers and distributors with cola syrup at a constant price *forever.* Of course, subsequent inflation would have caused Coca-Cola to lose large sums of money had they honored the contract. After much legal effort, Coke and its bottlers put an *inflation-escalator clause* in the contract. Another famous case concerned Westinghouse. It seems the firm had promised to deliver uranium to certain utilities at a fixed price. The price of uranium skyrocketed in the 1970s, making Westinghouse lose money on every shipment. Westinghouse defaulted on its agreement. The utilities took Westinghouse to court but did not recover anything near what Westinghouse owed them.

The mark-to-the-market provisions minimize the chance of default on a futures contract. If the price rises, the seller has an incentive to default on a forward contract. However, after paying the clearinghouse, the seller of a futures contract has little reason to default. If the price falls, the same argument can be made for the buyer. Because changes in the value of the underlying asset are recognized daily, there is no accumulation of loss, and the incentive to default is reduced.

Because of this default issue, forward contracts generally involve individuals and institutions who know and can trust each other. But as W. C. Fields said, "Trust every-

[3] The direction is reversed for the seller of a futures contract. However, the general point that the net present value of cash flows may differ between forward and futures contracts holds for sellers as well.

[4] See John C. Cox, John E. Ingersoll, and Steven A. Ross, "The Relationship between Forward and Future Prices," *Journal of Financial Economics* (1981).

body, but cut the cards." Lawyers earn a handsome living writing supposedly air-tight forward contracts, even among friends. The genius of the mark-to-the-market system is that it can prevent default where it is most likely to occur—among investors who do not know each other. Textbooks on futures contracts from one or two decades ago usually included a statement such as "No major default has ever occurred on the commodity exchanges." No textbook published after the Hunt Brothers defaulted on silver contracts in the 1970s can make that claim. Nevertheless, the extremely low default rate in futures contracts is truly awe-inspiring.

Futures contracts are traded in three areas: agricultural commodities, metals and petroleum, and financial assets. The extensive array of futures contracts is listed in Table 24.4.

TABLE 24.4 Futures Contracts Listed in *The Wall Street Journal*

Contract	*Contract Size*	*Exchange*
Agricultural (grain and oilseeds)		
Corn	5,000 bushels	Chicago Board of Trade (CBT)
Oats	5,000 bushels	CBT
Soybeans	5,000 bushels	CBT
Soybean meal	400 tons	CBT
Soybean oil	60,000 lbs.	CBT
Wheat	5,000 bushels	CBT
Wheat	5,000 bushels	Kansas City (KC)
Wheat	5,000 bushels	Minneapolis
Barley	20 metric tons	Winnipeg (WPG)
Flaxseed	20 metric tons	WPG
Rapeseed	20 metric tons	WPG
Wheat	20 metric tons	WPG
Rye	20 metric tons	WPG
Agricultural (livestock and meat)		
Cattle (feeder)	44,000 lbs.	Chicago Mercantile Exchange (CME)
Cattle (live)	40,000 lbs.	CME
Hogs	30,000 lbs.	CME
Pork bellies	40,000 lbs.	CME
Agricultural (food, fiber, and wood)		
Cocoa	10 metric tons	Coffee, Sugar and Cocoa Exchange (CSCE)
Coffee	37,500 lbs.	CSCE
Cotton	50,000 lbs.	New York Cotton Exchange (CTN)
Orange juice	15,000 lbs.	CTN
Sugar (world)	112,000 lbs.	CSCE
Sugar (domestic)	142,000 lbs.	CSCE
Lumber	150,000 board feet	CME
Metals and petroleum		
Copper (standard)	25,000 lbs.	Commodity Exchange in New York (CMX)
Gold	100 troy oz.	CMX
Platinum	50 troy oz.	New York Mercantile (NYM)
Palladium	100 troy oz.	NYM
Silver	5,000 troy oz.	CMX
Silver	1,000 troy oz.	CBT
Crude oil (light sweet)	1,000 barrels	NYM
Heating oil no. 2	42,000 gallons	NYM
Gas oil	100 metric tons	International Petroleum Exchange of London (IPEL)
Gasoline unleaded	42,000 gallons	NYM

TABLE 24.4 (Concluded)

Contract	Contract Size	Exchange
Financial		
British pound	62,500 pounds	International Monetary Market in Chicago (IMM)
Australian dollar	100,000 dollars	IMM
Canadian dollar	100,000 dollars	IMM
Japanese yen	12.5 million yen	IMM
Swiss franc	125,000 francs	IMM
German mark	125,000 marks	IMM
Eurodollar	$1 million	London International Financial Futures Exchange (LIFFE)
Financial		
Sterling	500,000 pounds	LIFFE
Treasury bonds	$1 million	LIFFE
Long gilt	250,000 pounds	LIFFE
Eurodollar	$1 million	IMM
U.S. Dollar Index	500 times Index	Financial Instrument Exchange in New York (FINEX)
CRB Index	500 times Index	New York Futures Exchange (NYFE)
Treasury bonds	$100,000	CBT
Treasury notes	$100,000	CBT
5-year Treasury notes	$100,000	CBT
5-year Treasury notes	$100,000	FINEX
Treasury bonds	$50,000	MCE
Treasury bonds	$1 million	IMM
Financial indexes		
Municipal bonds	1,000 times Bond Buyer Index	CBT
S&P 500 Index	500 times Index	CME
NYSE Composite	500 times Index	NYFE
Kansas City Value Line Index	500 times Index	KC
Major Market Index	250 times Index	CBT

Concept Questions

- What is a futures contract?
- How is a futures contract related to a forward contract?
- Why do exchanges require futures contracts to be marked to the market?

24.3 Hedging

Now that we have determined how futures contracts work, let us talk about hedging. There are two types of hedges, long and short. We discuss the short hedge first.

• ***Example***
In June, Bernard Abelman, a Midwestern farmer, anticipates a harvest of 50,000 bushels of wheat at the end of September. He has two alternatives:

1. *Write Futures Contracts against His Anticipated Harvest.* The September wheat contract on the Chicago Board of Trade is trading at $3.75 a bushel on June 1. He executes the following transaction:

Date of Transaction	*Transaction*	*Price per Bushel*
June 1	Write 10 September futures contracts	$3.75

He notes that transportation costs to the designated delivery point in Chicago are 30 cents/bushel. Thus, his net price per bushel is $3.45 = $3.75 − $0.30.

2. *Harvest the Wheat without Writing a Futures Contract.* Alternatively, Mr. Abelman could have harvested the wheat without benefit of a futures contract. The risk would be quite great here since no one knows what the cash price in September will be. If prices rise, he will profit. Conversely, he will lose if prices fall.

We say that strategy 2 is an unhedged position because there is no attempt to use the futures markets to reduce risk. Conversely, strategy 1 involves a hedge. That is, a position in the futures market offsets the risk of a position in the physical, that is, in the actual, commodity.

Though hedging may seem quite sensible to you, it should be mentioned that not everyone hedges. Mr. Abelman might reject hedging for at least two reasons.

First, he may simply be uninformed about hedging. We have found that not everyone in business understands the hedging concept. Many executives have told us that they do not want to use futures markets for hedging their inventories because the risks are too great. However, we disagree. While there are large price fluctuations in these markets, hedging actually reduces the risk that an individual holding inventories bears.

Second, Mr. Abelman may have a special insight or some special information that commodity prices will rise. He would not be wise to lock in a price of $3.75 if he expects the cash price in September to be well above this price.

The hedge of strategy 1 is called a **short hedge,** because Mr. Abelman reduces his risk by *selling* a futures contract. The short hedge is very common in business. It occurs whenever someone either anticipates receiving inventory or is holding inventory. Mr. Abelman was anticipating the harvest of grain. A manufacturer of soybean meal and oil may hold large quantities of raw soybeans, which are already paid for. However, the price to be received for meal and oil are not known because no one knows what the market price will be when the meal and oil are produced. The manufacturer may write futures contracts in meal and oil to lock in a sales price. An oil company may hold large inventories of petroleum to be processed into heating oil. The firm could sell futures contracts in heating oil in order to lock in the sales price. A mortgage banker may assemble mortgages slowly before selling them in bulk to a financial institution. Movements of interest rates affect the value of the mortgages during the time they are in inventory. The mortgage banker could sell Treasury-bond futures contracts in order to offset this interest-rate risk. (This last example is treated later in this chapter.) •

• ***Example***

On April 1, Moon Chemical agreed to sell petrochemicals to the U.S. government in the future. The delivery dates and the prices have been determined. Because oil is a basic ingredient of the production process, Moon Chemical will need to have large quantities of oil on hand. The firm can get the oil in one of two ways:

1. *Buy the Oil as the Firm Needs It.* This is an unhedged position because, as of April 1, the firm does not know the prices it will later have to pay for the oil. Oil is quite a volatile commodity, so Moon Chemical is bearing a good bit of risk. The key to this risk-bearing is that the sales price to the U.S. government has already been fixed. Thus, Moon Chemical cannot pass on increased costs to the consumer.

2. *Buy Futures Contracts.*[5] The firm can buy futures contracts with expiration months corresponding to the dates the firm needs inventory. The futures contract locks in the purchase price to Moon Chemical. Because there is a crude-oil futures contract for every month, selecting the correct futures contract is not difficult. Many other commodities have only five contracts per year, frequently necessitating buying contracts one month away from the month of production.

As mentioned earlier, Moon Chemical is interested in hedging the risk of fluctuating oil prices because it cannot pass any cost increases on to the consumer. Suppose, alternatively, that Moon Chemical was not selling petrochemicals on fixed contract to the U.S. government. Instead, imagine that the petrochemicals were to be sold to private industry at currently prevailing prices. The price of petrochemicals should move directly with oil prices, because oil is a major component of petrochemicals. Because cost increases are likely to be passed on to the consumer, Moon Chemical would probably not want to hedge in this case. Instead, the firm is likely to choose strategy 1, buying the oil as it is needed. If oil prices increase between April 1 and September 1, Moon Chemical will, of course, find that its inputs have become quite costly. However, in a competitive market, its revenues are likely to rise as well.

Strategy 2 is called a **long hedge** because one *purchases* a futures contract to reduce risk. In other words, one takes a long position in the futures market. In general, a firm institutes a long hedge when it is committed to a fixed sales price. One class of situations involves actual written contracts with customers, such as Moon Chemical had with the U.S. government. Alternatively, a firm may find that it cannot easily pass on costs to consumers or does not want to pass on these costs. For example, a group of students opened a small meat market called *What's Your Beef* near the University of Pennsylvania in the late 1970s.[6] You may recall that this was a time of volatile consumer prices, especially food prices. Knowing that their fellow students were particularly budget-conscious, the owners vowed to keep food prices constant, regardless of price movements in either direction. They accomplished this by purchasing futures contracts in various agricultural commodities. •

Concept Questions

- Define short and long hedges.
- Under what circumstances is each of the two hedges used?

24.4 Interest-Rate Futures Contracts

In this section we consider interest-rate futures contracts. Our examples deal with futures contracts on Treasury bonds because of their high popularity. We first price Treasury bonds and Treasury-bond forward contracts. Differences between futures and forward contracts are explored. Hedging examples are provided next.

[5] Alternatively the firm could buy the oil on April 1 and store it. This would eliminate the risk of price movement, because the firm's oil costs would be fixed upon the immediate purchase. However, this strategy would be inferior to strategy 2 in the common case where the difference between the futures contract quoted on April 1 and the April 1 cash price is less than storage costs.

[6] Ordinarily, an unusual firm name in this textbook is a tip-off that it is fictional. This, however, is a true story.

Pricing of Treasury Bonds

As mentioned earlier in the text, a Treasury bond pays semiannual interest over its life. In addition, the face value of the bond is paid at maturity. Consider a 20-year, 8-percent coupon bond that was issued on March 1. The first payment is to occur in six months, that is, on September 1. The value of the bond can be determined as

Pricing of a Treasury Bond:

$$P_{TB} = \frac{\$40}{1 + r_1} + \frac{\$40}{(1 + r_2)^2} + \frac{\$40}{(1 + r_3)^3} + \cdots + \frac{\$40}{(1 + r_{39})^{39}} + \frac{\$1{,}040}{(1 + r_{40})^{40}} \quad (24.1)$$

Because an 8-percent coupon bond pays interest of \$80 a year, the semiannual coupon is \$40. Principal and the semiannual coupons are both paid at maturity. As we mentioned in a previous chapter, the price of the Treasury bond, P_{TB}, is determined by discounting each payment on a bond at the appropriate spot rate. Because the payments are semiannual, each spot rate is expressed in semiannual terms. That is, imagine a horizontal term structure where the effective annual yield is 12 percent for all maturities. Because each spot rate, *r,* is expressed in semiannual terms, each spot rate is $\sqrt{1.12} - 1 = 5.83\%$. Because coupon payments occur every six months, there are 40 spot rates over the 20-year period.

Pricing of Forward Contracts

Now, imagine a *forward* contract where, on March 1, you agree to buy a new 20-year, 8-percent coupon Treasury bond in six months, that is, on September 1. As with typical forward contracts, you will pay for the bond on September 1, not March 1. The cash flows from both the Treasury bond issued on March 1 and the forward contract that you purchase on March 1 are presented in Figure 24.1. The cash flows on the Treasury bond begin exactly six months earlier than do the cash flows on the forward contract. The Treasury bond is purchased with cash on March 1 (date 0). The first coupon payment occurs on September 1 (date 1). The last coupon payment occurs at date 40, along with the face value of \$1,000. The forward contract compels you to pay

FIGURE 24.1 Cash Flows for Both a Treasury Bond and a Forward Contract on a Treasury Bond

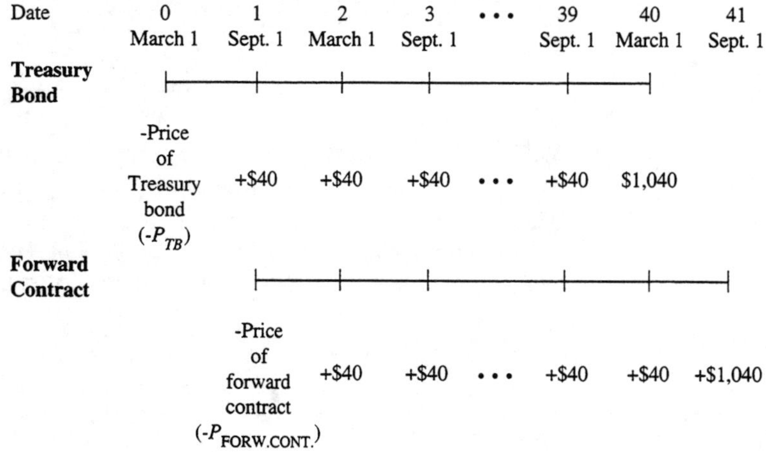

$P_{\text{FORW.CONT.}}$, the price of the forward contract, on September 1 (date 1). You receive a new Treasury bond at that time. The first coupon payment from the bond you receive occurs on March 1 of the following year (date 2). The last coupon payment occurs at date 41, along with the face value of \$1,000.

Given the 40 spot rates, equation (24.1) showed how to price a Treasury bond. How does one price the forward contract on a Treasury bond? Just as we saw earlier in the text that net-present-value analysis can be used to price bonds, we will now show that net-present-value analysis can be used to price forward contracts. Given the cash flows for the forward contract in Figure 24.1, the price of the forward contract must satisfy the following equation:

$$\frac{P_{\text{FORW.CONT.}}}{1+r_1} = \frac{\$40}{(1+r_2)^2} + \frac{\$40}{(1+r_3)^3} + \frac{\$40}{(1+r_4)^4} + \cdots + \frac{\$40}{(1+r_{40})^{40}} + \frac{\$1{,}040}{(1+r_{41})^{41}} \quad (24.2)$$

The right-hand side of equation (24.2) discounts all the cash flows from the delivery instrument (the Treasury bond issued on September 1) back to date 0 (March 1). Because the first cash flow occurs at date 2 (March 1 of the subsequent year), it is discounted by $1/(1+r_2)^2$. The last cash flow of \$1,040 occurs at date 41, so it is discounted by $1/(1 + r_{41})^{41}$. The left-hand side represents the cost of the forward contract as of date 0. Because the actual outpayment occurs at date 1, it is discounted by $1/(1 + r_1)$.

Students often ask, "Why are we discounting everything back to date 0, when we are actually paying for the forward contract on September 1?" The answer is simply that we apply the same techniques to equation (24.2) that we apply to all capital-budgeting problems; we want to put everything in today's (date 0's) dollars. Given that the spot rates are known in the market place, traders should have no more trouble pricing a forward contract by (24.2) than they would have pricing a Treasury bond by (24.1).

Forward contracts are similar to the underlying bonds themselves. If the entire term structure of interest rates unexpectedly shifts upward on March 2, the Treasury bond issued the previous day should fall in value. This can be seen from (24.1). A rise in each of the spot rates lowers the present value of each of the coupon payments. Hence, the value of the bond must fall. Conversely, a fall in the term structure of interest rates increases the value of the bond.

The same relationship holds with forward contracts, as can be seen from rewriting (24.2) as

$$P_{\text{FORW.CONT.}} = \frac{\$40 \times (1+r_1)}{(1+r_2)^2} + \frac{\$40 \times (1+r_1)}{(1+r_3)^3} + \frac{\$40 \times (1+r_1)}{(1+r_4)^4} + \cdots + \frac{\$40 \times (1+r_1)}{(1+r_{40})^{40}} + \frac{\$1{,}040 \times (1+r_1)}{(1+r_{41})^{41}} \quad (24.3)$$

We went from (24.2) to (24.3) by multiplying both the left- and the right-hand sides by $(1+r_1)$. If the entire term structure of interest rates unexpectedly shifts upward on March 2, the *first* term on the right-hand side of equation (24.3) should fall in value.[7] That is, both r_1 and r_2 will rise an equal amount. However, r_2 enters as a *squared* term, $1/(1 + r_2)^2$, so an increase in r_2 more than offsets the increase in r_1. As we move fur-

[7] We are assuming that each spot rate shifts the same amount. For example, suppose that, on March 1, $r_1 = 5\%$, $r_2 = 5.4\%$, and $r_3 = 5.8\%$. Assuming that all rates increase by ½ percent on March 2, r_1 becomes 5.5 percent (5% + ½%), r_2 becomes 5.9 percent and r_3 becomes 6.3 percent.

ther to the right, an increase in any spot rate, r_i, more than offsets an increase in r_1. Here, r_i enters as the ith power, $1/(1 + r_i)^i$. Thus, as long as the entire term structure shifts upward an equal amount on March 2, the value of a forward contract must fall on that date. Conversely, as long as the entire term structure shifts downward an equal amount on March 2, the value of a forward contract must rise.

Futures Contracts

The above discussion concerned a forward contract in U.S. Treasury bonds, that is, a forward contract where the deliverable instrument is a U.S. Treasury bond. What about a futures contract on a Treasury bond?[8] We mentioned earlier that futures contracts and forward contracts are quite similar, though there are a few differences between the two. First, futures contracts are generally traded on exchanges, whereas forward contracts are not traded on an exchange. In this case, the Treasury-bond futures contract is traded on the Chicago Board of Trade. Second, futures contracts generally allow the seller a period of time in which to deliver, whereas forward contracts generally call for delivery on a particular day. The seller of a Treasury-bond futures contract can choose to deliver on any business day during the delivery month.[9] Third, futures contracts are subject to the mark-to-the-market convention, whereas forward contracts are not. Traders in Treasury-bill futures contracts must adhere to this convention. Fourth, there is generally a liquid market for futures contracts allowing contracts to be quickly netted out. That is, a buyer can sell his futures contract at any time, and a seller can buy back her futures contract at any time. Conversely, because forward markets are generally quite illiquid, traders cannot easily net out their positions. The popularity of the Treasury-bond futures contract has produced liquidity even higher than that on other futures contracts. Positions in that contract can be netted out quite easily.

The above discussion is not intended to be an exhaustive list of differences between the Treasury-bond forward contract and the Treasury-bond futures contract. Rather, it is intended to show that both contracts share fundamental characteristics. Though there are differences, the two instruments should be viewed as variations of the same species, not different species. Thus, the pricing equation of (24.3), which is exact for the forward contract, should be a decent approximation for the futures contract.

Hedging in Interest-Rate Futures

Now that we have the basic institutional details under our belt, we are ready for examples of hedging using either futures contracts or forward contracts on Treasury bonds. Because the T-bond futures contract is extremely popular whereas the forward contract is traded sporadically, our examples use the futures contract.

• ***Example***
Ron Cooke owns a mortgage-banking company. On March 1, he made a commitment to loan a total of $1 million to various homeowners on May 1. The loans are 20-year mortgages carrying a 12-percent coupon, the going interest rate on mortgages at the time. Thus, the mortgages are made at par. Though homeowners would not use the term, we could say that he is buying a *forward contract* on a mortgage. That is, he

[8] Futures contracts on bonds are also called *interest-rate futures contracts.*

[9] Delivery occurs two days after the seller notifies the clearinghouse of her intention to deliver.

agrees on March 1 to give $1 million to his borrowers on May 1 in exchange for principal and interest from them every month for the next 20 years.

Like many mortgage bankers, he has no intention of paying the $1 million out of his own pocket. Rather, he intends to sell the mortgages to an insurance company. Thus, the insurance company will actually loan the funds and will receive principal and interest over the next 20 years. Mr. Cooke does not currently have an insurance company in mind. He plans to visit the mortgage departments of insurance companies over the next 60 days to sell the mortgages to one or many of them. He sets April 30 as a deadline for making the sale because the borrowers expect the funds on the following day.

Suppose that Mr. Cooke sells the mortgages to the Acme Insurance Co. on April 15. What price will Acme pay for the bonds?

You may think that the insurance company will obviously pay $1 million for the loans. However, suppose interest rates have risen about 12 percent by April 15. The insurance company will buy the mortgage at a discount. For example, suppose the insurance company agrees to pay only $940,000 for the mortgages. Because the mortgage banker agreed to loan a full $1 million to the borrowers, the mortgage banker must come up with the additional $60,000 ($1 million − $940,000) out of his own pocket.

Alternatively, suppose that interest rates fall below 12 percent by April 15. The mortgages can be sold at a premium under this scenario. If the insurance company buys the mortgages at $1.05 million, the mortgage banker will have made an unexpected profit of $50,000 ($1.05 million − $1 million).

Because Ron Cooke is unable to forecast interest rates, this risk is something that he would like to avoid. The risk is summarized in Table 24.5.

Seeing the interest-rate risk, students at this point may ask, "What does the mortgage banker get out of this loan to offset his risk-bearing?" Mr. Cooke wants to sell the mortgages to the insurance company so that he can get two fees. The first is an *origination fee,* which is paid to the mortgage banker from the insurance company on April 15, that is, on the date the loan is sold. An industry standard in certain locales is 1 percent of the value of the loan, that is $10,000 (1% × $1 million). In addition, Mr. Cooke will act as a collection agent for the insurance company. For this service, he will receive a small portion of the outstanding balance of the loan each month. For example, if he is paid 0.03 percent of the loan each month, he will receive $300 (0.03% × $1 million) in the first month. As the outstanding balance of the loan declines, he will receive less.

TABLE 24.5 Effects of Changing Interest Rate on Ron Cooke, Mortgage Banker

Mortgage interest rate on April 15	Above 12%	Below 12%
Sale price to Acme Insurance Company	Below $1 million (We assume $940,000)	Above $1 million (We assume $1.05 million)
Effect on mortgage banker	He loses because he must loan full $1 million to borrowers.	He gains because he loans only $1 million to borrowers.
Dollar gain or loss	Loss of $60,000 ($1 million − $940,000)	Gain of $50,000 ($1.05 million − $1 million)

The interest rate on March 1, the date when the loan agreement was made with the borrowers, was 12 percent. April 15 is the date the mortgages were sold to Acme Insurance Company.

Though Mr. Cooke will earn profitable fees on the loan, he bears interest-rate risk. He loses money if interest rates rise after March 1, and he profits if interest rates fall after March 1. To hedge this risk, he writes June Treasury-bond futures contracts on March 1. As with mortgages, Treasury-bond futures contracts fall in value if interest rates rise. Because he *writes* the contract, he makes money on these contracts if they fall in value. Therefore, with an interest-rate rise, the loss he endures in the mortgages is offset by the gain he earns in the futures market. Conversely, Treasury-bond futures contracts rise in value if interest rates fall. Because he writes the contracts, he suffers losses on them when rates fall. With an interest-rate fall, the profit he makes on the mortgages is offset by the loss he suffers in the futures markets.

The details of this hedging transaction are presented in Table 24.6. The column on the left is labeled "Cash markets," because the deal in the mortgage market is transacted off an exchange. The column on the right shows the offsetting transactions in the futures markets. Consider the first row. The mortgage banker enters into a forward contract on March 1. He simultaneously writes Treasury-bond futures contracts. Ten contracts are written because the deliverable instrument on each contract is $100,000 of Treasury bonds. The total is $1 million (10 × $100,000), which is equal to the value of the mortgages. Mr. Cooke would prefer to write May Treasury-bond futures contracts. Here, Treasury bonds would be delivered on the futures contract during the same month that the loan is funded. Because there is no May T-bond futures contract, Mr. Cooke achieves the closest match through a June contract.

If held to maturity, the June contract would obligate the mortgage banker to deliver Treasury bonds in June. Interest-rate risk ends in the cash market when the loans are sold. Interest-rate risk must be terminated in the futures market at that time. Thus, Mr. Cooke nets out his position in the futures contract as soon as the loan is sold to Acme Insurance. •

Risk is clearly reduced via an offsetting transaction in the futures market. However, is risk totally eliminated? Risk would be totally eliminated if losses in the cash markets were *exactly* offset in the futures markets and vice versa. This is unlike-

TABLE 24.6 Illustration of Hedging Strategy for Ron Cooke, Mortgage Banker

	Cash Markets	*Futures Markets*
March 1	Mortgage banker makes forward contracts to loan $1 million at 12 percent for 20 years. The loans are to be funded on May 1. No cash changes hands on March 1.	Mortgage banker writes 10 June Treasury-bond futures contracts.
April 15	Loans are sold to Acme Insurance Company. Mortgage banker will receive sale price from Acme on the May 1 funding date.	Mortgage banker buys back all the futures contracts.
If interest rates rise:	Loans are sold at a price below $1 million. Mortgage banker *loses* because he receives less than the $1 million he must give to borrowers.	Each futures contract is bought back at a price below the sales price, resulting in *profit.* Mortgage banker's profit in futures market offsets loss in cash market.
If interest rates fall:	Loans are sold at a price above $1 million. Mortgage banker *gains* because he receives more than the $1 million he must give to borrowers.	Each futures contract is bought back at a price above the sales price, resulting in *loss.* Mortgage banker's loss in futures market offsets gain in cash market.

ly to happen because mortgages and Treasury bonds are not identical instruments. First, mortgages may have different maturities than Treasury bonds. Second, Treasury bonds have a different payment stream than do mortgages. Principal is only paid at maturity on T-bonds, whereas principal is paid every month on mortgages. Because mortgages pay principal continuously, these instruments have a shorter *effective* time to maturity than do Treasury bonds of equal maturity.[10] Third, mortgages have default risk whereas Treasury bonds do not. The term structure applicable to instruments with default risk may change even when the term structure for risk-free assets remains constant. Fourth, mortgages may be paid off early and hence have a shorter *expected maturity* than Treasury bonds of equal maturity.

Because mortgages and Treasury bonds are not identical instruments, they are not identically affected by interest rates. If Treasury bonds are less volatile than mortgages, financial consultants may advise Mr. Cooke to write more than 10 T-bond futures contracts. Conversely, if these bonds are more volatile, the consultant may state that less than 10 futures contracts are indicated. An optimal ratio of futures contracts to mortgages will reduce risk as much as possible. However, because the price movements of mortgages and Treasury bonds are not *perfectly correlated,* Mr. Cooke's hedging strategy cannot eliminate all risk.

The above strategy is called a *short hedge* because Mr. Cooke sells futures contracts in order to reduce risk. Though it involves an interest-rate futures contract, this short hedge is analogous to short hedges in agricultural and metallurgical futures contracts. We argued at the beginning of this chapter that individuals and firms institute short hedges to offset inventory price fluctuation. Once Mr. Cooke makes a contract to loan money to borrowers, the mortgages effectively become his inventory. He writes a futures contract to offset the price fluctuation of his inventory.

We now consider an example where a mortgage banker institutes a long hedge.

• ***Example***

Margaret Boswell is another mortgage banker. Her firm faces problems similar to those facing Mr. Cooke's firm. However, she tackles the problems through the use of **advance commitments,** a strategy the opposite of Mr. Cooke's. That is, she promises to deliver loans to a financial institution *before* she lines up borrowers. On March 1, her firm agreed to sell mortgages to No-State Insurance Co. The agreement specifies that she must turn over 12-percent coupon mortgages with a face value of $1 million to No-State by May 1. No-State is buying the mortgages at par, implying that they will pay Ms. Boswell $1 million on May 1. As of March 1, Ms. Boswell had not signed up any borrowers. Over the next two months, she will seek out individuals who want mortgages beginning May 1.

As with Mr. Cooke, changing interest rates will affect Ms. Boswell. If interest rates fall before she signs up a borrower, the borrower will demand a premium on a 12-percent coupon loan. That is, the borrower will receive more than par on May 1.[11] Because Ms. Boswell receives par from the insurance company, she must make up the difference.

---

[10] Alternatively, we can say that mortgages have shorter duration than do Treasury bonds of equal maturity. A precise definition of duration is provided later in this chapter.

[11] Alternatively, the mortgage would still be at par if a coupon rate below 12 percent were used. However, this is not done since the insurance company only wants to buy 12-percent mortgages.

TABLE 24.7 Illustration of Advance Commitment for Margaret Boswell, Mortgage Banker

	Cash Markets	*Futures Markets*
March 1	Mortgage banker makes a forward contract (advance commitment) to deliver $1 million of mortgages to No-State Insurance. The insurance company will pay par to Ms. Boswell for the loans on May 1. The borrowers are to receive their funding from mortgage banker on May 1. The mortgages are to be 12-percent coupon loans for 20 years.	Mortgage banker buys 10 June Treasury-bond futures contracts.
April 15	Mortgage banker signs up borrowers to 12-percent coupon, 20-year mortgages. She promises that the borrowers will receive funds on May 1.	Mortgage banker sells all futures contracts.
If interest rates rise:	Mortgage banker issues mortgages to borrowers at a discount. Mortgage banker *gains* because she receives par from insurance company.	Futures contract is sold at a price below purchase price, resulting in *loss*. Mortgage banker's loss in futures market offsets gain in cash market.
If interest rates fall:	Loans to borrowers are issued at a premium. Mortgage banker *loses* becauses he receives only par from insurance company.	Futures contract is sold at a price above purchase price, resulting in *gain*. Mortgage banker's gain in futures market offsets loss in cash market.

Conversely, if interest rates rise, a 12-percent coupon loan will be made at a discount. That is, the borrower will receive less than par on May 1. Because Ms. Boswell receives par from the insurance company, the difference is pure profit to her.

The details are provided in the left-hand column of Table 24.7. As did Mr. Cooke, Ms. Boswell finds the risk burdensome. Therefore, she offsets her advance commitment with a transaction in the futures markets. Because she *loses* in the cash market when interest rates fall, she *buys* futures contracts to reduce the risk. When interest rates fall, the value of her futures contracts increases. The gain in the futures market offsets the loss in the cash market. Conversely, she gains in the cash markets when interest rates rise. The value of her futures contracts decreases when interest rates rise, offsetting her gain.

We call this a *long hedge* because Ms. Boswell offsets risk in the cash markets by buying a futures contract. Though it involves an interest-rate futures contract, this long hedge is analogous to long hedges in agricultural and metallurgical futures contracts. We argued at the beginning of this chapter that individuals and firms institute long hedges when their finished goods are to be sold at a fixed price. Once Ms. Boswell makes the advance commitment with No-State Insurance, she has fixed her sales price. She buys a futures contract to offset the price fluctuation of her raw materials, that is, her mortgages. •

Concept Questions

- How are forward contracts on bonds priced?
- What are the differences between forward contracts on bonds and futures contracts on bonds?
- Give examples of hedging with futures contracts on bonds.

24.5 Duration Hedging

The last section concerned the risk of interest-rate changes. We now want to explore this risk in a more precise manner. In particular, we want to show that the concept of duration is a prime determinant of interest-rate risk. We begin by considering the effect of interest-rate movements on bond prices.

The Case of Zero-Coupon Bonds

Imagine a world where the interest rate is 10 percent across all maturities. A one-year pure discount bond pays \$110 at maturity. A five-year pure discount bond pays \$161.05 at maturity. Both of these bonds are worth \$100, as given by[12]

Value of One-Year Pure Discount Bond:

$$\$100 = \frac{\$110}{1.10}$$

Value of Five-Year Pure Discount Bond:

$$\$100 = \frac{\$161.05}{(1.10)^5}$$

Which bond will change more when interest rates move? To find out, we calculate the value of these bonds when interest rates are either 8 or 12 percent. The results are presented in Table 24.8. As can be seen, the five-year bond has greater price swings than does the one-year bond. That is, both bonds are worth \$100 when interest rates are 10 percent. The five-year bond is worth more than the one-year bond when interest rates are 8 percent and worth less than the one-year bond when interest rates are 12 percent. We state that the five-year bond is subject to more price volatility. This point, which was mentioned in passing in an earlier section of the chapter, is not difficult to understand. The interest-rate term in the denominator, $1+r$, is taken to the fifth power for a five-year bond and only to the first power for the one-year bond. Thus, the effect of a changing interest rate is magnified for the five-year bond. The general rule is

[12] Alternatively, we could have chosen bonds that pay \$100 at maturity. Their values would be \$90.91 (\$100/1.10) and \$62.09 [\$100/(1.10)^5]. However, our comparisons to come are made easier if both have the same initial price.

TABLE 24.8 Value of a Pure Discount Bond as a Function of Interest Rate

Interest Rate	*1-Year Pure Discount Bond*	*5-Year Pure Discount Bond*
8%	$\$101.85 = \frac{\$110}{1.08}$	$\$109.61 = \frac{\$161.05}{(1.08)^5}$
10%	$\$100.00 = \frac{\$110}{1.10}$	$\$100.00 = \frac{\$161.05}{(1.10)^5}$
12%	$\$98.21 = \frac{\$110}{1.12}$	$\$91.38 = \frac{\$161.05}{(1.12)^5}$

For a given interest rate change, a five-year pure discount bond fluctuates more in price than does a one-year pure discount bond.

> The percentage price changes in long-term pure discount bonds are greater than the percentage price changes in short-term pure discount bonds.

The Case of Two Bonds with the Same Maturity but with Different Coupons

The previous example concerned pure discount bonds of different maturities. We now want to see the effect of different coupons on price volatility. To abstract from the effect of differing maturities, we consider two bonds with the same maturity but with different coupons.

Consider a five-year, 10-percent coupon bond and a five-year, 1-percent coupon bond. When interest rates are 10 percent, the bonds are priced at

Value of Five-Year, 10-Percent Coupon Bond:

$$\$100 = \frac{\$10}{1.10} + \frac{\$10}{(1.10)^2} + \frac{\$10}{(1.10)^3} + \frac{\$10}{(1.10)^4} + \frac{\$110}{(1.10)^5}$$

Value of Five-Year, 1-Percent Coupon Bond:

$$\$65.88 = \frac{\$1}{1.10} + \frac{\$1}{(1.10)^2} + \frac{\$1}{(1.10)^3} + \frac{\$1}{(1.10)^4} + \frac{\$101}{(1.10)^5}$$

Which bond will change more *in percentage terms* if interest rates change?[13] To find out, we first calculate the value of these bonds when interest rates are either 8 or 12 percent. The results are presented in Table 24.9. As we would expect, the 10-percent coupon bond always sells for more than the 1-percent coupon bond. Also, as we would

[13] The bonds are at different prices initially. Thus, we are concerned with percentage price changes, not absolute price changes.

TABLE 24.9 Value of Coupon Bonds at Different Interest Rates

Interest Rate	*5-Year, 10% Coupon Bond*
8%	$\$107.99 = \frac{\$10}{1.08} + \frac{\$10}{(1.08)^2} + \frac{\$10}{(1.08)^3} + \frac{\$10}{(1.08)^4} + \frac{\$110}{(1.08)^5}$
10%	$\$100.00 = \frac{\$10}{1.10} + \frac{\$10}{(1.10)^2} + \frac{\$10}{(1.10)^3} + \frac{\$10}{(1.10)^4} + \frac{\$110}{(1.10)^5}$
12%	$\$\ 92.79 = \frac{\$10}{1.12} + \frac{\$10}{(1.12)^2} + \frac{\$10}{(1.12)^3} + \frac{\$10}{(1.12)^4} + \frac{\$110}{(1.12)^5}$
Interest Rate	*5-year, 1% Coupon Bond*
8%	$\$\ 72.05 = \frac{\$1}{1.08} + \frac{\$1}{(1.08)^2} + \frac{\$1}{(1.08)^3} + \frac{\$1}{(1.08)^4} + \frac{\$101}{(1.08)^5}$
10%	$\$\ 65.88 = \frac{\$1}{1.10} + \frac{\$1}{(1.10)^2} + \frac{\$1}{(1.10)^3} + \frac{\$1}{(1.10)^4} + \frac{\$101}{(1.10)^5}$
12%	$\$\ 60.35 = \frac{\$1}{1.12} + \frac{\$1}{(1.12)^2} + \frac{\$1}{(1.12)^3} + \frac{\$1}{(1.12)^4} + \frac{\$101}{(1.12)^5}$

expect, each bond is worth more when the interest rate is 8 percent than when the interest rate is 12 percent.

We calculate percentage price changes for both bonds as the interest rate changes from 10 to 8 percent and from 10 to 12 percent. These percentage price changes are

	10% Coupon Bond	*1% Coupon Bond*
Interest rate changes from 10% to 8%:	$7.99\% = \frac{\$107.99}{\$100} - 1$	$9.37\% = \frac{\$72.05}{\$65.88} - 1$
Interest rate changes from 10% to 12%:	$-7.21\% = \frac{\$92.79}{\$100} - 1$	$-8.39\% = \frac{\$60.35}{\$65.88} - 1$

As can be seen, the 1-percent coupon bond has a greater percentage price increase than does the 10-percent coupon bond when the interest rate falls. Similarly, the 1-percent coupon bond has a greater percentage price decrease than does the 10-percent coupon bond when the interest rate rises. Thus, we say that the percentage price changes on the 1-percent coupon bond are greater than are the percentage price changes on the 10-percent coupon bond.

Duration

The question, of course, is "Why?" We can answer this question only after we have explored a concept called **duration.** We begin by noticing that any coupon bond is actually a combination of pure discount bonds. For example, the 5-year, 10-percent coupon bond is made up of five pure discount bonds:

1. A pure discount bond paying \$10 at the end of year 1.
2. A pure discount bond paying \$10 at the end of year 2.
3. A pure discount bond paying \$10 at the end of year 3.
4. A pure discount bond paying \$10 at the end of year 4.
5. A pure discount bond paying \$110 at the end of year 5.

Similarly, the five-year, 1-percent coupon bond is made up of five pure discount bonds. Because the price volatility of a pure discount bond is determined by its maturity, we would like to determine the average maturity of the five pure discount bonds that make up a five-year coupon bond. This leads us to the concept of duration.

We calculate average maturity in three steps. For the 10-percent coupon bond, we have these:

1. *Calculate Present Value of Each Payment.* We do this as

Year	*Payment*	*Present Value of Payment by Discounting at 10%*
1	\$ 10	\$ 9.091
2	10	8.264
3	10	7.513
4	10	6.830
5	110	68.302
		\$100.00

2. *Express the Present Value of Each Payment in Relative Terms.* We calculate the relative value of a single payment as the ratio of the present value of the payment to the value of the bond. The value of the bond is \$100. We have

Year	Payment	Present Value of Payment	Relative Value = $\frac{\text{Present Value of Payment}}{\text{Value of Bond}}$
1	$ 10	$ 9.091	$9.091/$100 = 0.09091
2	10	8.264	0.08264
3	10	7.513	0.07513
4	10	6.830	0.06830
5	110	68.302	0.68302
		$100.00	1.0

The bulk of the relative value, 68.302 percent, occurs at year 5 because the principal is paid back at that time.

3. *Weight the Maturity of Each Payment by Its Relative Value.* We have

$$4.1699 \text{ years} = 1 \text{ year} \times 0.09091 + 2 \text{ years} \times 0.08264 + 3 \text{ years} \times 0.07513 + 4 \text{ years} \times 0.06830 + 5 \text{ years} \times 0.68302$$

There are many ways to calculate the average maturity of a bond. We have calculated it by weighting the maturity of each payment by the payment's present value. We find that the *effective* maturity of the bond is 4.1699 years. Duration is a commonly used word for effective maturity. Thus, the bond's duration is 4.1699 years. Note that duration is expressed in units of time.[14]

Because the five-year, 10-percent coupon bond has a duration of 4.1699 years, its percentage price fluctuations should be the same as those of a zero-coupon bond with a duration of 4.1699 years.[15] It turns out that the five-year, 1-percent coupon bond has a duration of 4.8742 years. Because the 1-percent coupon bond has a higher duration than the 10-percent bond, the 1-percent coupon bond should be subject to greater price fluctuations. This is exactly what we found earlier. In general, we say:

> The percentage price changes of a bond with high duration are greater than the percentage price changes of a bond with low duration.

A final question: Why *does* the 1-percent bond have a greater duration than the 10-percent bond, even though they both have the same five-year maturity? As mentioned earlier, duration is an average of the maturity of the bond's cash flows, weighted by the present value of each cash flow. The 1-percent coupon bond receives only $1 in

[14] The mathematical formula for duration is

$$\text{Duration} = \frac{PV(C_1)1 + PV(C_2)2 + \cdots + PV(C_T)t}{PV}$$

and

$$PV = PV(C_1) + PV(C_2) + \cdots + PV(C_T)$$

$$PV(C_T) = \frac{C_T}{(1+r)^T}$$

Where C_T is the cash to be received in time T and r is the current discount rate.

Also note that in the above numerical example we discounted each payment by the interest rate of 10 percent. This was done because we wanted to calculate the duration of the bond before a change in the interest rate occurred. After a change in the rate to, say, 8 or 12 percent, all three of our steps would need to reflect the new interest rate. In other words, the duration of a bond is a function of the current interest rate.

[15] Actually, this relationship only exactly holds in the case of a one-time shift in a flat yield curve, where the change in the spot rate is identical for all different maturities.

each of the first four years. Thus, the weights applied to years 1 through 4 in the duration formula will be low. Conversely, the 10-percent coupon bond receives $10 in each of the first four years. The weights applied to years 1 through 4 in the duration formula will be higher.

Matching Liabilities with Assets

Earlier in this chapter we argued that firms can hedge risk by trading in futures. Because some firms are subject to interest-rate risk, we showed how they can hedge with interest-rate futures contracts. Firms may also hedge interest-rate risk by matching liabilities with assets. This ability to hedge follows from our discussion of duration.

• ***Example***

The Physical Bank of New York has the following market-value balance sheet:

PHYSICAL BANK OF NEW YORK
Market-Value Balance Sheet

	Market Value	*Duration*
Assets		
Overnight money	$ 35 million	0
Accounts-receivable–backed loans	$ 500 million	3 months
Inventory loans	$ 275 million	6 months
Industrial loans	$ 40 million	2 years
Mortgages	$ 150 million	14.8 years
	$1,000 million	
Liabilities and Owners' Equity		
Checking and savings accounts	$ 400 million	0
Certificate of deposits	$ 300 million	1 year
Long-term financing	$ 200 million	10 years
Equity	$ 100 million	
	$1,000 million	

The bank has $1,000 million of assets and $900 million of liabilities. Its equity is the difference between the two: $100 million ($1,000 million − $900 million). Both the market value and the duration of each individual item is provided in the balance sheet. Both overnight money and checking and savings accounts have a duration of zero. This is because the interest paid on these instruments adjusts immediately to changing interest rates in the economy.

The bank's managers think that interest rates are likely to move quickly in the coming months. Because they do not know the direction of the movement, they are worried that their bank is vulnerable to changing rates. They call in a consultant, James Charest, to determine hedging strategy.

Mr. Charest first calculates the duration of the assets and the duration of the liabilities.[16]

[16] Note that the duration of a group of items is an average of the durations of the individual items, weighted by the market value of each item. This is a simplifying step that greatly increases duration's practicality.

Duration of Assets:

$$2.56 \text{ years} = 0 \text{ years} \times \frac{\$35 \text{ million}}{\$1{,}000 \text{ million}} + \tfrac{1}{4} \text{ year} \times \frac{\$500 \text{ million}}{\$1{,}000 \text{ million}} + \tfrac{1}{2} \text{ year} \times \frac{\$275 \text{ million}}{\$1{,}000 \text{ million}} + 2 \text{ years} \times \frac{\$40 \text{ million}}{\$1{,}000 \text{ million}} + 14.8 \text{ years} \times \frac{\$150 \text{ million}}{\$1{,}000 \text{ million}} \quad (24.4)$$

Duration of Liabilities:

$$2.56 \text{ years} = 0 \text{ years} \times \frac{\$400 \text{ million}}{\$900 \text{ million}} + 1 \text{ year} \times \frac{\$300 \text{ million}}{\$900 \text{ million}} + 10 \text{ years} \times \frac{\$200 \text{ million}}{\$900 \text{ million}} \quad (24.5)$$

The duration of the assets, 2.56 years, equals the duration of the liabilities. Because of this, Mr. Charest argues that the firm is immune to interest-rate risk.

Just to be on the safe side, the bank calls in a second consultant, Gail Ellert. Ms. Ellert argues that it is incorrect to simply match durations, because assets total $1,000 million and liabilities total only $900 million. If both assets and liabilities have the same duration, the price change on a *dollar* of assets should be equal to the price change on a dollar of liabilities. However, the *total* price change will be greater for assets than for liabilities, because there are more assets than liabilities in this bank. The firm will be immune from interest-rate risk only when the duration of the liabilities is greater than the duration of the assets. Ms. Ellert states that the following relationship must hold if the bank is to be **immunized,** that is, immune to interest-rate risk:

$$\text{Duration of assets} \times \text{Market value of assets} = \text{Duration of liabilities} \times \text{Market value of liabilities} \quad (24.6)$$

She says that the bank should not *equate* the duration of the liabilities with the duration of the assets. Rather, using (24.6), the bank should match the duration of the liabilities to the duration of the assets. She suggests two ways to achieve this match.

1. *Increase the Duration of the Liabilities without Changing the Duration of the Assets.* Ms. Ellert argues that the duration of the liabilities could be increased to

$$\text{Duration of assets} \times \frac{\text{Market value of assets}}{\text{Market value of liabilities}} = 2.56 \text{ years} \times \frac{\$1{,}000 \text{ million}}{\$900 \text{ million}} = 2.84 \text{ years}$$

Equation (24.5) then becomes:

$$2.56 \times \$1 \text{ billion} = 2.84 \times \$900 \text{ million}$$

2. *Decrease the Duration of the Assets without Changing the Duration of the Liabilities.* Alternatively, Ms. Ellert points out that the duration of the assets could be decreased to

$$\begin{aligned}&\text{Duration of liabilities} \times \frac{\text{Market value of liabilities}}{\text{Market value of assets}}\\ &= 2.56 \text{ years} \times \frac{\$900 \text{ million}}{\$1{,}000 \text{ million}}\\ &= 2.30 \text{ years}\end{aligned}$$

Equation (24.6) then becomes:

$$2.30 \times \$1 \text{ billion} = 2.56 \times \$900 \text{ million} \bullet$$

Though we agree with Ms. Ellert's analysis, the bank's current mismatch was small anyway. Huge mismatches have occurred for real-world financial institutions, particularly savings and loans. S&Ls have frequently invested large portions of their assets in mortgages. The durations of these mortgages would clearly be above 10 years. Much of the funds available for mortgage lending were financed by short-term credit, especially savings accounts. As we mentioned, the duration of such instruments is quite small. A thrift institution in this situation faced a large amount of interest-rate risk, because any increase in interest rates would greatly reduce the value of the mortgages. Because an interest-rate rise would only reduce the value of the liabilities slightly, the equity of the firm would fall. As interest rates rose over much of the 1960s and 1970s, many S&Ls found that the market value of their equity approached zero.[17]

Duration and the accompanying immunization strategies are useful in other areas of finance. For example, many firms establish pension funds to meet obligations to retirees. If the assets of a pension fund are invested in bonds and other fixed-income securities, the duration of the assets can be computed. Similarly, the firm views the obligations to retirees as analogous to interest payments on debt. The duration of these liabilities can be calculated as well. The manager of a pension fund would commonly choose pension assets so that the duration of the assets is matched with the duration of the liabilities. In this way, changing interest rates would not affect the net worth of the pension fund.

Life insurance companies receiving premiums today are legally obligated to provide death benefits in the future. Actuaries view these future benefits as analogous to interest and principal payments of fixed-income securities. The duration of these expected benefits can be calculated. Insurance firms frequently invest in bonds where the duration of the bonds is matched to the duration of the future death benefits.

The business of a leasing company is quite simple. The firm issues debt to purchase assets, which are then leased. The lease payments have a duration, as does the debt. Leasing companies frequently structure debt financing so that the duration of the debt matches the duration of the lease. If the firm did not do this, the market value of its equity could be eliminated by a quick change in interest rates.

Concept Questions

- What is duration?
- How is the concept of duration used to reduce interest-rate risk?

[17] Actually, the market value of the equity could easily be negative in this example. However, S&Ls in the real world have an asset not shown on our market-value balance sheet: the ability to generate new, profitable loans. This should increase the market value of a thrift above the market value of its outstanding loans less its existing debt.

24.6 Swaps Contracts

Swaps are close cousins to forwards and futures contracts. Swaps are arrangements between two counterparties to exchange cash flows over time. There is enormous flexibility in the forms that swaps can take, but the two basic types are **interest-rate swaps** or **currency swaps.** Often these are combined when interest received in one currency is swapped for interest in another currency.

Interest-Rate Swaps

Like other derivatives, swaps are tools that firms can use to easily change their risk exposures and their balance sheets. Consider a firm that has borrowed and carries on its books an obligation to repay a 10-year loan for \$100 million of principal with a 9 percent coupon rate paid annually. Ignoring the possibility of calling the loan, the firm expects to have to pay coupons of \$9 million every year for 10 years and a balloon payment of \$100 million at the end of the 10 years. Suppose, though, that the firm is uncomfortable with having this large fixed obligation on its books. Perhaps the firm is in a cyclical business where its revenues vary and could, conceivably, fall to a point where it would be difficult to make the debt payment.

Suppose, too, that the firm earns a lot of its revenue from financing the purchase of its products. Typically, for example, a manufacturer might help its customers finance their purchase of its products through a leasing or credit subsidiary. Usually these loans are for relatively short time periods and are financed at some premium over the prevailing short rate of interest. This puts the firm in the position of having revenues that move up and down with interest rates while its costs are relatively fixed.

This is a classic situation where a swap can be used to offset the risk. When interest rates rise, it would have to pay more on the loan, but it would be making more on its product financing. What the firm would really prefer is to have a floating-rate loan rather than a fixed-rate loan. It can use a swap to accomplish this.

Of course, the firm could also just go into the capital markets and borrow \$100 million at a variable interest rate and then use the proceeds to retire its outstanding fixed-rate loan. While this is possible, it is generally quite expensive, requiring underwriting a new loan and the repurchase of the existing loan. The ease of entering into a swap is its inherent advantage.

The particular swap would be one that exchanged its fixed obligation for an agreement to pay a floating rate. Every six months it would agree to pay a coupon based on whatever the prevailing interest rate was at that time in exchange for an agreement from a counterparty to pay the firm's fixed coupon.

A common reference point for floating-rate commitments is called LIBOR. LIBOR stands for the London Interbank Offered Rate, and it is the rate that most international banks charge one another for dollar-denominated loans in the London market. LIBOR is commonly used as the reference rate for a floating-rate commitment, and, depending on the creditworthiness of the borrower, the rate can vary from LIBOR to LIBOR plus one point or more over LIBOR.

If we assume that our firm has a credit rating that requires it to pay LIBOR plus 50 basis points, then in a swap it would be exchanging its fixed 9 percent obligation for the obligation to pay whatever the prevailing LIBOR rate is plus 50 basis points. Figure 24.2 displays how the cash flows on this swap would work. In the figure we have assumed that LIBOR starts at 8 percent and rises for four years to 11 percent and then drops to 7 percent. As the figure illustrates, the firm would owe a coupon of $8.5\% \times \$100$ million = \$8.5 million in year 1, \$9.5 million in year 2, \$10.5 million

FIGURE 24.2 Fixed-for-Floating a Swap: Cash Flows ($million)

A. Swap						Coupons					
	Year	*1*	*2*	*3*	*4*	*5*	*6*	*7*	*8*	*9*	*10*
Fixed Obligation	9	9	9	9	9	9	9	9	9	9	+ 100
LIBOR Floating	−8.5	−9.5	−10.5	−11.5	−7.5	−7.5	−7.5	−7.5	−7.5	−7.5	+ 100
B. Original Loan											
Fixed Obligation	−9	−9	−9	−9	−9	−9	−9	−9	−9	−9	+100
Net Effect	−8.5	−9.5	10.5	11.5	7.5	7.5	7.5	7.5	7.5	7.5	+100

in year 3, and $11.5 million in year 4. The precipitous drop to 7 percent lowers the annual payments to $7.5 million thereafter. In return, the firm receives the fixed payment of $9 million each year. Actually, rather than swapping the full payments, the cash flows would be netted. Since the firm is paying variable and receiving fixed—which it uses to pay its lender—in the first year, for example, the firm owes $8.5 million and is owed by its counterparty who is paying fixed, $9 million. Hence, net, the firm would receive a payment of $.5 million. Since the firm has to pay its lender $9 million, but gets a net payment from the swap of $.5 million, it really only pays out the difference, or $8.5 million. In each year, then, the firm would effectively pay only LIBOR plus 50 basis points.

Notice, too, that the entire transaction can be carried out without any need to change the terms of the original loan. In effect, by swapping the firm has found a counterparty who is willing to pay its fixed obligation in return for the firm paying a floating obligation.

Currency Swaps

FX stands for foreign exchange, and currency swaps are sometimes called FX swaps. Currency swaps are swaps of obligations to pay cash flows in one currency for obligations to pay in another currency.

Currency swaps arise as a natural vehicle for hedging the risks in international trade. For example, suppose a U.S. firm sells a broad range of its product line in the German market. Every year the firm can count on receiving revenue from Germany in the German currency, Deutschemarks, or DM for short. We will study international finance later in this book, but for now we can just observe that, because exchange rates fluctuate, this subjects the firm to considerable risk.

If the firm produces its products in the United States and exports them to Germany, then the firm has to pay its workers and its suppliers in dollars. But, it is receiving some of its revenues in DM. The exchange rate between $ and DM changes over time. As the DM rises in value, the German revenues are worth more $, but as it falls they decline. Suppose that the firm can count on selling 100 million DM of goods each year in Germany. If the exchange rate is 2 DM for each $, then the firm will receive \$50 million. But, if the exchange rate were to rise to 3 DM for each \$, the firm would only receive \$33.333 million for its 100 million DM. Naturally the firm would like to protect itself against these currency swings.

To do so the firm can enter into a currency swap. We will learn more about exactly what the terms of such a swap might be, but for now we can assume that the swap is for five years at a fixed term of 100 million DM for \$50 million each year. Now, no matter what happens to the exchange rate between DM and \$ over the next five years, as long as the firm makes 100 million DM each year from the sale of its products, it will swap this for \$50 million each year.

We have not addressed the question of how the market prices swaps, either interest-rate swaps or currency swaps. In the fixed-for-floating example and in the currency swap, we just quoted some terms. We won't go into great detail on exactly how it is done, but we can stress the most important points.

Swaps, like forwards and futures, are essentially zero-sum transactions, which is to say that in both cases the market sets prices at a fair level, and neither party has any substantial bargain or loss at the moment the deal is struck. For example, in the currency swap, the swap rate is some average of the market expectation of what the exchange rate will be over the life of the swap. In the interest-rate swap, the rates are set as the fair floating and fixed rates for the creditor, taking account of the creditworthiness of the counterparties. We can actually price swaps fairly once we know how to price forward contracts. In our interest-rate swap example, the firm swapped LIBOR plus 50 basis points for a 9 percent, fixed rate, all on a principal amount of \$100 million. This is equivalent to a series of forward contracts extending out the life of the swap. In year one, for example, having made the swap, the firm is in the same position that it would be if it had sold a forward contract entitling the buyer to receive LIBOR plus 50 basis points on \$100 million in return for a fixed payment of \$9 million (9% on \$100 million). Similarly, the currency swap can also be viewed as a series of forward contracts.

Concept Question

- Show that a currency swap is equivalent to a series of forward contracts.

Exotics

Up to now we have dealt with the meat and potatoes of the derivatives markets, swaps, options, forwards, and futures. **Exotics** are the complicated blends of these that often produce the surprising results for the buyers.

One of the more interesting types of exotics is called an *inverse floater.* In our fixed-for-floating swap, the floating payments fluctuated with LIBOR. An inverse floater is one that fluctuates inversely with some rate such as LIBOR. For example, the floater might pay an interest of 20 percent minus LIBOR. If LIBOR is 9 percent, then the inverse pays 11 percent, and if LIBOR rises to 12 percent, the payments on the inverse would fall to 8 percent. Clearly the purchaser of an inverse profits from the inverse if interest rates fall.

Both floaters and inverse floaters have a supercharged version called *superfloaters* and *superinverses* that fluctuate more than one for one with movements in interest rates. As an example of a superinverse floater, consider a floater that pays an interest rate of 30 percent minus *twice* LIBOR. When LIBOR is 10 percent, the inverse pays

$$30\% - 2\times10\% = 30\% - 20\% = 10\%$$

and if LIBOR falls by 3 percent to 7 percent, then the return on the inverse rises by 6 percent from 10 percent to 16 percent,

$$30\% - 2\times 7\% = 30\% - 14\% = 16\%$$

Sometimes derivatives are combined with options to bound the impact of interest rates. The most important of these instruments are called *caps* and *floors.* A cap is so named because it puts an upper limit or a cap on the impact of a rise in interest rates. A floor, conversely, provides a floor below which the interest rate impact is insulated.

To illustrate the impact of these, consider a firm that is borrowing short-term and is concerned that interest rates might rise. For example, using LIBOR as the reference interest rate, the firm might purchase a 7 percent cap. The cap pays the firm the difference between LIBOR and 7 percent on some principal amount, provided that LIBOR is greater than 7 percent. As long as LIBOR is below 7 percent, the holder of the cap receives no payments.

By purchasing the cap the firm has assured itself that even if interest rates rise above 7 percent, it will not have to pay more than a 7 percent rate. Suppose that interest rates rise to 9 percent. While the firm is borrowing short-term and paying 9 percent rates, this is offset by the cap, which is paying the firm the difference between 9 percent and the 7 percent limit. For any LIBOR rate above 7 percent, the firm receives the difference between LIBOR and 7 percent, and, as a consequence, it has capped its cost of borrowing at 7 percent.

On the other side, consider a financial firm that is in the business of lending short-term and is concerned that interest rates—and, consequently, its revenues—might fall. The firm could purchase a floor to protect itself from such declines. If the limit on the floor is 7 percent, then the floor pays the difference between 7 percent and LIBOR whenever LIBOR is below 7 percent, and nothing if LIBOR is above 7 percent. Thus, if interest rates were to fall to, say, 5 percent while the firm is only receiving 5 percent from its lending activities, the floor is paying it the difference between 7 percent and 5 percent, or an additional 2 percent. By purchasing the floor, the firm has assured itself of receiving no less than 7 percent from the combination of the floor and its lending activities.

We have only scratched the surface of what is available in the world of derivatives. Derivatives are designed to meet marketplace needs, and the only binding limitation is the human imagination. Nowhere should the buyer's warning *caveat emptor* be taken more seriously than in the derivatives markets, and this is especially true for the exotics. If swaps are the meat and potatoes of the derivatives markets, then caps and floors are the meat and potatoes of the exotics. As we have seen, they have obvious value as hedging instruments. But, much attention has been focused on truly exotic derivatives, some of which appear to have arisen more as the residuals that were left over from more straightforward deals. We won't examine these in any detail, but suffice it to say that some of these are so volatile and unpredictable that market participants have dubbed them "toxic waste."

24.6 Summary and Conclusions

1. Firms hedge to reduce risk. This chapter shows a number of hedging strategies.
2. A forward contract is an agreement by two parties to sell an item for cash at a later date. The price is set at the time the agreement is signed. However, cash changes hands on the date of delivery. Forward contracts are generally not traded on organized exchanges.

3. Futures contracts are also agreements for future delivery. They have certain advantages, such as liquidity, that forward contracts do not. An unusual feature of futures contracts is the mark-to-the-market convention. If the price of a futures contract falls on a particular day, every buyer of the contract must pay money to the clearinghouse. Every seller of the contract receives money from the clearinghouse. Everything is reversed if the price rises. The mark-to-the-market convention prevents defaults on futures contracts.
4. We divided hedges into two types: short hedges and long hedges. An individual or firm that sells a futures contract to reduce risk is instituting a short hedge. Short hedges are generally appropriate for holders of inventory. An individual or firm that buys a futures contract to reduce risk is instituting a long hedge. Long hedges are typically used by firms with contracts to sell finished goods at a fixed price.
5. An interest-rate futures contract employs a bond as the deliverable instrument. Because of their popularity, we worked with Treasury-bond futures contracts. We showed that Treasury-bond futures contracts can be priced using the same type of net-present-value analysis that is used to price Treasury bonds themselves.
6. Many firms are faced with interest-rate risk. They can reduce this risk by hedging with interest-rate futures contracts. As with other commodities, a short hedge involves the sale of a futures contract. Firms that are committed to buying mortgages or other bonds are likely to institute short hedges. A long hedge involves the purchase of a futures contract. Firms that have agreed to sell mortgages or other bonds at a fixed price are likely to institute long hedges.
7. Duration measures the average maturity of all the cash flows in a bond. Bonds with high duration have high price variability. Firms frequently try to match the duration of their assets with the duration of their liabilities.
8. Swaps are agreements to exchange cash flows over time. The first major type is an interest-rate swap in which one pattern of coupon payments, say fixed payments, are exchanged for another, say, coupons that float with LIBOR. The second major type is a currency swap in which an agreement is struck to swap payments denominated in one currency for payments in another currency over time.

Key Terms

Hedging 654
Speculating 654
Forward contract 654
Taking delivery 654
Deliverable instrument 654
Making delivery 654
Cash transaction 655
Futures contract 655
Marked to the market 656
Short hedge 661
Long hedge 662
Advance commitments 668
Duration 672
Immunized 675
Swaps 677
Interest-rate swaps 677
Currency swaps 677
Exotics 679

Questions and Problems

Futures and Forward Contracts

24.1 Define:

a. Forward contract
b. Futures contract

24.2 Explain the three ways in which futures contracts and forward contracts differ.

24.3 The following table lists the closing prices for wheat futures contracts. Suppose you bought one contract at $5.00 at the opening of trade on March 15.

March 15	$5.03
March 16	$5.08
March 17	$5.12
March 18	$5.10
March 19	$4.98

a. Suppose that on March 18 you receive from your broker a notice of delivery on that day.
  i. What is the delivery price?
  ii. What price did you pay for wheat?
  iii. List the cash flows associated with this contract.

b. Suppose that on March 19 you receive from your broker a notice of delivery on that day.
  i. What is the delivery price?
  ii. What price did you pay for wheat?
  iii. List the cash flows associated with this contract.

24.4 Two days ago, you agreed to buy a 10-year, zero-coupon bond that would be issued in a year. Today, both the 1-year and 11-year spot rates unexpectedly shifted downward an equal amount. What should today's price of the forward contract be?

24.5 *a.* How is a short hedge created?
b. In what type of situation is a short hedge a wise strategy?
c. How is a long hedge created?
d. In what type of situation is a long hedge a wise strategy?

24.6 A speculator is an investor who uses his or her private information to profit from futures contracts. Mary Johnson is a speculator, who believes that wheat futures price will fall in a month. What position would Mary Johnson take?

24.7 A classmate of yours recently entered the import/export business. During a visit with him last week, he said to you, "If you play the game right, this is the safest business in the world. By hedging all my transactions in the foreign-exchange futures market, I eliminate all risk."

Do you agree with your friend's assessment of hedging? Why or why not?

24.8 This morning you agreed to buy a two-year Treasury bond six months from today. The bond carries a 10-percent coupon rate and has a $1,000 face. Below are listed the expected spot rates of interest for the life of the bond. These rates are semiannual rates.

Time from Today	*Semiannual Rate*
6 months	0.048
12 months	0.050
18 months	0.052
24 months	0.055
30 months	0.057

a. How much should you have paid for this forward contract?
b. Suppose that shortly after you purchased the forward contract, all semiannual rates increased 30 *basis points;* that is, the six-month rate increased from 0.048 to 0.051.
  i. State what you expect will happen to the value of the forward contract.
  ii. What is the value of the forward contract?

24.9 Derive the relationship between the spot price (S_0) and the futures price (F) by comparing the following two strategies:

Strategy 1: Buy the silver at S_0 today and hold it for one month.

Strategy 2: Take a long position on the silver futures contract expiring in one month. Lend money that will be equal to the futures price in one month. The lending rate for the period is the risk-free rate, r_f.

24.10 Aiko Miyazawa is a Japanese student, who is planning a one-year stay in America for studying English. She expects to leave for America in eight months. Since she is worried about the unstable exchange rates, she decided to lock-in the current exchange rates. What should Aiko's hedging position be?

24.11 After reading the text's example about Ron Cooke, the mortgage banker, you decide to enter the business. You begin small; you agree to provide $300,000 to an old college roommate to finance the purchase of her home. The loan is a 20-year loan and has a 10-percent interest rate. Ten percent is the current market rate of interest. For ease of computation, assume the mortgage payments are made annually. Your former roommate needs the money four months from today. You do not have $300,000, but you intend to sell the mortgage to MAX Insurance Corp. The president of MAX is also an old friend, so you know with certainty that he will buy the mortgage. Unfortunately, he is unavailable to meet with you until three months from today.

a. What is your former roommate's mortgage payment?
b. What is the most significant risk you face in this deal?
c. How can you hedge this risk?

24.12 Refer to question 24.11. There are four-month T-bond futures available. A single contract is for $100,000 of T-bonds.

a. Suppose that between today and your meeting with the president of MAX, the market rate of interest rises to 12 percent.
  i. How much is MAX's president willing to pay you for the mortgage?
  ii. What will happen to the value of the T-bond futures contract?
  iii. What is your net gain or loss if you wrote a futures contract?
b. Suppose that between today and your meeting with the president of MAX, the market rate of interest falls to 9 percent.
  i. How much is MAX's president willing to pay you for the mortgage?
  ii. What will happen to the value of the T-bond futures contract?
  iii. What is your net gain or loss if you wrote a futures contract?

Duration

24.13 Available are three zero-coupon, $1,000 face-value bonds. All of these bonds are initially priced using an 11-percent interest rate. Bond *A* matures one year from today, bond *B* matures five years from today, and bond *C* matures 10 years from today.

a. What is the current price of each bond?
b. If the market rate of interest rises to 14 percent, what are the prices of these bonds?
c. Which bond experienced the greatest percentage change in price?

24.14 Calculate the duration of a perpetuity that pays $100 at each year-end. Assume the annual discount rate of 12 percent. What if the discount rate is 10 percent?

24.15 Consider two four-year bonds. Each bond has a $1,000 face value. Bond *A*'s coupon rate is 7 percent, while bond *B*'s coupon rate is 11 percent.

a. What is the price of each bond when the market rate of interest is 10 percent?
b. What is the price of each bond when the market rate of interest is 7 percent?
c. Which bond experienced the greatest percentage change in price?
d. Explain your *c* result.

24.16 Calculate the duration of a three-year, $1,000 face-value bond with a 9-percent coupon rate, selling at par.

24.17 Calculate the duration of a four-year, $1,000 face-value bond with a 9-percent coupon rate, selling at par.

24.18 Calculate the duration of a four-year, $1,000 face-value bond with a 5-percent coupon rate, selling at par.

24.19 Mr. and Mrs. Chaikovski have a son who is going to enter a music college three years from today. Annual school expenses of $20,000 will occur at the beginning of each year for four years. What is the duration of Mr. and Mrs. Chaikovski's liability as parents? Assume the annual borrowing rate of 15 percent.

24.20 The following balance sheet is for Besdall Community Bank.

	Market Value	*Duration*
	Assets	
Federal funds deposits	$ 43 million	0
Accounts-receivable loans	615 million	4 months
Short-term loans	345 million	9 months
Long-term loans	55 million	5 years
Mortgages	197 million	15 years
	Liabilities and Equity	
Checking and savings deposits	$490 million	0
Certificates of deposit	370 million	18 months
Long-term financing	250 million	10 years
Equity	145 million	

a. What is the duration of Besdall's assets?

b. What is the duration of Besdall's liabilities?

c. Is Besdall Community Bank immune from interest-rate risk?

24.21 Refer to the previous problem. To what values must the durations of Besdall Community Bank change to make the bank immune from interest-rate risk if

a. Only the duration of the liabilities change?

b. Only the duration of the assets change?

24.22 Consider the following balance sheet for California Commercial Bank.

CALIFORNIA COMMERCIAL BANK
Market-value Balance Sheet

	Market Value (\$ million)	*Duration*
	Assets	
Overnight money	100	0
Loans	500	1 year
Mortgages	1,200	12 years
	1,800	
	Liabilities and Equity	
Checking and saving's account	300	0
Certificate of deposits	400	1.1 year
Long-term debt	500	18.9 years
Equity	600	
	1,800	

a. What is the duration of California's assets? What is the duration of liabilities?

b. Is the bank immunized from interest-rate risk?

CHAPTER

29 Mergers and Acquisitions

There is no more dramatic or controversial activity in corporate finance than the acquisition of one firm by another or the merger of two firms. It is the stuff of which reporters' dreams are made, and it is also an embarrassing source of scandal.

The acquisition of one firm by another is, of course, an investment made under uncertainty. The basic principle of valuation applies: A firm should be acquired if it generates a positive net present value to the shareholders of the acquiring firm. However, because the NPV of an acquisition candidate is very difficult to determine, mergers and acquisitions are interesting topics in their own right. Here are some of the special features of this area of finance:

1. The benefits from acquisitions are called *synergies.* It is hard to estimate synergies using discounted cash flow techniques.
2. There are complex accounting, tax, and legal effects when one firm is acquired by another.
3. Acquisitions are an important control device of shareholders. It appears that some acquisitions are a consequence of an underlying conflict between the interests of existing managers and of shareholders. Acquisition by another firm is one way that shareholders can remove managers with whom they are unhappy.
4. Acquisition analysis frequently focuses on the total value of the firms involved. But usually an acquisition will affect the relative values of stocks and bonds, as well as their total value.
5. Mergers and acquisitions sometimes involve unfriendly transactions. Thus, when one firm attempts to acquire another, it does not always involve quiet, gentlemanly negotiations. The sought-after firm may use defensive tactics, including poison pills, greenmail, and white knights.

This chapter starts by introducing the basic legal, accounting, and tax aspects of acquisitions. When one firm acquires another, it must choose the legal framework, the accounting method, and tax status. These choices will be explained throughout the chapter.

The chapter discusses how to determine the NPV of an acquisition candidate. The NPV of an acquisition candidate is the difference between the synergy from the merger and the premium to be paid. We consider the following types of synergy: (1) revenue enhancement, (2) cost reduction, (3) lower taxes, and (4) lower cost of capital. The premium paid for an acquisition is the price paid minus the market value of the acquisition prior to the merger. The premium depends on whether cash or securities are used to finance the offer price.

29.1 The Basic Forms of Acquisitions

There are three basic legal procedures that one firm can use to acquire another firm: (1) merger or consolidation, (2) acquisition of stock, and (3) acquisition of assets.

Merger or Consolidation

A **merger** refers to the absorption of one firm by another. The acquiring firm retains its name and its identity, and it acquires all of the assets and liabilities of the acquired firm. After a merger, the acquired firm ceases to exist as a separate business entity.

A **consolidation** is the same as a merger except that an entirely new firm is created. In a consolidation, both the acquiring firm and the acquired firm terminate their previous legal existence and become part of the new firm. In a consolidation, the distinction between the acquiring and the acquired firm is not important. However, the rules for mergers and consolidations are basically the same. Acquisitions by merger and consolidation result in combinations of the assets and liabilities of acquired and acquiring firms.

• ***Example***
Suppose firm *A* acquires firm *B* in a merger. Further, suppose firm *B* shareholders are given one share of firm *A*'s stock in exchange for two shares of firm *B*'s stock. From a legal standpoint, firm *A*'s shareholders are not directly affected by the merger. However, firm *B*'s shares cease to exist. In a consolidation, the shareholders of firm *A* and firm *B* would exchange their shares for the share of a new firm (e.g., firm *C*). Because the differences between mergers and consolidations are not all that important for our purposes, we shall refer to both types of reorganizations as mergers. •

There are some advantages and some disadvantages to using a merger to acquire a firm:

1. A merger is legally straightforward and does not cost as much as other forms of acquisition. It avoids the necessity of transferring title of each individual asset of the acquired firm to the acquiring firm.
2. A merger must be approved by a vote of the stockholders of each firm.[1] Typically, two thirds of the shares are required for approval. In addition, shareholders of the acquired firm have *appraisal rights.* This means that they can demand that their shares be purchased at a fair value by the acquiring firm. Often the acquiring firm and the dissenting shareholders of the acquired firm cannot agree on a fair value, which results in expensive legal proceedings.

Acquisition of Stock

A second way to acquire another firm is to purchase the firm's voting stock in exchange for cash, shares of stock, or other securities. This may start as a private offer from the management of one firm to another. At some point the offer is taken directly to the selling firm's stockholders. This can be accomplished by use of a tender offer. A **tender offer** is a public offer to buy shares of a target firm. It is made by one firm

[1] Mergers between corporations require compliance with state laws. In virtually all states the shareholders of each corporation must give their assent.

directly to the shareholders of another firm. The offer is communicated to the target firm's shareholders by public announcements such as newspaper advertisements. Sometimes a general mailing is used in a tender offer. However, a general mailing is very difficult because it requires the names and addresses of the stockholders of record, which are not usually available.

The following are factors involved in choosing between an acquisition of stock and a merger:

1. In an acquisition of stock, no shareholder meetings must be held and no vote is required. If the shareholders of the target firm do not like the offer, they are not required to accept it and they will not tender their shares.
2. In an acquisition of stock, the bidding firm can deal directly with the shareholders of a target firm by using a tender offer. The target firm's management and board of directors can be bypassed.
3. Acquisition of stock is often unfriendly. It is used in an effort to circumvent the target firm's management, which is usually actively resisting acquisition. Resistance by the target firm's management often makes the cost of acquisition by stock higher than the cost by merger.
4. Frequently a minority of shareholders will hold out in a tender offer, and thus the target firm cannot be completely absorbed.
5. Complete absorption of one firm by another requires a merger. Many acquisitions of stock end with a formal merger later.

Acquisition of Assets

One firm can acquire another firm by buying all of its assets. A formal vote of the shareholders of the selling firm is required. This approach to acquisition will avoid the potential problem of having minority shareholders, which can occur in an acquisition of stock. Acquisition of assets involves transferring title to assets. The legal process of transferring assets can be costly.

A Classification Scheme

Financial analysts have typically classified acquisitions into three types:

1. *Horizontal Acquisition.* This is an acquisition of a firm in the same industry as the acquiring firm. The firms compete with each other in their product market.
2. *Vertical Acquisition.* A vertical acquisition involves firms at different steps of the production process. The acquisition by an airline company of a travel agency would be a vertical acquisition.
3. *Conglomerate Acquisition.* The acquiring firm and the acquired firm are not related to each other. The acquisition of a food-products firm by a computer firm would be considered a conglomerate acquisition.

A Note on Takeovers

Takeover is a general and imprecise term referring to the transfer of control of a firm from one group of shareholders to another.[2] A firm that has decided to take over anoth-

[2] *Control* may be defined as having a majority vote on the board of directors.

FIGURE 29.1 Varieties of Takeovers

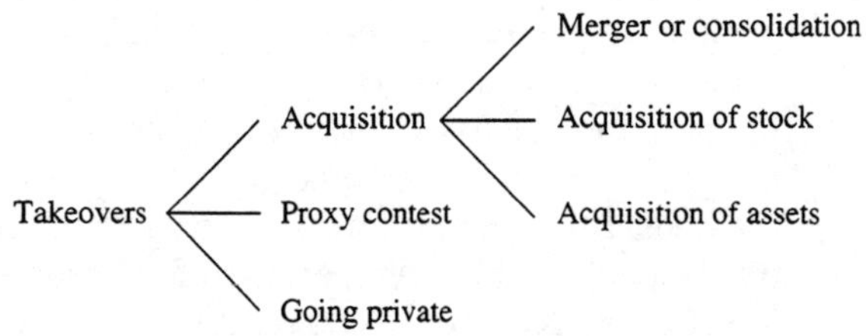

er firm is usually referred to as the **bidder.** The bidder offers to pay cash or securities to obtain the stock or assets of another company. If the offer is accepted, the target firm will give up control over its stock or assets to the bidder in exchange for the *consideration* (i.e., its stock, its debt, or cash).

For example, when a bidding firm acquires a target firm, the right to control the operating activities of the target firm is transferred to a newly elected board of directors of the acquiring firm. This is a takeover by acquisition.

Takeovers can occur by acquisition, proxy contests, and going-private transactions. Thus, takeovers encompass a broader set of activities than acquisitions. Figure 29.1 depicts this.

If a takeover is achieved by acquisition, it will be by merger, tender offer for shares of stock, or purchase of assets. In mergers and tender offers, the acquiring firm buys the voting common stock of the acquired firm.

Takeovers can occur with *proxy contests.* Proxy contests occur when a group of shareholders attempts to gain controlling seats on the board of directors by voting in new directors. A *proxy* authorizes the proxy holder to vote on all matters in a shareholders' meeting. In a proxy contest, proxies from the rest of the shareholders are solicited by an insurgent group of shareholders.

In *going-private transactions,* all the equity shares of a public firm are purchased by a small group of investors. The group usually includes members of incumbent management and some outside investors. The shares of the firm are delisted from stock exchanges and can no longer be purchased in the open market.

Concept Questions

- What is a merger? How does a merger differ from other forms of acquisition?
- What is a takeover?

29.2 The Tax Forms of Acquisitions

If one firm buys another firm, the transaction may be taxable or tax-free. In a *taxable acquisition,* the shareholders of the acquired firm are considered to have sold their shares, and they have realized capital gains or losses that will be taxed. In a taxable transaction, the *appraised value* of the assets of the selling firm may be revalued, as we explain below.

In a *tax-free acquisition,* the selling shareholders are considered to have exchanged their old shares for new ones of equal value, and they have experienced no capital gains or losses. In a tax-free acquisition, the assets are not revalued.

• ***Example***

Suppose that 15 years ago Bill Evans started Samurai Machinery (SM) and purchased plant and equipment costing $80,000. These have been the only assets of SM, and the company has no debts. Bill is the sole proprietor of SM and owns all the shares. For tax purposes the assets of SM have been depreciated using the straight-line method over 10 years, and have no salvage value. The annual depreciation expense was $8,000 ($80,000/10). The machinery has no accounting value today (i.e., it has been written off the books). However, because of inflation, the fair market value of the machinery is $200,000. As a consequence, the S. A. Steel Company has bid $200,000 for all of the outstanding stock of Samurai. •

Tax-Free Transaction

If Bill Evans receives *shares* of S. A. Steel worth $200,000, the IRS will treat the sale as a tax-free transaction. Thus, Bill will not have to pay taxes on any gain received from the stock. In addition, S. A. Steel will be allowed the same depreciation deduction that Samurai Machinery was allowed. Because the asset has already been fully depreciated, S. A. Steel will receive no depreciation deduction.

Taxable Transaction

If S. A. Steel pays $200,000 in *cash* for Samurai Machinery, it will be a taxable transaction. There will be a number of tax consequences:

1. In the year of the merger, Bill Evans must pay taxes on the difference between the merger price of $200,000 and his initial contribution to the firm of $80,000. Thus, his taxable income is $120,000 ($200,000 − $80,000).
2. S. A. Steel may *elect* to *write up* the value of the machinery. In this case, S. A. Steel will be able to depreciate the machinery from an initial tax basis of $200,000. If S. A. Steel depreciates straight-line over 10 years, depreciation will be $20,000 ($200,000/10) per year.

   If S. A. Steel elects to write up the machinery, S. A. Steel must treat the $200,000 write-up as taxable income immediately.[3]
3. Should S. A. Steel *not* elect the write-up, there is no increase in depreciation. Thus, depreciation remains zero in this example. In addition, because there is no write-up, S. A. Steel does not need to recognize any additional taxable income.

   Because the tax benefits from depreciation occur slowly over time and the taxable income is recognized immediately, the acquirer generally elects *not* to write up the value of the machinery in a taxable transaction.

Because the write-up is not allowed for tax-free transactions and generally not chosen for taxable ones, the only real tax difference between the two types of transactions concerns the taxation of the selling shareholders. Because these individuals can defer taxes under a tax-free situation but must pay taxes immediately under a taxable situation, the tax-free transaction has better tax consequences. The tax implications for both types of transactions are displayed in Table 29.1.

[3] Technically, Samurai Machinery pays this tax. However, because Samurai is now a subsidiary of S. A. Steel, S. A. Steel is the effective taxpayer.

TABLE 29.1 The Incremental Tax Consequences of S. A. Steel Company's Acquisition of Samurai Machinery

	Type of Acquisition	
Buyer or Seller	*Taxable Acquisition*	*Tax-Free Acquisition*
Bill Evans	Immediate tax on $120,000 ($200,000 − $80,000)	Capital gain tax not paid until Evans sells shares of S. A. Steel
S. A. Steel	S. A. Steel may elect to write up assets. Here: 1. Assets of Samurai written up to $200,000 (with useful life of 10 years). Annual depreciation expense is $20,000. 2. Immediate tax on $200,000 write-up of assets. Alternatively, S. A. Steel may elect not to write up assets. Here, there is neither additional depreciation nor immediate tax. Typically, acquirer elects *not* to write up assets.	No additional depreciation

S. A. Steel acquires Samurai Machinery for $200,000, which is the market value of Samurai's equipment. The book value of equipment is $0. Bill Evans started Samurai Steel 15 years ago with a contribution of $80,000.

The tax consequences of a tax-free acquisition are better than the tax consequences of a taxable acquisition, because the seller pays no immediate tax on a tax-free acquisition.

29.3 Accounting for Acquisitions

Earlier in this text we mentioned that firms keep two distinct sets of books: the stockholders' books and the tax books. The previous section concerned the effect of acquisitions on the tax books. We now consider the stockholders' books. When one firm acquires another firm, the acquisition will be treated as either a purchase or a pooling of interests on the stockholders' books.

The Purchase Method

The **purchase** method of reporting acquisitions requires that the assets of the acquired firm be reported at their fair market value on the books of the acquiring firm. This allows the acquiring firm to establish a new cost basis for the acquired assets.

In a purchase, an accounting term called *goodwill* is created. **Goodwill** is the excess of the purchase price over the sum of the fair market values of the individual assets acquired.

• ***Example***

Suppose firm *A* acquires firm *B*, creating a new firm, *AB*. Firm *A*'s and firm *B*'s financial positions at the date of the acquisition are shown in Table 29.2. The book value of firm *B* on the date of the acquisition is $10 million. This is the sum of $8 million in buildings and $2 million in cash. However, an appraiser states that the sum of the fair market values of the individual buildings is $14 million. With $2 million in cash, the sum of the market values of the individual assets in firm *B* is $16 million. This repre-

TABLE 29.2 Accounting for Acquisitions: Purchase (in $ millions)

Firm A				Firm B			
Cash	$ 4	Equity	$20	Cash	$ 2	Equity	$10
Land	16			Land	0		
Buildings	0			Buildings	8		
Total	$20		$20	Total	$10		$10

Firm AB			
Cash	$ 6	Debt	$19
Land	16	Equity	20
Buildings	14		
Goodwill	3		
Total	$39		$39

When the purchase method is used, the assets of the acquired firm (firm *B*) appear in the combined firm's books at their fair market value.

sents the value to be received if the firm is liquidated by selling off the individual assets separately. However, the whole is often worth more than the sum of the parts in business. Firm *A* pays $19 million in cash for firm *B*. This difference of $3 million ($19 million − $16 million) is goodwill. It represents the increase in value by keeping the firm intact as an ongoing business. Firm *A* issued $19 million in new debt to finance the acquisition. The last balance sheet in Table 29.2 shows what happens under purchase accounting.

1. The total assets of firm *AB* increase to $39 million. The buildings of firm *B* appear in the new balance sheet at their current market value. That is, the market value of the assets of the acquired firm become part of the book value of the new firm. However, the assets of the acquiring firm (firm *A*) remain at their old book value. They are not revalued upwards when the new firm is created.
2. The excess of the purchase price over the sum of the fair market values of the individual assets acquired is $3 million. This amount is reported as goodwill. Goodwill will be amortized over a period of years on the stockholders' books. However, the amortization expenses are *not tax deductible*. •

Pooling of Interests

Under a **pooling of interests,** the assets of the new firm are valued at the same level at which they were carried on the books of the acquired and acquiring firms. Using the previous example, assume that firm *A* issues common stock with a market value of $19 million to acquire firm *B*. Table 29.3 illustrates this merger.

The new firm is owned jointly by all the stockholders of the previously separate firms. The total assets and the total equity are unchanged by the acquisition. No goodwill is created. Furthermore, the $19 million used to acquire firm *B* does not appear in Table 29.3.

Purchase or Pooling of Interests: A Comparison

Pooling of interests is used when the acquiring firm issues voting stock in exchange for at least 90 percent of the outstanding voting stock of the acquired firm. Purchase

TABLE 29.3 Accounting for Acquisitions: Pooling of Interests (in $ millions)

	Firm A				Firm B		
Cash	$ 4	Equity	$20	Cash	$ 2	Equity	$10
Land	16			Land	0		
Buildings	0			Buildings	8		
Total	$20		$20	Total	$10		$10

	Firm AB		
Cash	$ 6	Equity	$30
Land	16		
Buildings	8		
Total	$30		$30

In a pooling of interests, the assets appear in the combined firm's books at the same value that they had in each separate firm's books prior to the merger.

accounting is generally used under other financing arrangements. Though there are many possible arrangements, the most common is that the acquiring firm distributes cash and bonds to obtain the assets or stock of the acquired firm.

We mentioned above that, in purchase accounting, goodwill is amortized over a period of years on the stockholders' books. Therefore, just like depreciation, the amortization expense reduces income on the stockholders' books. In addition, the assets of the acquired firm are written up on the stockholders' books in purchase accounting. This creates a higher depreciation expense for the combined firm than would be the case for a pooling. Due to both goodwill and asset write-ups, purchase accounting will usually result in lower reported income on the stockholders' books than will pooling.

The above paragraph concerns effects on the stockholders' books, not the tax books. Because the amount of tax-deductible expenses is not affected by the method of acquisition accounting, cash flows are not affected. Hence, the net present value of the acquisition should be the same whether pooling or purchase accounting is used.

Concept Question

- What is the difference between purchase accounting and pooling-of-interests accounting?

29.4 Determining the Synergy from an Acquisition

Suppose firm *A* is contemplating acquiring firm *B*. The value of firm *A* is V_A and the value of firm *B* is V_B. (It is reasonable to assume that, for public companies, V_A and V_B can be determined by observing the market price of the outstanding securities.) The difference between the value of the combined firm (V_{AB}) and the sum of the values of the firms as separate entities is the *synergy* from the acquisition:

$$\text{Synergy} = V_{AB} - (V_A + V_B)$$

The acquiring firm must generally pay a premium for the acquired firm. For example, if stock of the target is selling for $50, the acquirer might need to pay $60 a share, implying a premium of $10 or 20 percent. Firm *A* will want to determine the synergy before entering into negotiations with firm *B* on the premium.

The synergy of an acquisition can be determined from the usual discounted cash flow model:

$$\text{Synergy} = \sum_{t=1}^{T} \frac{\Delta \text{CF}_t}{(1 + r)^t}$$

where ΔCF_t is the difference between the cash flows at date t of the combined firm and the sum of the cash flows of the two separate firms. In other words, ΔCF_t is the incremental cash flow at date t from the merger. The term, r, is the risk-adjusted discount rate appropriate for the incremental cash flows. This is generally considered to be the required rate of return on the equity of the target.

From the chapters on capital budgeting we know that the incremental cash flows can be separated into four parts:

$$\Delta\text{CF}_t = \Delta\text{Rev}_t - \Delta\text{Costs}_t - \Delta\text{Taxes}_t - \Delta\text{Capital Requirements}_t$$

where ΔRev_t is the incremental revenue of the acquisition, ΔCosts_t is the incremental costs of the acquisition, ΔTaxes_t is the incremental acquisition taxes, and $\Delta\text{Capital Requirements}_t$ is the incremental new investment required in working capital and fixed assets.

29.5 Source of Synergy from Acquisitions

It follows from our classification of incremental cash flows that the possible sources of synergy fall into four basic categories: revenue enhancement, cost reduction, lower taxes, and lower cost of capital.[4]

Revenue Enhancement

One important reason for acquisitions is that a combined firm may generate greater revenues than two separate firms. Increased revenues may come from marketing gains, strategic benefits, and market power.

Marketing Gains

It is frequently claimed that mergers and acquisitions can produce greater operating revenues from improved marketing. Improvements can be made in the following:

[4] Many reasons are given by firms to justify mergers and acquisitions. When two firms merge, the boards of directors of the two firms adopt an *agreement of merger.* The agreement of merger of U.S. Steel and Marathon Oil is typical. It lists the economic benefits that shareholders can expect from the merger (key words have been italicized):

> U.S. Steel believes that the acquisition of Marathon provides U.S. Steel with an attractive opportunity to *diversify* into the energy business. Reasons for the merger include, but are not limited to, the facts that consummation of the merger will allow U.S. Steel to consolidate Marathon in U.S. Steel's federal *income tax return,* will also contribute to *greater efficiency,* and will enhance the ability to manage capital by permitting the movement of cash between U.S. Steel and Marathon. Additionally, the merger will eliminate the possibility of conflicts of interest between the interests of minority and majority shareholders and will enhance management flexibility. The acquisition will provide Marathon shareholders with a substantial premium over historic market prices for their shares. However shareholders will no longer continue to share in the future prospects of the company.

1. Previously ineffective media programming and advertising efforts.
2. A weak existing distribution network.
3. An unbalanced product mix.

Strategic Benefits

Some acquisitions promise a *strategic* advantage.[5] This is an opportunity to take advantage of the competitive environment if certain situations materialize. In this regard, a strategic benefit is more like an option than it is a standard investment opportunity. For example, imagine that a sewing machine company acquired a computer company. The firm will be well positioned if technological advances allow computer-driven sewing machines in the future. Michael Porter has used the word *beachhead* in his description of the process of entering a new industry to exploit perceived opportunities.[6] The beachhead is used to spawn new opportunities based on *intangible* relationships. He uses the example of Procter & Gamble's initial acquisition of the Charmin Paper Company as a beachhead that allowed Procter & Gamble to develop a highly interrelated cluster of paper products—disposable diapers, paper towels, feminine hygiene products, and bathroom tissue.

Market or Monopoly Power

One firm may acquire another to reduce competition. If so, prices can be increased and monopoly profits obtained. Mergers that reduce competition do not benefit society and may be challenged by the U.S. Department of Justice or the Federal Trade Commission.

The empirical evidence does not suggest that increased market power is a significant reason for mergers. If monopoly power is increased through an acquisition, all firms in the industry should benefit as the price of the industry's product is increased. However, Stillman's and Eckbo's examination of the share prices of firms that compete with the merger target when a merger announcement is made indicate that this is not the case.[7] They find no consistent tendency for the share prices of rivals to increase, and, thus, the Stillman-Eckbo data do not support the monopoly-power theory.

Cost Reduction

One of the most basic reasons to merge is that a combined firm may operate more efficiently than two separate firms. Thus, when Bank of America agreed to acquire Security Pacific, lower costs were cited as the primary reason. A firm can obtain greater operating efficiency in several different ways through a merger or an acquisition.

Economies of Scale

If the average cost of production falls while the level of production increases, there is said to be an economy of scale. Figure 29.2 illustrates that economies of scale result

---

[5] For a discussion of the financial side of strategic planning, see S. C. Myers, "Finance Theory and Finance Strategy," *Interfaces* 14 (January–February 1984), p. 1.

[6] M. Porter, *Competitive Advantage* (New York: Free Press, 1985).

[7] R. Stillman, "Examining Antitrust Policy toward Horizontal Mergers," *Journal of Financial Economics* 11 (April 1983); and E. B. Eckbo, "Horizontal Mergers, Collusion and Stockholder Wealth," *Journal of Financial Economics* 11 (April 1983).

FIGURE 29.2 Economies of Scale and the Optimal Size of the Firm

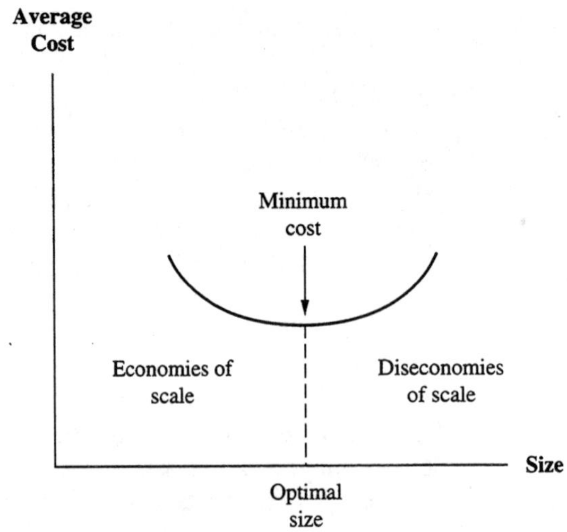

while the firm grows to its optimal size. After this point, diseconomies of scale occur. In other words, average cost increases with further firm growth.

Though the precise nature of economy of scale is not known, it is one obvious benefit of horizontal mergers. The phrase *spreading overhead* is frequently used in connection with economies of scale. This refers to the sharing of central facilities such as corporate headquarters, top management, and a large mainframe computer.

Economies of Vertical Integration

Operating economies can be gained from vertical combinations as well as from horizontal combinations. The main purpose of vertical acquisitions is to make coordination of closely related operating activities easier. This is probably the reason why most forest product firms that cut timber also own sawmills and hauling equipment. Economies from vertical integration probably explain why most airline companies own airplanes; it also may explain why some airline companies have purchased hotels and car-rental companies.

Technology transfers are another reason for vertical integration. Consider the merger of General Motors and Hughes Aircraft in 1985. An automobile manufacturer might well acquire an advanced electronics firm if the special technology of the electronics firm can improve the quality of the automobile.

Complementary Resources

Some firms acquire others to make better use of existing resources or to provide the missing ingredient for success. Think of a ski-equipment store that could merge with a tennis-equipment store to produce more even sales over both the winter and summer seasons—and better use of store capacity.

Elimination of Inefficient Management

There are firms whose value could be increased with a change in management. For example, Jensen and Ruback argue that acquisitions can occur because of changing technology or market conditions that require a restructuring of the corporation.[8] Incumbent managers in some cases do not understand changing conditions. They have trouble abandoning strategies and styles they have spent years formulating.

The oil industry is an example of managerial inefficiency cited by Jensen. In the late 1970s, changes in the oil industry included reduced expectations of the future price of oil, increased exploration and development costs, and increased real interest rates. As a result of these changes, substantial reductions in exploration and development were called for. However, many oil company managers were unable to "downsize" their firms. For example, a study by McConnell and Muscarella reports that the stock prices of oil companies tended to decrease with announcements of increases in exploration and development expenditures in the period 1975–1981.[9]

Acquiring companies sought out oil firms in order to reduce the investment levels of these oil companies.[10] For example, T. Boone Pickens of Mesa Petroleum perceived the changes taking place in the oil industry and attempted to buy several oil companies: Unocal, Phillips, and Getty. The results of these attempted acquisitions have been reduced expenditures on exploration and development and huge gains to the shareholders of the affected firms.

Mergers and acquisitions can be viewed as part of the labor market for top management. Jensen and Ruback have used the phrase *market for corporate control,* in which alternative management teams compete for the rights to manage corporate activities.

Tax Gains

Tax gains may be a powerful incentive for some acquisitions. The possible tax gains that can come from an acquisition are the following:

1. The use of tax losses from net operating losses.
2. The use of unused debt capacity.
3. The use of surplus funds.

Net Operating Losses

Sometimes firms have tax losses they cannot take advantage of. These tax losses are referred to as NOL (an acronym for net operating losses). Consider the situation of firm *A* and firm *B*.

Table 29.4 shows the pretax income, taxes, and after-tax income for firms *A* and *B*. Firm *A* will earn $200 under state 1 but will lose money under state 2. The firm will pay taxes under state 1 but is not entitled to a tax rebate under state 2. Conversely, firm *B* will pay tax of $68 under state 2. Thus, if firms *A* and *B* are separate, the IRS will obtain $68 in taxes, regardless of which state occurs. However, if *A* and *B* merge, the combined firm will pay $34 in taxes under both state 1 and state 2.

[8] M. C. Jensen and R. S. Ruback, "The Market for Corporate Control: The Scientific Evidence," *Journal of Financial Economics* 11 (April 1983); and M. C. Jensen, "Agency Costs of Free Cash Flow, Corporate Finance and Takeovers," *American Economic Review* (May 1986).

[9] J. J. McConnell and C. J. Muscarella, "Corporate Capital Expenditure Decisions and the Market Value of the Firm," *Journal of Financial Economics* 14 (1985).

[10] More than 26 percent of the total valuation of all takeover transactions involved a selling firm in the oil and gas industry in 1981–1984 [W. T. Grimm, *Mergerstat Review* (1985), p. 41].

TABLE 29.4 Tax Effect of Merger of Firms *A* and *B*

	Before Merger				*After Merger*	
	Firm *A*		**Firm *B***		**Firm *AB***	
	If State 1	*If State* 2	*If State* 1	*If State* 2	*If State* 1	*If State* 2
Taxable income	$200	−$100	−$100	$200	$100	$100
Taxes	68	0	0	68	34	34
Net income	$132	−$100	−$100	$132	$ 66	$ 66

Neither firm will be able to deduct its losses prior to the merger. The merger allows the losses from *A* to offset the taxable profits from *B*—and vice versa.

It is obvious that if firms *A* and *B* merge, they will pay lower taxes than if they remain separate. Without merger, they do not take advantage of potential tax losses.

The message of the preceding example is that firms need taxable profits to take advantage of potential tax losses. Mergers can sometimes accomplish this. However, there are two qualifications to the previous example:

1. The federal tax laws permit firms that experience alternating periods of profits and losses to equalize their taxes by carryback and carryforward provisions. A firm that has been profitable but has a loss in the current year can get refunds of income taxes paid in *three previous years* and can carry the loss *forward for 15 years.* Thus, a merger to exploit unused tax shields must offer tax savings over and above what can be accomplished by firms via carryovers.[11]
2. The IRS may disallow an acquisition if the principal purpose of the acquisition is to avoid federal tax. This is one of the Catch 22s of the Internal Revenue Code.

Unused Debt Capacity

We argued earlier in the text that the optimal debt-equity ratio is the one where the marginal tax benefit from additional debt is equal to the marginal increase in the financial distress costs from additional debt. Because some diversification occurs when firms merge, the cost of financial distress is likely to be less for the combined firm than is the sum of these present values for the two separate firms. Thus, the acquiring firm might be able to increase its debt-equity ratio after a merger, creating additional tax benefits—and additional value.[12,13]

[11] Under the 1986 Tax Reform Act a corporation's ability to carry forward net operating losses (and other tax credits) is limited when more than 50 percent of the stock changes hands over a three-year period.

[12] Unused debt capacity is cited as a benefit in many mergers. An example was the proposed merger of Hospital Corporation of America and American Hospital Supply Corporation in 1985. Insiders were quoted as saying that the combined companies could borrow as much as an additional $1 billion, 10 times the usual borrowing capacity of Hospital Corporation alone (*The Wall Street Journal,* April 1, 1985). (The merger never took place.)

[13] Michael C. Jensen ["Agency Costs of Free Cash Flow, Corporate Finance and Takeovers," *American Economic Review* (May 1986)] offers another reason why debt is frequently used in mergers and acquisitions. He argues that using more debt provides incentives for the new management to create efficiencies so that debt can be repaid.

Surplus Funds

Another quirk in the tax laws involves surplus funds. Consider a firm that has *free cash flow.* That is, it has cash flow available after payment of all taxes and after all positive net-present-value projects have been provided for. In this situation, aside from purchasing fixed-income securities, the firm has several ways to spend the free cash flow, including

1. Pay dividends
2. Buy back its own shares
3. Acquire shares in another firm

We have already seen in our previous discussion of dividend policy that an extra dividend will increase the income tax paid by some investors. Investors pay lower taxes in a share repurchase. However, this is not a legal option if the sole purpose is to avoid taxes that would otherwise have been paid by shareholders.

The firm can buy the shares of another firm. This accomplishes two objectives. First, the firm's shareholders avoid taxes from dividends that would have been paid. Second, the firm pays little corporate tax on dividends received from the shares of the firm it has purchased, because 70 percent of the dividend income received from the acquired firm is excluded from the corporate income tax. However, under Section 532 of the tax code the IRS might disallow the tax benefits from a continual strategy of this type.

Instead, the firm might make acquisitions with its excess funds. In a merger no taxes at all are paid on dividends remitted from the acquired firm, and the IRS would not question mergers of this type.

The Cost of Capital

The cost of capital can often be reduced when two firms merge because the costs of issuing securities are subject to economies of scale. As we observed in earlier chapters, the costs of issuing both debt and equity are much lower for larger issues than for smaller issues.

29.6 Calculating the Value of the Firm after an Acquisition

Now that we have listed the possible sources of synergy from a merger, let us see how one would value these sources. Consider two firms. Gamble, Inc., manufactures and markets soaps and cosmetics. The firm has a reputation for its ability to attract, develop, and keep talented people. The firm has successfully introduced several major products in the past two years. It would like to enter the over-the-counter drug market to round out its product line. Shapiro, Inc., is a well-known maker of cold remedies. Al Shapiro, the great-grandson of the founder of Shapiro, Inc., became chairman of the firm last year. Unfortunately, Al knows nothing about cold remedies, and as a consequence Shapiro, Inc., has had lackluster financial performance. For the most recent year, pretax cash flow fell by 15 percent. The firm's stock price is at an all-time low.

The financial management of Gamble finds Shapiro an attractive acquisition candidate. It believes that the cash flows from the combined firms would be far greater than what each firm would have alone. The cash flows and present values from the acquisition are shown in Table 29.5. The increased cash flows (CF_t) come from three benefits:

IN THEIR OWN WORDS . . . Michael C. Jensen on Mergers and Acquisitions

Economic analysis and evidence indicate that takeovers, LBOs, and corporate restructurings are playing an important role in helping the economy adjust to major competitive changes in the last two decades. The competition among alternative management teams and organizational structures for control of corporate assets has enabled vast economic resources to move more quickly to their highest-valued use. In the process, substantial benefits for the economy as a whole as well as for shareholders have been created. Overall gains to selling-firm shareholders from mergers, acquisitions, leveraged buyouts and other corporate restructurings in the 12-year period 1977–1988 total over $500 billion in 1988 dollars. I estimate gains to buying-firm shareholders to be at least $50 billion for the same period. These gains equal 53 percent of the total cash dividends (valued in 1988 dollars) paid to investors by the entire corporate sector in the same period.

Mergers and acquisitions are a response to new technologies or market conditions which require a strategic change in a company's direction or use of resources. Compared to current management, a new owner is often better able to accomplish major change in the existing organizational structure. Alternatively, leveraged buyouts bring about organizational change by creating entrepreneurial incentives for management and by eliminating the centralized bureaucratic obstacles to maneuverability that are inherent in large public corporations.

When managers have a substantial ownership interest in the organization, the conflicts of interest between shareholders and managers over the payout of the company's free cash flow are reduced. Management's incentives are focused on maximizing the value of the enterprise, rather than building empires—often through poorly conceived diversification acquisitions—without regard to shareholder value. Finally, the required repayment of debt replaces management's discretion in paying dividends and the tendency to overretain cash. Substantial increases in efficiency are thereby created.

Michael C. Jensen is Edsel Bryant Ford Professor of Business Administration at Harvard University. An outstanding scholar and researcher, he is famous for his path-breaking analysis of the modern corporation and its relations with its stockholders.

1. *Tax Gains.* If Gamble acquires Shapiro, Gamble will be able to use some tax-loss carryforwards to reduce its tax liability. The additional cash flows from tax gains should be discounted at the cost of debt capital because they can be determined with very little uncertainty. The financial management of Gamble estimates that the acquisition will reduce taxes by $1 million per year in perpetuity. The relevant discount rate is 5 percent, and the present value of the tax reduction is $20 million.
2. *Operating Efficiencies.* The financial management of Gamble has determined that Gamble can take advantage of some of the unused production capacity of Shapiro. At times Gamble has been operating at full capacity with a large backlog of orders. Shapiro's manufacturing facilities, with a little reconfiguration, can be used to produce Gamble's soaps. Thus, more soaps and cold remedies can be produced without adding to the combined firm's capacity and cost. These operating efficiencies will increase after-tax cash flows by $1.5 million per year. Using Shapiro's discount rate and assuming perpetual gains, the PV of the unused capacity is determined to be $10 million.
3. *Strategic Fit.* The financial management of Gamble has determined that the acquisition of Shapiro will give Gamble a strategic advantage. The management of Gamble believes that the addition of the Shapiro Bac-Rub ointment for sore backs to its existing product mix will give it a better chance to launch successful new skin-care cosmetics if these markets develop in the

TABLE 29.5 Acquisition of Shapiro, Inc., by Gamble, Inc.

	Net Cash Flow per Year (perpetual)	*Discount Rate*	*Value*
Gamble, Inc.	$10.0 million	0.10	$100 million
Shapiro, Inc.	4.5 million	0.15	30 million*
Benefits from acquisition:	5.5 million	0.122	45 million
Strategic fit	3.0 million	0.20	15 million
Tax shelters	1.0 million	0.05	20 million
Operating efficiencies	1.5 million	0.15	10 million
Gamble-Shapiro	20.0 million	0.114	175 million

* The market value of Shapiro's outstanding common stock is $30 million; 1 million shares are outstanding.

future. Management of Gamble estimates that there is a 50-percent probability that $6 million in after-tax cash flow can be generated with the new skin-care products. These opportunities are contingent on factors that cannot be easily quantified. Because of the lack of precision here, the managers decided to use a high discount rate. Gamble chooses a 20-percent rate, and it estimates that the present value of the strategic factors is $15 million (0.50 × $6 million/0.20).

Avoiding Mistakes

The Gamble-Shapiro illustration is very simple and straightforward. It is deceptive because the incremental cash flows have already been determined. In practice an analyst must estimate these cash flows and determine the proper discount rate. Valuing the benefits of a potential acquisition is harder than valuing benefits for standard capital-budgeting projects. Many mistakes can be made. Following are some of the general rules:

1. *Do Not Ignore Market Values.* In many cases it is very difficult to estimate values using discounted cash flows. Because of this, an expert at valuation should know the market prices of comparable opportunities. In an efficient market, prices should reflect value. Because the market value of Shapiro is $30 million, we use this to estimate Shapiro's existing value.
2. *Estimate Only Incremental Cash Flows.* Only incremental cash flows from an acquisition will add value to the acquiring firm. Thus, it is important to estimate the cash flows that are incremental to the acquisition.
3. *Use the Correct Discount Rate.* The discount rate should be the required rate of return for the incremental cash flows associated with the acquisition.[14] It should reflect the risk associated with the *use* of funds, not their *source.* It would be a mistake for Gamble to use its own cost of capital to value the cash flows from Shapiro.
4. *If Gamble and Shapiro Combine, There Will Be Transactions Costs.* These will include fees to investment bankers, legal fees, and disclosure requirements.

[14] Recall that the required rate of return is sometimes referred to as the *cost of capital,* or the *opportunity cost of capital.*

29.7 A Cost to Stockholders from Reduction in Risk

The previous section discussed gains to the firm from a merger. In a firm with debt, these gains are likely to be shared by both bondholders and stockholders. We now consider a benefit to the bondholders from a merger, which occurs at the expense of the stockholders.

When two firms merge, the variability of their combined values is usually less than would be true if the firms remained separate entities. A reduction of the variability of firm values can occur if the values of the two firms are less than perfectly correlated. The reduction in variability can reduce the cost of borrowing and make the creditors better off than before. This will occur if the probability of financial distress is reduced by the merger.

Unfortunately, the shareholders are likely to be worse off. The gains to creditors are at the expense of the shareholders if the total value of the firm does not change. The relationship among the value of the merged firm, debt capacity, and risk is very complicated. We now consider two examples.

The Base Case

Consider a base case where two all-equity firms merge. Table 29.6 gives the net present values of firm *A* and firm *B* in three possible states of the economy—prosperity, average, and depression. The market value of firm *A* is \$60, and the market value of firm *B* is \$40. The market value of each firm is the weighted average of the values in each of the three states. For example, the value of firm *A* is

$$\$60 = \$80 \times 0.5 + \$50 \times 0.3 + \$25 \times 0.2$$

The values in each of the three states for firm *A* are \$80, \$50, and \$25, respectively. The probabilities of each of the three states occurring are 0.5, 0.3, and 0.2, respectively.

When firm *A* merges with firm *B*, the combined firm *AB* will have a market value of \$100. There is no synergy from this merger, and consequently the value of firm *AB* is the sum of the values of firm *A* and firm *B*. Stockholders of *B* receive stock with a value of \$40, and therefore stockholders of *A* have a value of \$100 − \$40 = \$60. Thus, stockholders of *A* and *B* are indifferent to the proposed merger.

One Firm Has Debt

Alternatively, imagine firm *A* has some debt and some equity outstanding before the merger.[15] Firm *B* is an all-equity firm. Firm *A* will default on its debt in state 3 because the net present value of firm *A* in this state is \$25, and the value of the debt claim is \$40. As a consequence, the full value of the debt claim cannot be paid by firm *A*. The creditors take this into account, and the value of the debt is \$37 (\$40 × 0.5 + \$40 × 0.3 + \$25 × 0.2).

Though default occurs without a merger, no default occurs with a merger. To see this, notice that, when the two firms are separate, firm *B* does not guarantee firm *A*'s debt. That is, if firm *A* defaults on its debt, firm *B* does not help the bondholders of firm *A*. However, after the merger the bondholders can draw on the cash flows from

[15] This example was provided by David Babbel.

TABLE 29.6 Stock-Swap Mergers

	NPV			
	State 1	*State* 2	*State* 3	*Market Value*
Base case: two all-equity firms before merger				
Firm *A*	$ 80	$50	$25	$ 60
Firm *B*	$ 50	$40	$15	$ 40
Probability	0.5	0.3	0.2	
After merger*				
Firm *AB*	$130	$90	$40	$100
Firm *A*, equity and risky debt before merger				
Firm *B*, all-equity before merger				
Firm *A*	$ 80	$50	$25	$ 60
Debt	$ 40	$40	$25	$ 37
Equity	$ 40	$10	$0	$ 23
Firm *B*	$ 50	$40	$15	$ 40
After merger†				
Firm *AB*	$130	$90	$40	$100
Debt	$ 40	$40	$40	$ 40
Equity	$ 90	$50	$ 0	$ 60

Value of debt rises after merger. Value of original stock in acquiring firm falls correspondingly.

* Stockholders in *B* receive stock value of $40. Therefore, stockholders of *A* have a value of $100 − $40 = $60 and are *indifferent to merger.*

† Because firm *B*'s stockholders receive stock in firm *A* worth $40, original stockholders in firm *A* have stock worth $20 ($60 − $40). Gains and losses from merger are

$20 − $23 = −$3: Therefore, stockholders of *A* lose $3.
$40 − $37 = $3: Therefore, bondholders of *A* gain $3.

both *A* and *B*. When one of the divisions of the combined firm fails, creditors can be paid from the profits of the other division. This mutual guarantee, which is called the *coinsurance effect,* makes the debt less risky and more valuable than before.

The bonds are worth $40 after the merger. Thus, the bondholders of *AB* gain $3 ($40 − $37) from the merger.

The stockholders of firm *A* lose $3 ($20 − $23) from the merger. That is, firm *A*'s stock is worth $23 prior to the merger. The stock is worth $60 after the merger. However, stockholders in firm *B* receive $40 of stock in firm *A*. Hence, those individuals who were stockholders in firm *A* prior to the merger have stock worth only $20 ($60 − $40) after the merger.

There is no net benefit to the firm as a whole. The bondholders gain the coinsurance effect, and the stockholders lose the coinsurance effect. Some general conclusions emerge from the preceding analysis.

1. Bondholders in the aggregate will usually be helped by mergers and acquisitions. The size of the gain to bondholders depends on the reduction of bankruptcy states after the combination. That is, the less risky the combined firm is, the greater are the gains to bondholders.
2. Stockholders of the acquiring firm will be hurt by the amount that bondholders gain.
3. The conclusions apply to mergers and acquisitions where no synergy is present. In the case of synergistic combinations, much depends on the size of the synergy.

How Can Shareholders Reduce Their Losses from the Coinsurance Effect?

The coinsurance effect allows some mergers to increase bondholder values by reducing shareholder values. However, there are at least two ways that shareholders can reduce or eliminate the coinsurance effect. First, the shareholders in firm *A* could retire its debt *before* the merger announcement date and reissue an equal amount of debt after the merger. Because debt is retired at the low, pre-merger price, this type of refinancing transaction can neutralize the coinsurance effect to the bondholders.

Also, note that the debt capacity of the combined firm is likely to increase because the acquisition reduces the probability of financial distress. Thus, the shareholders' second alternative is simply to issue more debt after the merger. An increase in debt following the merger will have two effects, even without the prior action of debt retirement. The interest deduction from new corporate debt raises firm value. In addition, an increase in debt after merger raises the probability of financial distress, thereby reducing or eliminating the bondholders' gain from the coinsurance effect.

29.8 Two "Bad" Reasons for Mergers

Earnings Growth

An acquisition can create the appearance of earnings growth, which may fool investors into thinking that the firm is worth more than it really is. Suppose Global Resources, Ltd., acquires Regional Enterprises. The financial positions of Global and Regional before the acquisition are shown in Table 29.7. Regional has had very poor earnings growth and sells at a price-earnings ratio much lower than that of Global. The merger creates no additional value. If the market is smart, it will realize that the combined firm is worth the sum of the values of the separate firms. In this case, the market value of the combined firm will be $3,500, which is equal to the sum of the values of the separate firms before the merger.

At these values, Global will acquire Regional by exchanging 40 of its shares for 100 Regional shares,[16] so that Global will have 140 shares outstanding after the merger. Because the stock price of Global after the merger is the same as before the merger, the price-earnings ratio must fall. This is true because the market is smart and recognizes that the total market has not been altered by the merger. This scenario is represented by the third column of Table 29.7.

Let us now consider the possibility that the market is fooled. One can see from Table 29.7 that the acquisition enables Global to increase its earnings per share from $1 to $1.43. If the market is fooled, it might mistake the 43-percent increase in earnings per share for true growth. In this case, the price-earnings ratio of Global may not fall after the merger. Suppose the price-earnings ratio of Global remains equal to 25. The total value of the combined firm will increase to $5,000 (25 × $200), and the stock price per share of Global will increase to $35.71 ($5,000/140). This is reflected in the last column of Table 29.7.

This is earnings-growth magic. Like all good magic, it is an illusion and the shareholders of Global and Regional will receive something for nothing. This may work for a while, but in the long run the efficient market will work its wonders and the value will decline.

[16] This ratio implies a fair exchange because a share of Regional is selling for 40 percent ($10/$25) of the price of a share of Global.

TABLE 29.7 Financial Positions of Global Resources and Regional Enterprises

	Global Resources before Merger	*Regional Enterprises before Merger*	**Global Resources after Merger** *The Market is "Smart"*	**Global Resources after Merger** *The Market is "Fooled"*
Earnings per share	$ 1.00	$ 1.00	$ 1.43	$ 1.43
Price per share	$ 25.00	$ 10.00	$ 25.00	$ 35.71
Price-earnings ratio	25	10	17.5	25
Number of shares	100	100	140	140
Total earnings	$ 100	$ 100	$ 200	$ 200
Total value	$2,500	$1,000	$3,500	$5,000

Exchange ratio: 1 share in Global for 2.5 shares in Regional.

Diversification

Diversification often is mentioned as a benefit of one firm acquiring another. Earlier in this chapter, we noted that U.S. Steel included diversification as a benefit in its acquisition of Marathon Oil. In 1982 U.S. Steel was a cash-rich company (over 20 percent of its assets were in the form of cash and marketable securities). It is not uncommon to see firms with surplus cash articulating a need for diversification.

However, we argue that diversification, by itself, cannot produce increases in value. To see this, recall that a business's variability of return can be separated into two parts: (1) what is specific to the business and called *unsystematic,* and (2) what is *systematic* because it is common to all businesses.

Systematic variability cannot be eliminated by diversification, so mergers will not eliminate this risk at all. By contrast, unsystematic risk can be diversified away through mergers. However, the investor does not need widely diversified companies such as General Electric to eliminate unsystematic risk. Shareholders can diversify more easily than corporations by simply purchasing common stock in different corporations. For example, the shareholders of U.S. Steel could have purchased shares in Marathon if they believed there would be diversification gains in doing so. Thus, diversification through conglomerate merger may not benefit shareholders.[17]

Diversification can produce gains to the acquiring firm only if two things are true:

1. Diversification decreases the unsystematic variability at lower costs than by investors via adjustments to personal portfolios. This seems very unlikely.
2. Diversification reduces risk and thereby increases debt capacity. This possibility was mentioned earlier in the chapter.

Concept Question

- Why can a merger create the appearance of earnings growth?

[17] Recent evidence suggests that diversification can actually hurt shareholders. Randall Mork, Andrei Shleifer, and Robert W. Vishney ["Do Managerial Objectives Drive Bad Acquisitions," *Journal of Finance* 45 (1990), pp. 31–48] show that shareholders did poorly in firms that diversified by acquisition in the 1980s.

29.9 The NPV of a Merger

Firms typically use NPV analysis when making acquisitions.[18] The analysis is relatively straightforward when the consideration is cash. The analysis becomes more complex when the consideration is stock.

Cash

Suppose firm A and firm B have values as separate entities of \$500 and \$100, respectively. They are both all-equity firms. If firm A acquires firm B, the merged firm AB will have a combined value of \$700 due to synergies of \$100. The board of firm B has indicated that it will sell firm B if it is offered \$150 in cash.

Should firm A acquire firm B? Assuming that firm A finances the acquisition out of its own retained earnings, its value after the acquisition is[19]

$$\begin{array}{c}\text{Value of}\\ \text{firm } A \text{ after}\\ \text{the acquisition}\end{array} = \begin{array}{c}\text{Value of}\\ \text{combined firm}\end{array} - \begin{array}{c}\text{Cash}\\ \text{paid}\end{array}$$

$$= \$700 - \$150$$

$$= \$550$$

Because firm A was worth \$500 prior to the acquisition, the NPV to firm A's stockholders is

$$\$50 = \$550 - \$500 \tag{29.1}$$

Assuming that there are 25 shares in firm A, each share of the firm is worth \$20 (\$500/25) prior to the merger and \$22 (\$550/25) after the merger. These calculations are displayed in the first and third columns of Table 29.8. Looking at the rise in stock price, we conclude that firm A should make the acquisition.

We spoke earlier of both the synergy and the premium of a merger. We can also value the NPV of a merger to the acquirer as

$$\begin{array}{c}\text{NPV of a merger}\\ \text{to acquirer}\end{array} = \text{Synergy} - \text{Premium}$$

Because the value of the combined firm is \$700 and the premerger values of A and B were \$500 and \$100, respectively, the synergy is \$100 [\$700 − (\$500 + \$100)]. The premium is \$50 (\$150 − \$100). Thus, the NPV of the merger to the acquirer is

$$\begin{array}{c}\text{NPV of merger}\\ \text{to firm } A\end{array} = \$100 - \$50 = \$50$$

One caveat is in order. This textbook has consistently argued that the market value of a firm is the best estimate of its true value. However, we must adjust our analysis when discussing mergers. If the true price of firm A *without the merger* is \$500, the market value of firm A may actually be above \$500 when merger negotiations take place. This

[18] The NPV framework for evaluating mergers can be found in S. C. Myers, "A Framework for Evaluating Mergers," in *Modern Developments in Financial Management,* ed. by S. C. Myers (New York: Praeger, 1976).

[19] The analysis will be essentially the same if new stock is issued. However, the analysis will differ if new debt is issued to fund the acquisition because of the tax shield to debt. An adjusted present value (APV) approach would be necessary here.

TABLE 29.8 Cost of Acquisition: Cash versus Common Stock

	Before Acquisition		After Acquisition: Firm A		
	(1)	*(2)*	*(3)*	*(4)* Common Stock:† Exchange Ratio (0.75:1)	*(5)* Common Stock:† Exchange Ratio (0.6819:1)
	Firm A	*Firm* B	*Cash**		
Market value (V_A, V_B)	$500	$100	$550	$700	$700
Number of shares	25	10	25	32.5	31.819
Price per share	$ 20	$ 10	$ 22	$ 21.54	$ 22

* Value of firm *A* after acquisition: cash

$$V_A = V_{AB} - \text{Cash}$$
$$\$550 = \$700 - \$150$$

†Value of firm *A* after acquisition: common stock

$$V_A = V_{AB}$$
$$\$700 = \$700$$

occurs because the market price reflects the possibility that the merger will occur. For example, if the probability is 60 percent that the merger will take place, the market price of firm *A* will be

$$\begin{matrix} & \text{Market value of firm } A \text{ with merger} & \times & \text{Probability of merger} & + & \text{Market value of firm } A \text{ without merger} & \times & \text{Probability of no merger} \\ \$530 = & \$550 & \times & 0.60 & + & \$500 & \times & 0.40 \end{matrix}$$

The managers would underestimate the NPV from merger in equation (29.1) if the market price of firm *A* is used. Thus, managers are faced with the difficult task of valuing their own firm without the acquisition.

Common Stock

Of course, firm *A* could purchase firm *B* with common stock instead of cash. Unfortunately, the analysis is not as straightforward here. In order to handle this scenario, we need to know how many shares are outstanding in firm *B*. We assume that there are 10 shares outstanding, as indicated in column 2 of Table 29.8.

Suppose firm *A* exchanges 7.5 of its shares for the entire 10 shares of firm *B*. We call this an exchange ratio of 0.75:1. The value of each share of firm *A*'s stock before the acquisition is $20. Because 7.5 × $20 = $150, this exchange *appears* to be the equivalent of purchasing firm *B* in cash for $150.

This is incorrect: The true cost is greater than $150. To see this, note that firm *A* has 32.5 (25 + 7.5) shares outstanding after the merger. Firm *B* shareholders own 23 percent (7.5/32.5) of the combined firm. Their holdings are valued at $161 (23% × $700). Because these stockholders receive stock in firm *A* worth $161, the cost of the merger to firm *A*'s stockholders must be $161, not $150.

This result is shown in column 4 of Table 29.8. The value of each share of firm *A*'s stock after a stock-for-stock transaction is only $21.54 ($700/32.5). We found out earlier that the value of each share is $22 after a cash-for-stock transaction. The difference is that the cost of the stock-for-stock transaction to firm *A* is higher.

This nonintuitive result occurs because the exchange ratio of 7.5 shares of firm *A* for 10 shares of firm *B* was based on the *premerger* prices of the two firms. However, since the stock of firm *A* rises after the merger, firm *B* stockholders receive more than $150 in firm *A* stock.

What should the exchange ratio be so that firm *B* stockholders receive only $150 of firm *A*'s stock? We begin by defining α, the proportion of the shares in the combined firm that firm *B*'s stockholders own. Because the combined firm's value is $700, the value of firm *B* stockholders after the merger is

Value of Firm *B* Stockholders after Merger:

$$\alpha \times \$700$$

Setting $\alpha \times \$700 = \$150$, we find that $\alpha = 21.43\%$. In other words, firm *B*'s stockholders will receive stock worth $150 if they receive 21.43 percent of the firm after merger.

Now we determine the number of shares issued to firm *B*'s shareholders. The proportion, α, that firm *B*'s shareholders have in the combined firm can be expressed as

$$\alpha = \frac{\text{New shares issued}}{\text{Old shares + New shares issued}} = \frac{\text{New shares issued}}{25 + \text{New shares issued}}$$

Plugging our value of α into the equation yields

$$0.2143 = \frac{\text{New shares issued}}{25 + \text{New shares issued}}$$

Solving for the unknown, we have

$$\text{New shares} = 6.819 \text{ shares}$$

Total shares outstanding after the merger is 31.819 (25 + 6.819). Because 6.819 shares of firm *A* are exchanged for 10 shares of firm *B*, the exchange ratio is 0.6819:1.

Results at the exchange ratio of 0.6819:1 are displayed in column 5 of Table 29.8. Each share of common stock is worth $22, exactly what it is worth in the stock-for-cash transaction. Thus, given that the board of firm *B* will sell its firm for $150, this is the fair exchange ratio, not the ratio of 0.75:1 mentioned earlier.

Cash versus Common Stock

Whether to finance an acquisition by cash or by shares of stock is an important decision.[20] The choice depends on several factors, as follows:

1. *Overvaluation.* If in the opinion of management the acquiring firm's stock is overvalued, using shares of stock can be less costly than using cash.
2. *Taxes.* Acquisition by cash usually results in a taxable transaction. Acquisition by exchanging stock is tax free.
3. *Sharing Gains.* If cash is used to finance an acquisition, the selling firm's shareholders receive a fixed price. In the event of a hugely successful merger, they will not participate in any additional gains. Of course, if the acquisition is not a success, the losses will not be shared and shareholders of the acquiring firm will be worse off than if stock were used.

[20] All-cash transactions are much more common than all-stock transactions. In 1985, only about 10 percent of acquisitions were financed by all stock (see *Mergers and Acquisitions,* "Almanac and Review: 1985").

Concept Question

- In an efficient market with no tax effects, should an acquiring firm use cash or stock?

29.10 Defensive Tactics

Target-firm managers frequently resist takeover attempts. Resistance usually starts with press releases and mailings to shareholders that present management's viewpoint. It can eventually lead to legal action and solicitation of competing bids. Managerial action to defeat a takeover attempt may make target shareholders better off if it elicits a higher offer premium from the bidding firm or another firm. Of course, management resistance may simply reflect pursuit of self-interest at the expense of shareholders. That is, the target managers may resist a takeover in order to preserve their jobs. In this section we describe various defensive tactics that have been used by target-firm managements to resist unfriendly takeover attempts.

The Corporate Charter

The corporate charter refers to the articles of incorporation and corporate bylaws that govern the firm. The corporate charter establishes the conditions that allow a takeover. Firms frequently amend corporate charters to make acquisitions more difficult. For example, usually two-thirds of the shareholders of record must approve a merger. Firms can make it more difficult to be acquired by requiring 80-percent approval. This is called a *supermajority amendment.* Another device is to *stagger* the election of the board members, which increases the difficulty of electing a new board of directors quickly. DeAngelo and Rice, and Linn and McConnell examine the adoption of anti-takeover amendments related to the corporate charter on stock prices of the adopting firms and find no adverse effect.[21]

Repurchase Standstill Agreements

Managers may arrange a *targeted repurchase* to forestall a takeover attempt. In a targeted repurchase, a firm buys back its own stock from a potential bidder, usually at a substantial premium. These premiums can be thought of as payments to potential bidders to delay or stop unfriendly takeover attempts. Critics of such payments label them *greenmail.*

In addition, managers of target firms may simultaneously negotiate standstill agreements. *Standstill agreements* are contracts where the bidding firm agrees to limit its holdings of another firm. These agreements usually lead to cessation of takeover attempts, and announcement of such agreements has had a negative effect on stock prices.

- ***Example***

On April 2, 1986, Ashland Oil, Inc., the nation's largest independent oil refiner, had 28 million shares outstanding. The company's stock price closed the day before at $49¾

[21] H. DeAngelo and E. M. Rice, "Antitakeover Charter Amendments and Stockholder Wealth," *Journal of Financial Economics* 11 (April 1983); and S. G. Linn and J. J. McConnell, "An Empirical Investigation of the Impact of Antitakeover Amendments on Common Stock Prices," *Journal of Financial Economics* 11 (April 1983).

per share on the New York Stock Exchange. On April 2, Ashland's board of directors made two decisions:

1. The board approved management's agreement with the Belzberg family of Canada to buy, for $51 a share, the Belzbergs' 2.6 million shares in Ashland. This was part of a standstill agreement that ended a takeover skirmish in which the Belzberg family offered $60 per share for all of the common stock of Ashland.
2. The board authorized the company to repurchase 7.5 million shares (27 percent of the outstanding shares) of its stock. The board simultaneously approved a proposal to establish an employee stock-ownership plan to be funded with 5.3 million shares of Ashland stock.

The result of these two actions was to make Ashland invulnerable to unfriendly takeover attempts. In effect, the company was selling about 20 percent of its stock to the employee stock-ownership plan. Earlier Ashland had put in place a provision that said 80 percent of the stockholders have to approve a takeover. Ashland's stock price fell by $0.25 over the next two days. Because this move can probably be explained by random error, there is no evidence that Ashland's actions reduced shareholder value. •

Exclusionary Self-Tenders

An *exclusionary self-tender* is the opposite of a targeted repurchase. Here, the firm makes a tender offer for a given amount of its own stock while excluding targeted stockholders.

In one of the most celebrated cases in financial history, Unocal, a large integrated oil firm, made a tender offer for 29 percent of its shares while excluding its largest shareholder, Mesa Partners II (led by T. Boone Pickens). Unocal's self-tender was for $72 per share, which was $16 over the prevailing market price. It was designed to defeat Mesa's attempted takeover by Unocal by transferring wealth, in effect, from Mesa to Unocal's other stockholders.

Going Private and Leveraged Buyouts

Going private refers to what happens when the publicly owned stock in a firm is purchased by a private group, usually composed of existing management. As a consequence, the firm's stock is taken off the market (if it is an exchange-traded stock, it is delisted) and is no longer traded. Thus, in going-private transactions, shareholders of publicly held firms are forced to accept cash for their shares.

Going-private transactions are frequently *leveraged buyouts* (LBOs). In a leveraged buyout, the cash-offer price is financed with large amounts of debt. LBOs have recently become quite popular because the arrangement calls for little equity capital. This equity capital is generally supplied by a small group of investors, some of whom are likely to be managers of the firm being purchased.

The selling stockholders are invariably paid a premium above market price in an LBO, just as they are in a merger.[22] As with a merger, the acquirer profits only if the synergy created is greater than the premium. Synergy is quite plausible in a merger of

---

[22] H. DeAngelo, L. DeAngelo, and E. M. Rice, "Going Private: Minority Freezeouts and Shareholder Wealth," *Journal of Law and Economics* 27 (1984). They show that the premiums paid to existing shareholders in LBOs and other going-private transactions are about the same as in interfirm acquisitions.

two firms, and we delineated a number of types of synergy earlier in the chapter. However, it is much more difficult to explain synergy in an LBO, because only *one* firm is involved.

There are generally two reasons given for the ability of an LBO to create value. First, the extra debt provides a tax deduction, which, as earlier chapters suggested, leads to an increase in firm value. Most LBOs are on firms with stable earnings and with low to moderate debt. The LBO may simply increase the firm's debt to its optimum level. In fact, Congress has recently taken a skeptical look at LBOs, partly because the increase in debt reduces the U.S. Treasury's tax revenues.

Second, the LBO usually turns the previous managers into owners, thereby increasing their incentive to work hard. The increase in debt is a further incentive because the managers must earn more than the debt service to obtain any profit for themselves.

Though it is easy to value the additional tax shields from an LBO, it is quite difficult to value the gains from increased efficiency. Nevertheless, this increased efficiency is considered to be at least as important as the tax shield in explaining the LBO phenomenon.[23]

Of course, one cannot be entirely sure that LBOs create value at all, because the stock price cannot be observed once the company has been taken private. Though one frequently hears of LBO investors achieving great wealth, this is only casual empirical evidence. There may be an equal number of LBO investors who are left with little value after purchasing a company at a premium. The full story on LBOs has certainly not been told at this point.

Other Devices and Jargon of Corporate Takeovers

As corporate takeovers have become more common, a new lexicon has developed. The terms are colorful, and some are listed here:

1. **Golden parachutes.** Some target firms provide compensation to top-level management if a takeover occurs. For example, when the Scoville board endorsed a $523 million tender offer by First City Properties, it arranged for 13 top executives to receive termination payments of about $5 million. This can be viewed as a payment to management to make it less concerned for its own welfare and more interested in stockholders when considering a takeover bid. Alternatively, the payment can be seen as an attempt to enrich management at the stockholders' expense.
2. **Crown jewels.** Firms often sell major assets—crown jewels—when faced with a takeover threat. This is sometimes referred to as the *scorched earth strategy.*
3. **Poison pill.** Poison pill is a term taken from the world of espionage. Agents are supposed to bite a pill of cyanide rather than permit capture. Presumably this prevents enemy interrogators from learning important secrets. In finance, poison pills are used to make a stock repellent to others. A poison pill is generally a right to buy shares in the merged firm at a bargain price. The right is granted to the target firm's shareholders, contingent on another firm

[23] For the academic community's view of LBOs, see "A Discussion of Corporate Restructuring," *Midland Corporate Finance Journal* (Summer 1984), which features a roundtable discussion by a number of prominent university professors.

acquiring control.[24] The right dilutes the stock so much that the bidding firm loses money on its shares. Thus, wealth is transferred from the bidder to the target.

Concept Question

- What can a firm do to make a takeover less likely?

29.11 Some Evidence on Acquisitions

One of the most controversial issues surrounding our subject is whether mergers and acquisitions benefit shareholders.

Do Acquisitions Benefit Shareholders?

Much research has attempted to estimate the effect of mergers and takeovers on stock prices of the bidding and target firms. These studies are called *event studies* because they estimate abnormal stock-price changes on and around the offer-announcement date—the event. Abnormal returns are usually defined as the difference between actual stock returns and a market index, to take account of the influence of marketwide effects on the returns of individual securities.

An overview of the evidence is reported in Jensen and Ruback. Tables 29.9 and 29.10 summarize the results of numerous studies that look at the effects of mergers and tender offers on stock prices. Table 29.9 shows that the shareholders of target companies in successful takeovers achieve large abnormal returns. When the takeover is done by merger the gains are 20 percent, and when the takeover is done by tender offer the gains are 30 percent.

The shareholders of bidding firms do not fare nearly as well. According to the studies summarized in Table 29.9, bidders experience abnormal returns of 4 percent in tender offers, and in mergers the percentage is zero. These numbers are sufficiently small to leave doubt about the effect on bidders. Table 29.10 shows that the shareholders of firms involved in unsuccessful takeover attempts experience small negative returns in both mergers and tender offers. What conclusions can be drawn from Tables 29.9 and 29.10?

1. The results of all event studies suggest that the shareholders of target firms achieve substantial gains as a result of successful takeovers.[25] The gains appear to be larger in tender offers than in mergers. This may reflect the fact that takeovers sometimes start with a friendly merger proposal from the bidder to the management of the target firm. If management rejects the offer, the bidding firm may take the offer directly to the shareholders with an unfriendly tender offer. The target management may actively oppose the offer with defensive tactics. This often has the result of raising the tender offer

[24] P. H. Malatesta and R. A. Walkling, "Poison Pill Securities: Stockholder Wealth, Profitability and Ownership Structure," *Journal of Financial Economics* (January/March 1988). The authors conclude that the poison pill reduces stockholder wealth. Also see R. A. Walkling and M. Long, "Agency Theory, Managerial Welfare and Takeover Bid Resistance," *Rand Journal of Economics* (Spring 1984).

[25] This has been a consistent finding in all merger studies. G. Mandelker, "Risk and Return: The Case of the Merging Firm," *Journal of Financial Economics* (1974), was one of the first to document the premiums to acquired firms.

TABLE 29.9 Abnormal Stock-Price Changes Associated with Successful Corporate Takeover Bids

Takeover Technique	*Target*	*Bidders*
Tender offer	30%	4%
Merger	20%	0
Proxy contest	8%	n.a.

n.a. = Not applicable.

Modified from Michael C. Jensen and Richard S. Ruback, "The Market for Corporate Control: The Scientific Evidence," *Journal of Financial Economics* 11 (April 1983), pp. 7, 8. © Elsevier Science Publishers B. V. (North-Holland).

TABLE 29.10 Abnormal Stock-Price Changes Associated with Unsuccessful Corporate Takeover Bids

Takeover Technique	*Target*	*Bidders*
Tender offer	−3%	−1%
Merger	−3%	−5%
Proxy contest	8%	n.a.

n.a. = Not applicable

Modified from Michael C. Jensen and Richard S. Ruback, "The Market for Corporate Control: The Scientific Evidence," *Journal of Financial Economics* 11 (April 1983), pp. 7, 8. © Elsevier Science Publishers B. V. (North-Holland).

from the bidding firm, and thus, on the average, friendly mergers are arranged at a lower premium than unfriendly tender offers.

2. The shareholders of bidding firms earn comparatively little from takeovers. They earn an average of only 4 percent from tender offers and do not appear to earn anything from mergers. In fact, in a study by Asquith the shareholders of acquiring firms in successful mergers experienced significantly abnormal losses after the announcement of the merger.[26] These findings are a puzzle.
   a. One possible explanation is that anticipated merger gains were not completely achieved, and thus shareholders experienced losses. Managers of bidding firms may have hubris and tend to overestimate the gains from acquisition.[27]
   b. The bidding firms are usually much larger than the target firms. Thus, the dollar gains to the bidder may be approximately the same as the dollar gains to the shareholders of the target firm at the same time that the *percentage* returns are much lower for the bidding firms.

[26] P. Asquith, "Merger Bids, Uncertainty and Stockholder Returns," *Journal of Financial Economics* 11 (April 1983).

[27] R. Roll, "The Hubris Hypothesis of Corporate Takeover," *Journal of Business* (April 1986).

c. Management may not be acting in the interests of shareholders when it attempts to acquire other firms. Perhaps it is attempting to increase the size of its firm, even if this reduces its value.

d. Several studies indicate that the returns of bidding firms cannot be measured very easily. Malatesta, and Schipper and Thompson show that many of the gains to the shareholders of bidding firms come when acquisition programs commence. The incremental effect of each acquisition on stock price may be very small, because the stock price at commencement reflects the anticipated gains from future acquisitions.[28]

3. The return to the shareholders of targets of unsuccessful merger, measured from the offer date to the cancellation date, is negative. Thus, all the initial gains are lost over the time period during which the merger failure becomes known. The overall average return to shareholders of unsuccessful tender offers is about the same as for unsuccessful merger attempts. However, the story is more complicated. Bradley, Desai, and Kim report that how well shareholders of target firms do in unsuccessful tender offers depends on whether or not future takeover offers are forthcoming. They find that target-firm shareholders realize additional positive gains when a new offer is made but lose everything previously gained if no other offer occurs.[29]

Concept Question

- What does the evidence say about the benefits of mergers and acquisitions?

29.12 The Japanese Keiretsu

In Japan it has been unusual for firms to grow by large-scale mergers and acquisitions. However, in the late 1980s several Japanese firms acquired large U.S. firms.[30] Most notably, Sony acquired CBS Records in November 1987 and Columbia Pictures in September 1989. Sony's acquisition of Columbia Pictures for $3.45 billion is the largest Japanese acquisition of a U.S. firm. The second largest was Bridgestone Corporation acquisition of Firestone Tire and Rubber for $2.6 billion in March 1988.

The most interesting Japanese business combinations involve reciprocal shareholding and trading agreements. These networks are called **keiretsu** and involve a group of firms affiliated around a large bank, industrial firm, or trading firm. The Mitsubishi and the Mitsui keiretsu groups are shown in Figure 29.3.

Participation in the Mitsubishi or Mitsui keiretsu implies significant reciprocal ownership of common stock. It is widely understood that firms within the keiretsu are not to sell these cross-held shares.

Nobody knows for sure what the main benefit of the keiretsu is. However, one of the most important features of the keiretsu is the relationship between the industrial

[28] P. H. Malatesta, "The Wealth Effect of Merger Activity and the Objective Function of Merging Firms," *Journal of Financial Economics* 11 (April 1983); and K. Schipper and R. Thompson, "Evidence on the Capitalized Value of Merger Activity for Acquiring Firms," *Journal of Financial Economics* 11 (April 1983).

[29] M. Bradley, A. Desai, and E. H. Kim, "The Rationale behind Interfirm Tender Offers: Information or Synergy," *Journal of Financial Economics* 11 (April 1983).

[30] W. Carl Kester, *Japanese Takeovers the Global Contest for Corporate Control*, Cambridge, Mass.: 1991 (Harvard Business School Press). Chapter 5 describes the acquisition experience of several Japanese firms.

FIGURE 29.3 Japanese Keiretsu

Financial Services	Mitsubishi Bank Mitsubishi Trust & Banking Meiji Mutual Life Tokio Marine & Fire	Mitsui Taiyo Kobe Bank Mitsui Trust & Banking Mitsui Mutual Life Taisho Marine & Fire
Computers, Electronics, and Electrical Equipment	Mitsubishi Electric	Toshiba
Cars	Mitsubishi Motors	Toyota Motor*
Trading and Retailing	Mitsubishi	Mitsui Mitsukoshi
Food and Beverage	Kirin Brewery	Nippon Flour Mills
Construction	Mitsubishi Construction	Mitsui Construction Sanki Engineering
Metals	Mitsubishi Steel Mfg. Mitsubishi Materials Mitsubishi Aluminum Mitsubishi Cable Industries	Japan Steel Works Mitsui Mining & Smelting
Real Estate	Mitsubishi Estate	Mitsui Real Estate Development
Oil and Coal	Mitsubishi Oil	
Rubber and Glass	Asahi Glass	
Chemicals	Mitsubishi Kasei Mitsubishi Petrochemical Mitsubishi Gas Chemical Mitsubishi Plastics Industries Mitsubishi Kasei Polytec	Mitsui Toatsu Chemicals Mitsui Petrochemical Industries
Fibers and Textiles	Mitsubishi Rayon	Toray Industries
Pulp and Paper	Mitsubishi Paper Mills	Oji Paper
Mining and Forestry		Mitsui Mining Hokkaido Colliery & Steamship
Industrial Equipment	Mitsubishi Heavy Industries Mitsubishi Kakoki	Mitsui Engineering & Shipbuilding
Cameras and Optics	Nikon	
Cement		Onoda Cement
Shipping and Transportation	Nippon Yusen Mitsubishi Warehouse & Transportation	Mitsui OSK Lines Mitsui Warehouse

This table describes the network of firms in the Mitsubishi and Mitsui keiretsu.
* Companies affiliated with more than one group.
Source: *Fortune* (July 15, 1991), p. 81.

firms and the financial institutions. For example, Mitsubishi Motors may have an extensive relationship with Mitsubishi Trust and Banking, Jeiji Mutual Life, and Tokio Marine and Fire. This connection between industrial firms and financial institutions within the group may benefit the group by reducing the costs of financial distress that come from getting creditors to agree to a restructuring if one of the keiretsu members gets into financial trouble.[31] Reaching an agreement between Mitsubishi Bank and

[31] This is the argument of Takeo Hoshi, Anil K. Kashyup, and David Scharfstein, "The Role of Banks in Reducing Financial Distress in Japan." A paper in the Finance and Economic Discussion Series, No. 134, Federal Reserve Board, Washington, D.C. (October 1990). See also, W. Carl Kester, "Japanese Corporate Governance and the Conservation of Value in Financial Distress," *Journal of Applied Corporate Finance* (Summer 1991).

Mitsubishi Motors will be easier if Mitsubishi Motors gets into trouble because both are in the Mitsubishi keiretsu.

Concept Questions

- Can you describe a keiretsu?
- What is a benefit of a keiretsu?

29.13 Summary and Conclusions

1. One firm can acquire another in several different ways. The three legal forms of acquisition are merger and consolidation, acquisition of stock, and acquisition of assets. Mergers and consolidations are the least costly to arrange from a legal standpoint, but they require a vote of approval by the shareholders. Acquisition by stock does not require a shareholder vote and is usually done via a tender offer. However, it is difficult to obtain 100-percent control with a tender offer. Acquisition of assets is comparatively costly because it requires more difficult transfer of asset ownership.
2. Mergers and acquisitions require an understanding of complicated tax and accounting rules. Mergers and acquisitions can be taxable or tax-free transactions. In a taxable transaction, each selling shareholder must pay taxes on the stock's capital appreciation. Should the acquiring firm elect to write up the assets, additional tax implications arise. However, acquiring firms do not generally elect to write up the assets for tax purposes. The selling stockholders do not pay taxes at the time of a tax-free acquisition.

   Accounting for mergers and acquisitions involves a choice of the purchase method or the pooling-of-interests method. The choice between these two methods does not affect after-tax cash flows of the combined firm. However, most financial managers prefer the pooling-of-interests method, because net income of the combined firm under this method is higher than it is under the purchase method.
3. The synergy from an acquisition is defined as the value of the combined firm (V_{AB}) less the value of the two firms as separate entities (V_A and V_B), or

   $$\text{Synergy} = V_{AB} - (V_A + V_B)$$

   The shareholders of the acquiring firm will gain if the synergy from the merger is greater than the premium.
4. The possible benefits of an acquisition come from the following:
   a. Revenue enhancement
   b. Cost reduction
   c. Lower taxes
   d. Lower cost of capital

   In addition, the reduction in risk from a merger may actually help bondholders and hurt stockholders.
5. Some of the most colorful language of finance stems from defensive tactics in acquisition battles. *Poison pills, golden parachutes, crown jewels,* and *greenmail* are terms that describe various antitakeover tactics. These tactics are discussed in this chapter.
6. The empirical research on mergers and acquisitions is extensive. Its basic conclusions are that, on average, the shareholders of acquired firms fare very well, while the shareholders of acquiring firms do not gain much.
7. The keiretsu is a Japanese form of business networks. It involves reciprocal shareholding and agreements among member firms.

Key Terms

Suggested Readings

A readable book on how to quantify the value from mergers and acquisitions:
Rappaport, A. *Creating Shareholder Value: The New Standard for Business Performance.* New York: Free Press, 1986: Chapter 9.

Some good articles on mergers and acquisitions appear in
Stein, J. M., and D. H. Chew, eds. *The Revolution in Corporate Finance.* New York: Basil Blackwell, 1986.
"A Symposium on the Market for Corporate Control: The Scientific Evidence." *Journal of Financial Economics* (April 1983).
"A Symposium on the Distribution of Power among Corporate Managers, Shareholders and Directors." *Journal of Financial Economics* (January/March 1988).

Questions and Problems

The Basic Forms of Acquisitions

29.1 The Lager Brewing Corporation has acquired the Philadelphia Pretzel Company in a vertical merger. Lager Brewing has issued $300,000 in new long-term debt to pay for its purchase. ($300,000 is the purchase price.) Construct the balance sheet for the new corporation if the merger is treated as a purchase for accounting purposes. The balance sheets shown here represent the assets of both firms at their true market values. Assume these market values are also the book values.

LAGER BREWING
Balance Sheet
(in thousands)

Current assets	$400	Current liabilities	$200
Other assets	100	Long-term debt	100
Net fixed assets	500	Equity	700
Total	$1,000	Total	$1,000

PHILADELPHIA PRETZEL
Balance Sheet
(in thousands)

Current assets	$80	Current liabilities	$80
Other assets	40	Equity	120
Net fixed assets	80		
Total	$200	Total	$200

29.2 Suppose the balance sheet for Philadelphia Pretzel in problem 29.1 shows the assets at their book value and not their market value of $240,000. Construct the balance sheet for the new corporation. Again, treat the transaction as a purchase.

29.3 Keep the assumptions of 29.2. Construct the balance sheet for the new corporation. Use pooling interest method to treat the transaction.

Source of Synergy from Acquisitions

29.4 Indicate whether you think the following claims regarding takeovers are true or false. In each case provide a brief explanation for your answer.

a. By merging competitors, takeovers have created monopolies that will raise product prices, reduce production, and harm consumers.

b. Managers act in their own interest at times and, in reality, may not be answerable to shareholders. Takeovers may reflect runaway management.

c. In an efficient market, takeovers would not occur because market price would reflect the true value of corporations. Thus, bidding firms would not be justified in paying premiums above market prices for target firms.

d. Traders and institutional investors, having extremely short time horizons, are influenced by their perceptions of what other market traders will be thinking of stock prospects and do not value takeovers based on fundamental factors. Thus, they will sell shares in target firms despite the true value of the firms.

e. Mergers are a way of avoiding taxes because they allow the acquiring firm to write up the value of the assets of the acquired firm.

f. Acquisitions analysis frequently focuses on the total value of the firms involved. An acquisition, however, will usually affect relative values of stocks and bonds, as well as their total value.

Calculating the Value of the Firm after an Acquisition

29.5 The following table shows the projected cash flows and their respective discount rates after the acquisition of Small Fry Co. by Whale Co. Fill in the blanks and calculate the stock price of the new firm if it has $100 million of debt and 5 million shares of stock outstanding.

	Net Cash Flow Per Year (Perpetual) (in $million)	*Discount Rate (%)*	*Value (in $million)*
Small Fry Co.	8	16%	?
Whale Co.	20	10	?
Benefits from Acquisition	5	?	42.5
Revenue Enhancement	2.5	?	12.5
Cost Reduction	2	10	?
Tax Shelters	0.5	5	?
Whale-Co.	33	?	?

A Cost to Stockholders from Reduction in Risk

29.6 The Chocolate Ice Cream Company and the Vanilla Ice Cream Company have agreed to merge and form Fudge Swirl Consolidated. Both companies are exactly alike except that they are located in different towns. The end-of-period value of each firm is determined by the weather, as shown.

State	*Probability*	*Value*
Rainy	0.1	$100,000
Warm	0.4	200,000
Hot	0.5	400,000

The weather conditions in each town are independent of those in the other. Furthermore, each company has an outstanding debt claim of $200,000. Assume that no premiums are paid in the merger.

a. What is the distribution of joint values?

b. What is the distribution of end-of-period debt values and stock values after the merger?

c. Show that the value of the combined firm is the sum of the individual values.

d. Show that the bondholders are better off and the stockholders are worse off in the combined firm than they would have been if the firms remained separate.

29.7 Cholern Electric Company (CEC) is a public utility that provides electricity to the central Colorado area. Recent events at its Mile-High Nuclear Station have been discouraging. Several shareholders have expressed concern over last year's financial statements.

Income Statement Last Year (in millions)		**Balance Sheet End of Year (in millions)**	
Revenue	$110	Assets	$400
Fuel	50	Debt	300
Other expenses	30	Equity	100
Interest	30		
Net income	$0		

Recently, a wealthy group of individuals has offered to purchase one half of CEC's assets at fair market price. Management recommends that this offer be accepted because, "We believe our expertise in the energy industry can be better exploited by CEC if we sell our electricity generating and transmission assets and enter the telecommunications business. Although telecommunications is a riskier business than providing electricity as a public utility, it is also potentially very profitable."

Should the management approve this transaction? Why or why not?

Two "Bad" Reasons for Mergers

29.8 Refer to the Global Resources example in section 29.8 of the text. Suppose that instead of 40 shares, Global exchanges 100 of its shares for the 100 shares of Regional. The new Global Resources will now have 200 shares outstanding and earnings of $200. Assume the market is smart.

a. Calculate Global's value after the merger.

b. Calculate Global's earnings per share.

c. Calculate Global's price per share.

d. Redo your answers to (*a*), (*b*), and (*c*) if the market is fooled.

29.9 Coldran Aviation has voted in favor of being bought out by Arcadia Financial Corporation. Information about each company is presented below.

	Arcadia Financial	*Coldran Aviation*
Price-earnings ratio	16	10.8
Number of shares	100,000	50,000
Earnings	$225,000	$100,000

Stockholders in Coldran Aviation will receive six-tenths of a share of Arcadia for each share they hold.

a. How will the earnings per share (EPS) for these stockholders be changed?

b. What will be the effect on the original Arcadia stockholders of changes in the EPS?

The NPV of a Merger

29.10 Fly-By-Night Couriers is analyzing the possible acquisition of Flash-in-the-Pan Restaurants. Neither firm has debt. The forecasts of Fly-By-Night show that the purchase would increase its annual after-tax cash flow by $600,000 indefinitely. The current market value of Flash-in-the-Pan is $20 million. The current market value of

Fly-By-Night is $35 million. The appropriate discount rate for the incremental cash flows is 8 percent.

a. What is the synergy from the merger?

b. What is the value of Flash-in-the-Pan to Fly-By-Night?

Fly-By-Night is trying to decide whether it should offer 25 percent of its stock or $15 million in cash to Flash-in-the-Pan.

c. What is the cost to Fly-by-Night of each alternative?

d. What is the NPV to Fly-by-Night of each alternative?

e. Which alternative should Fly-By-Night use?

29.11 Freeport Manufacturing is considering making an offer to purchase Portland Industries. The treasurer of Freeport has collected the following information:

	Freeport	*Portland*
Price-earnings ratio	15	12
Number of shares	1,000,000	250,000
Earnings	$1,000,000	$750,000

The treasurer also knows that securities analysts expect the earnings and dividends (currently $1.80 per share) of Portland to grow at a constant rate of 5 percent each year. Her research indicates, however, that the acquisition would provide Portland with some economies of scale that would improve this growth rate to 7 percent per year.

a. What is the value of Portland to Freeport?

b. If Freeport offers $40 in cash for each outstanding share of Portland, what would the NPV of the acquisition be?

c. If instead Freeport were to offer 600,000 of its shares in exchange for the outstanding stock of Portland, what would the NPV of the acquisition be?

d. Should the acquisition be attempted, and if so, should it be a cash or stock offer?

e. Freeport's management thinks that 7-percent growth is too optimistic and that 6 percent is more realistic. How does this change your previous answers?

29.12 Harrods PLC has a market value of £600 million and 30 million shares outstanding. Selfridge Department Store has a market value of £200 million and 20 million shares outstanding. Harrods is contemplating acquiring Selfridge Department Store. Harrods' CFO concludes that the combined firm with synergy will be worth £1 billion and Selfridge can be acquired at a premium of £100 million.

a. If Harrods offers 15 million shares to exchange for the 20 million shares of Selfridge, what will after-acquisition stock price of Harrods be?

b. To make the value of stock offer equivalent to a cash offer of £300 million, what would be the proper exchange ratio of the two stocks?

29.13 Company *A* is contemplating acquiring company *B*. Company *B's* projected revenues, costs, and required investments appear in the following table. The table also shows sources for financing company *B's* investments if *B* is acquired by *A*. The table incorporates the following information.

> Company *B* will immediately increase its leverage with a $110 million loan, which would be followed by a $150 million dividend to company *A*. (This operation will increase the debt-to-equity ratio of company *B* from 1/3 to 1/1.)
>
> Company *A* will use $50 million of tax-loss carryforwards available from the firm's other operations.

The terminal, total value of company *B* is estimated to be $900 million in five years, and the projected level of debt then is $300 million.

The risk-free rate and the expected rate of return on the market portfolio are 6 percent and 14 percent, respectively. Company *A* analysts estimate the weighted average cost of capital for their company to be 10 percent. The borrowing rate for both companies is 8 percent. The beta coefficient for the stock of company *B* (at its current capital structure) is estimated to be 1.25.

The board of directors of company *A* is presented with an offer for $68.75 per share of company *B*, or a total of $550 million for the 8 million shares outstanding.

Evaluate this proposal. The table produced below may help you.

Projections for Company *B* if Acquired by Company *A* (in $ millions)

	Year 1	*Year 2*	*Year 3*	*Year 4*	*Year 5*
Sales	800	900	1,000	1,125	1,250
Production costs	562	630	700	790	875
Depreciation	75	80	82	83	83
Other expenses	80	90	100	113	125
EBIT	83	100	118	139	167
Interest	19	22	24	25	27
EBT	64	78	94	114	140
Taxes	32	39	47	57	70
Net income	32	39	47	57	70
Investments:					
Net working capital	20	25	25	30	30
Net fixed assets	15	25	18	12	7
Total	35	50	43	42	37
Sources of financing:					
Net debt financing	35	16	16	15	12
Profit retention	0	34	27	27	25
Total	35	50	43	42	37

Cash flows—Company *A*

	Year 0	*Year 1*	*Year 2*	*Year 3*	*Year 4*	*Year 5*
Acquisition of *B*	—					
Dividends from *B*	150	—	—	—	—	—
Tax-loss carryforwards			25	25		—
Terminal value	—	—	—	—	—	—
Total	—	—	—	—	—	—

Defensive Tactics

29.14 List the defensive tactics commonly used by target-firm managers to resist unfriendly takeover attempts.

Appendix 29A

The U.S. Steel Acquisition of Marathon Oil

U.S. Steel Corporation's takeover of Marathon Oil Company, the nation's 17th largest oil firm, for a total purchase consideration of $6.5 billion is one of the largest takeovers in U.S. corporate history. Interestingly, it followed closely on the heels of Du Pont's $7.5 billion acquisition of Conoco, and at least one key investment banker was involved in both takeovers.

In this appendix we analyze in detail the abnormal returns associated with 16 significant announcements over a five-month period for the major players in the Marathon takeover game. We also examine the cumulative returns to the stockholders of the different participating firms. Our study concludes with some explanations of Marathon's substantial revaluations and other theories to explain why Mobil and U.S. Steel actively pursued an acquisition that seemed to lower shareholder wealth.

Our framework of analysis is patterned very closely after Richard S. Ruback's work on the Conoco and Cities Service takeovers.

Brief Description of the Acquisition

In the summer of 1981, Marathon Oil Company commissioned the First Boston Corporation to prepare an analysis of the underlying asset value of Marathon based solely on publicly available information. Before First Boston could complete the study, Mobil Corporation announced a tender offer for Marathon's common equity, thus launching one of the most eventful takeover stories in American corporate history.

On October 30, 1981, Mobil bid $85 per share for up to 40 million shares of Marathon's common equity. Before the announcement, Marathon stock traded for about $64 per share on the New York Stock Exchange. Before trading on the new information commenced, Marathon management rejected Mobil's offer as grossly inadequate and began seeking a white knight merger candidate. When trading began on Monday, November 2, 1981, Marathon's shares shot up immediately to the $90-per-share range for a one-day abnormal excess return of more than 30 percent. The market reacted to Mobil's offer by bidding Mobil's common stock down to $25⅜ for a one-day abnormal return of −4.26 percent. (November 2, 1981, was also the ex-dividend date for a $0.50 per share dividend declared earlier. The share price, however, fell $⅝.) These data suggest that the market viewed the possible acquisition of Marathon by Mobil at $85 per share as a near-zero net-present-value transaction for Mobil. The dramatic response of Marathon's share price was very likely caused by anticipation of more bidding. These traders were not to be disappointed.

On November 9, the management of U.S. Steel Corporation expressed an interest in acquiring Marathon. The possible takeover price was rumored to be $100 per share in cash and notes. Presumably because the market actually valued this offer as less than Mobil's offer, Marathon's common stock showed an abnormal return for the day of −2.91 percent. The effect of the rumors on U.S. Steel's share price was insignificant, so it may be concluded that the market felt that the transaction at this price would be a zero net-present-value transaction for U.S. Steel as well.

During subsequent negotiations, U.S. Steel raised its price and actually tendered $125 per share for up to 30 million shares of Marathon stock on November 18. On the next trading day Marathon showed a one-day abnormal excess return on its share price of almost 35 percent; again the market roared its approval for the reevaluation of Marathon. U.S. Steel's common, however, showed significantly negative abnormal returns in response to this news. This indicates that the market believed U.S. Steel overbid for Marathon. Mobil's share price showed no significant abnormal return on November 18 and 19.

However, on November 25, Mobil raised its bid to $126 per share, and the market responded by lowering the value of both Mobil and U.S. Steel by significant amounts. Apparently the market believed that at this price the merger was unattractive for both Mobil and U.S. Steel. Marathon's stock fell in price by a significant amount in response to Mobil's offer, perhaps because Mobil's offer and U.S. Steel's offer were valued nearly equally by the market, and this signaled the end of the bidding and the end of speculating in Marathon.

In fact, on November 30, Mobil was prohibited by the courts for antitrust reasons from pursuing Marathon any further, and a merger between U.S. Steel and Marathon was eventually consummated on March 11, 1982.

Conclusion

As Table 29A.1 shows, the cumulative abnormal returns for Marathon for the period from the beginning of the third quarter of 1981 to the merger date were more than 59 percent. This is

TABLE 29A.1 Summary of Abnormal Returns for Firms Involved in the Takeover of Marathon Oil Company

Firm	*Holding Period*	*Cumulative Abnormal Return**
Marathon Oil Company	July 2, 1981–March 11, 1982	59.1%
Mobil Corporation	July 2, 1981–March 11, 1982	−7.1
U.S. Steel Corporation	July 2, 1981–March 11, 1982	−4.7
Gulf Oil Corporation	July 2, 1981–February 1, 1982	0.5

* Notes on calculations follow:

1. Daily returns on stocks were adjusted for market returns according to the capital-asset-pricing model as follows:

$$PE_{jt} = R_{jt} - \hat{\beta}_j R_{mt}$$

where PE_{jt} is the prediction error for firm j on day t; R_{jt} is the unadjusted return for firm j on day t; β_j is firm j's beta; and R_{mt} is the return on the Standard & Poor's 500-stock index on day t. This approach assumes that the effect of firm alpha is negligible and that the risk-free rate can be disregarded.

2. The cumulative abnormal daily returns were calculated as follows:

$$\left[\prod_{t=t_1}^{t_2} (1 + PE_{jt})\right] - 1$$

where t_2 is the date for which the cumulative abnormal return is required, and t_1 is July 2, 1981.

3. The t-statistics were approximated as follows:

$$t = \frac{PE_{jt}}{\sigma_j}$$

where σ_j is the square root of the residual variance of the market-model regression.

4. The beta values used in the calculations are as follows:

Marathon	1.22
Mobil	0.98
U.S. Steel	1.02
Gulf	1.08

consistent with other findings, which have shown significant positive abnormal returns for the targets of takeover activity.[32]

The cumulative abnormal returns for U.S. Steel and Mobil were, respectively, −4.65 percent and −7.13 percent for the same period. Again, these results are consistent with other studies showing significantly negative abnormal returns for bidding and acquiring firms.

These results support the notion that the real winners in takeover battles such as this are the shareholders of target firms and those traders who identify undervalued firms that will become takeover targets, buy their stock before bidding begins, and hold it until just after the last bid is made.

U.S. Steel's acquisition of Marathon is puzzling. Its shareholders fared poorly. The transaction may reflect the inherent conflict of interests between managers and shareholders and how they are sometimes resolved.

Chronology of the Events in the Acquisition of Marathon Oil Company

July 15, 1981—Marathon Oil arranges $5 billion in credit. *The Wall Street Journal* reports that the rumored takeover target is expected to use the loan for purchases or other defensive tactics.

[32] P. Dodd, "Merger Proposals, Management Discretion, and Stockholder Wealth," *Journal of Financial Economics* (June 1980).

July 20, 1981—Gulf Oil raises a $5 billion line of credit. *The Wall Street Journal* speculates that Gulf might be preparing to take over another oil company.

July 22, 1981—Mobil continues to fight for Conoco. Mobil raises cash price for Conoco further to $105 per share.

July 28, 1981—U.S. Steel profit doubles from 1980 second quarter.

August 3, 1981—Mobil raises bid for Conoco to $115 per share.

August 11, 1981—Dome Petroleum announces plans to acquire the remaining 47 percent of Hudson Bay Oil and Gas Company from Marathon.

September 3, 1981—Mobil gets a temporary stay of an order that could have forced it to pay up to $50 million to other refiners. The order stems from the U.S. Department of Energy's efforts to end its entitlement program.

September 9, 1981—Marathon Oil announces it will accept offers for two Canadian units: Marathon Petroleum Canada, Ltd., and Pan-Ocean Oil, Ltd.

October 28, 1981—U.S. Steel's earnings increase fourfold over previous year's depressed levels to $187.8 million in the third quarter.

October 29, 1981—Marathon Oil agrees to buy Husky Oil's U.S. unit for $650 million. The transaction is expected to be completed in mid-December. Mobil's earnings fall 30 percent, mainly because of a 53-percent fall in foreign profits.

October 30, 1981—Mobil tenders for up to 40 million shares of Marathon at $85 per share.

October 31, 1981—Marathon's board rejects Mobil's offer as being grossly inadequate and not in the best interest of the company and its shareholders.

November 1, 1981—Marathon institutes action in federal district court alleging that the effect of the proposed acquisition of the company by Mobil may be to lessen competition or to tend to create a monopoly in violation of Section 7 of the Clayton Act.

November 2, 1981—Pennzoil expresses an interest in acquiring Marathon.

November 9, 1981—U.S. Steel contacts Marathon with a view to a possible takeover and/or merger.

November 18, 1981—U.S. Steel and Marathon enter into an agreement of merger, pursuant to which the former (through a subsidiary) makes a tender offer for 30 million shares of the latter at a price of $125 per share. Gulf Oil makes an oral offer to purchase about 50 percent of Marathon's shares for between $130 and $140 per share.

November 24, 1981—Mobil files suit against Marathon, U.S. Steel, etc., and court orders defendants to suspend merger activities.

November 25, 1981—Mobil makes a new tender offer for 30 million shares of Marathon at $126 per share.

November 27, 1981—Court amends its order, pending disposal of Mobil's case against U.S. Steel and Marathon, now permitting U.S. Steel to solicit tenders.

November 30, 1981—Federal district court prohibits Mobil from acquiring any shares of Marathon.

December 1, 1981—Mobil is denied appeal to stay a temporary restraining order blocking its $6.5 billion acquisition of Marathon. Preliminary injunctions issued by court in respect of above.

December 3, 1981—Marathon drops its proposed $650 million purchase of Husky Oil's U.S. unit. Mobil signals that it expects to have another oil company, believed to be Amerada Hess, as a partner in its hostile bid for Marathon.

December 6, 1981—U.S. Steel gains a clear lead in the takeover contest for Marathon. Its $125-per-share bid draws far more than the 30 million shares it sought. Its offer also clears an FTC review.

December 7, 1981—Mobil is denied a request to have a federal court block U.S. Steel's rival bid. Separately, Mobil attempts to satisfy antitrust objections by agreeing to sell certain Marathon assets to Amerada Hess.

December 8, 1981—Marathon's stockholders tender 90 percent of their shares in response to U.S. Steel's offer for 50 percent. The FTC decides to challenge Mobil's acquisition proposal on antitrust grounds. Mobil hints it might seek to acquire U.S. Steel. Mobil and Amerada Hess sign agreement.

December 9, 1981—Mobil says it might seek to buy 25 percent of U.S. Steel's 89.9 million outstanding shares. The holding could be used to force U.S. Steel to sell Marathon Oil to Mobil if U.S. Steel wins the takeover battle over Marathon.

December 13, 1981—An appeals court in Cincinnati rules that U.S. Steel cannot buy Marathon shares until five working days after the court decides on two Mobil appeals against federal court rulings in Ohio. Meanwhile, the FTC files the promised antitrust case against Mobil.

December 23, 1981—A federal appeals court upholds the district court ruling blocking Mobil, on antitrust grounds, from acquiring Marathon shares. Court also invalidates the Yates option and the stock option, which were integral aspects of U.S. Steel's friendly offer. Court seems to invite others to bid for the nation's 17th largest oil firm. On December 24, U.S. Steel gives up its rights under both options.

December 27, 1981—U.S. Steel could buy control of Marathon as early as the next week under an order issued by a federal judge in Columbus, Ohio. The ruling allows U.S. Steel to begin buying Marathon shares after midnight, January 6, unless rival suitor Mobil gets a delay or a new bidder for Marathon emerges.

December 29, 1981—Mobil asks the Supreme Court to review a lower court's antitrust ruling blocking its proposed $6.5 billion takeover of Marathon. It also petitions Justice Sandra O'Connor, asking that U.S. Steel be enjoined from buying Marathon shares until its first request is considered by the High Court.

December 30, 1981—Mobil, rebuffed by Chief Justice Warren Burger on procedural grounds (he said Mobil should first take its request to a lower court), will ask an appeals court to delay U.S. Steel's plans to buy a controlling stake in Marathon.

January 4, 1982—Mobil loses appeal.

January 5, 1982—Mobil renews emergency Supreme Court plea to block U.S. Steel's purchase of Marathon stock, which can begin January 6 at midnight.

January 6, 1982—Mobil's petition is denied by Justice Burger.

January 7, 1982—U.S. Steel begins to purchase Marathon shares at $125 per share. Mobil considers buying 25 percent of U.S. Steel.

January 10, 1982—Mobil continues to hint that it will purchase 15 to 25 percent of U.S. Steel's shares.

January 13, 1982—Two Marathon Oil shareholders file suit to block U.S. Steel's acquisition of the company. They claim that the second part of the takeover (including the note swap) is unfair and inadequate.

January 24, 1982—Marathon Oil's net falls 28 percent to $40.1 million, reflecting one-time changes related to its merger into U.S. Steel and accounting adjustments.

January 26, 1982—U.S. Steel's fourth-quarter net falls 46 percent to $101.8 million, reflecting a sharp drop in demand.

February 2, 1982—First Boston gives a written opinion confirming the fairness of U.S. Steel's offer.

February 15, 1982—Marathon announces a final $0.50-per-share dividend payable ex February 16, 1982, on March 10, 1982.

March 11, 1982—Merger between U.S. Steel and Marathon is approved by more than two thirds of Marathon's shareholders.

CHAPTER

30 Financial Distress

This chapter discusses financial distress, private workouts, and bankruptcy. A firm that does not generate enough cash flow to make a contractually required payment, such as an interest payment, will experience financial distress. A firm that defaults on a required payment may be forced to liquidate its assets. More often, a defaulting firm will reorganize its financial structure. Financial restructuring involves replacing old financial claims with new ones and takes place with private workouts or legal bankruptcy. Private workouts are voluntary arrangements to restructure a company's debt, such as postponing a payment or reducing the size of the payment. Sometimes a private workout is not possible and formal bankruptcy is required. The largest formal bankruptcy in U.S. financial history occurred in April 1987 when Texaco filed Chapter 11 bankruptcy. (See Table 30.1 for information on the largest U.S. bankruptcies.)

30.1 What Is Financial Distress?

Financial distress is surprisingly hard to define precisely. This is true partly because of the variety of events befalling firms under financial distress. The list of events is almost endless but here are some examples:

Dividend reductions
Plant closings
Losses
Layoffs
CEO resignations
Plummeting stock prices

Financial distress is a situation where a firm's operating cash flows are not sufficient to satisfy current obligations (such as trade credits or interest expenses) and the firm is forced to take corrective action.[1] Financial distress may lead a firm to default on a contract, and it may involve financial restructuring between the firm, its creditors, and its equity investors. Usually the firm is forced to take actions that it would not have taken if it had sufficient cash flow.

[1] This definition is close to the one used by Karen Wruck, "Financial Distress: Reorganization and Organization Efficiency," *Journal of Financial Economics* 27 (1990), p. 425.

TABLE 30.1 The Largest U.S. Bankruptcies

Firm	*Liabilities (in $ millions)*	*Bankruptcy Date*
Texaco (including subsidiaries)	21,603	April 1987
Executive Life Insurance	14,577	April 1991
Mutual Benefit Life	13,500	July 1991
Campeau (Allied & Federated)	9,947	January 1990
First Capital Holdings	9,291	May 1991
Baldwin United	9,000	September 1983
Continental Airlines (II)	6,200	December 1990
Lomas Financial	6,127	September 1989
Macy's	5,300	January 1992
Columbia Gas	4,998	July 1991
LTV (including LTV International NV)	4,700	July 1986
Maxwell Communication	4,100	December 1991
TWA	3,470	January 1992
Southland	3,380	October 1990
Penn Central Transportation	3,300	June 1970
Eastern Airlines	3,196	March 1989
Drexel Burnham Lambert	3,000	February 1990
Pan Am World Airlines	3,000	January 1991
Interco	2,213	May 1990
Laventhol & Horwath	2,000	November 1990
Wickes	2,000	April 1982
Global Marine	1,800	January 1986
ITEL	1,700	January 1981
Public Service, New Hampshire	1,700	January 1988
Continental Information Systems	1,669	January 1989
Integrated Resources	1,600	February 1990
Revco	1,500	July 1988

Source: Supplied by Edward I. Altman.

Our definition of financial distress can be expanded somewhat by linking it to insolvency. Insolvency is defined in *Black's Law Dictionary* as[2]

> Inability to pay one's debts; lack of means of paying one's debts. Such a condition of a woman's (or man's) assets and liability that the former made immediately available would be insufficient to discharge the latter.

This definition has two general themes, stocks and flows.[3] These two ways of thinking about insolvency are depicted in Figure 30.1. The stock-based insolvency occurs when a firm has negative net worth, and so the value of assets is less than the value of its debts. Flow-based insolvency occurs when operating cash flow is insufficient to meet current obligations. Flow-based insolvency refers to the inability to pay one's debts.

[2] Taken from *Black's Law Dictionary*, 5th ed. (St. Paul, Minn: West Publishing Company), p. 716.

[3] Edward Altman was one of the first to distinguish between stock-based insolvency and flow-based insolvency. See Edward Altman, *Corporate Financial Distress: A Complete Guide to Predicting, Avoiding and Dealing with Bankruptcy* (New York: John Wiley & Sons, 1983).

FIGURE 30.1 Insolvency

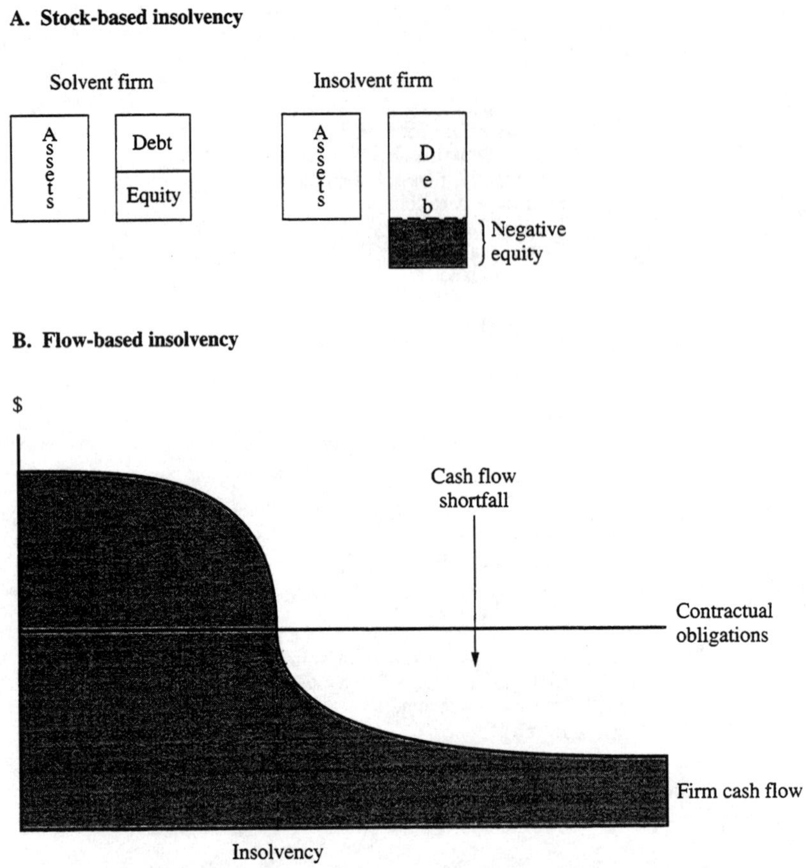

Stock-based insolvency occurs when the value of the assets of a firm are less than the value of the debts. This implies negative equity. Flow-based insolvency occurs when firm cash flows are insufficient to cover contractually required payments.

Concept Questions

- Can you describe financial distress?
- What are stock-based insolvency and flow-based insolvency?

30.2 What Happens in Financial Distress?

In the early 1990s Trans World Airline, Inc. (TWA) experienced financial distress. It lost money in 1989, 1990, and 1991 and steadily lost market share to its rivals United, American, and Delta. Having seen Eastern and Pan Am disappear, airline travelers had good reason to be nervous about buying tickets from TWA.

In the summer of 1991 TWA General Counsel Mark A. Buckstein bet Carl Icahn, TWA owner and CEO, $1,000 that the airline would be forced into involuntary bankruptcy by September 1991.[4] Icahn argued that he could arrange a private restructuring and avoid formal bankruptcy. Icahn won the bet, but TWA eventually filed for bankruptcy on January 31, 1992. Icahn was quoted as saying the bankruptcy reorganization would give TWA the time it needed to turn the firm around. The odds favored Icahn because financial distress does not usually result in a firm's death. (TWA was reorganized in 1993. Icahn resigned as CEO and gave up all ownership claims.)

Firms deal with financial distress in several ways such as

1. Selling major assets.
2. Merging with another firm.
3. Reducing capital spending and research and development.
4. Issuing new securities.
5. Negotiating with banks and other creditors.
6. Exchanging equity for debt.
7. Filing for bankruptcy.

Items (1), (2), and (3) concern the firm's assets. Items (4), (5), (6), and (7) involve the right-hand side of the firm's balance sheet and are examples of financial restructuring. Financial distress may involve both asset restructuring and financial restructuring (i.e., changes on both sides of the balance sheet).

Some firms may actually benefit from financial distress by restructuring their assets. In an earlier chapter we showed that, in 1986, Goodyear Tire and Rubber's levered recapitalization changed the firm's behavior and forced the firm to dispose of unrelated businesses. Goodyear's cash flow was not sufficient to cover required payments, and it was forced to sell its noncore businesses. For some firms financial distress may bring about new organizational forms and new operating strategies. However, in this chapter we focus on financial restructuring.

Financial restructuring may occur in a private workout or a bankruptcy reorganization under Chapter 11 of the U.S. Bankruptcy Code. Figure 30.2 shows how large public firms move through financial distress. Approximately one half of the financial restructurings have been done via private workouts. Most large public firms (83 percent) that file for Chapter 11 bankruptcy are able to reorganize and continue to do business.[5]

Financial distress can serve as a firm's "early warning" system for trouble. Firms with more debt will experience financial distress earlier than firms with less debt. However, firms that experience financial distress earlier will have more time for private workouts and reorganization. Firms with low leverage will experience financial distress later and, in many instances, be forced to liquidate.

Concept Questions

- Why doesn't financial distress always cause firms to die?
- What is a benefit of financial distress?

[4] The bet was reported in "Carl has 9 lives but he is betting up to 8½," *Business Week*, February 24, 1992.

[5] Only about 15 percent of all firms (public or private) going through a Chapter 11 bankruptcy are successfully reorganized.

FIGURE 30.2 What Happens in Financial Distress

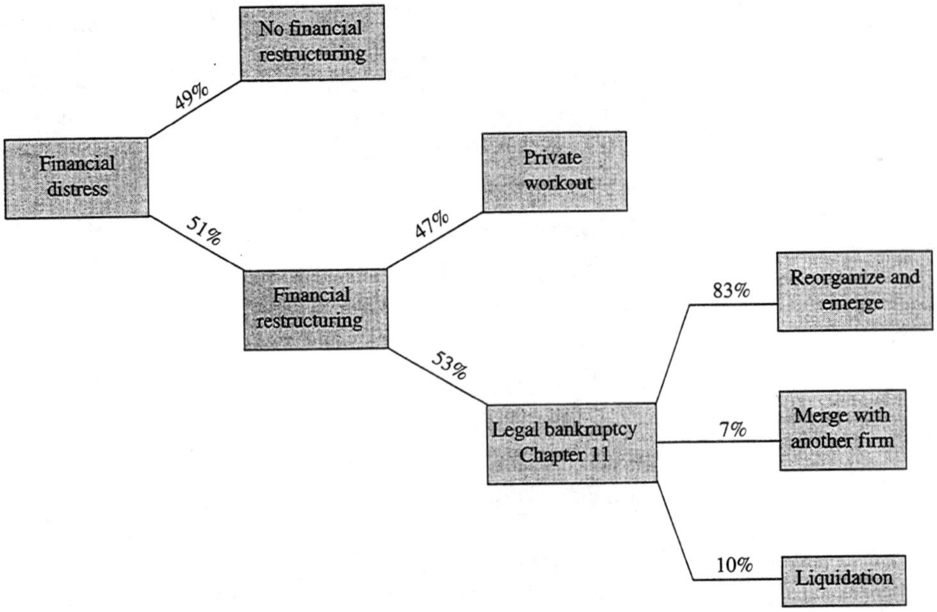

Source: Karen H. Wruck, "Financial Distress: Reorganization and Organizational Efficiency," *Journal of Financial Economics* 27, (1990), Figure 2. See also Stuart C. Gilson; Kose John; and Larry N. P. Lang, "Troubled Debt Restructurings: An Empirical Study of Private Reorganization of Firms in Defaults," *Journal of Financial Economics* 27, (1990); and Lawrence A. Weiss, "Bankruptcy Resolution: Direct Costs and Violation of Priority of Claims," *Journal of Financial Economics* 27, (1990).

30.3 Bankruptcy Liquidation and Reorganization

Firms that cannot or choose not to make contractually required payments to creditors have two basic options: liquidation or reorganization. This section discusses bankruptcy liquidation and reorganization.

Liquidation means termination of the firm as a going concern; it involves selling the assets of the firm for salvage value. The proceeds, net of transactions costs, are distributed to creditors in order of established priority.

Reorganization is the option of keeping the firm a going concern; it sometimes involves issuing new securities to replace old securities.

Liquidation and formal reorganization may be done by bankruptcy. *Bankruptcy* is a legal proceeding and can be done voluntarily with the corporation filing the petition or involuntarily with the creditors filing the petition.

Bankruptcy Liquidation

Chapter 7 of the Bankruptcy Reform Act of 1978 deals with "straight" liquidation. The following sequence of events is typical:

1. A petition is filed in a federal court. Corporations may file a voluntary petition, or involuntary petitions may be filed against the corporation.
2. A trustee-in-bankruptcy is elected by the creditors to take over the assets of the debtor corporation. The trustees will attempt to liquidate the assets.

3. When the assets are liquidated, after payment of the costs of administration, assets are distributed among the creditors.
4. If any assets remain, after expenses and payments to creditors, they are distributed to the shareholders.

Conditions Leading to Involuntary Bankruptcy

An involuntary bankruptcy petition may be filed by creditors if both the following conditions are met:

1. The corporation is not paying debts as they become due.
2. If there are more than 12 creditors, at least three with claims totaling $5,000 or more must join in the filing. If there are fewer than 12 creditors, then only one with a claim of $5,000 is required to file.

Priority of Claims

Once a corporation is determined to be bankrupt, liquidation takes place. The distribution of the proceeds of the liquidation occurs according to the following priority:

1. *Administration expenses,* associated with liquidating the bankrupt's assets.
2. Unsecured claims arising after the filing of an involuntary bankruptcy petition.
3. Wages, salaries, and commissions, not to exceed $2,000 per claimant, earned within 90 days before the filing date.
4. Contributions to employee benefit plans arising within 180 days before the filing date.
5. Consumer claims, not exceeding $900.
6. Tax claims.
7. Secured and unsecured creditors' claims.
8. Preferred stockholders' claims.
9 Common stockholders' claims.

The priority rule in liquidation is the **absolute priority rule** (APR).

One qualification to this list concerns secured creditors. Liens on property are outside APR ordering. However, if the secured property is liquidated and provides cash insufficient to cover the amount owed them, the secured creditors join with unsecured creditors in dividing the remaining liquidating value. In contrast, if the secured property is liquidated for proceeds greater than the secured claim, the net proceeds are used to pay unsecured creditors and others.

• ***Example***

The B. O. Drug Company is to be liquidated. Its liquidating value is $2.7 million. Bonds worth $1.5 million are secured by a mortgage on the B. O. Drug Company corporate headquarters building, which is sold for $1 million; $200,000 is used to cover administrative costs and other claims (including unpaid wages, pension benefits, consumer claims, and taxes). After paying $200,000 to the administrative priority claims, the amount available to pay secured and unsecured creditors is $2.5 million. This is less than the amount of unpaid debt of $4 million. •

Under APR all creditors must be paid before shareholders, and the mortgage bondholders have first claim on the $1 million obtained from the sale of the headquarters building.

The trustee has proposed the following distribution:

Type of Claim	Prior Claim	Cash Received under Liquidation
Bonds (secured by mortgage)	$1,500,000	$1,500,000
Subordinated debentures	2,500,000	1,000,000
Common stockholders	10,000,000	0
Total	$14,000,000	$2,500,000

Calculation of the distribution	
Cash received from sale of assets available for distribution	$2,500,000
Cash paid to secured bondholders on sale of mortgaged property	1,000,000
Available to bond- and debenture holders	$1,500,000
Total claims remaining ($4,000,000 less payment of $1,000,000 on secured bonds)	3,000,000
Distribution of remaining $1,500,000 to cover total remaining claims of $3,000,000	

Type of claim remaining	Claim on Liquidation Proceeds	Cash Received
Bonds	$ 500,000	$ 500,000
Debentures	2,500,000	1,000,000
Total	$3,000,000	$1,500,000

Bankruptcy Reorganization

Corporate reorganization takes place under Chapter 11 of the Federal Bankruptcy Reform Act of 1978. The general objective of a proceeding under Chapter 11 is to plan to restructure the corporation with some provision for repayment of creditors. A typical sequence of events follows:

1. A voluntary petition can be filed by the corporation, or an involuntary petition can be filed by three or more creditors (or one creditor if the total creditors are fewer than 12—see the previous section). The involuntary petition must allege that the corporation is not paying its debt.
2. A federal judge either approves or denies the petition. If the petition is approved, a time for filing proofs of claims and of shareholders is set.
3. In most cases, the corporation (the "debtor in possession") continues to run the business.
4. The corporation is given 120 days to submit a reorganization plan.
5. Creditors and shareholders are divided into classes. A class of creditors accepts the plan if two-thirds of the class (in dollar amount) and one-half of the class (in number) have indicated approval.
6. After acceptance by creditors, the plan is confirmed by the court.
7. Payments in cash, property, and securities are made to creditors and shareholders. The plan may provide for the issuance of new securities.

• ***Example***

Suppose B. O. Drug Co. decides to reorganize under Chapter 11. Generally, senior claims are honored in full before various other claims receive anything. Assume that the "going concern" value of B. O. Drug Co. is $3 million and that its balance sheet is as shown:

Assets	$3,000,000
Liabilities	
Mortgage bonds	1,500,000
Subordinated debentures	2,500,000
Stockholders' equity	−1,000,000

The firm has proposed the following reorganization plan:

Old Security	*Old Claim*	*New Claim with Reorganization Plan*
Mortgage bonds	$1,500,000	$1,500,000
Subordinated debentures	2,500,000	1,500,000

and a distribution of new securities under new claim with reorganization plan:

Old Security	*Receives under Proposed Reorganization Plan*
Mortgage bonds	$1,000,000 in 9% senior debentures
	$500,000 in 11% subordinated debentures
Debentures	$1,000,000 in 8% preferred stock
	$500,000 in common stock

However, it will be very difficult for the firm to convince secured creditors (mortgage bonds) to consent to accepting unsecured debentures of equal face value. In addition, the corporation may wish to allow the old stockholders to retain some participation in the firm. Needless to say, this would be a violation of the absolute priority rule and the holders of the debentures would not be happy. •

Absolute Priority Rule

The absolute priority rule states that senior claims are fully satisfied before junior claims receive anything.

Deviation from Rule

Equityholders	Expectation: No payout Reality: Payout in 81 percent of cases
Unsecured creditors	Expectation: Full payout after secured creditors Reality: Violation in 78 percent of cases
Secured creditors	Expectation: Full payout Reality: Full payout in 92 percent of cases

Reasons for Violations

Creditors want to avoid the expense of litigation. Debtors are given a 120-day opportunity to cause delay and harm value.

Managers often own equity and demand to be compensated.

Bankruptcy judges like consensual plans and pressure parties to compromise.

Source: Lawrence A. Weiss, "Bankruptcy Resolution: Direct Costs and Violation of Priority of Claims," *Journal of Financial Economics* 27 (1990).

Concept Questions

- What is bankruptcy?
- What is the difference between liquidation and reorganization?

30.4 Private Workout or Bankruptcy: Which Is Best?

A firm that defaults on its debt payments will need to restructure its financial claims. The firm will have two choices: formal bankruptcy or **private workout.** The previous section described two types of formal bankruptcies: bankruptcy liquidation and bankruptcy reorganization. This section compares private workouts with bankruptcy reorganizations. Both types of financial restructuring involve exchanging new financial claims for old financial claims. Usually senior debt is replaced with junior debt and debt is replaced with equity. Much recent academic research has described what happens in private workouts and formal bankruptcies.[6]

- Historically, one half of financial restructurings have been private but, recently, formal bankruptcy has dominated.
- Firms that emerge from private workouts experience stock-price increases that are much greater than those for firms emerging from formal bankruptcies.
- The direct costs of private workouts are much less than the costs of formal bankruptcies (about 10 percent).
- Top management usually loses pay and sometimes jobs in both private workouts and formal bankruptcies.

These facts, when taken together, seem to suggest that a private workout is much better than a formal bankruptcy. We then ask the question: Why do firms ever use formal bankruptcy to restructure?

The Marginal Firm

For the average firm a formal bankruptcy is more costly than a private workout, but for other firms formal bankruptcy is better. Formal bankruptcy allows firms to issue debt that is senior to all previously incurred debt. This new debt is "debtor in possession" (DIP) debt. For firms that need a temporary injection of cash, DIP debt makes bankruptcy reorganization an attractive alternative to a private workout. There are some tax advantages to bankruptcy. Firms do not lose tax carryforwards in bankruptcy, and the tax treatment of the cancellation of indebtness is better in bankruptcy. Also, interest on prebankruptcy unsecured debt stops accruing in formal bankruptcy.

Holdouts

Bankruptcy is usually better for the equity investors than it is for the creditors. Using DIP debt and stopping prebankruptcy interest helps the stockholders and hurts the creditors. As a consequence, equity investors can usually hold out for a better deal in

[6] For example, see Stuart Gilson, "Managing Default: Some Evidence on How Firms Choose Between Workouts and Bankruptcy," *Journal of Applied Corporate Finance* (Summer 1991); and Stuart C. Gilson, Kose John, and Larry N. P. Lang, "Troubled Debt Restructuring: An Empirical Study of Private Reorganization of Firms in Defaults," *Journal of Financial Economics* 27 (1990).

bankruptcy. The absolute priority rule, which favors creditors over equity investors, is usually violated in formal bankruptcies. One recent study found that in 81 percent of recent bankruptcies the equity investor obtained some compensation.[7] Under Chapter 11 the creditors are often forced to give up some of their seniority rights to get management and the equity investors to agree to a deal.

Complexity

A firm with a complicated capital structure will have more trouble putting together a private workout. Firms with secured creditors and trade creditors such as Macy's and Carter Hale will usually use formal bankruptcy because it is too hard to reach an agreement with many different types of creditors.

Lack of Information

There is an inherent conflict of interest between equity investors and creditors, and the conflict is accentuated when both have incomplete information about the circumstances of financial distress. When a firm initially experiences a cash flow shortfall, it may not know whether the shortfall is permanent or temporary. If the shortfall is permanent, creditors will push for a formal reorganization or liquidation. However, if the cash flow shortfall is temporary, formal reorganization or liquidation may not be necessary. Equity investors will push for this viewpoint. This conflict of interest cannot easily be resolved.

These last two points are especially important. They suggest that financial distress will be more expensive (cheaper) if complexity is high (low) and information is incomplete (complete). Complexity and lack of information make cheap workouts less likely.

Concept Questions

- What are two ways a firm can restructure its finances?
- Why do firms use formal bankruptcy?

30.5 Prepackaged Bankruptcy[8]

On October 1, 1986, the Crystal Oil Company filed for protection from its creditors under Chapter 11 of the U.S. Bankruptcy Code. Given the firm's heavy indebtedness, perhaps the outcome was not very surprising. However, less than three months later Crystal Oil came out of bankruptcy with a different capital structure. This surprised many people because, traditionally, bankruptcy has been very costly and often takes many years to emerge from. Crystal Oil avoided a lengthy bankruptcy by negotiating a reorganization plan with its creditors several months before the bankruptcy filing date.

[7] Lawrence A. Weiss, "Bankruptcy Dissolution: Direct Costs and Violation of Priority and Claims," *Journal of Financial Economics* 23 (1990).

[8] John McConnell and Henri Servaes "The Economics of Pre-packaged Bankruptcy," *Journal of Applied Corporate Finance* (Summer 1991), describe prepackaged bankruptcy and the Crystal Oil Company.

TABLE 30.2 Recent Prepackaged Bankruptcies of Large U.S. Firms

Firm	*Business*	*Filing Dates*	*Approved Date*
Memorex Telex	Computer equipment	January 6, 1992	February 7, 1992
Taj Mahal	Casino	August 8, 1991	October 4, 1991
JPS Textiles	Textiles	February 7, 1991	March 21, 1991
Southland	7-11 convenience stores	October 24, 1990	March 5, 1991

This new reorganization arrangement has been called **prepackaged bankruptcy.** Table 30.2 lists several recent prepackaged bankruptcies of large firms. Prepackaged bankruptcy is a combination of private workout and legal bankruptcy. In prepackaged bankruptcy the firm and most of its creditors agree to private reorganization outside formal bankruptcy. After the private reorganization is put together (i.e., prepackaged), the firm files a formal bankruptcy under Chapter 11.

Prepackaged bankruptcy arrangements require that most creditors reach agreement privately. Prepackaged bankruptcy doesn't seem to work when there are thousands of reluctant trade creditors, such as in the case of a retail trading firm like Macy's and Revco D. S.

The main benefit of prepackaged bankruptcy is it forces holdouts to accept a bankruptcy reorganization. If a large fraction of a firm's creditors can agree privately to a reorganization plan, the holdout problem may be avoided. It makes a reorganization plan in formal bankruptcy easier to put together.[9]

Concept Questions

- What is prepackaged bankruptcy?
- What is the main benefit of prepackaged bankruptcy?

30.6 The Decision to File for Bankruptcy: The Case of Revco[10]

Revco D. S. has a special place in the history of finance. It was both one of the largest leveraged buyouts and one of the largest bankruptcies in U.S. financial history.

In July 1988, Revco filed for bankruptcy under Chapter 11 of the U.S. Bankruptcy Code. At the time of its bankruptcy it was one of the largest retail drugstore chains in the United States. Revco's bankruptcy came at the end of four very turbulent years.

Up to 1984 the shareholders of Revco had reason to be pleased with its operating results. By 1984 Revco was operating approximately 2,000 stores in 30 states. Its gross profit margins averaged close to 7 percent. From 1971 to 1984 Revco had grown in sales and profits in excess of 20 percent per annum. In January 1984, its stock traded

[9] The original reorganization plan of Crystal Oil was accepted by the public creditors, but it was not accepted by the secured creditors. During bankruptcy a slightly revised plan was "crammed down" on the secured creditors. A bankruptcy court can force creditors to participate in a reorganization if it can be shown that the plan is "fair and equitable."

[10] See Karen H. Wruck, "What Really Went Wrong at Revco," *Journal of Applied Corporate Finance* (Summer 1991), pp. 71–92. This article contains an excellent description of the troubles of Revco.

at an all-time high of $37.50. Revco's financial difficulty began in the spring of 1984.[11]

1. In April 1984, E-Ferol, a vitamin product manufactured by a Revco subsidiary, was allegedly linked to 38 infant deaths and was recalled.
2. In May 1984, Revco acquired Odd Lot Trading, Inc., for over $100 million of Revco common stock. The acquisition gave Barnard Marden and Isaac Perlmutter, owners of Odd Lot Trading, 12 percent ownership in Revco. However, Perlmutter and Marden were not passive investors, and they had many new ideas for "improving" Revco. Eventually, hostility broke out between Perlmutter and Marden and Stanley Dworkin, the CEO of Revco.
3. In 1985 Revco's competitors, Rite-Aid and Ecker, adopted aggressive pricing tactics in an attempt to gain market share.
4. In July 1985, Revco bought out Marden's and Perlmutter's stakes in Revco for $98 million.
5. On December 29, 1986, Revco announced a leveraged buyout (LBO) with a private investor group. Because of the LBO, Revco's long-term debt increased from $44.7 million in 1985 to over $700 million after the LBO in 1986. Eventually, its total debt rose to $1.3 billion, and, in April 1988, Revco announced that it could not make the interest payment on its subordinated notes.
6. In March 1987, Revco decided to change its strategic orientation. Instead of "everyday low prices" on a narrow product line, Revco expanded its product line to include TVs, furniture, and appliances, and used selective promotions.
7. The new strategic orientation did not work, and Revco generated large losses in 1987.
8. In July 1988, Revco filed for bankruptcy under Chapter 11 of the Bankruptcy Code.
9. Four years later, Revco emerged from bankruptcy.

Why did Revco file for formal bankruptcy instead of private restructuring? What were the costs of the Revco bankruptcy? There are no easy answers to these questions.

1. *The Direct Costs of Bankruptcy.* Formal bankruptcy can be expensive and time-consuming. Revco was in Chapter 11 bankruptcy for almost four years and paid out over $40.5 million in direct bankruptcy costs (2.7 percent of the buyout price).[12] Below are some of the direct bankruptcy fees (in millions).

Law firms	
Baker & Hostetler	$ 7.5
Fried Frank	3.2
Accounting firms	
Arthur Andersen	7.4
Ernst & Young	4.2
Investment bankers	
Lazard Freres	3.5
Other	14.3
	$40.5

[11] Stephen Phillips, "Revco, Anatomy of an LBO that Failed," *Business Week* (October 3, 1988) describes the troubles of Revco.

[12] George Anders, "Revco Saga: On How the Buy Out Bonanza Became a Frenzy of Fees in Chapter," *The Wall Street Journal* (May 16, 1991).

2. *The Indirect Costs of Financial Distress.* There are many indirect costs of financial distress, including management distractions, loss of customers, and loss of reputation. The indirect costs of financial distress may occur whether or not formal bankruptcy is declared. In the case of Revco, financial distress caused a costly change in management and strategic direction.
3. *The Costs of a Complicated Financial Structure.* Firms such as Revco that have bank loans, senior subordinated debt, and junior subordinated debt will have a very hard time getting all claimholders to agree to an out-of-court settlement. For a retailer like Revco private agreements are especially difficult because of the large number of trade creditors. It is axiomatic that the more complicated a firm's financial structure, the more difficult it will be to work out private arrangements to avoid bankruptcy. Conflicts between managers, shareholders, and creditors make reaching a private agreement difficult. There is a natural tendency for each group to try to gain value at the expense of the others.

Concept Questions

- Why did it take Revco D. S. so long to emerge from bankruptcy?
- What are some of the costs of the Revco D. S. bankruptcy?

30.7 Summary and Conclusions

This chapter examines what happens when firms experience financial distress.

1. Financial distress is a situation where a firm's operating cash flow is not sufficient to cover contractual obligations. Financially distressed firms are often forced to take corrective action and undergo financial restructuring. Financial restructuring involves exchanging new financial claims for old ones.
2. Financial restructuring can be accomplished with a private workout or formal bankruptcy. Financial restructuring can involve liquidation or reorganization. However, liquidation is not common.
3. Corporate bankruptcy involves Chapter 7 liquidation or Chapter 11 reorganization. An essential feature of the U.S. Bankruptcy Code is the absolute priority rule. The absolute priority rule states that senior creditors are paid in full before junior creditors receive anything. However, in practice the absolute priority rule is often violated.
4. A new form of financial restructuring is prepackaged bankruptcy. It is a hybrid of a private workout and formal bankruptcy.
5. One of the most well-known bankruptcies involved Revco D. S. Revco's bankruptcy was long and costly. The main reason was Revco's complicated financial structure, which made agreement among creditors very difficult.

Key Terms

Financial distress 808
Liquidation 812
Reorganization 812
Absolute priority rule 813
Private workout 816
Prepackaged bankruptcy 818

Suggested Readings

An excellent book on financial distress by one of the leading authorities is
Altman, Edward I. *Corporate Financial Distress: A Complete Guide to Predicting, Avoiding and Dealing with Bankruptcy* (New York: John Wiley & Sons, 1983).

Many recent academic articles on financial distress can be found in
Jenson, Michael, and Richard Rubeck, eds. "Symposium on the Structure and Governance of Enterprise Part II." *Journal of Financial Economics* 27 (1990). Articles by Lawrence Weiss, Stuart G. Gilson, Kose John, Larry N. P. Lang, Steven Kaplan, David Reishus, Frank Easterbrook, and Karen H. Wruck appear.

Questions and Problems

Financial Distress?

30.1 Define financial distress using the stock-based and flow-based approaches.

30.2 What are some benefits of financial distress?

Bankruptcy Liquidation and Reorganization

30.3 When the Beacon Computer Company (BCC) filed for bankruptcy under Chapter 7 of the U.S. Bankruptcy Code, it had the following balance sheet:

Liquidating Value		*Claims*	
Net realizable assets	\$5,000	Trade credit	\$1,000
		Secured notes (by a mortgage)	1,000
		Senior debenture	3,000
		Junior debenture	1,000
		Equity	(−1,000)

As trustee, what distribution of liquidating value do you propose?

30.4 When the Master Printing Company filed for bankruptcy, it filed under Chapter 11 of the U.S. Bankruptcy Code. Its balance sheet is shown below:

Assets		*Claims*	
Going concern value	\$15,000	Mortgage bonds	\$10,000
		Senior debenture	6,000
		Junior debenture	4,000
		Equity	(−5,000)

As trustee, what reorganization plan would you accept?

Private Workout or Bankruptcy: Which Is Best?

30.5 Explain the following two terms.

a. APR

b. DIP

30.6 Why do so many firms file for legal bankruptcy when private workouts are so much less expensive?

APPENDIX 30A

PREDICTING CORPORATE BANKRUPTCY: THE Z-SCORE MODEL[13]

Many potential lenders use credit scoring models to assess the credit worthiness of prospective borrowers. The general idea is to find factors that enable the lenders to discriminate between good and bad credit risks. To put it more precisely, lenders want to identify attributes of the borrower that can be used to predict default or bankruptcy.

Edward Altman has developed a model using financial statement ratios and multiple discriminant analyses to predict bankruptcy for publicly traded manufacturing firms. The resultant model is of the form:

$$Z = 3.3\,\frac{\text{EBIT}}{\text{Total assets}} + 1.2\,\frac{\text{Net working capital}}{\text{Total assets}}$$

$$+\,1.0\,\frac{\text{Sales}}{\text{Total assets}} + .6\,\frac{\text{Market value of equity}}{\text{Book of debt}}$$

$$+\,1.4\,\frac{\text{Accumulated retained earnings}}{\text{Total assets}}$$

where Z is an index of bankruptcy.

A score of Z less than 2.675 indicates that a firm has a 95 percent chance of becoming bankrupt within one year. However, Altman's results show that in practice the area between 1.81 and 2.99 should be thought of as a gray area. In actual use, bankruptcy would be predicted if $Z \leq 1.81$ and nonbankruptcy if $Z \geq 2.99$. Altman shows that bankrupt firms and nonbankrupt firms have very different financial profiles one year before bankruptcy. These different financial profits are the key intuition behind the Z-score model and are depicted in Table 30A.1.

Altman's original Z-score model requires a firm to have publicly traded equity and be a manufacturer. He uses a revised model to make it applicable for private firms and nonmanufacturers. The resulting model is

$$Z = 6.56\,\frac{\text{Net working capital}}{\text{Total assets}} + 3.26\,\frac{\text{Accumulated retained earnings}}{\text{Total assets}}$$

$$+\,1.05\,\frac{\text{EBIT}}{\text{Total assets}} + 6.72\,\frac{\text{Book value of equity}}{\text{Total liabilities}}$$

where $Z < 1.23$ indicates a bankruptcy prediction,
$1.23 \geq Z \leq 2.90$ indicates a gray area,
and $Z > 2.90$ indicates no bankruptcy.

- ***Example***

The U.S. Composite Corporation is attempting to increase its line of credit with the First National State Bank. The director of credit management of First National State Bank uses the Z-score model to determine credit worthiness. The U.S. Composite Corporation is not a publicly traded firm so that the revised Z-score model must be used.

The balance sheet and income statement of the U.S. Composite Corporation are in Tables 2.1 and 2.2 (Chapter 2).

[13] Edward I. Altman, *Corporate Financial Distress and Bankruptcy.* John Wiley & Sons, N.Y. (1993) chapter 3.

TABLE 30A.1 Financial Statement Ratios One Year Before Bankruptcy: Manufacturing Firms

	Average Ratios One Year Before Bankruptcy Of	
	Bankrupt Firms	*Non Bankrupt Firms*
$\frac{\text{Net working capital}}{\text{Total assets}}$	−6.1%	41.4%
$\frac{\text{Accumulated retained earnings}}{\text{Total assets}}$	−62.6%	35.5%
$\frac{\text{EBIT}}{\text{Total assets}}$	−31.8%	15.4%
$\frac{\text{Market value of equity}}{\text{Total liabilities}}$	40.1%	247.7%
$\frac{\text{Sales}}{\text{Assets}}$	150%	190%

Source: Edward I. Altman. *Corporate Financial Distress and Bankruptcy.* John Wiley & Sons (1993), Table 3.1, p. 109.

The first step is to determine the value of each of the financial statement variables and in the revised Z-score model.

(millions)

$$\frac{\text{Net working capital}}{\text{Total assets}} = \frac{275}{1879} = .146$$

$$\frac{\text{Accumulated retained earnings}}{\text{Total assets}} = \frac{390}{1879} = .208$$

$$\frac{\text{EBIT}}{\text{Total assets}} = \frac{219}{1879} = .117$$

$$\frac{\text{Book value of equity}}{\text{Total liabilities}} = \frac{805}{588} = 1.369$$

The next step to calculate the revised Z-score is

$$\begin{aligned} Z = {} & 6.56 \times .146 + 3.26 \times .208 \\ & +1.05 \times .117 + 6.72 \times 1.369 \\ & = 10.96 \end{aligned}$$

Finally, we determine that the Z-score is above 2.9, and we conclude that U.S. Composite is a good credit risk.